JOHN EVELYN
AND HIS MILIEU

Engraved portrait of John Evelyn by Robert Nanteuil, 1650
(British Library, Add. MS 78426).

JOHN EVELYN AND HIS MILIEU

Essays edited by
FRANCES HARRIS & MICHAEL HUNTER

THE BRITISH LIBRARY
2003

© 2003 The Contributors

First published 2003 by
The British Library
96 Euston Road
London NW1 2DB

British Library Cataloguing in Publication Data
A CIP record for this volume is available
from The British Library

ISBN 0 7123 4817 4

Designed by John Trevitt
Typeset by Norman Tilley Graphics, Northampton
Printed in England by St Edmundsbury Press, Bury St Edmunds

CONTENTS

CONTENTS

NOTES ON CONTRIBUTORS

DOUGLAS CHAMBERS is Professor Emeritus of the University of Toronto. His works include *The Planters of the English Landscape Garden* (New Haven & London: Yale University Press, 1993), and he is currently preparing an edition of Evelyn's letterbooks and correspondence.

EDWARD CHANEY is Professor of Fine and Decorative Arts at Southampton Institute. His works include *The Evolution of the Grand Tour: Anglo-Italian Cultural Relations since the Renaissance* (London: Frank Cass, 1998), and *Inigo Jones's Roman Sketchbook*, Roxburghe Club (2003, forthcoming).

GILLIAN DARLEY is an architectural and landscape historian. She is the author of *John Soane, Accidental Romantic* (New Haven & London: Yale University Press, 1999), and is currently writing a life of John Evelyn for Yale University Press.

MIRJAM FOOT is Professor of Library and Information Studies at University College, London. Her works include *Studies in the History of Bookbinding* (Aldershot: Scolar Press, 1993) and *The History of Bookbinding as a Mirror of Society* (London: The British Library, 1998).

CAROL GIBSON-WOOD is Professor at the Department of History in Art, and Lansdowne Chair in Fine Arts, University of Victoria, B.C. Her works include *Jonathan Richardson: Art Theorist of the English Enlightenment* (New Haven & London: Yale University Press, 2000).

EDWARD GREGG is Professor of History at the University of South Carolina. A new edition of his *Queen Anne* was published by Yale University Press in 2001, and jointly with Clyve Jones he is editing the journal of Sir John Evelyn, 1st Bart.

ANTONY GRIFFITHS is Keeper of Prints and Drawings at the British Museum. His works include *The Print in Stuart Britain 1603-1689* (London: British Museum, 1998).

FRANCES HARRIS is a curator of Manuscripts at the British Library and author of *Transformations of Love: the Friendship of John Evelyn and Margaret Godolphin* (Oxford University Press, 2003).

MICHAEL HUNTER is Professor of History at Birkbeck College, University of London. His works include *Science and Society in Restoration England* (Cambridge University Press, 1981), and, with Edward D. Davis, Antonio Clericuzio, and Lawrence M. Principe, the Pickering & Chatto editions of the *Works* and *Correspondence* of Robert Boyle (London: 1999-2001).

MARK LAIRD is an historic gardens consultant and senior lecturer in landscape history at Harvard University, and author of *The Flowering of the Landscape Garden: English Pleasure Grounds, 1720-1800* (Philadelphia: University of Pennsylvania Press, 1999).

GILES MANDELBROTE is a curator of Rare Books at the British Library and co-editor of, among other works, *A Radical's Books: the Library Catalogue of Samuel Jeake of Rye* (Woodbridge: Brewer, 1999).

STEVEN PINCUS is Associate Professor of History at the University of Chicago. He is author of *Protestantism and Patriotism: Ideology and the Making of English Foreign Policy 1650-1668* (Cambridge University Press, 1996) and is working on a study of the ideologies of Revolution of 1688-9.

JOHN SPURR is Reader in History at the University of Wales, Swansea. His works include *The Restoration Church of England* (New Haven & London: Yale University Press, 1991) and *England in the 1670s* (Oxford: Blackwell, 2000).

ISABEL SULLIVAN is archivist at the Surrey History Centre and has responsibility for the Evelyn estate and manorial records there.

SUSAN WHYMAN is author of *Sociability and Power in Late Stuart England: the Cultural Worlds of the Verneys 1660-1720* (Oxford University Press, 1999), and is working on a cultural history of letter-writing.

GILLIAN WRIGHT is a Post-Doctoral Researcher with the Perdita Project on Early Modern Women's Manuscripts, Nottingham Trent University.

ABBREVIATIONS
USED IN THE NOTES

BL   British Library
Evelyn, *Diary*   *The Diary of John Evelyn*, ed. by E. S. de Beer, 6 vols
              (Oxford: Clarendon Press, 1955)

INTRODUCTION

MICHAEL HUNTER AND
FRANCES HARRIS

THE ESSAYS WHICH MAKE UP THIS VOLUME are based on the proceedings of the conference, 'John Evelyn and his Milieu', held at The British Library on 17-18 September 2001.[1] What in turn prompted the convening of this conference was the variety of important new research and archival discoveries which have been stimulated by the Library's acquisition of, first, an important portion of the Evelyn library in 1977-8 and then the Evelyn manuscripts and family archive in March 1995. We will return later in this Introduction to the circumstances in which these acquisitions occurred.

The core of these collections, printed and manuscript, are of course those of John Evelyn, 'the diarist', himself, the main subject of this volume. His correspondence, literary manuscripts, and personal and official papers make up 227 'volumes' of the total of 525 'volumes' in which the archive is now arranged, and nine of the fourteen essays here printed have their focus on him. The remainder of the archive is made up of the papers of earlier and later generations of his family and that of his wife, extending the time-span back to the sixteenth century and forward to the eighteenth and nineteenth centuries.[2] Of particular importance for the later period are the extensive archive of Evelyn's beloved grandson and heir (and fellow diarist), Sir John Evelyn, 1st Baronet, and a group of papers relating to William Bray and William Upcott, the prime movers in the publication of Evelyn's diary and correspondence in the nineteenth century. The subsidiary groups of family papers have also proved a rich source of research material.[3] Two of the essays below are based on the surviving manuscripts of Evelyn's daughters, one focuses on the 1st Baronet, and two more span several generations. This is appropriate, because it signals a family background of which Evelyn himself was always aware, and a concern for continuity which is much in evidence in the solicitude that he showed for his children and favourite grandchild. It was reciprocated in turn by the care with which his family preserved his literary remains.

During his lifetime and for more than a century after his death, Evelyn was chiefly known as a writer on – and practitioner of – forestry and horticulture, as a pioneering advocate of the arts, and as a significant member of the circle that founded the Royal Society. It was thus that he was remembered in the eighteenth century in such compendia as the influential *Biographia Britannica*; the lengthy account of him there by Dr John Campbell is mainly devoted to a summary of his published writings. Best known of these was his *Sylva: or, a Discourse of Forest Trees*, in fact he became known to his descendants as 'Sylva Evelyn'.[4] Though this book originated in 1664 as a joint enterprise of the nascent Royal Society in circumstances which will be considered more fully below, it was increasingly transformed by Evelyn into an artefact of his own. He made lengthy additions to successive editions (1670, 1679, and 1706), greatly elaborating the main text and adding separate works of his own as appendices [Fig. 1]. Then in the late eighteenth century it was the subject of a lavish annotated edition by the York physician and agriculturalist, Dr Alexander Hunter, first published in 1776 and reprinted a number of times thereafter.[5]

Evelyn's reputation was transformed almost overnight, however, by the publication in 1818 of his diary (under the title *Memoirs Illustrative of the Life and Writings of John Evelyn*), followed the next year by a second edition in the same lavish quarto format [Fig. 2]. It was this which turned him from a minor worthy into one of the most famous of all seventeenth-century Englishmen. His friend Samuel Pepys, of course, underwent a similar trans-formation. Indeed, it is interesting that the success of Evelyn's *Memoirs* was a significant stimulus to the decipherment of Pepys's diary and its publication under the editorship of Lord Braybrooke in 1825.[6] The Evelyn edition, which included a selection of his correspondence, was principally the work of William Bray, a Surrey lawyer and antiquary who acted as solicitor to the then Lady Evelyn. He was assisted by William Upcott, librarian of the London Institution, who was subsequently to produce an edition of Evelyn's miscel-laneous published writings in 1825.[7] Upcott had been appointed by Lady Evelyn in 1813 at Bray's suggestion to arrange and catalogue the family books. He was also an autograph collector whose enthusiasm for adding to his personal holdings sometimes outran his moral sense. He accumulated a suspiciously large number of Evelyn manuscripts (though he claimed to have had a general permission from Lady Evelyn for doing so), many of which were bought back by the family at the sale of his collections in 1846, following his death the previous year. Further items were acquired for the (then) British Museum Department of Manuscripts and now form the earliest portion of the British Library's Evelyn collections.[8]

Bray's original edition of the diary was reprinted in smaller format in 1827. A new edition by the historian and biographer, John Forster, was then published in 1850-2, in which the apparatus was extended and a much larger selection of correspondence included.[9] Thereafter it was reprinted many times throughout the nineteenth century and into the twentieth. One reason

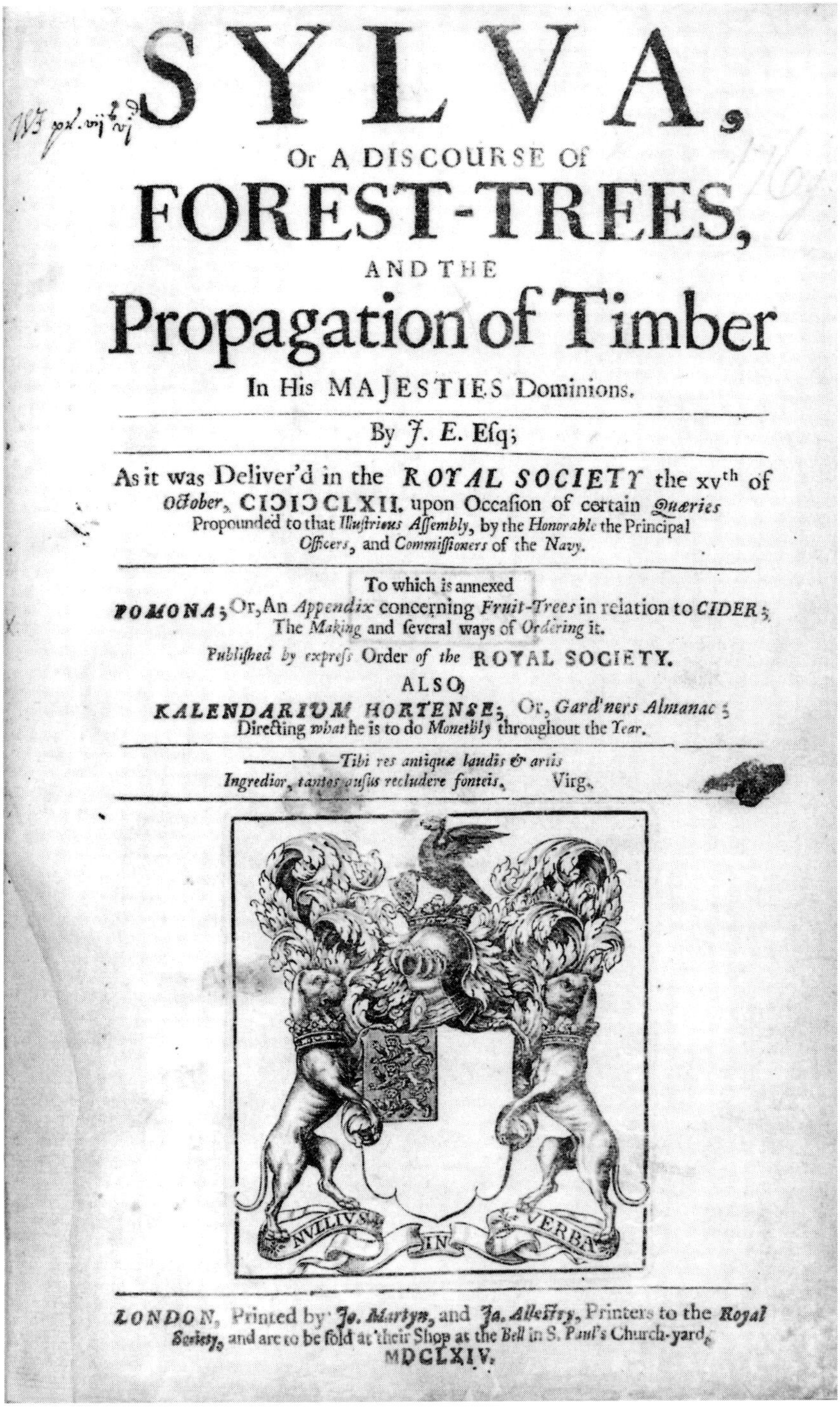

SYLVA,

Or A DISCOURSE Of

FOREST-TREES,

AND THE

Propagation of Timber

In His MAJESTIES Dominions.

By *J. E.* Esq;

As it was Deliver'd in the *ROYAL SOCIETY* the xv^th of
October, CIƆIƆCLXII, upon Occasion of certain *Quæries*
Propounded to that *Illustrious Assembly*, by the *Honorable* the Principal
Officers, and *Commissioners* of the Navy.

To which is annexed
POMONA; Or, An *Appendix* concerning *Fruit-Trees* in relation to *CIDER*;
The *Making* and several ways of *Ordering* it.

Published by express Order *of the* ROYAL SOCIETY.

ALSO,

KALENDARIUM HORTENSE; Or, *Gard'ners Almanac*;
Directing *what he is to do Monethly* throughout the *Year*.

———— *Tibi res antiquæ laudis & artis*
Ingredior, tantos ausus recludere fonteis. Virg.

LONDON, Printed by *Jo. Martyn*, and *Ja. Allestry*, Printers to the *Royal*
Society, and are to be sold at their Shop at the Bell in S. *Paul's* Church-yard,
MDCLXIV.

Fig. 1: Title-page of the first edition of Evelyn's *Sylva* (1664).

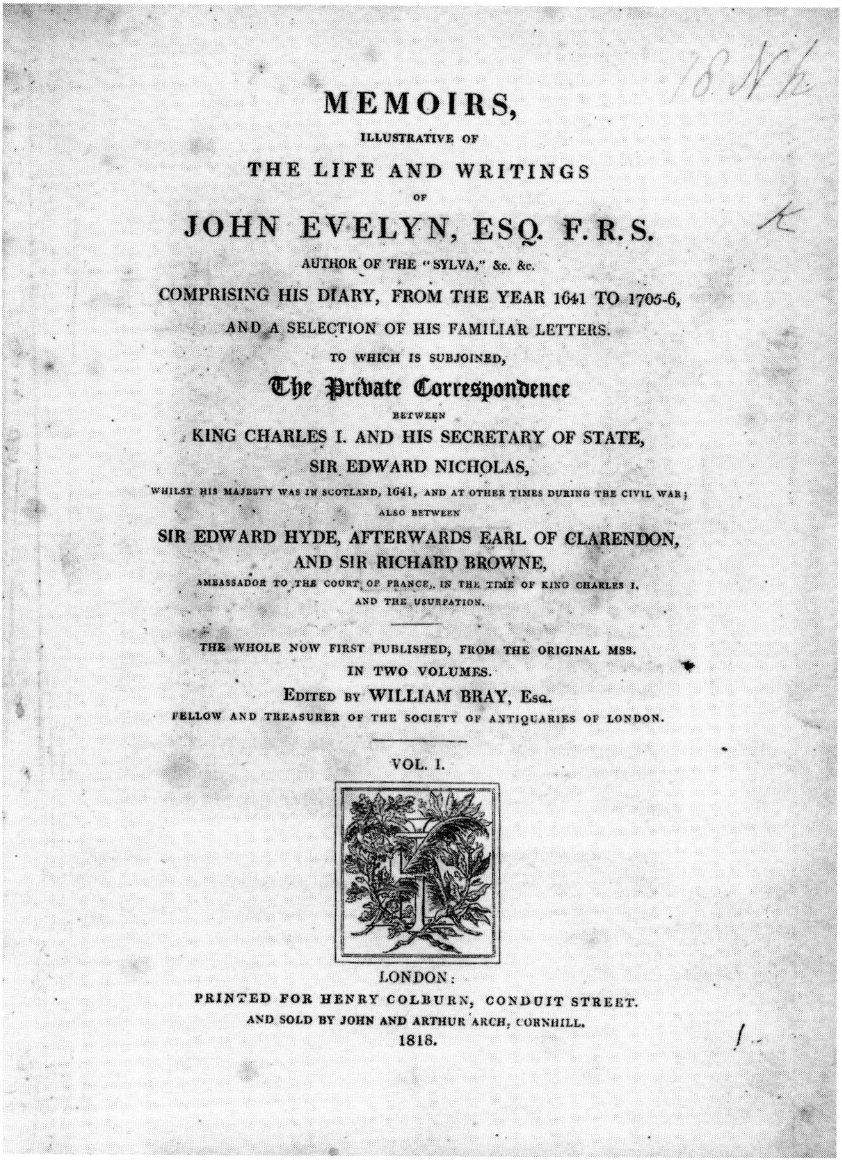
MEMOIRS,
ILLUSTRATIVE OF
THE LIFE AND WRITINGS
OF
JOHN EVELYN, ESQ. F.R.S.
AUTHOR OF THE "SYLVA," &c. &c.
COMPRISING HIS DIARY, FROM THE YEAR 1641 TO 1705-6,
AND A SELECTION OF HIS FAMILIAR LETTERS.
TO WHICH IS SUBJOINED,
The Private Correspondence
BETWEEN
KING CHARLES I. AND HIS SECRETARY OF STATE,
SIR EDWARD NICHOLAS,
WHILST HIS MAJESTY WAS IN SCOTLAND, 1641, AND AT OTHER TIMES DURING THE CIVIL WAR;
ALSO BETWEEN
SIR EDWARD HYDE, AFTERWARDS EARL OF CLARENDON,
AND SIR RICHARD BROWNE,
AMBASSADOR TO THE COURT OF FRANCE, IN THE TIME OF KING CHARLES I.
AND THE USURPATION.

THE WHOLE NOW FIRST PUBLISHED, FROM THE ORIGINAL MSS.
IN TWO VOLUMES.
EDITED BY WILLIAM BRAY, ESQ.
FELLOW AND TREASURER OF THE SOCIETY OF ANTIQUARIES OF LONDON.

VOL. I.

LONDON:
PRINTED FOR HENRY COLBURN, CONDUIT STREET.
AND SOLD BY JOHN AND ARTHUR ARCH, CORNHILL.
1818.

Fig. 2: Title-page of the first edition of Evelyn's diary, edited by William Bray with assistance of William Upcott, 1818.

for its extraordinary success was its intrinsic interest; another was that it presented a figure who was very much to the taste of nineteenth-century, and especially Victorian, readers. This was made plain at a very early stage by a reference in Sir Walter Scott's *Kenilworth* (1821) to 'the celebrated Mr Evelyn, whose "Silva" is still the manual of British planters; and whose life, manners, and principles, as illustrated in his Memoirs, ought equally to be the manual of English gentlemen'. And it was amplified by Upcott, who described Evelyn as 'The amiable, accomplished, and worthy Patriot and Philosopher',

whose life offers the most perfect model of what an English gentleman should be: who living was an example of public and private virtue, and who dying bequeathed this golden sentence to be inscribed on his tomb for the advantage of posterity: 'In an age of extraordinary events and revolutions, he learnt that all is vanity which is not honest, and that there is no solid wisdom but in real piety.'[10]

The early-twentieth-century littérateur, Bonamy Dobrée, once dubbed Joseph Addison 'The First Victorian', with reference to the huge cult that the first editor of *The Spectator* enjoyed in the Victorian period; he saw Addison as exemplifying the complacency, confidence, and mild hypocrisy that he saw as characteristic of the Victorians.[11] Arguably, the Evelyn of the diary would have been equally well-suited to this title, and his claim to it was reinforced by a deeply sentimental reading of another text, his *Life of Mrs Godolphin*, which was newly discovered at this time. Written shortly after her death in 1678 for private circulation amongst her friends and family, this account of Evelyn's pact of spiritual friendship with a young woman of the Restoration court was not a biography in any modern sense; its models were those of Roman Catholic hagiography, the memorial sermon, and puritan exemplary lives. Unknown outside the families of the author and subject for two and a half centuries, the manuscript eventually came into the hands of one of Evelyn's descendants, Edward Venables Vernon-Harcourt, Archbishop of York, and was published for the first time under his auspices in 1847. The Victorians relished the poignant story of the devout young Anglican woman, a beacon of purity in an ungodly court, of her religious vocation, domestic virtue, and early death in childbirth, and the work, like the diary, ran to several popular editions.

So harmoniously did Evelyn fit into the Victorian image of late-seventeenth-century English culture that an essentially Victorian view of him survived well into the twentieth century – in Lord Ponsonby's biography of him, published in 1933, for instance[12] – while vestiges of it still remain in the popular conception of Evelyn today. It was therefore perhaps only to be expected that the twentieth century would see a reaction, in the context of the rejection of Victorian values associated with the Bloomsbury circle and most cuttingly expressed by Lytton Strachey in his *Eminent Victorians* of 1918. It is not coincidental that the first critical appraisal of Evelyn took the form of an essay by Virginia Woolf, 'Rambling around Evelyn', written in 1920 and included in *The Common Reader* of 1925. We quote a few memorable phrases:

Evelyn was no genius. His writing is opaque rather than transparent; we see no depths through it, nor any very secret movements of mind or heart. ... He was, we cannot help suspecting, something of a bore, a little censorious, a little patronising, a little too sure of his own merits, and a little obtuse to those of other people. Or what is the quality, or absence of quality, that checks our sympathies? Partly, perhaps, it is due to some inconsistency which it would be harsh to call by so strong a name as hypocrisy.[13]

A more sustained assault, explicitly inspired by Virginia Woolf, came from the somewhat unexpected figure of W. G. Hiscock, deputy librarian of Christ Church, Oxford, who wrote two books, *John Evelyn and Mrs Godolphin* in 1951, and *John Evelyn and his Family Circle* in 1955. Hiscock had earlier published *A Christ Church Miscellany* in 1946, for which he had been given an honorary Oxford M.A. That he should develop this further interest is not entirely surprising, for in 1949 the Evelyn Papers had been deposited at Christ Church by Jack Evelyn, a descendant of the diarist and himself a Christ Church graduate. Hiscock therefore had access to Evelyn's manuscripts, and he attempted to use them to get behind the image presented in the *Diary* and the *Life of Mrs Godolphin*. He explained how his work was 'based, in part, on the hitherto unpublished material recently made accessible at Christ Church by the kindness of Mr John Evelyn. ... In many instances – particularly in personal matters – the letters of the Evelyn circle provide a necessary and illuminating corrective to the Victorian eulogy of the Diarist.'[14] He then went on to argue that what Evelyn described as a 'holy friendship' with Margaret Godolphin had actually been a kind of spiritual seduction on his part; that he had played on her religious susceptibilities to try to prevent her from marrying the man she loved, and strove to conceal this afterwards from her husband, whose patronage he sought.

Hiscock's realization that Evelyn's correspondence and devotional papers were in many respects a richer and more revealing source than his diary was well founded, but the methods he used to exploit his new material were misguided. He frequently over-interpreted his evidence. His determination to incriminate Evelyn was too obvious, and his interpretation of Margaret Godolphin's every religious aspiration as a symptom of neurosis was too crude. In his determination to treat the friendship as a post-Victorian episode, he ignored its actual context in the pre- and post-Reformation debate concerning marriage and the long tradition of friendships between men and women in religious settings, going back to patristic literature, in which Evelyn himself explicitly placed it. In fact Evelyn had made no attempt to conceal the intensity of the friendship from his family or friends. His wife was to some extent included in it and so, at his own fervent request, was Margaret Godolphin's widower (a fact Hiscock must have been aware of, but scarcely alluded to). Of course the friendship with a beautiful and devout young woman was fraught with human difficulties; the later confessional notes in which Evelyn castigated himself for his excessive affection for her, first publicized by Hiscock (though without divulging them correctly), are a clear indication of these. Yet there is no doubt that it was conducted within the norms of its own day, and what is chiefly interesting about it is how it serves to illuminate these.[15] Hiscock's interpretation, which has never fully found favour, was criticized in detail in a series of articles by Esmond de Beer in *Notes and Queries* in 1960.[16]

By this time, de Beer had brought out his definitive edition of Evelyn's *Diary*, published in six volumes by the Clarendon Press at Oxford in 1955. All those who study the period will be familiar with this work and will have gone to its capacious index and annotations for information, not just about Evelyn but about virtually every aspect of late-seventeenth-century England. Undoubtedly, it is one of the masterpieces of editing of the twentieth century, and is in many ways exemplary.[17] Its principal flaw is that it makes no use whatever of the Evelyn archive. This was hardly de Beer's fault, since, although his edition was not published till 1955, it was largely completed some years before that. The index alone (which comprises the whole of the sixth volume) took him three years to complete, and the bulk of the work on the edition was done in the 1930s, when the Evelyn Papers were not available for study. Nonetheless, this is a serious shortcoming, and there are many places in his annotations where de Beer could have elucidated entries in the *Diary* more effectively if he had had access to the manuscripts.

Indeed, for all its value as a source on many aspects of late-seventeenth-century history, this famous text often cries out to be elucidated, contextualized, and, up to a point, corrected. Of course, some of the defects of the *Diary* as a text are well known, especially the problems that arise from the extent to which, for much of the period it covers – up to about 1683 – it is not strictly contemporary, but written up from original notes with a dose of hindsight many years after the events recorded. In this respect its first appearance in print as Evelyn's *Memoirs*, rather than his *Diary*, was justified. There are thus often 'know-all' comments, particularly concerning political and other developments of the Interregnum and Restoration, as where the first meeting of the Long Parliament on 3 November 1640 is described as 'the beginning of all our sorrows for twenty yeares after'.[18] There is also the *Diary*'s tone. It is, of course, a rather spare document, describing events telegraphically and selectively, so that in it we are given a view of some two-thirds of a century, in contrast to Pepys's record of almost comparable length of just over nine years. This means that Evelyn often understates things, leaving himself uncommitted in ways that allow the reader to invest his comments with a significance that he may or may not have intended, but for which he retrospectively gains credit – hence partly explaining its appeal to the Victorians. Yet, as will become apparent again and again in the essays below, recourse to his archive makes Evelyn seem a more, rather than a less, interesting person, and the *Diary* an even more interesting text as a kind of authentic yet coded statement, to be deciphered by recourse to this wider range of material. Indeed, this challenge of using the vast archive to place it in context, which de Beer never attempted and which Hiscock tried to rise to without much success, is the major task awaiting any student or biographer of Evelyn.

Since de Beer's time, the Evelyn manuscripts have become progressively more available for research. We have already mentioned how they were deposited at Christ Church in 1949, initially in the custody of W. G. Hiscock, whose own works helped to publicize them. Although the want of a complete and accessible catalogue limited knowledge of their richness, there was scholarly access from this time onwards. J. P. Kenyon, for example, used them in the 1950s for his fine biography of Robert Spencer, 2nd Earl of Sunderland, whose wife was amongst the little coterie of high church women who looked to Evelyn as their mentor in his later years.[19] Researchers at Christ Church from the 1970s to the early 1990s, including the present editors, benefited from the knowledgeable help of the deputy librarian, John Wing. In 1987 Peter Beal included a valuable list of Evelyn's manuscripts at Christ Church and elsewhere in his *Index of English Literary Manuscripts*.[20] A transcript of the archive's most famous unpublished manuscript, the unfinished gardening encyclopaedia, 'Elysium Britannicum', was begun by John Ingram and has since appeared in print, providing a wealth of new evidence for Evelyn's place in garden history.[21]

However, this trajectory was interrupted by the initially sad, but ultimately triumphant, history of the Evelyn heirlooms in the latter part of the twentieth century. In the mid-1970s tax complications over the Evelyn inheritance brought about the threat of sales. When the news of this broke in 1976, a frantic discussion ensued among the 'heritage lobby' of the day, but relatively little could be done due to the absence of the bodies that have since come into existence to deal with such emergencies – notably the National Heritage Memorial Fund, inaugurated only in 1981. Hence, first some of the family portraits and furniture were dispersed, along with Evelyn's collection of prints, while finally, in four major sales between June 1977 and November 1978, the Evelyn Library went under the hammer. Fortunately something was salvaged. Evelyn's two cabinets went respectively to the Victoria and Albert and the Geffrye Museums, while the most interesting portrait of him, by Robert Walker of 1649, was purchased by the National Portrait Gallery. Then the British Library was able to acquire the most interesting portion of the library, in the form of the books with Evelyn's annotations. Nevertheless, much of great interest was dispersed, and Evelyn's copies of some key books are now untraceable.[22]

But when it was decided in the early 1990s that the manuscripts should also be sold, there was, fortunately, to be no such dispersal as overtook the other collections. They were offered by private treaty sale to the British Library, which with the help of the National Heritage Memorial Fund, was able to purchase them *in toto* for the nation.[23] They have been accessible at the Library ever since, where they have now been catalogued fully for the first time. The essays that make up this volume are the product of this increased scholarly knowledge and use. It is hoped they will serve both to make the riches of this exceptional addition to the national collections more widely known, and to stimulate further research.

The volume opens with an essay by Douglas Chambers inspired by Evelyn's letterbooks, at least as important a part of his life record in their way as the more famous *Diary*. These are the pair of folio volumes into which Evelyn copied, sometimes in revised form, a large selection of the many letters that he wrote in the course of his life, which Douglas Chambers is currently editing for publication. The essay begins with an interesting digression on Evelyn's use of the word 'Impertinence', which he deploys in a number of letters, apparently somewhat whimsically and inconsistently (perhaps intending to fit what he conceived to be the preoccupations of his recipient), but which often denotes the affairs of the public sphere which drew him away from the more satisfying private world of the intellect. It then moves on to discuss Evelyn as a letter-writer, explaining how the letterbooks were a repository, not only of the actual communications that he dispatched, but of epistles, 'letter-essays', in Chambers' apt phrase. These Evelyn polished, revised, and preserved, but in some cases, though they are addressed to named individuals such as Samuel Pepys, probably never sent. As Chambers points out, in this Evelyn was modelling his letters on the epistolary genre in its own right, which extended back through Renaissance figures like Erasmus and Lipsius to such authors as Cicero, Seneca, and the younger Pliny in classical antiquity. To these figures Evelyn evidently likened himself, seeing the 'studiolum' in which he wrote as comparable to Cicero's in his villa at Tusculanum.

With Edward Chaney's essay we go back to Evelyn's formative continental travels in the 1640s, as written up fully (if not always entirely accurately) in his *Diary*. Chaney focuses on the episode in 1645-6 when the ageing Earl of Arundel took the youthful Evelyn under his wing and introduced him to the cultural treasures of northern Italy, as recorded in the 'Remembrances of things worth seeing in Italy' that the Earl vouchsafed him. Chaney uses this to give a revisionist account of Arundel's Italian travels as a whole, taking us back to the early decades of the seventeenth century. This is appropriate both because his advice to Evelyn was based on a lifetime's experience of Italian art and architecture, and because this takes us to the heart of English exposure to Italian classicism through Arundel and his protégé, Inigo Jones. Matters were complicated by Arundel's clandestine Roman Catholicism and his consequent need to be less than perfectly open about his movements. Through impressive sleuthing, of which he gives a witty and entertaining account, Chaney is able to revise a number of mistaken statements made in the past and throw new light on an episode in cultural history which also illuminates Evelyn's later role in this field.

In terms of Evelyn's activity as a connoisseur and collector, an equally crucial episode was the time that he spent in Paris from 1649 to 1652. It was at this point that he first seems to have developed his penchant for elaborate bindings, inspired by his father-in-law, Sir Richard Browne, as Mirjam Foot illustrates in her paper. Thereafter, and not least after their return to England – in 1652 in Evelyn's case and at the Restoration in Browne's – both men continued to indulge their tastes in fine bindings.

In addition, from his Parisian days onwards, Evelyn built up a serious collection of books, a substantial number of which were present in the Christie's sales, and of which the British Library holdings preserve the most significant sample. Indeed, as Giles Mandelbrote emphasizes in his essay, this was very much a working library, devoted to the pursuit of knowledge: relatively few items in it were chosen purely for show, and Evelyn's preference was for reliable, up-to-date books rather than choicer, older ones. The library was also elaborately classified and catalogued, and Evelyn's assiduity in using his books is witnessed by the extensive annotations that they often display. These range from curt notes to the effect that he had read a book, to extensive marginal markings, sometimes reflecting successive perusals of the volume; their fly-leaves often have lists of references or record ancillary information from Evelyn's own experience. As such, the extant books provide an unusual insight into early modern reading habits, and this gives a special significance to the British Library's holding. The commonplace books which came to the British Library as part of the Evelyn archive illustrate a further stage in the processing of Evelyn's reading which these annotations began. Overall, as Mandelbrote illustrates, the book acquisitions of 1977-8 dovetail neatly with his archive acquired in 1995.

The Christie's sales also form the subject of the first section of the next essay, by Antony Griffiths, who opens his evaluation of Evelyn's role in the history of the print in the seventeenth century with a heart-breaking account of the dispersal of his print collection. Using the auction catalogues of these, along with such sources as the section on prints in Evelyn's library catalogue of 1687 (the text of which is appended to his essay), Griffiths is able to give a sense for the first time of the scale, quality, and purpose of Evelyn's collecting. He also provides evidence of the period in which Evelyn chiefly formed his collection, the climax coming (as with his book-collecting) during his Parisian years, when he became a noted patron of print-makers. At the same time he is shown to have become quite a respectable print-maker in his own right. By the mid-1650s, however, Evelyn had ceased either to make prints or even to collect them, and Griffiths points out that it was just at this time, as either therapy or record, that he wrote his classic treatise, *Sculptura*.

Probably Evelyn's greatest claim to distinction in a particular field was in that of gardening, both as theorist and as creator of one of the best-known gardens in seventeenth-century England, at Sayes Court in Deptford.[24] This is quite well documented, with several plans and descriptions surviving from different times in Evelyn's life, while further light is thrown on it by his *Elysium Britannicum*. Hitherto, studies of the garden have focused on its design, and on the influences on it from Evelyn's experiences in Italy and France.[25] But here Mark Laird gives an arresting study of the instability of the garden, its vulnerability both to its less than satisfactory local environment, down-river from London and adjacent to the dockyard, and to the buffetings that it received from the extreme climatic conditions at the end of the Little Ice Age. Quite apart from the beached whale of 1658 with which he begins, Laird gives a vivid account of slugs, caterpillars, frosts, and other perils to the garden, at the same time exploring Evelyn's ambivalence towards birds, those 'winged choristers' whom he alternately celebrated for their song and deprecated for their taste for ripening fruit. Above all, he shows how it is likely that Evelyn's replanting of the garden in the 1680s was the result of the damage caused to the formal garden that he had first laid out in the 1650s by strong winds and extreme frosts, which meant that he had literally to go back to the drawing-board.

A less familiar aspect of Evelyn is his importance as a lay Anglican, significant not least because he left so much detailed evidence of his private and public observance. His devotional manuscripts, the largest single portion of his archive, include his copiously annotated Bible, sermon notes, the draft of his 'History of Religion' and various shorter essays, as well as a wealth of meditations, private 'offices', and prayers, many of them associated with his friendship with Margaret Godolphin. John Spurr's essay uses these to explore the nature of Evelyn's Anglicanism, pointing out that Evelyn himself strongly believed in the need to rationalize the basis of one's beliefs and left considerable evidence of how he did so. He emphasizes the importance of the 1650s, when the Church of England was under persecution, in strengthening Evelyn's emotional loyalty to a suffering church and prompting him to develop a private devotional world to compensate for the lack of public ritual. He also shows how after the Restoration this somewhat oppositional stance was continued in Evelyn's cultivation of a lay religious coterie in the inhospitable environment of the court. Focussing on the sermon notes in particular, he suggests that in many cases Evelyn was not simply recording, but rather assimilating and transforming the preachers' texts into his own devotional prose.

The following chapter, by Gillian Darley, gives a masterly account of a further important aspect of Evelyn's life that has been underplayed hitherto: his activity as a public servant responsible for sick and wounded seamen and prisoners of war during the second and third Dutch Wars in 1664-7 and 1672-4. In this capacity he soon found himself at the mercy of the inefficiency, makeshift, and sheer chaos which was typical of government administration in early Restoration England, and his letters rapidly become a catalogue of complaints, mounting at times, especially during the plague year of 1665, to a shrill climax. Yet he did more than complain, as Gillian Darley also shows; his experiences impressed him with the crying need for a proper infrastructure and building programme, for the benefit not just of the sick and wounded but of the nation at large, and he found time to plan for this even during the worst of his difficulties. The latter part of her essay is devoted to an account of his later efforts to this end, culminating in the great hospitals of Chelsea and Greenwich, in the planning of which he played a significant role.

In his arresting essay, Steven Pincus takes issue with those who have seen Evelyn as a politically conservative figure. On the basis particularly of a lengthy letter to an unidentified aristocrat that Evelyn wrote in the aftermath of William of Orange's invasion in November 1688 and which he sub-sequently copied into his letterbook, Pincus argues that, on the contrary, he had quite a radical agenda for national reform. This reflected his disillusionment with the policies and attitudes of first Charles II and then James II, which led him to develop links with political and commercial figures of a strongly Whig complexion, and with low churchmen like John Tillotson and Thomas Tenison. As a result, his prescriptions for change were quite at odds with those of the Tories and crypto-Jacobites with whom he has sometimes been linked, including proposals for electoral reform, for a land registry, for religious toleration and moral reform, and for a wholesale reorientation of foreign and commercial policy, including unification with the United Provinces. All told, it is a remarkable combination, which challenges traditional stereotypes.

In the remaining essays, we move away from Evelyn himself to his descendants. First, Gillian Wright complements John Spurr's account of

Evelyn's own piety by providing a detailed study of the surviving devotional manuscripts of his eldest daughter Mary, who died of smallpox in 1685 at the age of nineteen. Evelyn's 'Directions for the Employment of Your Time', which Mary herself expanded with 'Necessary Additions', provide evidence of how closely her father supervised her devotional regime, but also how she adapted it to her own needs. Gillian Wright analyses Mary's small books of devotional notes, to show how completely she embraced the 'Holy Living' movement of Restoration Anglicanism, using the works of Jeremy Taylor and Simon Patrick, and less predictably François de Sales, to devise what she called a daily 'Methodical Course of Holy Living'. Like John Spurr in his discussion of Evelyn's sermon-book, she concludes that Mary Evelyn's notes from whatever source were transformed into seamless devotional texts for her personal use, indicating the completeness of her assimilation of what she read and heard.

Susanna Draper was the only one of the diarist's children who survived her parents and lived into old age. Scarcely more than a name till now, she emerges from Carol Gibson-Wood's study of the family letters as a significant amateur painter, whose story provides fresh evidence of a female role which was not uncommon but is often difficult to document. Although she was regarded by her parents as the least promising of their three daughters, she became the focus of their attention in their desolation following the deaths in rapid succession of the devout and accomplished Mary and her wayward sister Elizabeth, when Susanna was fifteen. Initially as a means of personal improvement, they encouraged her talent for drawing and painting, and this support was continued after her marriage by a mother-in-law who shared her interests. As Carol Gibson-Wood points out, the correspondence gives clear indications of the enhanced status that Susanna Draper achieved in her family, both as an accomplished and reliable copyist and for her contacts with the commercial art world. This throws important light on the respect accorded to amateur painting at this period; all the more valuable because of the rarity of such a sustained body of evidence.

An archive in which the correspondence of several generations of a highly literate and communicative family is carefully preserved also offers an ideal case-study for the importance of letter-writing in the formation of family identity and the social education of children. In her essay on this subject Susan Whyman extends her work on the Verney family archive by showing how successive generations of Evelyns, male and female, were tutored in letter-writing and the conventions and networks of the polite world. As she points out, the transformation into adulthood is literally visible in the transition in such documents from ill-formed and blotted letters to elegant script and finely-turned phrases. The diarist's correspondence with his son and grandson provide especially telling examples, and Susan Whyman's evidence reinforces Douglas Chambers's conclusion from his study of Evelyn's letterbooks, of the primary importance in this epistolary training (at least for boys) of classical models such as Cicero and Pliny.

A further case study is provided by the diarist's grandson, the third John Evelyn, afterwards 1st Baronet, whose education forms the focus of Edward Gregg's essay. Closely directed by his grandfather rather than his ailing or absent father, he progressed from Eton to Oxford, through the series of educative tours within his native country, to a settlement in marriage with the niece of Evelyn's long-standing patron (and Margaret Godolphin's widower), Sidney, Lord Godolphin. These domestic travels were a substitute for the Grand Tour in Europe which the family thought too risky in wartime for its sole surviving male heir, and initiated the series of journals, now being edited for the first time, which Sir John Evelyn was to continue intermittently for a large part of his life. Edward Gregg shows how he emerged from his grandfather's tutelage as his ideal exemplar of paterfamilias, gentleman scholar, public servant, and country squire, not only achieving the balance which the diarist had aimed at less successfully in his own life, but carrying it forward into the eighteenth century.

Drawing on the extensive deeds and manorial records of the Evelyns' estates at the Surrey History Centre, Isabel Sullivan traces the history and fortunes of different branches of the family, including the Wotton Evelyns, from which the diarist sprang. In the process she makes the important point that, for all the diarist's travels and long residence elsewhere, his native county of Surrey and Wotton especially were his 'most cherished' places. She also points out that it was the family's uninterrupted residence there over several centuries which ensured the survival of so many generations of family papers largely intact. She ends fittingly with an account of the role of the indefatigable Surrey solicitor and family friend, William Bray, a key figure for county history, in the publication of Evelyn's *Diary*, which has ensured his fame ever since.

One of the questions asked at the final session of the conference from which these essays derive was the very pertinent one: how important was John Evelyn and why? This is a complex matter. What is not in doubt is how extraordinarily well-connected he was with the leading personalities and events of his age. This is the image of him that has long been familiar from his *Diary*, on the basis of which David Howarth has called him 'the great minute-taker of Restoration culture'.[26] With due allowance for the extent to which that famous text may exaggerate Evelyn's own significance by placing him in the foreground to a disproportionate extent, his range of contacts is undoubtedly confirmed and extended by the new evidence provided by the contributors to this book. This importance was enhanced by his very long and active life. It is notable that the records of his last decades have provided as much new material for the essays below as those of his formative and middle years. Evelyn, who had witnessed Charles I ride in state to open Parliament, was in attendance at the courts of each of the late Stuart monarchs, and devised a programme of reform for William of Orange. He had close links with successive generations of the aristocratic families (the Howards are a case in point) and close friendships with both men and women. He associated with Hartlib's circle and with many of the most eminent early Fellows of the Royal Society.

It is important to recognize Evelyn's limitations: he was tangential to the politics of the period, in the sense that, for all his courtly contacts, he never became a Member of Parliament or a political activist: his political views, though well informed, remained slightly aloof from the hurly-burly of Whig–Tory confrontation, and this partly explains their character. Equally, no one pretends that Evelyn was a great thinker like Robert Boyle, or even William Petty. Indeed, he would have been the first to admit this, as is seen in the deferential terms in which he advertises his acquaintance with such men. As a thinker, he always tended to the syncretic, preferring to reconcile disparate positions rather than to subject them to the rigour that made possible some of the spectacular intellectual break-throughs of his age.

On the other hand, he clearly played a crucial role in shaping English culture in his period. Perhaps most significant was his role as a writer or translator of a wide range of books on different aspects of the arts and connoisseurship, many of them being among the earliest works on such topics in English. A case in point is his *Sculptura*, which, as Antony Griffiths points out, has been unfairly maligned by its successors, who could take for granted Evelyn's pioneering work in bringing together information about prints and print-makers that had never been previously collected. His *Numismata* (1697) is a similarly significant book, in this case in its exposition of the rationale of collecting coins and medals and a range of ancillary topics. Added to these are his translations of works on related subjects from French: Gabriel Naudé's manual of librarianship, Roland Fréart, sieur de Chambray's *Parallel of the Antient Architecture with the Modern*, and his *Idea of the Perfection of Painting*, all of them providing an exposition of principles from which he rightly saw that his fellow countrymen would benefit. In horticulture, too, his own compositions, especially the incomplete but extraordinarily rich *Elysium Britannicum*, were supplemented by translations of Nicolas de Bonnefons' *The French Gardiner* and Jean de la Quintinye's *The Compleat Gard'ner*.

Evelyn enhanced this literary activity by his more practical role as a consultant. This is well illustrated by the advice that he gave Samuel Pepys on matters of connoisseurship in the series of letters over many years that has recently been usefully collected by Guy de la Bédoyère.[27] But it is also evident in advice that he gave earlier and more widely on a great range of matters to do with collecting, taste, and design: to such eminent figures as the Earl of Clarendon on his picture gallery and on the encouragement of reliable editions of classical texts, to Lord Arlington on his library and his park at Euston (only one of many such landscape consultancies), and to Charles II himself on his cabinet and menagerie.[28] Added to this is his more public role in architectural and environmental matters: seeking to enhance the European standing of London by recommending improvements in its air and amenities, and later by planning and implementing such major institutional initiatives as the royal hospitals at Chelsea and Greenwich.[29]

Evelyn also has a subtler, perhaps even insidious role, in terms of the realignment of cultural priorities that occurred in late-seventeenth-century England, a shift which Michael Leslie has well described, away from the millenarian and egalitarian goals of mid-century reformers like Samuel Hartlib and his associates to the more elitist, more Latinate culture which was to dominate the Augustan period.[30] In this connection, and particularly in terms of the stress on gentility which characterized the period, it is possible retrospectively to underestimate the role of a man like Evelyn, who could achieve things in the fields that interested him which eluded humbler practitioners, ever on the verge of poverty. His social standing allowed him effortlessly to bridge the gap between connoisseurship and the practice of art. He was able to recognize and encourage promising talent, from the famous case of his discovery of Grinling Gibbons, as recounted in the *Diary*,[31] to that of his own daughter, unknown till divulged by Carol Gibson-Wood in this volume, at the same time providing a rationale for this through his writings. Douglas Chambers's and Susan Whyman's depictions of Evelyn as an upholder of the traditions of the epistolary culture of his day and Edward Gregg's account of his education of his grandson: these also illustrate the conviction that he shared with many contemporaries of the way in which politeness should be achieved through careful and repeated emulation of classical and other models.

This also helps to make sense of Evelyn's role in relation to the early Royal Society. To some extent, this reflected his acknowledged authority in matters of connoisseurship and the arts; *Sculptura* was presented as part of the Society's 'History of Trades' programme. It was also Evelyn who helped the Society to choose an appropriate symbolic crest and motto, and who provided a visual image of the Society in the form of the pictorial frontispiece to Thomas Sprat's *History of the Royal Society* of 1667.[32] When a manual on the cultivation and uses of timber was to be published under the Society's auspices in 1664, it is revealing that he should have been chosen to use his 'exquisite pen' and his horticultural prowess to give appropriate form to the disparate body of data that he and other Fellows of the Society had brought together, and to enhance this in later editions. It was this which enabled *Sylva* to reach its intended gentry audience, and Evelyn is rightly celebrated for his central role in one of the most successful examples of the collaboration that characterized the Royal Society in its early years.[33] Beyond that, his significance to the Society is more as a stalwart, part of the remarkable core of original members who were still surprisingly central to it as late as 1700. As some of the leading Fellows in the Society's earliest years died, Evelyn himself increasingly came to the fore, serving as Secretary in the 1670s, and taking it upon himself to devote a lengthy addition to the preface of the third edition of *Sylva* to a defence of the Society against its fashionable detractors.[34]

All this links with recent work such as J. M. Levine's *Between Ancients and Moderns*, in which Evelyn has a prominent role as a man torn between excitement in the intellectual ambitions of his own, Baconian age, and the legacy of classical antiquity, one of the most typical examples of what Levine characterizes as the 'Baroque' culture of his period.[35]

As this suggests, Evelyn's greatest significance may be as a representative, almost an emblematic figure: a spokesman of both his own and the coming age. As the essays of John Spurr and Steven Pincus indicate, this was as true of his political and religious as of his intellectual life. The breadth of his interests and concerns, his sense of mission, his belief in intellectual communities, and most of all the hospitality of mind which made him able to assimilate, contain, reconcile, and transmit so many opposing influences: all these qualities make the copious records he left us of his long life and preoccupations not just valuable for biographical study, but an immensely rich source for the period in which he lived. Together, they provide us with a more complete view than any other source of the cultivated late Stuart Englishman. As the following essays in their different ways demonstrate, to study the man and his records is to study his age.

NOTES

1 They include two papers (those of Susan Whyman and Edward Gregg) which were intended for the conference but could not be delivered there by their authors, who were unable to travel from the USA in the aftermath of the events in New York and Washington on 11 September 2001.

2 For an overview, see Theodore Hofmann, and others, *John Evelyn in the British Library* (London: British Library Publications, 1995).

3 For the correspondence of Evelyn's wife, see Frances Harris, 'The Letterbooks of Mary Evelyn', *English Manuscript Studies*, 6 (1998), 202-15.

4 *Biographia Britannica*, ed. by [William Oldys & Joseph Towers], 6 vols (London: 1747-66), III, 1849-72. For contemporary comment on the link

between Evelyn's garden-making and his 'book of forest trees', see Roger North, *The Lives of the Norths,* ed. by A. Jessopp, 3 vols (London: Bell, 1890), I, 375.

5   For an account of this and Evelyn's other writings, see Sir Geoffrey Keynes, *John Evelyn: a Study in Bibliophily with a Bibliography of his Writings,* 2nd edn (Oxford: Clarendon Press, 1968).

6   For a discussion, see *The Diary of Samuel Pepys,* ed. by Robert Latham & William Matthews, 11 vols (London: Bell & Hyman, 1970-83), I, pp. lxxv-vi.

7   BL Add. MSS 78577-9 of the Evelyn Papers contain transcripts and notes in Bray's hand, confirming his leading role in the project; see also Isabel Sullivan's essay below. Upcott was inclined to exaggerate his role in the affair in his later accounts of it, for instance in that quoted at length in *Diary,* I, 53-4.

8   *John Evelyn in the British Library,* pp. 64-71. On Upcott see A. N. L. Munby, *The Cult of the Autograph Letter in England* (London: Athlone Press, 1962), ch. 2.

9   This edition contained over twice as many of Evelyn's letters as the first; it also included an extensive selection of the correspondence of Mary Evelyn. No significant additions were made to subsequent editions.

10 Sir Walter Scott, *Kenilworth,* 3 vols (Edinburgh, 1821), II, 18-19; *The Miscellaneous Writings of John Evelyn,* ed. by William Upcott (London: Henry Colburn, 1825), pp. vii, xxiii.

11 Bonamy Dobrée, *Essays in Biography, 1680-1726* (London: Humphrey Milford, 1925), pp. 201ff.

12 Arthur Ponsonby, *John Evelyn* (London: Heinemann, 1933).

13 Virginia Woolf, *The Common Reader* (London, 1925, repr. 1929), pp. 117-18.

14 W. G. Hiscock, *John Evelyn and his Family Circle* (London: Routledge, 1955), p. vi.

15 Frances Harris, *Transformations of Love: the Friendship of John Evelyn and Margaret Godolphin* (Oxford University Press, 2003).

16 E. S. de Beer, 'John Evelyn: Mr W. G. Hiscock's Account of Him', *Notes and Queries,* 205 (1960), 203-6, 243-8, 284-6. For Hiscock's response, see ibid., 476-7.

17 If anything, it is sometimes over-annotated, for instance when Evelyn mentions Michelangelo's tomb to Julius II in Rome and de Beer gives a lengthy note on it: *Diary,* II, 278.

18 *Diary,* II, 26; cf. ibid., I, 69ff.

19 J. P. Kenyon, *Robert Spencer, 2nd Earl of Sunderland* (London: Longmans, 1958).

20 Peter Beal, *Index of English Literary Manuscripts,* 3 vols (London: Mansell, 1980-93), II: *1625-1700,* Pt 1 (1987), 461-87.

21 *Elysium Britannicum or The Royal Gardens,* ed. by John Ingram (Philadelphia: University of Pennsylvania Press, 2001).

22 *The Evelyn Library,* Christie's, London, 4 parts, 22-23 June 1977, 30 Nov.- 1 Dec. 1977, 15-16 March 1978, 12-13 July 1978; *John Evelyn in the British Library,* pp. 74-102. Subsidiary sales of books were on 12 Oct. 1977 and 8 Nov. 1978. The principal Christie's sales at which Evelyn material other than books appeared occurred on 17-18, 23-24 and 31 March, 20, 22 April, 10 May 1977.

23 The deeds and manorial records relating to the Surrey estates went on deposit to the Surrey History Centre.

24 On Evelyn as theorist, see John Dixon Hunt, *Greater Perfections: the Practice of Garden Theory* (London: Thames & Hudson, 2000), pp.180-200.

25 See esp. Mark Laird, 'Parterre, Grove and Flower Garden: European Horticulture and Planting Design in John Evelyn's Time', in *John Evelyn's 'Elysium Britannicum' and European Gardening*, ed. by Therese O'Malley & Joachim Wolschke-Bulmahn (Washington, D.C.: Dumbarton Oaks, 1998), pp. 171-219.

26 David Howarth, *Lord Arundel and his Circle* (New Haven & London: Yale University Press, 1985), p. 126.

27 *Particular Friends: The Correspondence of Samuel Pepys and John Evelyn*, ed. by Guy de la Bédoyère (Woodbridge: Boydell, 1997).

28 BL Add. MS 78298 and *Diary and Correspondence of John Evelyn*, ed. by William Bray (London: Bohn, 1859), III, 189-93: Evelyn to Clarendon, 18 March, 27 Nov. 1667; BL Add. MS 78317: Evelyn to Arlington, 16 October 1671 (draft on the formation of a library); Douglas Chambers, *The Planters of the English Landscape Garden* (New Haven & London: Yale University Press, 1993), pp. 35-6; *Diary and Correspondence*, ed. Bray, III, 135-6 and Add. MS 78298: Evelyn to Thomas Chiffinch, [1662] and 4 Feb. 1665. See further, in general, Maria Zytaruk, 'Occasional *Specimens*, not Compleat Systemes': John Evelyn's Culture of Collecting', *Bodleian Library Record*, 17 (2001), 185-212.

29 Mark Jenner, 'The Politics of London Air: John Evelyn's *Fumifugium* and the Restoration', *Historical Journal*, 38 (1995), 535-51; see also Gillian Darley's essay below.

30 Michael Leslie, '"Bringing Ingenuity into Fashion": the 'Elysium Britannicum' and the Reformation of Husbandry', in *John Evelyn's 'Elysium Britannicum'* (see n.25 above), pp. 131-52.

31 *Diary*, III, 567-8.

32 The significance of the image is not reduced by the fact that it was originally intended for a different book, an apology for the Society by John Beale, and was only re-routed to Sprat's book when that proved abortive; see Michael Hunter, *Science and Society in Restoration England* (Cambridge: Cambridge University Press, 1981), pp. 194-7. For the 'History of Trades', see ibid., ch. 4.

33 Ibid., pp. 93, 100-1. For a further appraisal of *Sylva* see W. T. Lynch, *Solomon's Child: Method in the Early Royal Society of London* (Stanford: Stanford University Press, 2001), ch. 2.

34 Michael Hunter, *The Royal Society and its Fellows 1660-1700*, 2nd edn (Oxford: British Society for the History of Science, 1994), pp. 32, 41, 142-3.

35 J. M. Levine, *Between the Ancients and the Moderns: Baroque Culture in Restoration England* (New Haven & London: Yale University Press, 1999), chs 1-2.

'EXCUSE THESE IMPERTINENCES'

Evelyn in his Letterbooks

DOUGLAS CHAMBERS

JOHN EVELYN is a chameleon: a man whose work ranges over more than twenty fields and many different sorts of discourse. This is nowhere more evident than in his letters, especially in the 810 letters of which he chose to keep copies in his two surviving volumes of letterbooks. These, however, reflect the same desire for orderly knowledge and arrangement that is reflected in his summary notes (called 'Adversaria') on the books that he read: a 'Method and orderly reduction', as he called it in a letter to his elder brother George, and 'one of the greatest restitutions of our losse in Paradyse'.[1] Not surprisingly, this 'method' is also reflected in the way in which the daily entries of all kinds in his *Diary* make their way into the letters and are further recycled in books: the essay on ice houses for Boyle's *New Experiments and Observations Touching Cold* (1665), for example.[2]

On 15 November 1699, less than a decade before the end of his life, Evelyn wrote (not entirely candidly) at the beginning of his second letter-book:

I did not enter any of these Letters (or what are copied in two other Volumes) with the least Intention to make them publique but for my own satisfaction, and to looke now and then backe upon what has past in my private Concerne and Conversations, many of them being Impertinencys, and therefore may be dispos'd of as my Heirs think fit.[3]

What I would like to discuss is the meaning (for him) of the word 'impertinencys', and how that word is a clue to the nature of his letters generally; that is, to how we might read them.

If Evelyn is protean in his published works (as Horace Walpole complained about *Numismata*), he is even more so in his manuscripts, and especially those of his letters. A surprising number of these letters exist in at least three versions (none of them identical), and even the version entered into the letterbooks has frequently been subsequently altered and annotated by him. (This is a subject that Michael Hunter addressed in his treatment of Evelyn's partly autobiographical letter to William Wotton.)[4]

What surely many (if not most) of us have noted in him is his gust for revision: his inability to leave anything alone – or rather his insistence on seeing what he wrote as part of a dialogue, both among his own acquaintance and with the advancing state of knowledge. This is a state of mind foreign to our latter-day world of settled taxonomies (or was until DNA's 'new philosophy' unsettled our categories). Perhaps in botany at least we can begin again to see something useful in that dismissed category, curiosity, and (in the process) regain the sense of interchange that Marvell celebrated in the 'curious peach' of his poem 'Upon Appleton House'. For Marvell the peach was at once a rare curiosity of nature and at the same time a living thing animated by curiosity to reach itself into the poet's hand.[5] Marvell is engaged in a literally animated dialogue. Speculations, as Evelyn's friend Sir Thomas Browne also observed, look both outwards and inwards. The Mirror looks back at the inquiring observer. To such minds the words 'pertinence' and 'impertinence' depend very much on what Donne called 'the looker on in these actions': 'pertinent' or 'pertaining to' what? Evelyn certainly used the word 'impertinent' in its modern sense some of the time. Writing, for instance, to Lady Berkeley in 1684 about the manners of the contractors who were then building Berkeley Square for her, he could reprove their impertinence to her in the modern sense of that word.[6] He could also use the word (slightly more elusively) to dismiss what he considered the crazed ravings of William Stubbe, the persistent critic of the Royal Society, or to reprove what he considered the hack-work of the French polymath, Samuel de Sorbière.[7] He even feared that his own abortive history of the Dutch Wars was full of historical material about the English navy that might not be pertinent to his subject, and he later described it to Pepys (who lost the manuscript) as 'a fardle of impertinences'.[8]

In most of his letters, though, 'impertinence' is his word to describe everything but the public life that he was drawn into almost from the moment of Charles II's Restoration: a time in which declining a knighthood did not exempt him (as he had once hoped) from royal appointments to state commissions. That public life consumed much of his time and money, primarily on the Commission for Sick and Wounded Seamen in the second and third Dutch Wars, as did his subsequent term as one of the commissioners of the Privy Seal in the years 1685-7, when his conscience was agonized in the slippery negotiations of that difficult time.

Tellingly, in the famous letter to Boyle outlining his thoughts about the Royal Society as a sort of monastic withdrawal, he excuses himself from the common charge of impertinence by drawing attention to the literal impertinence of the world in relation to spiritual and intellectual things. His Royal Society proposal (Evelyn claims) is 'pertinent' to the truth,

and therefore, far from being the Effect either of an impertinent or trifling spirit, but the results of mature and frequent reasoning: And Sir, is not this the same that many noble personages did, at the confusion of the Empire by the barbarous Goths, when St. Hierome, Eustochius and others retired from the impertinencies of the World to the sweete recesses and societys of the East.[9]

In spite of the establishment of the Royal Society in 1661, such 'sweete recesses and societys' were not to become commonplace for him until his close friendship with Pepys from the mid-1660s onwards. And it was in this latter half of his life that such other protégé-correspondents as Francis Godolphin, Charles Spencer, and Robert Berkeley became the substitutes not just for his poor unsatisfactory son, John, but for that remembered world of the virtuoso: the magical years of his continental grand tour in the 1640s. One of his companions at that time had been Robert Heath, a distant cousin whom he described as 'my worthy learned friend' and one of the 'banish'd company' from England. In two letters to Heath in 1659 – about the use of accents in ancient Hebrew – Evelyn first uses the word 'impertinencys' to describe the learned preoccupations that were to occupy his mind for the rest of his life.[10]

By 1659 he had published his translation of book one of Lucretius's *De rerum natura* and six other works, but it was only with the Restoration and the establishment of the Royal Society that he came to see that his learned interest in curiosities would be seen as 'impertinencies' both to the new science and to the *realpolitik* of Restoration public life. A letter to Lord Arlington in 1661, sending him an account of the quarrel between the French and Spanish ambassadors in that year, is an ironic rendering of Evelyn's sense of his own self-exile from that public world:

I have no greater ambitions to serve, then such as prompt me to gratitude. I have Sir, spent much time amongst Bookes, and other impertinences; and want the Politure, which those who have the honor to converse with you receive, which makes me sometimes emulous of their good fortune, who having stations at Court can cultivate those shining talents which wee that are poore Country Gentlemen, may not hope to aspire to.[11]

It was plainly no dishonour to Evelyn to abjure the world of the town and courtly mouse with its 'politure' and 'good fortune'. Better bookish 'impertinences' than to aspire to such 'shining talents'! One of the 'impertinences' he had in mind would have been his translation of Naudé's *Instructions Concerning Erecting of a Library*, which was printing at the very time of this letter: a book which he was to dedicate to a very different sort of statesman (and former fellow exile), Lord Clarendon.

When, in December of that year, he sent a copy to court of his *Tyrannus, or the Mode* (an attack on the taste in London for absurd French fashions) it was in the recognition that that sort of publication was just the sort of raillery that would be to the court's taste. To Lord Arlington he wrote:

If this innocent exercise I presume to put into your hands afford his Majestie the least Diversion, I am to Sacrifice to the Addresse which shall present it: Be pleas'd therefore to take some lucky opportunity of reading it to him: if he smile, mention your humble servant; if he frowne, conceale his name, and pardon the presumption: It is with you onely he dares trust his fame: and as he finds the returne in this; so is resolv'd to publish to the World to whom he is indebted for it. I would not have you thinke I preserve the least fondnesse for this Trifle, farther then as an Essay; call it a Rhapsody or what you please.[12]

What Evelyn publishes to the world is a list of fashionable follies gleaned from the court itself. What a long way this 'rhapsody' or illusion is from the world of learning that he shared with (for example) Sir Kenelm Digby to whom he wrote (echoing Naudé) in the following May about 'what Bookes had bin publish'd amongst us during these late Yeares' and how they might be catalogued.[13]

Within the next year he had translated the relation of China by Janus Dousa or van der Does (a work never published), corresponded with Thomas Pierce on ecclesiastical controversies, and sent plants and seeds to Cowley.[14] In all of these letters he described his interests as trifles or impertinences, but they were so only in a world in which learning was a peripheral 'impertinence'. Indeed in his ode to Cowley on the garden (a work later 'recycled' to Flower Hyde), Evelyn celebrated (in the midst of the plague) the archetypal topos of innocent retreat from the world. And yet he was able to describe its subject as 'the formes and impertinences of my manner of life'.[15] Evelyn's friend Sir Roger L'Estrange, in his *Seneca's Morals By Way of Abstract* (published in 1678 and reaching ten editions by 1711), was to ensure that Augustan withdrawal was the model: a model in which learned 'impertinencies' could be weighed against the world's vanities.

Even the assembling of the material for his 'Elysium Britannicum', Evelyn describes (in a letter to Lord Sandwich in 1667 about Spanish gardens and the Spanish seed-drill or 'sembrador') as 'my impertinencies amongst your publique weighty concernes'. And he would use the same sort of diction in asking Richard Stokes about getting seeds from the Holy Land for the same work.[16] Only to such an epistolary friend as John Beale could Evelyn use the phrase 'the impertinencies of my life in this place' to refer to the frequent interruptions of his life in Sayes Court that took him from his real vocation, reading and writing.[17] To Thomas Lloyd, an unidentifiable correspondent from Whitminster in Gloucestershire, it is Evelyn's inquiries for 'Elysium Britannicum' that are 'impertinences'.[18] To his good friend Thomas Clifford (as to Beale) Evelyn's 'conversation sometimes amongst Bookes to redeeme my tyme from other Impertinences' is in contrast to the quotidien matters of the world. And to his son John who knows his mind and temper, he can write of the sorrows and impertinencies of this world.[19]

Indeed it was the death of his close friends, beginning with Margaret Godolphin in 1678, that initiated an elegiac strain in his letters. 'We have lately lost as many Friends, as there are Months,' he writes to Anne Sylvius in 1679.[20] What he called these 'unavoidable Impertinences'[21] (life's transience) were to recur as a theme for the rest of his life in the annual letters to Lord Godolphin on the anniversary of Margaret's death.

Those letters he referred to as 'my Impertinencies', as he would the two letters to Godolphin on the death of Charles II in 1685. But for Evelyn the *real* impertinences were the affairs of the public world. 'You and I,' he writes to Godolphin at that time of threatened political upheaval, 'have pass'd through so many changes, and irreparable losses, as ought, by this time to have exhausted all our passions for the things and enjoyments of this vaine and empty world.'[22] Over against this, like the refugee saints of the late Roman empire (or Plato's philosopher come to that), is Evelyn's sense of withdrawal to the *hortus conclusus* of his garden and the pertinent world of knowledge that could be cultivated (in both senses) within it. Evelyn's frequently iterated description of himself as 'a planter of coleworts' (cabbages) draws attention to his withdrawal to an elysian world that is both classical and biblical, Edenic and Virgilian.

Annabel Patterson's *Censorship and Interpretation* (especially the chapter called 'Letters to Friends: the Self in Familiar Form') is primarily addressed to considerations of the self in epistolary writing and to the ways in which oppositional writing deploys the letter.[23] Her account of the way in which letters became vehicles for political debate during the Civil War and, in the hands of opposition writers in the 1670s a genre in their own right, also provides a useful map within which to place Evelyn's epistolary practice. Certainly it was shaped in the 1640s by the need to write royalist letters to his father-in-law in France, quite literally in code.[24] It was also probably influenced by the sophisticated epistolary conventions with which Evelyn would have been familiar at the French court. Arising out of the salons there, these conventions had produced writing manuals for letters that were to result in the publication of three significant collections of letters in 1668-9 and lay the groundwork of the epistolary novel.[25]

But with none of Evelyn's correspondents did the essay-epistle flourish as it did in the correspondence with Pepys. Beginning in the 1660s as a practical exchange about the Commission for Sick and Wounded Seamen from the Dutch Wars, it became by the 1680s an occasion for the longest letters that Evelyn wrote: on the history of the navy and naval combat in antiquity, dogs at war, the collecting of medals, books, coins and prints, and the nature of the English language.[26] When he writes to Pepys in 1683 about what might be discovered on the expedition to Tangier, it is for both ancient coins and inscriptions as well as modern plants that he asks assistance. And he does so not only with reference to the interest of classical authors, but in their epistolary manner:

Had you time, I dare say, your Curiosity would among other things carry you to the Inquiry after *Medalls* and Inscriptions[27] frequently dug up about the old Tingis[28] Mr: Streeter[29] will not be unmindfull of a poore *Gard'ner*, if he happen on any Kernels, or seedes, of such Trees and Plants especially sempervirent) as grow about that Citty: Were it not posible to discover whether any of those *Citern* [citron] *Trees* are extant, that of old grew about the Foote of *Mont Atlas*? (not far from *Tangir*) and were heretofore in deliciis for their politure[30] and natural machinations,[31] to that degree, as estimated worth their weight in Gold? *Cicero* had a Table of one that cost him *Ten-thousand Sestertias*, and another (I read of) valued at 140000 sestertias which at 3 pence per sestertia amounted to a pretty Summ, and one of the *Ptolomies* had yet another of far greater price[32] insomuch as when they us'd to reproch their Wives for their prodigality and Lux in *Pearls* and Points,[33] they would briskly retort, and turne the *Tables* on their *Husbands*. Now for that some copies in Pliny read *Cedria*, others *Citria*, it would be inquir'd what sort of *Cedar* (if any) grows there: But I am growing to be impertinent and beg pardon.[34]

Evelyn shares many of Pliny's interests and concerns: politics, the advancement of young men's careers, the arts, retirement, the extended family, and natural history. And it is no diminution of his grief at the death of his daughter Mary to note that his letter about her death sounds remarkably like that of Pliny's on the death of a friend's daughter (*Epistolae* 5.16). Pliny even provides a model for the ancients and moderns controversy (6.11); and many of his letters – the one about his uncle's library and reading habits, for example (3.5) – sound suspiciously like the sort of essay-letter on that subject that Evelyn wrote to Pepys. Perhaps nothing puts Evelyn closer to Pliny than Pliny's concern with narrative and revision. His arrangement of his letters to form a narrative and his rewriting of his speeches is reflected in Evelyn's rewriting of his own letters in his two letterbooks. Although Cicero wrote from his estate at Tusculum, it was the younger Pliny (modelling himself on Cicero) who provided what are still regarded as models of such description (*Epistolae*, 2.17 and 5.6). Indeed it has been argued that these letters are only models of the sort of thing one *might* write about an estate. As written and topographical texts they were constantly argued over in the seventeenth century and are certainly detectable both in Evelyn's description of his own estate and in those of others. His 1686 letter to his young protégé, Robert Berkeley, for example, describes gardens worth visiting in the Netherlands.[35]

Nothing better characterizes this double sense of address to both ancient and modern audiences in Evelyn's correspondence than a letter he ostensibly sent to Pepys on 20 June 1687:

It has often come into my mind, that observation of Velleius Paterculus (speaking of the greate Scipio) as often as you have come into my thoughts (which is I assure very often) that never any body did more worthily Imploy the Intervale of Buisinesse: ...

[No man more than Scipio ever relieved the impositions of an active life by a more elevated use of his leisure time, or was more constant in his devotion either to the arts of war or peace. Always involved in the pursuit of arms or his studies, he was either training his body by exposure to danger or his mind to learning.] Thus you, either to the Affaires of the Navy, or to the Culture of the mind, by reading, and studying and encouraging all that is great, and becoming a generous Soule: No person that I know of has more fortunately pass'd the Adventures of an unquiet and tumultuary Age, and in so buisy a station, if that may be so calld, which is so full of motion, as that which is upon the floods and waters.[36]

There is no evidence that this letter (like several addressed to Pepys) was ever sent. It seems as much an encomium in the style of Seneca or Pliny – to be addressed to a man such as Pepys – as a letter: almost as if Evelyn required a notional correspondent to whom to write this kind of address.

Cicero himself, in the *Epistulae ad Familiares* (*Familiar Letters*, II.4), tells Curionus that letters are not for seeking simple pieces of information; that's what servants are for. But the kind of letters that please him, Cicero says, are the intimate and humorous or the austere and serious. Cicero also notes that letters, 'except when they deal with some subject above their natural level', have a looser texture and peculiar rhythms, 'the structural cohesion being loose rather than non-existent'.[37] Cicero's letters set the tone for the learned epistle and it is his gravity of subject that characterizes most of Evelyn's letter-essays.

In his 'Notes towards the Study of the Renaissance Letter', an account of the neo-Latin letter, Claudio Guillén elaborates the genre and context to which Evelyn's essay-letters to Pepys also belong: 'an ideal of friendship … and the pursuit of scholarship join these men, who share items of philological or philosophical knowledge, erudite commentaries, travel descriptions, the incidents of vanity, and fluctuations of fame'.[38] What I am drawing attention to is the conscious literary language of self-definition, and the corollary implications for what Evelyn writes of himself in his letters. In 1694 he wrote to Pepys (now living in retirement at Clapham, as Evelyn was at Wotton) about the sense of collegiality that had prevailed among their circle in the 1680s in Surrey Street:

I have now in prospect of my exalted *Studiolum* here, Water, Woods, Meadow and other Circumstances of Solitude; I have also a pretty Collection of Books, which I brought along with me: But there is no such thing as a Mr. *Pepys* nor Dr. *Gale* within 20 Miles north of me, nor within a Thousand of any other point of the Compas.[39]

Reading Aulus Gellius, Evelyn thinks of the learned *convivia* of his friends in London in terms of that classical model: affable dialogue, but also about the serious business of the reformation of knowledge.

I wish we had more of these *Attic Nights*,[40] and glad I am to find they are come into fashion; nor do I looke on them as Scraps; but as *Bellaria*, and *Cupediæ* [sweetmeats

27

and delicacies], which exceedingly refresh with their pretty Varietie, when one has ben Tir'd with moyling, and turning over the Rubbish you justly Complaine of; and which after all the Toile, and Time repaies one with so little solid Advantage: With you therefore I have a thousand times deplor'd, that there has as yet ben so little don towards the Ridding us of this monstrous and unprofitable Lumber: Indeede honest Gesner[41] has don his part, and by his Example shew'd what others might do; and such as of late have taken paines in the Histories of Animals and Plants: Dr. Pell[42] left a Diatyposis [Gk: *diatuposis*] of what he pretended to have don in the Mathematic Cycle; and the late *Bishop of Chester*[43] (our never to be forgotten Friend) in the prælimina[r]ie to his Essay of the *Real Character*, scor'd-out many most usefull Tables, preparatory to such a Work: I meane not to the Knowledge of Words and Language onely, but of real Things, greately conducing to such an undertaking.[44]

But such a reformation of knowledge does not imply ridding inquiry of the sorts of speculation that also occupied Boyle (to his early editors' chagrin): the loves of the angels, for example. It is Hamlet's speculations that linger in a letter to Pepys in 1690 about the interpretation of dreams.

'Tis now mithinks, so *long* since I saw my *Friend*, that I cannot but inquire after his health: If he Aske what I am doing here so long? *Sarcinam componere* [bundling up my cares]: I am making my *Fardle* of *Impertinences*, that I may march with the lesse Incumbrance: ... I *dream'd* last night (for you know, I have little else to entertaine you with for the most part besides *Dreames*) that you sent me word you would *dine* with me to day: which, according to the *Oneirocritics* (or as *Homer* his ... (dreams, or castles in the air) are to be *Interpreted* by the *Contrary*) and by that *Rule*, I should dine with Mr. *Pepys*: But since the times of *Joseph* and *Daniel*,[45] I have found them oft mistaken, and the truth is, I am Ingag'd to dine *at White-hall* to day, though I assure you, I had rather eate a *sallad* on a *Joynt-stoole* with you, and *Dr. Gale*, than with all the *pompe* of Courts.[46]

These are dreams, but they are also 'lies like truth'. Far from the world of courts Evelyn writes of bundling up his scattered writings and putting them into some order. They may be 'impertinencies' to the world, but they are his 'cares'. It is a cliché of criticism that neo-classicism belongs to the age of Pope. But Evelyn's whole career is modelled on the '*procul discordibus armis*' section of *Georgic II*, in which Virgil celebrates the wise man's withdrawal from the corruption of courts and towns to a life of reflection and modest aspiration.

As early as 1653, the year after he came back to live in England and to make what accommodation he could with what he always called 'the rebels', he wrote to his friend Jasper Needham at his ancestral home, Wotton in Surrey. There (with his elder brother and his cousin) he had already redesigned some of the gardens in a neo-classical manner, as he would do nearby in the 1660s for Henry Howard, the future duke of Norfolk and son of his mentor, Lord Arundel. For him he would create a reconstruction of Virgil's tomb at Posilippo. Evelyn's picture of all this to Needham is classical, humanist, sylvan, and exotic all at once.

Imagine yet, how my thoughts waite on you into the grounds, and about the fountaines; how they assent in your preferring of that Tulip, or this Anemonie; that I breath the same ayre, commend the same prospect, philosophize in the same peristyle, upon that artificial Iris which the sunn reflects from the watry girandola below it, or the beauties of those faire Nymphs which admire it [and he goes on to quote Virgil on Dido's palace].[47]

In 1690 he wrote two joking letters to his honorary grandson, the eleven-year-old Francis Godolphin, about the boy's trip to the family home at Breage in Cornwall. The first prompted Francis to send Evelyn an account of his journey: the earliest such account by an English child that I know of.[48] Evelyn replied, thanking him for his epistolary journal in the terms both of ancient and modern learning. It is a letter that both plays with the curriculum of Francis's education and endorses it: a playfulness that reveals Evelyn's ironic stance about letter-writing itself.

Never did *Aldrovandus*[49] who writ of *Birds, Beasts* and *Fishes, Men,* Mer-Maids and *Monsters*; no nor *Ulysses* of *Ithaca Multorum mores homines qui vidit, et Urbes*, in all his ten-yeares *Errors* and *Ramblings* (himselfe so *transmogrified* at his Returne, as no living *Creature* knew him, but his *old* Dog) and that all the World has for *above 3000* yeares cryed-up for so renown'd a *Leg-stretcher*; I say, Neither of these, have ever left to *posterity*, such an Account of his Travells, as my deare *Grand-child* has don.[50]

In the 1690s Evelyn also had high hopes for Charles Spencer, the future 3rd Earl of Sunderland, who corresponded with him in Latin. In 1694, when Charles was nearing his majority, Evelyn referred to the Spencers' home as the 'Althorpian Tempe', a place where learned conversation was common-place.[51] Here is a place where ancients and moderns are at one, not least in the business of letter-writing:

Having now tempted, and sufficiently provok'd your Lordship in *Plautus, Cicero, Pliny, Seneca, Lipsius*[52] etc. (for your Lordship is master of all styles) I give it over: on my word, your Lordship has tam'd the shrew, and 'tis more than time for me to leave off the Pedant, and write hence foreward in my mother tongue: And now I think on't, I cannot a little wonder, that whilst there are extant so many Volumes of Letters and familiar Epistles, in the politer modern Languages Italian, Spanish, French, we should have so few tollerable ones of our owne country now extant who have adorned the part of Elegancy, so proper, and so becoming persons of the noblest quality, and men of Businesse, and Erudition too, as well, as Lovers, and Courters of the faire sex.

What Evelyn then offers is a survey of vernacular letter-writing as an art: an art that he had practised for over half a century and of whose conventions he was thoroughly aware:

Sir *Francis Bacon*,[53] *Dr. Don*[54] and I hardly remember any else, who have publish'd any thing of considerable, and they but gleanings of our Cabbal men,[55] who have put many things in an heape, without much choice or fruite: Especialy as to Culture of the Style or Language; The Genius of the Nation being almost another thing, than it was at that time: *James Howel* publish'd his *Ho-Elianæ*, for which he indeede was laught at; not for his Letters, which acquaint us with a number of passages, worthy to be known, and had never else ben preserved, but for that pedant, and the many impertinent Bookes, the poore Gent. was faine mercenarily to put out, that he might Eate bread in the late times:[56]

Donne himself was a commentator on letter-writing and rehearses the examples of antiquity in a letter to his father-in-law, Sir George More:

What treasures of Morall knowledge are in *Senecaes* Letters to onely one *Lucilius*? and what of Naturall in *Plinies*? how much of the storie of the time, is in *Ciceroes* Letters? … The Evangiles and Acts, teach us what to beleeve, but the Epistles of the Apostles what to do. And those who have endeavoured to dignifie *Seneca* above his worth, have no way fitter, then to imagine Letters between him and S. *Paul.*[57]

Similarly, what Evelyn says about the art of letter-writing by his predecessors and contemporaries gives insight into the way he thought about his own composition.

Yet, I say, even those letters, are worthy the reading, for the Matter and Subject of divers of them: Familiar Letters of that, and other Kinds your Lordship knowes comprehende all the kinds *Deliberative, Demonstrative, Judiciary*, and what ever else can fall under the compass of Rhetorick. There were nothing I thinke more conducible to the Improvement of our Young Gent, be his aime whatsoever in the state publique or private Capacity, than an easy and natural style in writing letters, nor any exercise by which he may better discover his abillities, or improve those who reade them: What should we have don with-out *Ciceros*,[58] and the younger *Plinies*?[59] to name no more, because they are incomparably the best, and of the later Centuries, *Erasmus*,[60] to this time: I am bold to affirme, that there is more good Learning to be gotten from Epistles, than from all the rest of their Workes, more of the Soule, and most intimate thoughts, and deepest knowledge of the writers: *St. Cyprian, St. Augustine*, St. *Hierome*, etc. of the Fathers, *Calvine, Melanchton, Vives, Politianus, Grotius, Salmasius*, our owne Countryman *Ascham*,[61] etc. Let not therefore the *Aretines, Bentivoglias, Balzacs, Voitures*,[62] and the rest Transalpines and exotics, forever cary it away from England, where were the language cultivated with that sort of Exercise and Conversation, I should not question, its being equal to any of the most celebrated abroade: When therefore your Lordship shall think fit to descend so low, as to believe it not unworthy your Reflection; (You who are so perfect a Master in the learned Tongues) how would you imbellish your native Language, and set an emulous example to others, revive the dul and torpent age, and put it out of Debt by the product of a native Stock of our owne, and as I said, the most usefull.[63]

Evelyn, like Donne, would have heard the Pauline epistles regularly as part of the liturgy of the church and was familiar with the patristic commentary on them. Moreover, Lipsius's sense of letters, not as an aspect of oratory but of discourse, was based on Erasmus's translation of the first sentence of the gospel of *John* where the Greek *logos* was translated not as *verbum* (word) but *sermo* (discourse).[64] Lipsius's definition of the letter not as a branch of oratory but as a 'message of the mind', and the mind of one withdrawn from the world of affairs, is Stoic in origin and close to Evelyn's ideal. Like Evelyn too, Lipsius seems to have revised his letters and to have used them to discuss education and style. Whether as a pedagogical manual or as a scholarly critique of manuals of letter-writing, Lipsius's *Epistolica* looked back to Cicero and classical practice.

The most influential treatise in the tradition of the reformed epistle of the Renaissance, however, was Erasmus's *De Conscribendis Epistolis* (1522), of which Evelyn owned the 1530 Paris edition. It was a work designed as much for pedagogy as for practice. Echoing Cicero, Erasmus recognized that letters were not oratory and that therefore the three traditional divisions of classical oratory into demonstrative, deliberative, and judicial were not adequate for the epistle. If 'no topic is excluded from the letter form', he argues, 'and if, in addition the mode of expression must never be at variance with the nature of the subject, how, I ask you, can a single style be devised for such an infinitely varied content?'[65] His subsequent division of the subject into more than seventy kinds of letters suggests the range of possible kinds, many of them strikingly similar to the sorts of letters Evelyn was to write to his correspondents more than a century later: letters of dissuasion and consolation; of petition and recommendation; of advice, complaint, or entreaty; of instruction, thanks, or congratulation. But what are closest to Evelyn's favourite sort of letter – the letters of discussion or information – are inevitably so varied that Erasmus's only advice is that they be straight-forward and clear. The *De Conscribendis Epistolis* was republished thirty times in Erasmus's lifetime and (like his *De Copia Verborum ac Rerum* which Evelyn echoes in a letter to Pepys on language)[66] continued to be very influential after his time. From the *Lettere di diversi nobilissimi uomini e chiari ingegni*, published in Venice in 1542, to Abraham Fleming's collection of the translated letters of Cicero, Pliny, and others, in *A Panoplie of Epistles* in 1576, classical letter-writers were held up as the models of the school-room.

Erasmus's catalogue of the various kinds of modern letters was followed closely by English writers of epistolary theory in the later sixteenth century: William Fullwood's *Enimie of Idleness* (1568), Angell Day's *The English Secretorie* (1586, 1592),[67] John Hoskyn's *Directions for Speech and Style* (*c.*1599), and even Jonson's *Discoveries* (1641). By the end of the century, however, Erasmus's work had been overlaid by Justus Lipsius's *Epistolica Institutio* (1591), not least in Lipsius's continuing to stress the difference between an epistle and an oration: a distinction that went back to Demetrius's ancient Greek work, *On Style*. This distinction had been eroded by the formulaic rhetoric of the mediaeval *ars dictaminis* tradition: a tradition that one critic has called 'a rhetorical deadend unparalleled in the arts of discourse'.[68] Like Erasmus's work, Lipsius's *Epistolica Institutio*, though based on such a work as Cicero's *De Oratore*, takes its manner from Horace's *Ars poetica*, which is itself cast as a letter. And his sympathies are with the Cicero who writes to Papirus Paetus 'my letters I generally compose in the language of everyday life' (*Ad Familiares* 9.21), or with the Seneca who says to Lucilius, 'I prefer that my letters should be just what my conversation would be if you and I were sitting in one another's company or taking long walks together – spontaneous and easy' (*Ad Lucilium Epistulae Morales*, 75).

What many of these letters exemplify is an overlap between *literae* (learned writing) and *epistolae* (correspondence). The English language elides these two meanings in the one word 'letters', though Ted Hughes's collection of posthumous poems to his wife, Sylvia Plath, called *Birthday Letters*,[69] is a reminder of the word's continuing ambivalence. Moreover the classical models that lurk in Evelyn's epistolary practice are dialectical. In her study, *Eros the Bittersweet*, the contemporary poet and classical scholar, Anne Carson, has remarked on the ancient Greek sense that ideas are 'part of a process that is necessarily lived out in space and time'. 'Letters stand oblique to the action,' she points out, 'and unfold a three-cornered relation: A writes to C about B, or B reads a letter from C in the presence of A, and so on'; a collection of such letters is not a simple narrative compilation, but demands an 'act of communication as an intimate collusion between writer and reader'.[70]

On 3 December 1686 Evelyn wrote to Lord Danby who, as Lord Treasurer before his fall from power in 1679, had been responsible for the preservation of royal woods and forests. His subject is the revived Augustanism that he, Cowley, and Waller had hoped for at the Restoration court:

yet had *Augustus* and other mighty Princes, their Malles *Additus* and would sometimes heare Pöems recited, and *Scipio* would converse with *Lælius*, & some-times with *Lucilius* too: *Cicero, Hortensius* & the Purpl'd Senators in the midst of Buisinesse & State Affairs, went often to their *Tusculans* and *Wimbledons* to irrigate and refresh the *Platanus* with those very hands, they sign'd the Fate of Empires, and controll'd the World.[71]

Pliny's Tusculum and Danby's Wimbledon (a former palace of Charles I's wife) are part of one continuum for Evelyn. If England is to become the Empire of Great Britain that James I envisaged, it must place itself within the discourse of that older empire. Two years later Evelyn writes to Flower Hyde and quotes Cicero 'for [he says] you read his Worke, and understand him too'.[72]

In the same year he wrote to Lady Sunderland of retirement to the country in terms that would have suited Horace or Pliny the Younger or even the Virgil of the *Georgics* (2.459):

I have preferr'd the Recesse of neere Thirty-Yeares ... [and] have found nothing Solid, nothing stable, and worth all this hurry, disquiet, and expense of Time, but the pursuite of Moderate Things for this Life ... Piety, Sincerity, Justice, Temperance, and all that *Series* and Chaine of the *Moral Vertues* (recommended to us, as well by the wiser Heathen, as by *God* himselfe and the very dictates of Nature) are the onely meanes of obtaining that Tranquill and happy state, a prudent man would choose.[73]

The more than 800 letters in the letterbooks show Evelyn revising and reusing letters, creating effectively a parallel (and often scholarly) auto-biography to the (largely public) life that he offers in his better-known *Diary*. This is 'life-writing' of a highly conscious and literary kind. As such, these letters constitute a literary document, a corpus, as the letters of Cicero, Seneca, and Pliny also do: not simply a record of the busy affairs of a very long life, but a dialectic of the various stages of his own life amid the 'hypertexts' of his friends' letters and the letters of antiquity that are his models.

NOTES

1 BL Add. MS 78298: to George Evelyn, 15 Oct. 1658 (no. 143). The numbers following this and later citations of the letters are those assigned to them in my forthcoming edition of Evelyn's letterbooks (formerly Christ Church MSS 39 a, b, now BL Add. MSS 78298-9).
2 Ibid.: to Robert Boyle, 21 Oct. 1664 (no. 224).
3 BL Add. MS 78299, f. iii. The reference to 'two other Volumes' apparently refers to the division of the two bound letterbooks into three sections, 'Liber I', 'Liber II' and 'Liber III', of which the last (letters in English) is by far the longest, taking up most of the first and all of the second letterbook. It is not clear how Evelyn imagined that some letters in these continuously written volumes could be removed without destroying others.
4 'John Evelyn's letter to William Wotton, 29 March, 1696', in *Robert Boyle by Himself and his Friends*, ed. by Michael Hunter (London: Pickering & Chatto, 1994), pp. 84-90.
5 This interchange between the botanic and the human world is the subject of Michael Pollan's *The Botany of Desire* (London: Bloomsbury, 2000).
6 BL Add. MS 78299: to Lady Berkeley, 26 July 1684 (no. 483).
7 BL Add. MS 78298: to John Beale, 27 July 1670; to Thomas Sprat, 31 Oct. 1664 (nos 331, 223).
8 Ibid.: to Clifford, 14 Nov. 1671 (no. 345); BL Add. MS 78299: to Pepys, 5 Dec. 1681 (no. 438).
9 BL Add. MS 78298: to Boyle, 3 Sept. 1659 (no. 159).
10 Ibid.: to Heath, 26 Feb., 3 March 1659 (nos 153, 154).
11 Ibid.: to Arlington, 7 Oct. 1661 (no. 191).
12 Ibid.: to Arlington, 4 Dec. 1661 (no. 193).
13 Ibid.: to Digby, 15 May 1662 (no. 197).

14 Ibid.: to Dousa, 13 Sept. 1662; to Thomas Pierce, 17 Sept. 1663; to Cowley, 20 March 1663 (nos 200, 212, 202).

15 Ibid.: to Cowley, 24 Aug. 1666 (no. 278).

16 Ibid.: to Sandwich, 13 Dec. 1667; to Richard Stokes, 21 Aug. 1668 (nos 300, 308).

17 Ibid.: to Beale, 27 Aug. 1668 (no. 310).

18 Ibid.: to Thomas Lloyd, 16 Oct. 1668 (no. 312).

19 Ibid.: to Clifford, 1 Feb. 1669; to his son, [*c.* April 1679] (nos 315, 404).

20 BL Add. MS 78299: to Lady Sylvius, 4 May 1679 (no. 406).

21 Ibid.: to Lady Berkeley, 28 Aug. 1680 (no. 423).

22 Ibid.: to Godolphin, 19 Dec. 1681, 11 Feb., 20 March 1685 (nos 440, 495, 499).

23 Madison, WI: University of Wisconsin Press, 1984.

24 BL Add. MS 34702, ff. 23-222.

25 See Elizabeth J. MacArthur, *Extravagant Narratives: Closure and Dynamics in the Epistolary Form* (Princeton, N.J.: Princeton University Press, 1990), ch. 1.

26 *Particular Friends: The Correspondence of Samuel Pepys and John Evelyn*, ed. by Guy de la Bédoyère (Woodbridge: Boydell, 1997), letters C1, C7-C10; C14; C47; C49.

27 Evelyn's correspondence with Pepys about this resulted in his *Numismata: a Discourse of Medals* (London: B. Tooke, 1697).

28 The ancient name for Tangiers. See Pliny, *Natural History*, V.14, and XIII.91.

29 Apparently a mistake for Henry Sheeres, FRS and military engineer.

30 'Delightful, and valued for their polish'.

31 A mistake for 'maculations' (as in the original letter): markings for which this wood was highly valued (see Pliny, *Natural History*, XIII.96). In fact, Cicero's table cost half a million sesterces (see *Particular Friends*, p. 144).

32 Pliny cites Ptolemy of Mauretania as owning the largest citrus-wood table that he knows of. Cicero refers to such a table in the *Verrine Orations*, IV.27 (17).

33 Lace or needlework.

34 BL Add. MS 78299: to Pepys, 10 Aug. 1683 (no. 463).

35 Ibid.: to Berkeley, 16 July 1686 (no. 540).

36 Ibid.: 20 June 1687 (no. 567); *Particular Friends*, p. 177: C38. The translation of the original Latin in square brackets is mine.

37 *Institutio Oratoria*, trans. by H. E. Butler (London: Heinemann, 1922), III; IX.iv.19. Giles Constable warns that there is a danger in imposing our retro-spective categories on these letters. Not only is there 'no clear line [that] can be drawn between the "historical" and "literary" aspects of mediaeval [Latin] letters', but even in Roman epistles it is not true that some were 'literary and intended for publication and that [others were] unliterary and intended for the addressee only'; *Letters and Letter Collections,* Typologie Des Sources du Moyen Âge Occidental, Fasc. 17 (Turnhout, Belgium: Editions Brepolis, 1976), p. 22.

38 Claudio Guillén, *Renaissance Genres: Essays on Theory, History, and Interpret-ation*, Harvard English Studies 14 (Cambridge, MA: Harvard University Press, 1986), p. 91.

39 BL Add. MS 78299: to Pepys, 30 May 1694 (no. 707).

40 Aulus Gellius's *Noctes Atticae* (*c.*180 AD) is a collection of notes on reading.

41 Conrad Gesner; probably his *Catalogus Plantarum* (Zurich, 1542).

42 John Pell wrote an *Idea of Mathematicks* (1639), which was published in 1650 as

an appendix to J. Dury, *The Reformed Librarie-Keeper* (1650).

43 John Wilkins.

44 BL Add. MS 78299: to Pepys, 2 Sept. 1694 (no. 718).

45 Two Old Testament prophets associated with the interpretation of dreams.

46 BL Add. MS 78299: to Pepys, 2 Oct. 1690 (no. 636).

47 BL Add. MS 78298: to Needham, 16 June 1653 (no. 67). See also my 'The Tomb in the Landscape: John Evelyn's Garden at Albury', *Journal of Garden History*, 1 (1981), 37-51. My reading of this garden as an invocation of Virgil has been challenged by Carola and Alastair Small in 'John Evelyn and the Garden of Epicurus', *Journal of the Warburg and Courtauld Institute*, 60 (1997), 194-214. In that Virgil himself invoked Epicurus's garden of retirement in the *Georgics*, I do not find their reading persuasive.

48 BL Add. MS 78307: Francis Godolphin to Evelyn, 5 July 1690.

49 Ulisse Aldrovandi was a natural historian who published on birds (1599), fish (1613), animals (1637), and monsters (1642). An anthology of his work was published in 1642. His namesake, Ulysses, is described by Horace (*Ars Poetica* 142) as one who 'saw the customs of men and cities', a paraphrase of the opening words of the *Odyssey*.

50 BL Add. MS 78299: to Francis Godolphin, 9 Aug. 1690 (no. 633).

51 Ibid.: to Spencer, Aug. 1694 (no. 717).

52 Ibid.: to Spencer, 15 Jan. 1692 (no. 665). All these Latin authors were read for their style. A copy of the 1596 Louvain edition of Lipsius's *Epistolarum centuriae duae* is listed in Evelyn's library catalogue of *c.*1687, BL Add. MS 78632. Lipsius was a modern follower of Plautus and wrote in a terse style.

53 Bacon's *Scrinia Ceciliana: Mysteries of State and Government* (London, 1663) contained many of his previously unpublished letters.

54 The 1651 edition of John Donne's *Letters to Severall Persons of Honour* is listed in Evelyn's library catalogue of *c.*1687.

55 *Cabala, sive Scrinia sacra: Mysteries of State and Government: in Letters of Illustrious Persons* (London, 1654).

56 Four of Howell's political works are listed in Evelyn's library catalogue of *c.*1687.

57 *Letters to Severall Persons of Honour* (London, 1651), pp. 105-6. Although many seventeenth-century readers continued to believe that the correspondence between St Paul and Seneca was genuine, Erasmus had attacked its legitimacy in his 1529 catalogue of Seneca's works. Nonetheless, he regarded Seneca's letters as exemplary models of letter-writing; see Lisa Jardine, *Erasmus, Man of Letters* (Princeton, N.J.: Princeton University Press, 1995), chs 5 and 6, and Anthony Grafton, *Forgers and Critics* (Princeton, N.J.: Princeton University Press, 1990).

58 Of Cicero's *Familiar Letters* Evelyn had the 1599 Leiden and the 1578 Paris edition as well as the English edition translated by John Webbe in his library. He also had the 1595 Leiden edition of Cicero's *Letters to Brutus* and the 1547 Paris edition of the *Letters to Atticus*. Entries for these and works cited in the following notes appear in his library catalogue of *c.*1687.

59 Evelyn had the 1659 edition of Pliny's *Letters* in his library.

60 Of Erasmus's *Letters*, Evelyn had the 1521 Basle edition and the 1552 Antwerp edition as well as the 1546 Antwerp edition of Erasmus's *Concerning the Writing of Letters* in his library.

61 Of the ancient fathers of the church the following are listed in Evelyn's library

catalogue of *c.*1687: the 1682 edition of Cyprian's *Opera*; two editions of Augustine's *Meditations* (though not his *Liber Epistolarum*); Calvin's *Epistolae et Responsa* (Lausanne, 1576); Juan Luis Vives's *Dialogues* (Paris, 1566); Angelo Politiano's *Opera omnia* (Basle, 1553); Hugo Grotius's *Epistolae ad Gallos* (Leiden, 1650); Salamasius's *Epistolae* (Leiden, 1656). Neither the letters of Roger Ascham nor those of Pietro Aretino appear in the catalogue.

62 Evelyn's library catalogue contains an edition of Cardinal Bentivoglio's *Lettere* (Paris 1635), three volumes of Sieur de Balzac's *Lettres* (Paris, 1634, 1642, 1647), and two other editions (Paris, 1658, 1659), and the 1676 edition of the *Oeuvres* of Vincent de Voiture.

63 BL Add. MS 78299: to Lord Spencer, 15 Jan. 1692 (no. 665).

64 Evelyn owned Erasmus's *Paraphraseon in Novum Testamentum* (Basle, 1524).

65 *De Conscribendis Epistolis*, in *Collected Works of Erasmus: Literary and Educational Writings*, 3, transl. & ed. by Charles Fantazzi (Toronto: University of Toronto Press, 1985), XXV, 12.

66 BL Add. MS 78299: to Pepys, 1 Oct. 1689 (no. 622); cf. *Particular Friends*, pp. 208-10: C49.

67 In 'The Complete Letter Writer in England 1586-1800', *Smith College Studies in Modern Languages*, 15 (1934), 21-2, Katherine Hornbeak points out, however, that Day's division of letters into four forms – demonstrative, deliberative, judicial, and familiar – resurrects the divisions of ancient oratory that Erasmus rejected as inappropriate.

68 James Murphy, *Rhetoric in the Middle Ages* (Berkeley: University of California Press, 1974), p. 261. In this account of Lipsius, I am indebted to the preface to Lipsius's *Principles of Letter-Writing: a Bilingual Text*, ed. & transl. by R. V. Young & M. Thomas Hester (Carbondale, IL: Southern Illinois University Press, 1996). In his earlier *Questiones Epistolicae*, Lipsius prefers the style of Cicero's letters to that of his orations. Lipsius was preceded in some of his reforms by Vives, but Vives had already been overshadowed by Erasmus. Also influential in this debate about epistolary style were the letters of Augustine, Jerome, and Cassiodorus, as well as the discussion of letter-writing in Quintilian's *Institutio Oratoria*, 9.4.19.

69 In the poem, 'Your Paris', Hughes extends the genre's play with its audience further to imagine Plath writing to her father and imagining Paris as 'a desk in a *pension* / Where your letters / Waited for him unopened'; *Birthday Letters* (London: Faber, 1998), p. 38. In *Experiences in Translation*, trans. by Alastair Maclean (Toronto: University of Toronto Press, 2001), p. 7, Umberto Eco cites William Weaver, the translator of his *Foucault's Pendulum*, on the difficulty of translating the word '*lettera*' into English. Whereas Italian uses the same word for contemporary communications and for the writings of St Paul, traditional English uses the word 'Epistles' for the latter.

70 *Eros the Bittersweet* (Princeton, 1986; repr. Normal, IL; Dalkey Archive Press, 1998), pp. 91, 99.

71 BL Add. MS 78299: to Danby, 3 Dec. 1686 (no. 555).

72 Ibid.: to Lady Clarendon, 12 Oct. 1688 (no. 594).

73 Ibid.: to Lady Sunderland, 23 Dec. 1688 (no. 603).

EVELYN, INIGO JONES, AND THE COLLECTOR EARL OF ARUNDEL

EDWARD CHANEY

THOMAS HOWARD, the 2nd, 14th, or occasionally even the 24th Earl of Arundel, known to posterity more conveniently as the 'Collector Earl', died in Padua on 24 September 1646 (4 October by the modern calendar) [Fig. 1]. Four years later, a great-niece, Lady Catherine Whetenhall, née Talbot, died in childbirth in the same city on her way home after a pilgrimage to Rome. Her Catholic chaplain, Father Richard Lassels, wrote a diary account of her tour which he eventually expanded into a comprehensive guide-book. Published posthumously as *The Voyage of Italy* both in Paris and London in 1670, this became the standard Grand Tour *vade mecum*, still being used by Whigs and Jacobites alike until well into the eighteenth century. It was indeed used extensively by John Evelyn to write up his purportedly 1640s travel diaries. In describing the Basilica of Sant'Antonio in Padua, the small but once slightly more elaborate plaque marking the spot beneath which Arundel's intestines are buried provided Lassels with the opportunity to wax lyrical about his two favourite subjects, Italy and Roman Catholicism. Since his remark about Arundel's religion was omitted in the published version, I quote here from the 1664 manuscript:

In the cloister in the monastery, are seen many tombes of learned men: and in that quarter of the cloister which lyeth upon the Church, I found written upon a black marble stone, these words: Interiora Thomae Howardi Comitis Arondeliae: that is: *The bowels of the Earle of Arondel, late Lord Marshal of England*. No wonder if his bowels be enchased in marble after his death who in his lifetime loved marbles *con todas sus [...] entrannjos with his whole bowels*, as the Spaniards say. His *Marmora Arondeliana* commented upon by learned Selden, shewed this sufficiently. <In this one thing he was happyer than the other antiquarians of his country and time: that by loving *Antiquityes* so much as he did he fell in love with the best piece of antiquity, the ancient Faith.> He dyed here in Padua, and yet in a manner at home, because he had made Italy familiar to him whiles he lived at home.[1]

In the interests of rhetoric here, Lassels rather glossed over the extent of Arundel's previous familiarity both with Italy (which he had visited at least twice prior to his final journey) and with Roman Catholicism, in which religion his widowed mother, Anne Dacre, a devout and devoted single parent and a major benefactress of the Jesuits, had brought him up.[2] On

Fig. 1: François Dieussart, *Thomas Howard, 14th Earl of Arundel, c.*1636.
(Ashmolean Museum, Oxford).

30 June 1614, when he was in Rome with Inigo Jones (a month after two other members of Arundel's entourage, Tobie Matthew and George Gage, were ordained as priests by Cardinal Bellarmine), the Spanish ambassador, Gondomar reported from London to his master Philip III, 'This Earl of Arundel has been in Italy three years, together with his wife and children [*su muger y sus hijos*], with the king's permission to have the opportunity to see Italy but the more certain reason is to enable him to live as a Catholic in public.'[3]

On Christmas Day 1616, after returning from Italy and joining the Privy Council, Arundel ostensibly conformed to the Anglican rite, but clearly remained a 'church papist'. Described as 'the head of the Catholics' by the Venetian ambassador in 1616, twenty-one years later the papal nuncio would still report that he was 'reputed a Catholic in secret'.[4] Though described as a Puritan by the same papal nuncio, Inigo Jones was considered by Christopher Wren and George Vertue to have died a Roman Catholic and was probably born one. His Christian name (with which Ben Jonson had such cruel fun once their friendship had collapsed) was inherited from his father. Yñigo senior probably had a Spanish godfather; it is even possible that he was named after that most famous Yñigo of all, Ignatius Loyola. His son was called Ignatius by fellow Catholic Edmund Bolton, and 'Ignatius Architectus' by his friend Thomas Coryate when he Latinized his name. On the tomb he designed for George Chapman in the form of a Roman altar, he called himself 'Ignatius Jonesius Architectus Regius'.[5]

Lord Arundel's father was named (like Philip Sidney three years earlier) after Philip II himself, who stood as his godfather on 2 July 1557, the day before he left England and his ailing wife, Queen Mary, forever. In 1625, with assistance from his 'most approved good friend' Inigo Jones, Arundel arranged for his father's remains to be removed from the Tower burial grounds to the Fitzalan Chapel adjoining Arundel Castle.[6] The father is now (since 1970) a Catholic saint, St Philip Howard. Arundel's eldest son, James, died a Catholic in Ghent in 1623 on his way back from Italy with the Countess. His youngest son, William, Viscount Stafford, who was to describe Arundel as 'the best father and friend to his children that ever lived', was imprisoned in Heidelburg for 'vice', but executed in London for his religion, an innocent victim of the so-called Popish plot.[7] Two of Arundel's grandsons by his middle son and eventual heir Henry Frederick, Lord Maltravers, became Dominican friars, Philip the eldest eventually becoming a Cardinal.

That Lassels is correct in saying that Arundel himself died a Catholic is confirmed by a letter of 22 December 1646 written by the Father General of the Jesuits, Vincenzo Caraffa, in response to one from the English Jesuit Henry Silesden: 'I rejoice greatly to hear in yours of the 11 November that the Earl died in the bosom of the Supreme Catholic Church. Moreover, as I am not ignorant of the merits of that noble family towards our humble order, I will gladly apply to the relief of his soul a thousand masses and as many rosaries.'[8]

In January of the previous year, two young Englishmen had signed the visitors' book of the University of Padua.[9] The first was Roger Pratt, who was to become our most influential architect after Inigo Jones and prior to Christopher Wren.[10] The second was Arundel's grandson, Henry Howard ('Henrico Howardo'), the future 6th Duke of Norfolk who was to donate his grandfather's inscribed marbles to the University of Oxford and his great library to the Royal Society, which, after the Great Fire of 1666 destroyed its headquarters, met as his guests at Arundel House[11] [Fig. 2]. Both of these historic gifts were entrepreneured by John Evelyn, who arrived in Padua a few months after Pratt. Evelyn later described Pratt as having been his 'old friend and fellow traveller (co-habitant and contemporary at Rome)',[12] and kept in touch with him after he left Rome, forwarding his greetings, via a Mr Collyer in Livorno, in a letter dated 25 November 1644.[13] He was later to praise the Palladian mansion that Pratt designed for Lord Clarendon in Piccadilly as 'the most useful, gracefull and magnificent house in England', and sat on various building commissions with him.[14]

Evelyn had left Rome on 18 May 1645. 'Being disappointed of Monies long expected' and therefore obliged to return to Livorno, he had to exclude the Holy House of Loreto from his return itinerary via Lucca, Florence, and Bologna, and arrived in Venice about a fortnight later. In mid June he spent a 'day in rambling' around Padua after a journey from Venice up the Brenta canal; but on 29 July he returned, signed the University register (adding his name with the star symbol or pentacle on the verso of the same leaf of the *Registro* [Fig. 3]), and the next day was invited to dinner and matriculated the same afternoon, 'being resolved to spend some moneths here at study, especially Physic & Anatomie, of both which here were now the most famous Professors then in Europe'.[15] Two days later Arundel invited Evelyn to accompany him on a sight-seeing stroll around Padua (to which I shall return). Over the next few months in Padua, Evelyn would consolidate a friendship with Arundel, become an acquaintance of his 'most worthy' son, Lord Maltravers, and the life-long confidant, if eventually somewhat jaundiced critic, of his grandson Henry. From the 1650s to the 1670s Evelyn helped to design Italianate features, first at Wotton and then in the Arundels' garden at Albury, inspired in part by the Giusti gardens in Verona (which had been praised by both Coryate and Arundel himself).[16] On 1 August 1662 he entertained five of Arundel's grandsons at Sayes Court: Henry (godson of Henrietta Maria); 'Philip the priest' (the Queen's almoner and future Cardinal); the scholar-hermit Charles Howard of Greystoke (godson of the

Fig. 2: Abraham Blooteling after Sir Peter Lely, *Henry Howard, 6th Duke of Norfolk*. Engraving, 1678 (Robert Harding Collection).

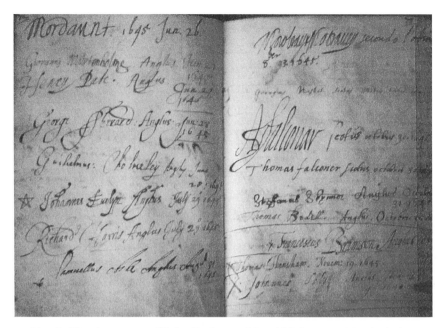

Fig. 3: The signatures of John Evelyn and Lord Maltravers, Matriculation register-book of the University of Padua. Bibliotheca del. Seminario Patavino, Codice 634, pp. 72-3.

King and grandfather of the 10th Duke), whose 'extraordinary' garden at Deepdene near Wotton Evelyn greatly admired and advised upon;[17] Edward, who never married, and the Douai-educated soldier and future Jacobite Bernard Howard of Glossop, the youngest of this group, who nevertheless had other siblings, including Francis, the future Dominican, and Esmé, who was the youngest son. Henry's two sons, Henry, the future 7th Duke, and Thomas, the future Jacobite, with whom John Evelyn junior was being educated, came with them, and stayed behind at Sayes Court.[18] It was soon after this visit, however, that Evelyn's conformist religious anxiety overcame his somewhat *arriviste* pleasure in having his son educated 'amongst Mr Howard's Children at Arundel house [and] for feare of their perverting him, in the popish religion, I was forc'd to take him home'.[19] This did not, however, prevent him dedicating his 1668 translation of Fréart's *Idée de la perfection de la peinture* to Henry.[20]

But Evelyn came to disapprove of Henry's morals even more than his popishness. On 23 January 1678 he dined with the now Duke of Norfolk, 'being the first time I had seen him since the Death of his elder Bro. Who died at Padoa in Italy where as being lunatic, he had kept above 30 yeares: The Duke had now newly declard his Marriage to that infamous Woman his Concubine, whom he promised me he never would marry.'[21] It had been in

October 1671 that Evelyn first registered (in the privacy of his diary) his disgust at Henry's revelation of his plan to marry his eldest son 'to one of the King's natural daughters by the Dutchesse of Cleveland' and to maintain as his own mistress 'that idle Creature & Common –', Jane Bickerton, daughter of a gentleman of the king's wine-cellar. 'I was sorry at heart,' he writes, 'to hear what now in confidence he confessed to me; that a person & a family (which I so much honoured for the sake of that noble & illustrious friend of mine, his Grandfather) should dishonor and polute them both, with those base, & vicious Courses he of late had taken & was falln into.'[22]

This provides the background for a rare attempt at a joke in the diary, albeit a somewhat bitter one given Arundel's lifelong quest to earn immortal fame by his collecting and patronage of art, and to re-establish the glories of the Howard Dukes of Norfolk. In May 1683, a year before Henry died, knowing how little he cared about his grandfather's collections, Evelyn asked him if he would: 'part with any of his *Cartoones* & other Drawings of *Raphael* & and the great masters: He answered me, he would part with, & sell any thing for mony, but his *Wife* (The *Dutchesse* &c) who stood neere him; & I thought with my selfe, That if I were in his condition, it should be the first thing I would be glad to be part with.'[23]

Arundel and Evelyn had similar motives for leaving England once the Long Parliament began to bare its teeth. Both felt insufficient enthusiasm for the King's cause to risk their families' estates, all of which were in areas controlled by the Parliament. On 12 May 1641 on Tower Hill, the twenty-year-old Evelyn and his older brother George witnessed 'the fatal Stroake, which sever'd the wisest head in England from the Shoulders of the Earl of Strafford'.[24] It had been Arundel's unpleasant duty to preside over Strafford's trial, an event which, like the execution itself, was recorded in an etching by his servant and Evelyn's friend, Wenceslaus Hollar. The following month Evelyn came up to London again, this time with his sister Jane, and sat for his portrait by Arundel's resident artist and curator Hendrick van der Borcht, 'which I presented her, being her request upon my resolutions to absent my selfe from this ill face of things at home, which gave umbrage to wiser then my selfe, that the Medaill was turning, and our calamities but yet in their infancy'[25] [Fig. 4].

Evelyn travelled first to Amsterdam and then toured the other major Dutch and Flemish cities, ending up in Dort to be present at the reception of Marie de Medicis, from which city she 'design'd for Collin (Cologne), conducted by the Earle of Arundell'.[26] Evelyn may have met Arundel in Dort, for his 'De Vita Propria' has it that the coach in which he and John Caryll travelled from Brussels to Ghent was in fact requested by Arundel. In any event, the assiduous Evelyn certainly travelled from Ghent to Ostend and thence to Dunkirk and across to Dover, to Gravesend and up the

Fig. 4: Hendrick van der Borcht, John Evelyn, holding a Drawing of
Circe and the Pigs (National Portrait Gallery).

Thames, in Arundel's company.[27] He took his leave at Arundel Stairs and
retired to his lodgings at the Middle Temple at 'about two in the morning'.
He then returned to his brother's estate at Wotton, in Surrey, at about the
same time as Arundel returned to his country house, Albury, just six miles
to the west of Wotton.[28] On Sunday afternoon, 7 November 1641, Evelyn
'went to give my L: Martial a Visite at Albury', an historic visit in view of his
involvement in the garden which was to follow.

Evading the conflict between King and Parliament, Evelyn covers the year
1642 in less than a page of his diary, noting that on 3 October (actually the
23rd) 'was fought that signal Battaile at Edgehill'.[29] Then after months of
'perpetuall motions hitherto betweene Lond: and Wotton', partly in order to
avoid swearing the Presbyterian Covenant, he obtained a licence from the
King 'to travel againe', and sailed from Dover for Calais in company with his

Balliol friend James Thicknesse.[30] He was to remain abroad for the next five years. With even less hesitation than Evelyn and prior to the outbreak of Civil War, Arundel also decided to return to the continent. In February 1642, after entertaining the young Prince William of Orange at Arundel House following his marriage to Charles's daughter Mary, Arundel and at least one each of his sons and grandsons accompanied the Princess, together with Henrietta Maria, to the Hague. He then moved to Catholic Antwerp where his younger son, Lord Stafford, wrote to Lady Arundel asking her to join them there.[31]

I believe that Arundel may have arrived with his grandsons in Italy during the winter of 1644/5, considerably earlier than previously supposed. He was certainly in Milan in April 1645 and in Piacenza later that spring, touring with at least three of his grandsons, Thomas, Henry, and Philip. I have also found evidence of his visiting Florence in this period,[32] and suspect that he discreetly visited Rome in April (when one of his grandsons, perhaps Henry, 'Illustrissimus ... Catholicus Anglus', dined at the English College there), before returning to Piacenza and then retiring more publicly to Padua where he spent the remainder of his life.[33] The dining companion of Arundel's 'nepos' at the College was the urbane Benedictine, John Wilfrid, and it is probably no coincidence that on Evelyn's first morning in Rome, ironically 5 November 1644, he 'got acquaintance with several persons that had long lived [there] being especially recommended to Father John a Benedictine Monke, and superior of his Order for the English Colledg of Doway; a Person (to say truth) of singular learning, Religion, and humanity'.[34] Evelyn was to seek out this learned monk again and had long since left Rome by the time Henry Howard dined with his future brother-in-law, Sir Kenelm Digby's son, at the English College there.[35]

In 1636, when he had gone on an embassy to the Emperor Ferdinand II at Linz, Arundel had left his eldest surviving son, Lord Maltravers, in charge of most of his affairs, including those connected with collecting. In a typical letter, Maltravers told the agent William Petty, that the 'Master Surveyor' (Inigo Jones) was 'madde to see' the collection of drawings he had sent from Naples and urged him to continue his efforts to obtain the *Meleager* in Rome (the 'Adonis of Parrian Marble' that Evelyn was to admire at 'the palace of Signor Pichini').[36] He wrote letters both from Arundel House and his own property at Lothbury in the City of London. Two years later Jones designed a new house and office block for Maltravers's Lothbury property, which were both revolutionary in their astylar simplicity. It is not clear whether they were actually built, but the similar structure seen in Hollar's print of the courtyard of Arundel House clearly was and in view of the rarity of this style before the Civil Wars may also be attributed to Jones.[37]

In 1642 Arundel again left Maltravers (now Lord Mowbray and

Maltravers) in charge of affairs at home, tacitly approving when he chose
to fight for the King at Edgehill, Banbury, and elsewhere. By the end of 1643
Maltravers was writing from royalist Oxford that whichever way the Civil
War went, 'this is like to be a most miserably wasted Kingdom'.[38] With the
prospects of peace and a return home receding, Arundel moved south from
Antwerp to Rheims. In September 1644 we now find him writing to the
English resident in Paris that he had decided to continue his travels in search
of 'some quiett and cheape place where I may have some horse-manship for
my children'.[39] That he was in fact heading for Italy and still motivated by his
love of collecting is revealed in one of Richard Symonds notebooks: Nicholas
Lanier's uncle Jerome informing Symonds that he and Arundel, 'were in
agreement to go into Italy this year of 1644 to buy drawings and pictures'.[40]
With conspiracy pamphlets such as William Prynne's cunningly entitled
Romes Master-peece (1643) inflaming opinion at home against the Arundels,
it is not surprising that he was discreet to the point of deliberately misleading
correspondents (and consequently historians) as to his whereabouts throughout this period.[41]

Having probably left England with the royalist exodus after Newcastle's
defeat at Marston Moor (Arundel Castle had fallen the previous year),
Maltravers joined his father and sons in Italy by September 1645 at the latest.
In their two-volume *House of Howard*, Brenan and Statham say that he
hastened to Padua from England in 1646 just 'in time to be present at his
father's deathbed', and all subsequent biographers have followed suit.[42]
In fact we find Maltravers sightseeing in Venice with John Evelyn on
29 September 1645, a full year before his father's death. Given that this
Michaelmas Day visit was to an important collection of sculpture and medals
already known to Arundel (the Contarini-Ruzini collection), and that Evelyn
had already spent a day sightseeing in Padua with Arundel two months
previously, it is probable both that father and son had already met and
that the Venetian visit had been suggested by Arundel himself. Evelyn and
Maltravers returned to Padua within a day or two of this visit and on
3 October, as a rather mature thirty-seven-year-old, the latter signed the
same *Registro* of students at the University of Padua that he had signed with
his elder brother James, more than a quarter of a century earlier. On the last
day of October he formally matriculated in the faculty of law, his name just
recognisable in Andrich's printed list as 'Moubrae Matcaners' (for Mowbray
Maltravers). In August 1646 'Barones Maubery et Somerset' dined with
John Caryll at the English College, Rome, so it is from there that he would
have returned to Padua on hearing of his father's final illness.[43]

On his return to Padua, Evelyn fell seriously ill. On his recovery, he was
visited by Henry Howard and several other Englishmen recently arrived
from Venice with whom he then hired a house, 'neere St. Catherins over

against the Monasterie of Nunns' in what is now Via Cesare Battisti, 'where we lived very nobly'. On his birthday, 31 October, the friendly nuns sent him 'flowers of silk-work'. Evelyn recalls that he and his friends 'were very studious all this Winter till Christmas, when on Twelfe day we invited all the English & Scots in Towne (the Earle of Arundel excepted) to a Feast, which sunk our excellent Wine considerably'.[44] Arundel was perhaps too frail or merely melancholy to attend Evelyn's party, but in other respects he made himself available to this Surrey neighbour throughout the latter's nine months' residence in the Veneto. On the morning of 1 August 1645, two days after matriculating at the University, Evelyn had been invited to call on him. With that meritocratic lack of snobbery that gives the lie to Clarendon's portrait of an arrogant and pretentious aristocrat (based I suspect on his having been snubbed when, as Mr Hyde M.P., he had been a young critic of the crown),

the *Earle of Arundel* ... [that] famous Collector of Paintings and Antiquities, invited me to go with him to see the Garden of *Mantua*, where as one enters stands a huge Collosse of Hercules. From hence to a place where was a roome cover'd with a noble Cupola built purposly for Musique, the fillings up, or Core 'twixt the Walls were of urnes & earthen potts for the better sounding, it was also well painted.

After dinner we walked to the Palace of *Foscari all'Arena*, there remaining yet some appearances of an antient theater, though serving now for a Court onely before the house. There were kept in it two *Eagles*, a crane, a Mauritanian Sheepe, a stag, and sundry foule as in a Vivarie.[45]

Here for once, thanks to being personally guided by Arundel, Evelyn departs from his usual anthologizing of guidebooks (including Lassels's *Voyage*, which was published a quarter of a century after his supposed visit). Ironically this rare piece of authenticity has caused even more confusion than usual for both Evelyn's and Arundel's biographers, as well for as the most recent editor of Arundel's *Remembrances*; for all have concluded that after dinner the fragile Arundel and never very *sportif* Evelyn strolled from Padua the sixty-odd miles to Mantua, even to the extent of identifying the building with the noble cupola as the Palazzo Te.[46] In fact the so-called Gardens of Mantua, or as it should be, Mantoa, were and still are in Padua itself, immediately south east of the Eremitani, behind the courtyard of the Palazzo Mantoa-Benavides. In any case Evelyn elsewhere expresses his regret at not visiting Mantua, Parma, or Piacenza through fear of banditi.[47] 'The Colosse of Hercules' in the courtyard itself (now shrouded in ancient scaffolding) is by Bartolomeo Ammanati and at nine metres tall a distinctive feature [Fig. 5].

The domed and elaborately decorated music room, to which Evelyn next refers, is the celebrated Odeon near the Santo, designed in 1530-4 by Giovanmaria Falconetto in collaboration with his friend and patron, Alvise

Fig. 5: Bartolomeo Ammanati's statue of Hercules in the courtyard in front of the garden of the Palazzo Mantoa-Benavides (Edward Chaney).

Fig. 6: The Scrovegni Chapel and remains of the Arena, Padua (Edward Chaney).

Cornaro, in the courtyard behind the discreet façade of the Palazzo Giustiniani-Giusti.[48] It is very likely that Arundel would have been introduced to both this and Falconetto's loggia (1524), which functioned as a private theatre, by his own architectural protégé Inigo Jones, who would have known it from Book VII of Serlio's *Architettura*. Finally, 'the Palace of Foscar all'Arena' was none other than the once magnificent Palazzo Foscari or Scrovegni, to which Giotto's Scrovegni or Arena Chapel was then attached (and which Arundel had attempted to buy or rent) [Fig. 6]. The 'court before the house' was the space created by the remains of the first-century Roman amphitheatre. Given Arundel's familiarity with Vasari, dating at least as far back as his travels with Inigo Jones, it would be fascinating to know whether he drew Evelyn's attention to Giotto's great fresco cycle or indeed showed him the now badly bomb-damaged Mantegnas in the almost adjacent church of the Eremitani. Evelyn mentions Giotto's *Navicella* mosaic in his diary account of Rome (albeit mistranslating Pompilio Totti's guide-book long after his visit), and in his 'Account of Architects' attached to his translation of Fréart. He admires a Mantegna in Paris and later praises the *Triumphs of Caesar* which Cromwell kept back from the sale of the late King's goods and are thus still at Hampton Court.[49]

As well as Arundel, his son Maltravers, and grandsons, and Roger Pratt, Evelyn befriended the recently exiled Royalist poet and plotter, Edmund Waller, in Italy. That Waller also associated with the Howard family in Padua emerged years later when he testified in Parliament that Arundel's grandson, Thomas, now the fifth Duke of Norfolk, was already insane in 1646. That he also benefited from Arundel's artistic expertise is implicit in Evelyn's diary, for Waller was with Evelyn when the latter assiduously followed Arundel's instructions as to what to see in northern Italy on the first leg of their journey home (including Palladian Vicenza, the Arena, and the Giusti Gardens of Verona, and even a proto-Romantic appreciation of natural landscape in Cavalcassele near Lake Garda). Waller eventually designed a sub-Palladian country house for himself at Hall Barn, Beaconsfield (where thanks to his grandson some of the Arundel Marbles came to rest).[50]

Evelyn, meanwhile, was to design some of the most dramatic neo-classical features of the garden which Henry Howard inherited at Albury, the Surrey 'Cottage' in which Arundel had hoped to end his days. An Italianate garden building, however, can be seen in the vineyard by the canal in an etching by Hollar which is usually dated 1645 [Fig. 7]. This cannot therefore be the tunnel inspired by the Grotta di Posillipo, which dates from Henry Howard's tenancy in the 1660s, but was presumably built before Arundel and Hollar went abroad. John Harris has therefore suggested it may be an unknown work by Inigo Jones for Arundel.[51] There is a post-1645 letter from Arundel to Evelyn which might explain both its function, and an earlier reference by

Fig. 7: Wenceslaus Hollar, The grotto at Albury Park, Surrey. Etching,
Antwerp 1645 (Robert Harding Collection).

Arundel to his 'Alpine Cell' at Albury dated 9 August 1646, by which time
Evelyn had probably only just reached Paris with Waller. Arundel hopes they
are both safely in England and that 'y[o]u will there remember me that I may
hope to see my poore littel Cottage of Allberrye to my comforte. I had a
Conserve for Snowe there w[hic]h did not hold it well. I desire it might be
amended, and an other made to keepe Ice in.'[52] One can indeed see that
if this was intended as an ice-house the structure was too exposed to have
functioned well. That Evelyn was interested in such structures is clear from
his 'Account of the Snow-pits in Italy', sent to Boyle in October 1664 and
published in Boyle's *New Experiments and Observations touching Cold* the
following year.[53]

On the morning Evelyn left Padua in April 1646, he was invited to breakfast with Arundel:

It was *Easter* Monday, that I was invited to Breakfast at the Earle of *Arundels*, I took
my leave of him in his bed, where I left that great & excellent Man in teares upon
some private discourse of the crosses had befaln his Illustrious family: particularly the
undutifullnesse of his Grandson *Philips* turning *Dominican* Frier ... the unkindnesse
of his *Countesse*, now in Holland; The miserie of his Countrie, now embroil'd in a
Civil War &c: after which he causd his Gentleman to give me Directions all written
with his owne hand, what curiosities I should enquire after in my Journey, & so
injoyning me to write sometimes to him, I departed.[54]

Evelyn was escorted to his coach by Henry Howard and John Digby, who had returned to Padua from Rome earlier in the year. The *Remembrances* which Arundel wrote out for Evelyn consisted of two pages of messages for servants and friends in England and six and a half pages of advice as to what to see in northern Italy on the way home. The first stop west of Padua and thus the first place to be described by Arundel was Vicenza. He may have visited Vicenza on his brief trip to the Veneto in 1612, but the first time he would have inspected its Palladian buildings with care was in the following year when he returned to Italy with Inigo Jones. On the endpaper opposite the title-page of his 1601 edition of Palladio's *Quattro Libri,* now at Worcester College, Oxford, Jones recorded this historic moment: 'Vicenza Mundaie the 23 September 1613'. The first Palladian building that Jones (and thus, I believe, Arundel also) inspected was the Teatro Olimpico, no doubt encouraged by the excellent description which Jones's friend Thomas Coryate, plagiarizing the Vicentine edition of Schott's *Itinerarii Italiae,* had published in the *Crudities* two years earlier. (We know that Jones knew the *Crudities* because he contributed a satirical poem to its preface, while Evelyn used Coryate extensively in his account of the Veneto.) What Jones wrote immediately beneath this date reveals that he had already begun acquiring original drawings by Palladio and his circle: 'The Theater of Palladios ordering the front of the sceane of Bricke Covered with Stuco full of ornament and Stattues as in the designe I have.'[55] This large and important drawing (now in the library of the Royal Institute of British Architects) is thought to have been prepared by Palladio's son, Marcantonio, on his father's instruction and presents two alternative designs for the proscenium and seating before Scamozzi completed the work, adding the illusionist avenues.[56]

In attempting to date Jones's acquisition of a group of Palladio's drawings formerly belonging to Sir Henry Wotton, John Newman has cited this inscription as 'independent confirmation that Jones [had] access to original drawings by Palladio in England before his second Italian journey' (that is, this 1613-14 journey with Arundel).[57] But Jones could have acquired this and other drawings during the previous two months in Venice and Padua, where he and the Arundels had arrived on 20 July. While they had to visit Rome incognito due to its still being off limits for Englishmen, in Venice they were lavishly entertained by the Doge and Senate and given a farewell party by Gregorio Barbarigo, whose servant Francesco Vercellini they eventually inherited. Ten days before the date of Jones's annotation, Arundel wrote to Sir Robert Cotton from Padua asking him to 'pick out some story of my Ancestors' which he 'could have painted in Venice', adding that Cotton should 'send it in writing and direct up to Mr Richard Willoughby in case I be not here'. Willoughby had been Coryate's guide around Padua in 1608 and is thanked as such in the *Crudities*.[58] Coryate's account of the advantages of the porticoed pavements of Padua, may have encouraged Inigo Jones and Arundel, who between them dominated the new commission for building, to design such a portico around the piazza at Covent Garden. Arundel was clearly intending to leave Venice when he wrote this letter to Cotton, and by 30 September Dudley Carleton reported that he had set out for Florence, 'having left his lady at a villa hereby towards Cataio' (more likely to be Scamozzi's Villa Molin, which is on the Canale Battaglia between Cataio and Padua, than the 350-room Castello of Cataio itself as has been suggested).[59] This makes it all the more likely that Arundel visited Vicenza on 23 September with Jones as their first stop after Padua.

By taking Jones on tour with them following the deaths in 1612 of Lord Salisbury, who encouraged him to take up architecture in the first place, and Prince Henry, who made him his Surveyor of Works, the Arundels became Jones's principal private patrons. Their primary acquaintance with him prior to this would have been as performers in Jones's royal masques, Arundel appearing in *Hymenaei* as early as February 1606 before he was married. Two drawings of 1609 for Lady Arundel's costume in *The Masque of Queens* survive at Chatsworth. By 1617, however, when Arundel wrote a will on the eve of a journey to Scotland, he described Jones as 'my most approoved good friend', and asked him 'to continewe to my wife & my children as he hath bin unto me'. In 1621 Arundel arranged for him to become M.P. for his Sussex constituency of New Shoreham. He continued his patronage throughout the 1630s and was still corresponding with Jones at the end of his life.[60]

During 1613-14 it would clearly have been the Arundels who provided the wherewithal for Jones to acquire what became the largest collection of Palladio drawings in existence. This consists of approximately 250 sheets, many of which are now in the RIBA, and when it was acquired by Lord Burlington with Jones's own drawings in the early eighteenth century it provided the major inspiration for that especially Anglo-Saxon phenomenon, the so-called Palladian Revival. Arundel himself ended up with two chests of drawings by Scamozzi, whom Jones met in the Veneto on the return journey from Rome in August 1614.[61]

Given all this, Arundel would surely have thought back to his first encounters with Palladian Vicenza in Jones's company, when he jotted down his notes for John Evelyn: 'The prime things to be seene are the buildings ordered by Andrea Palladio the great Architect borne there, of which the prime are the Theatro with the Scene, which is the finest in Italy of that kinde.' Arundel then recommended Palladio's modernised Basilica and what he called the 'private pallace ... to Conte Teine wanting the least [i.e., almost complete] w[hi]ch stands within the Citty neare the gate by which the

Coaches passe usually for Verona', as well as 'the great garden of Conte Valmarano being just without the wall'. By this Arundel means neither Palladio's Palazzo Thiene, nor the gardens of the (later) Villa Valmarana (as stated by his editor). The palace just inside the walls is Scamozzi's Palazzo Bonin, formerly Thiene,[62] and the 'great garden of Conte Valmarana' is the no longer very great garden immediately outside the walls, accessible through a separate gate in the wall and now called the Giardino Salvi. The Palazzo Bonin is clearly the 'Pallas' referred to by Jones in his 13 August 1614 marginalia. Having met and spoken with Scamozzi on Friday 1 August, Jones identified this as the 'great Pallas begun by Scamozio but the order within agreith not with that without which is an Ionicke Portico that within is Dorricke and lower'.[63]

Having misread Arundel's 'Teine' as 'Oleine'and probably missed both Palazzi as a result, Evelyn 'would now very faine have visited a Palace call'd the Rotunda, which was a Mile out of Towne', as Arundel next advised; 'but one of our Companions hasting to be gon, and little minding anything save drinking & folly, causd us to take coach sooner than we should'.[64] Thus Evelyn, and probably Waller (who was apparently not the guilty party), never saw Palladio's exquisite Villa which Jones, and we may now assume Arundel also, visited on their second day in Vicenza, 24 September 1613. The enormous influence of this building, above all in Britain and America, owes much to this moment, though Coryate had published a description two years earlier.

Arundel's talents as patron and collector, and Jones's as designer and architect, came to full maturity during this 1613-14 tour. It may for these reasons be considered the most culturally significant Grand Tour ever undertaken, its somewhat incoherent echo in the relevant part of Evelyn's cut-and-paste diary a faint taste of things to come, as interesting for de Beer's footnotes as for the text itself. Given his later claims to architectural expertise and his admiration of Jones, Evelyn's lack of interest in or understanding of the importance of Palladio is notable. Interestingly Waller served with Evelyn on the Restoration commission for reforming 'the buildings, wayes, streets and incumbrances', set up in 1662.[65] Both were of that generation, however, which paid less regard to Palladio than the generations either before or immediately after.

Jones and Arundel never met again, even though they continued to correspond and may have had a go-between in the person of Evelyn. Evelyn certainly got to know another of Arundel's protégés even before his return home, the 'very honest simple well meaning' Wenceslaus Hollar. He says in his diary that Hollar was 'perverted at last by the Jesuits at Antwerp to change his religion', but John Aubrey supposed him to have been a Catholic 'ever since he came to Arundel House'; though both de Beer and Hollar's

Fig. 8: Wenceslaus Hollar, after Sir Anthony van Dyck, self-portrait
with a sunflower. Etching, 1644 (Robert Harding Collection).

biographer Richard Pennington are reluctant to accept that he was a
Catholic at all. In fact in 1656, the year in which Evelyn employed Hollar
to etch the frontispiece to his essay on Lucretius, Hollar was indicted for
being present 'at the hearing of a mass' at the lodging of the Venetian
ambassador.[66]

In conclusion, two further etchings by Hollar are relevant: Van Dyck's
self-portrait with a sun-flower and Cornelius Schut's rather awkward posthumous tribute to Arundel. The latter was dedicated to the Countess of
Arundel by the same Hendrick van der Borcht who had painted Evelyn's
portrait at Arundel House prior to his first journey abroad in 1641, and
subsequently sold him and his brother pictures and visited collections with
him in Paris.[67] Hollar's poignant image of Van Dyck, however, was dedicated
by Van der Borcht to Evelyn himself [Fig. 8]. The wording, which praises

Evelyn as a great lover of the arts and is dated 1644, suggests that Evelyn was already emulating Arundel before he renewed his acquaintance in Italy. In Florence in 1644 he purchased nineteen pietra dura panels from Domenico Benotti 'for a Cabinet' and in Rome the following year he pioneeringly patronized Carlo Maratti.[68] But Evelyn's concluding encounters in the Veneto with the greatest English patron and virtuoso of his age, confirmed his own aspiration to become a cosmopolitan virtuoso and collector, thus able to play a crucial role in preserving what was best about the reign of Charles I through the reigns of his heirs.[69]

NOTES

I should like to thank Ann Barnes, Robert Harding, Frances Harris and Sara Rodger for their help in preparing this paper for publication.

1 Now in the Osborn Collection, Beinecke Library, Yale University. The sentence between < > was omitted in the version, designed to be acceptable to a Protestant readership, published in Paris in 1670. For Lassels, Catherine Whetenhall *et al.*, see Edward Chaney, *The Grand Tour and the Great Rebellion* (Geneva: Slatkine, 1985), passim; for Arundel, see Mary Hervey, *The Life, Correspondence and Collections of Thomas Howard, Earl of Arundel* (Cambridge: Cambridge University Press, 1921) and David Howarth, *Lord Arundel and his Circle* (New Haven & London: Yale University Press, 1985). For evidence that Arundel's plaque was once more elaborate, see Bernardo Gonzati, La Basilica di S.Antonio di Padova (Padua: A. Bianchi, 1852), II, 278.

2 In 1622, she founded the English College of the Society of Jesus in Ghent.

3 Gondomar seems to have been counting Arundel's 1612 journey to Italy here as continuous with his 1613-14 one, perhaps because he knew that the first journey was planned to be a longer one and that when Arundel was obliged to return to England prematurely on the death of Prince Henry he intended to resume his Grand Tour; see *Spain and the Jacobean Catholics*, ed. by A. J. Loomie, Catholic Record Society, 68 (1978), II, 37-9. Sir Dudley Carleton also refers to Arundel's being with his family; ibid., 40, n. 6.

4 S. N. D. [Rose Meeres], *Sir William Howard, Viscount Stafford 1612-1680* (London: Sands, 1929), p. 19; Ruth Elizabeth Grun, 'A Study in Seventeenth-Century English Recusancy', Ph.D. diss. (Bryn Mawr, 1956); Chaney, *The Grand Tour and the Great Rebellion*, p. 304; Godfrey Anstruther, *A Hundred Homeless Years: English Dominicans 1558-1658* (London: Blackfriars, 1958), pp. 196-7.

5 Once in the graveyard of St Giles's but now in the church; see E. Chaney, *Inigo Jones's Roman Sketchbook*, Roxburghe Club (2003, forthcoming).

6 John Newman, 'A Draft Will of Lord Arundel', *Burlington Magazine*, 122 (1973), 692-96.

7 S. N. D., *Sir William Howard*, pp. 15, 39 (for his imprisonment); see also Evelyn, *Diary*, IV, 234.

8 Edward Chaney, 'Thomas Howard, 14th Earl of Arundel by François Dieussart', *Apollo*, 144 (1996), 49-50.

9 This register was begun as a matriculation record. It was published by Horatio

Brown in Venice in 1921 as *Inglesi e Scozzesi all'Università di Padova dell'anno 1618 sino al 1765*. I have used the original manuscript in the Seminario Patavino (Padua), which includes some details not included by Brown. I thank Monsignor Pier Gios, Librarian of the Seminario, for permission to photograph this.

10 R. T. Gunther, *The Architecture of Roger Pratt* (Oxford: Oxford University Press, 1928); Howard Colvin, *Biographical Dictionary of British Architects 1600-1840*, 3rd edn (New Haven & London: Yale University Press, 1995), pp. 777-9; Chaney, *The Grand Tour and the Great Rebellion*, p. 344, for his dining at the English College at Rome. He also signs a draft pawn agreement for the young Duke of Buckingham in The Hague on 20 April 1649 (Bodleian Library, Clarendon MSS, XXXVII, fol. 77); cf. Philip McEvansoneya, 'The Sequestration and Dispersal of the Buckingham Collection', *Journal of the History of Collectons*, 8 (1996), 148.

11 Linda Levy Peck, 'Uncovering the Arundel Library at the Royal Society: Changing Meanings of Science and the Fate of the Norfolk Donation', *Notes and Records of the Royal Society of London*, 53 (1998), 3-24.

12 *Diary and Correspondence of John Evelyn*, ed. by William Bray (London: Bohn, 1859), III, 177: Evelyn to Cornbury, 20 Jan. 1666; see also Gunther, *Roger Pratt*, p. 3.

13 BL Add. MS 78315.

14 *Diary and Correspondence*, ed. Bray, III, 177: Evelyn to Cornbury, 20 Jan. 1666.

15 Registro, p. 72 (Brown, no. 334); cf. Evelyn, *Diary*, II, 464. Evelyn describes both events as if they took place on the same day, but his signature is clearly dated 29 July, while his matriculation is recorded in his diary and in the surviving documents itself as the 30th. De Beer points out (n. 2) 'a man named Richard Harris appears in both lists on the same days, and was perhaps a travelling companion at this time'. Harris, who became consul of the English and Scots nation at the University, seems to have remained in Padua and together with the distinguished professor of anatomy, Johann Vesling, signs a medical report confirming the insanity of Arundel's eldest grandson, Thomas (Arundel Castle Archives). Other relevant signatories of the Padua *Registro* include Thomas Henshaw (19 Nov. 1645), whom Evelyn met in Pisa in Oct. 1644, '& from whose Company I never parted till more than a yeare after'; and the son of Strafford's chief adviser, Sir George Radcliffe, Thomas, who signed on 10 July together with the sons of Strafford and the Duke of Buckingham. Evelyn dined with Sir George Radcliffe in Oct. 1649 (*Diary*, II, 564), Thomas having witnessed his will on 27 June (III, 12).

16 Douglas Chambers, 'The Tomb in the Landscape: John Evelyn's Garden at Albury', *Journal of Garden History*, 1 (1981), 37-54; Michael Charlesworth, 'A Plan by John Evelyn of Henry Howard's Garden at Albury Park, Surrey', in *John Evelyn's Elysium Britannicum and European Horticulture*, ed. by Therese O'Malley & Joachim Wolschke-Bulmahn (Washington, D.C.: Dumbarton Oaks, 1998), pp. 289-93.

17 *Sylva* (1664), in *The Writings of John Evelyn*, ed. by Guy de la Bédoyère (Woodbridge: Boydell, 1995), p. 231; Evelyn, *Diary*, I, 154.

18 Evelyn, *Diary*, III, 329; Anstruther, *Hundred Homeless Years* (see n. 4 above), ch. 9, and the annotated copy of Henry Howard of Corby's *Memorials of the Howard Family* (1834) at Arundel Castle.

19 Evelyn, *Diary*, III, 326.

20 *An Idea of the Perfection of Painting* (London: Henry Herringman, 1668), translated from the first edition of 1662.

21 Evelyn, *Diary*, IV, 127-8.

22 Ibid., III, 592-3.

23 Ibid., IV, 312: 'In conclusion he told me, if he might sell them altogether, he would; but that the late Sir Peter Lely (our famous painter) had gotten some of his best.' Evelyn later expanded on this in his 12 August 1689 letter to Samuel Pepys: 'That great lover of antiquity, Thomas Earl of Arundel, had a very rich collection as well of medals, as other intaglios, belonging to the cabinet he purchased of Daniel Nice at the cost of ten thousand pounds, which, with innumerable other rarities, have been scattered'; *Particular Friends*, ed. by Guy de la Bédoyère (Woodbridge: Boydell, 1997), pp. 188-204.

24 Evelyn, *Diary*, II, 28.

25 Ibid., II, 28-9; cf. Chaney, *The Grand Tour and the Great Rebellion*, p. 307, and Robert Harding, 'John Evelyn, Hendrick van der Borcht the Younger, and Wenceslaus Hollar', *Apollo*, 144 (Aug. 1996), 39-44.

26 Ibid., II, 57. For what is probably the second of two Van der Borcht portraits of Evelyn, see Edward Chaney & G. Worsdale, *The Stuart Portrait: Status and Legacy* (Southampton: City Art Gallery, 2001), pp. 24-8. I thank Nigel Hughes for the suggestion that the drawing held by the fashionably dressed Evelyn may depict Circe and the swine. For Evelyn's consciousness of Circe in the context of fashion, see *Tyrannus and the Mode* (1661), in *Writings*, ed. by de la Bédoyère (see n. 17 above), p. 164: 'Methinks a French Taylor with his Ell in his hand looks like the enchantress Circe over the Companions of Ulysses and changes them into as many formes.'

27 Ibid., I, 47; cf. II, 29.

28 Ibid., II, 76-7, and n. for Arundel's incomplete acquisition of the property in 1638.

29 Ibid., II, 79.

30 Ibid., I, 55-6.

31 Arundel travelled to Mechlin and Louvain in August 1642 but then returned to Antwerp where he had left Stafford; see Anstruther, *Hundred Homeless Years* (see n. 4 above), pp. 194-214.

32 Diarii di Etichetta, Archivio di Stato di Firenze, Miscellanea Medicea, 436, fol. 130 (28 July 1645), describing the reception of the Duke of Buckingham and his brother 'come si era fatto al Sr. Conte d'Arundel'; Chaney, *The Grand Tour and the Great Rebellion*, pp. 312-13.

33 Reference to Arundel's being in Piacenza, whence he had sent William Petty and John Price in search of drawings in 1637, is based on letters in the Vatican Library from him to Cardinal Francesco Barberini, July-Oct. 1645 (Barberini Latini, 7378, fols. 1-5); cf. Howarth, *Arundel* (see n. 1 above), p. 247, who claims that Lady Arundel visited Rome in 1642 (p. 212). These sit uncomfortably with Evelyn's dating of his walk with Arundel on 1 Aug. 1645; cf. *Dominicana*, Catholic Record Society, 25 (1925), and Anstruther, *Hundred Homeless Years*, pp. 194-221. It is possible, albeit incompatible with Anstruther's account, that the 'Illustrissimus Dominus Howardius nepos Comitis de Arundeli Catholicus Anglus', who dines in the college 'circa initium Aprilis' is Philip, the future cardinal (VEC MS *Pilgrim-Book*, p. 135).

34 Evelyn, *Diary*, II, 213.

35 VEC *Pilgrim-Book*, p. 136 (17 July 1645). Evelyn left Rome on 18 May 1645.

36 Lassels later remarked on Arundel having offered twelve thousand crowns for the *Adonis* and the *Venus* in the Palazzo Pighini near the Palazzo Farnese (*Voyage*, II, 224). George Conn noted that Arundel insisted that the former statue represented Meleager rather than Adonis. Given Lassels's account, de Beer is incorrect (*Diary*, II, 217) in saying that Evelyn's reference to Arundel's attempt to purchase it for 'a great price' is original, even if he may indeed also 'have heard of the negotiation from Arundel himself'.

37 Giles Worsley, *Classical Architecture in Britain: the Heroic Age* (New Haven & London: Yale University Press, 1995), pp. 9-10.

38 Hervey, *Arundel*, p. 441. He secured the Earldom of Norfolk for his father on 6 June 1644.

39 BL Add. MS 78193: Arundel to Sir Richard Browne, 29 Sept. 1644. On 14 October, still in Rheims, he writes that he 'long[s] very much to have letters from my wife'.

40 BL Harleian MSS 1991, fol. 33. Jerome had named his son Arundel, who probably therefore stood as godfather, see *Anthony van Dyck*, ed. by A. K. Wheelock, S. J. Barnes, & J. Held (Washington, D.C.: National Gallery of Art, 1990), p. 207. In his *Remembrances* Arundel asks Evelyn to commend him to 'good Mr Jerome Laniere'.

41 Prynne, *Romes Master-peece*, p. 22, refers to Lady Arundel as the 'strenuous She-Champion of the Popish Religion' and to Lord Arundel's intention of going to Rome to seek support against Parliament.

42 M. A. Tierney *The History and Antiquities of the Castle and Town of Arundel*, 2 vols (London: Nicol, 1834), I, 500; Gerald Brenan & E. P. Statham, *The House of Howard*, 2 vols (London: Hutchinson, 1907), II, 570; John Martin Robinson, *The Dukes of Norfolk* (Chichester: Phillimore, 1995), p. 118.

43 Gianluigi Andrich, *De natione Anglica et Scota juristarum Universitatis Patavinae* (Padua, 1892), and VEC MS *Pilgrim-Book*, p. 143. For the various John Carylls, including Evelyn's travelling companion, see Chaney, *The Grand Tour and the Great Rebellion*, pp. 74, 240, 307, 364.

44 Evelyn, *Diary*, II, 473. His account of his lodgings is confused, as he says he moved from Pozzo Pinti (Via Posso Dipinto) to near St Catherines, yet Santa Caterina is in fact in the former Via Pozzo Dipinto.

45 Evelyn, *Diary*, II, 466-7.

46 *Remembrances of Things Worth Seeing in Italy Given to John Evelyn 25 April 1646 by Thomas Howard, 14th Earl of Arundel*, ed. by John Martin Robinson, Roxburghe Club (1987), p. 19, follows Howarth, *Arundel*, p. 214, in assuming that they walked to the Palazzo Te in Mantua.

47 Evelyn, *Diary*, II, 490.

48 Via Cesaroti 37, sometimes called the Casa Angelici. See the illustrations in *Padova: Ritratto di una Città*, ed. by Sergio Bettini (Padua: Neri Pozza, 1973), figs 193-9.

49 Evelyn, *Diary*, II, 113, 265; III, 323. For an engraving of the palazzo Foscari all'Arena, which once dwarfed the Scrovegni chapel, see *Padova*, ed. by Bettini, fig. 109.

50 Chaney, *The Grand Tour and the Great Rebellion*, p. 308.

51 *The Artist and the Country House* (London: Sotheby Parke Bernet, 1979), pp. 30-1.

52 *Catalogue of the Collection of Autograph Letters and Historical Documents Formed ... by Alfred Morrison*, ed. by A. W. Thibaudeau, 6 vols (London, 1883-97), I, 40: Arundel to Evelyn, 9 Aug. 1646.

53 Ice-houses were to become increasingly common in Restoration England. Evelyn had 'laied in Snow to coole our drink' as well as having 'bought some Sheepe, Poultry, Bisquit, Spirits & a little Cabinet of Drouggs &c' in Venice in June 1645 when preparing for a voyage to Jerusalem, only cancelled due to the English captain receiving orders to take provisions to Candia, then besieged by the Turks (*Diary*, II, 451-2). For his letter to Boyle on the subject, see BL Add. MS 72198: 21 Oct. 1664.

54 Evelyn, *Diary*, II, 479. De Beer here points out that Easter Monday fell on 2 April New Style and that his chronology at this time is uncertain.

55 *Inigo Jones on Palladio, Being the Notes by Inigo Jones in the Copy of I Quattro Libri dell Architettura di Andrea Palladio 1601 in the Library of Worcester College Oxford*, ed. by Bruce Allsopp, 2 vols (Oxford; Oriel Press, 1970), I, 1.

56 Douglas Lewis, *The Drawings of Palladio* (Washington, D.C.: International Exhibition, 1981).

57 John Newman, 'Inigo Jones's Architectural Education', *Architectural History*, 35 (1992), 49.

58 Edward Chaney, *The Evolution of the Grand Tour*, 2nd edn (London: Frank Cass, 2000), p. 173; *Coryat's Crudities* (London, 1611), I, 298.

59 Jennifer Fletcher, 'The Arundels in the Veneto', *Apollo*, 144 (August 1996), 63-9.

60 See Arundel's letter on the decline of Italian art cited by John Webb, in his *Vindication of Stone-Heng Restored* (London, 1665), pp. 182-6.

61 On 11 Aug. 1614 Sir Dudley Carleton reported that Arundel had asked him for his house in Padua to spend the season there; *CSP Venetian 1613-15*, p. 174.

62 Evelyn, *Diary*, II, 483, n. 8; Ottavio Bertotti Scamozzi, *Il forestiere istruito ... della città di Vicenza* (Vicenza, 1761), pp. 56-7.

63 *Inigo Jones on Palladio*, I, 2.

64 Evelyn, *Diary*, II, 484.

65 Ibid., III, 319.

66 Ibid., I, 21; Chaney, *The Grand Tour and the Great Rebellion*, pp. 322-3.

67 Gertrude Wilmers, *Cornelis Schut (1597-1655)* (Turnhout, 1996), pp. 49-51, and Harding, 'John Evelyn, Hendrick van der Borcht the Younger, and Wenceslaus Hollar', p. 40. For a reference to the Countess apparently back in England in February 1652, see Lodewijk Huygens, *The English Journal 1651-52*, ed. by A. G. H. Bachrach & R. G. Collmer (Leiden: Brill, 1982), p. 218. It is possible that Huygens has confused the 'dochter van de Graef van Shrewesburrij' with Maltravers's wife, now also called the Countess of Arundel, but the daughter of the Duke of Lennox, whom Evelyn met at Albury on 28 Sept. 1648 (*Diary*, II, 543).

68 Anthony Radcliffe & Peter Thornton, 'John Evelyn's Cabinet', *Connoisseur* (April 1978), 256-61, Antony Griffiths, 'The Arch of Titus by Carlo Maratti', *The National Art Collections Fund Annual Review* (1992), 35-7, and *The Evolution of English Collecting*, ed. by E. Chaney (New Haven & London: Yale University Press, 2003), pp. 6-7.

69 'The Earl of Arundel had several Gravers constantly at work with a design to make a large volume of prints of all his pictures drawings and other rarities which

Mr Evelyn had collected all that were done & are now in the possession of his Grandson, Sr John Evelyn': George Vertue, *Vertue Notebooks*, I, Walpole Society, 18 (1929-30), 47.

JOHN EVELYN'S BOOKBINDINGS[1]

MIRJAM FOOT

WHEN GABRIEL NAUDÉ, the learned librarian of Richelieu and Mazarin, issued the second edition of his *Advis pour dresser une bibliothèque* in 1644, John Evelyn was in Paris at the time. Whether he read it then or later, he was clearly taken by this manual on how to build up and arrange a library, for he translated it into English in 1658 and published it in 1661.

Although Evelyn followed much of Naudé's advice, especially in the complex arrangement of his books, he paid only partial attention to his contempt for the book's exterior; as when Naudé admonished the reader to

retrench and cut off all the superfluous expences, which many prodigally and to no purpose bestow upon the binding and ornaments of their Books, ... it becoming the ignorant onely to esteem a Book for its cover; ... so that it is a great deal better, and more necessary, ... to have a good quantity of Books, well and ordinarily bound, than to have a little Chamber or Cabinet full of [books] washed, gilded, ruled, and enriched with all manner of nicity, lux and superfluity.[2]

Evelyn did indeed possess a 'good quantity of Books, well and ordinarily bound', but he also had several that would have been too luxurious for Naudé's taste. Some of these were presented to him; others he bought for himself, ready-bound in blind- or gold-tooled English sprinkled or plain calf. But he also ordered finely decorated bindings to be made for special occasions, such as that on his manuscript 'Life of Mrs Godolphin', made in London after *c.*1688 of red goatskin, elaborately tooled in gold with fleurons, curls, and with the smaller version of Evelyn's monogram in the centre.[3] A beautifully tooled red goatskin binding covering a *Common Prayer* and *Psalmes* (London, 1639) was made in Paris *c.*1651 for his wife, Mary.[4]

The finest bindings Evelyn possessed he either inherited from or was given by his father-in-law, Sir Richard Browne, since July 1641 'the King's resident at the Court of France'. In the autumn of 1643 Evelyn went to Paris, where he visited the English ambassador and struck up an acquaintance that deepened into friendship. For the next four years Evelyn travelled on the Continent and in 1647 he married Browne's daughter, Mary. He returned to England, but was again in Paris from mid-summer 1649 till early in 1652.

When back in England he settled at Browne's former estate, Sayes Court in Deptford, where Browne later came to live with his son-in-law.

There is no doubt that Browne's taste in books, and in particular in fine bindings, influenced Evelyn's collecting habits. Browne had the better taste, or at least spent more money on his bindings, which he had made in Paris, and often lavishly decorated in gold with the small solid fleurons and curl tools that were then the height of fashion. He was explicit in his ownership, using two different monograms, two Bs addorsed and a monogram combining the letters of his own name and that of his wife Elizabeth (RBE). He also used his coat of arms in two different versions: a plain shield (*or*) charged with a chief (*sable*) and surmounted by a vulture, an augmentation granted to him by a warrant dated 6 January 1649/50, and a more complex version, of which the 1649/50 augmentation formed the first quarter, with above it his motto, 'Domino potiora'.

Not all Browne's bindings were equally elaborate. A copy of Henricus Oraeus, *Nomenclator praecipuorum* (Hanover, 1619) in black goatskin is simply tooled with fillets and his BB monogram at the corners of the panel and in the centre, where it is surrounded by a common French device, the s fermé, interpreted by G. D .Hobson as 'fermesse', symbolizing loyalty.[5] Evelyn later owned this book and had it inscribed in his catalogue. A much grander example, also showing the BB monogram, but here surrounded by an elaborate design of gold-tooled solid curls and fleurons, occurs on a 1636 London *Book of Common Prayer*, bound in Paris probably in the 1640s [Fig. 1]. That Browne did not lose the taste for fine bindings once he had joined his King in England is shown by the bindings he had made in London, such as that on a copy of René Rapin's *Of Gardens,* translated by John Evelyn jr. (London, 1673), bound in gold-tooled red goatskin, combining the BB monogram, Browne's simple coat of arms, and the arms with all the quarterings with typical London tools of the 1670s. This may have been a present from the translator to his grandfather.[6]

Like his father-in-law, Evelyn also used two different monograms and two different versions of his coat of arms, and he too had some of his books bound in Paris and others in London. They are far more difficult to locate than Browne's because the tools of the monogram and arms block that Evelyn used most frequently were cut in London and the additional decorative tooling is largely limited to the spine panels. Moreover, I think that either Evelyn himself or his amanuensis and secretary, Richard Hoare (whom he employed from the late 1640s to the early 1650s), instructed the binders, and especially the London binders, not only what ownership tools to use, but in certain matters of detail concerning the end-bands and end-leaves.

It seems that Evelyn was taken by the French habit of using fine comb-marbled paper for pastedowns, combined with white paper for free end-

Fig. 1: A binding made in Paris in the1640s for Sir Richard Browne:
The Booke of Common Prayer, London, 1636. Red goatskin, tooled in
gold to an elaborate centre- and corner-design with curls and fleurons
surrounding Browne's BB monogram. 350 × 235 × 40 mm
(British Library, C.67.g.2).

leaves, and that he often asked his London craftsmen to do the same, although this was not a habit in England at the time. Similarly, we almost always find the same end-band construction on bindings Evelyn had made in Paris and in London. They are sewn in coloured silk, double, finished with a bead, over a main core of rolled paper which was cut off and not laced in, while the coloured silk was tied down at intervals into the sections. *Per contra*, certain typically French sewing and lacing-in techniques (e.g. through three holes) were not copied in London, probably because these were hidden features. Not only the tooling and the structural details suggest where the books were bound. Their indication is supported by Evelyn's inscriptions, stating that certain books were bought in Paris and others in London, often giving a date, sometimes a price, and a note that he had read the book and when. Presents were also inscribed, not only with the name of the donor, but often with the place and date of the gift.

There are also some tantalizing references in letters from Richard Hoare. On 13 July 1650 he wrote from Paris: 'Mr. R. tells me you shall have the stampe of your cipher for your Books this weeke, and if I can possible you shall have a proofe sent you by the next opportunity.' This next opportunity arose on 27 July, for a letter of some 3 weeks later states, 'I have in my letter of the 27 July sent you enclosed a proof of that Stamp for your Books which Mr. R. cut for which he asks a round price.' Hoare goes on to dispute the price as too high and then continues: 'The book binder is not so honest I supposed he was for notwithstanding his quotidian promises to me, he has not done a Stich in your Bookes'.[7] Two and a half years later, when both the secretary and his master were back in England, Hoare wrote from London on 10 January 1653, 'Returning yesterday from Waltham to London I by chance mett with your Book-binder, who told mee he hath beene at Deptford to render you the manuscript, but finding you not at home carried it back with him. He therefore hath desired mee to convey it to you, which I have here inclosed. The price of the binding thereof … amounts to the sum of five shillings, and whether it be worth so much you may easily judge.'[8] It is clear from these letters that Evelyn had one of his monograms cut in Paris and that he employed a Parisian binder as well as a London one.

Let us now look at Evelyn's ownership tools themselves. On the bindings made for him that I have seen, both in the British Library and elsewhere, he most frequently used a simple monogram consisting of the entwined letters IE between a palm and a laurel branch. There is a larger and a smaller version. He also regularly used a large coat of arms: a griffin passant and a chief with a martlet for difference, surmounted by a griffin displayed, with below the arms his motto 'omnia explorate meliora retinete', the whole surrounded by a wreath of palm and laurel branches. The idea of setting his monogram or coat of arms on his books did not come from Browne. In 1640 Thomas

Simon, later chief engraver to the King, cut for Evelyn the IE monogram between palm and laurel branches in two sizes; he also cut Evelyn's large coat of arms, as well as a smaller and simpler version of the arms, consisting of an oval with a part-pearl edge, with the same charges, and Evelyn's crest: on a wreath a griffin passant.

Among the Evelyn Papers is a piece of paper with smoke impressions of these tools, and a note in Evelyn's hand, 'stamps for the Bookbinder ingraved by Mr Symonds his Ma[jesty']s. Gr: at the Tower: 1641'.[9] From the fact that both monogram tools and both versions of the arms were used in combination with French decorative tools and that they occur on bindings of books that Evelyn had acquired and read in Paris, it is clear that he owned his ownership tools himself and that he simply gave them to a bookbinder with the books to be bound. All five tools also occur on bindings made after 1653, when Evelyn had returned to England, in combination with identifiable London decorative tools.

I do not know whether the same was the case with the monogram 'Mr. R.' cut for him in Paris in 1650, as this tool cannot be identified with any certainty. There is a different IE monogram, a more complex one, showing the entwined initials crossed by two palm branches and surrounded by oak and laurel branches. Alas, I have found it on only seven bindings, always in combination with the simpler IE monogram, used on books with imprints ranging from 1623 to 1649, one of which was bought in London in 1640.[10] The binding on [H. Grotius], *La vérité de la réligion Chrestienne* [Paris, ?1640], is tooled in gold with fillets and both simple and complex monograms [Fig. 2]. At the end of the text Evelyn wrote 'per legi Pa[ris] 1647', and on the first free end-leaf: 'E Libris Evelyni Parisijs 1647 / Ex dono d:d: Browne Barronetti', followed by his motto. Although Browne was not formally created a Baronet until 1 September 1649, Evelyn may have reflected Charles I's intention expressed in a dormant warrant of February 1643. But it does look as if the complex monogram was used before 1650 and it is therefore unlikely to be the one referred to in Hoare's letter as cut by 'Mr. R.' in Paris.

The simpler IE monogram, cut in London, was sometimes used on its own, just with the addition of a few fillets, as on a copy of a collection of works by Malvezzi (n.p., n.d.), one of which at least Evelyn read in 1646, bound in marbled calf [Fig. 3]. The tooling on the spine compartments suggests that it was made in Paris. More often this monogram is found in combination with one or other of the coats of arms or the more complex monogram. Both sizes are frequently used on the compartments of the spine, sometimes alternating with the griffin crest. The oval coat of arms block occurs both by itself, as cut by Simon, or – more often – inside a large wreath tool which incorporates the second part of Evelyn's motto. I have

Fig. 2: A binding made in Paris, presented to John Evelyn by Sir Richard Browne, 1647: [H. Grotius], *La vérité de la réligion Chrestienne* [Paris, ?1640]. Brown mottled calf, tooled in gold with fillets and two versions of Evelyn's monogram. 177 × 120 × 38 mm (British Library, Eve.a.70).

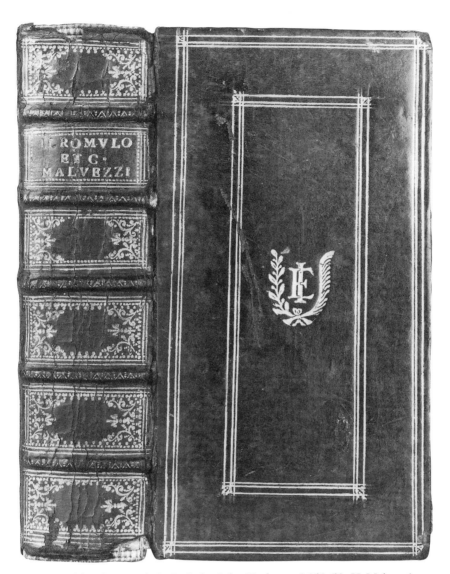

Fig. 3: A binding made in Paris for John Evelyn, *c.*1650-52: V. Malvezzi, *Il Romulo* [and four other works], n.p., n.d. Brown marbled calf, tooled in gold with fillets and Evelyn's simple monogram. 143 × 80 × 43 mm (British Library, Eve.a.5).

found the block without the wreath on three bindings only. One is certainly English and was produced after 1647, the other two were made in the early 1650s, probably in Paris.[11] The arms block was used inside the wreath, both in Paris, on books Evelyn inscribed as having been bought there (in 1647 and 1650)[12] and in London.

Five bindings covering books printed in Oxford and London between 1644 and 1650,[13] show these two tools. One of these, on H. Hammond's *The Christians Obligations to Peace and Charity* (London, 1649), like the others bound in brown marbled calf and like them also decorated with the small simple monogram as well as the crest at the corners of the panel and in the compartments of the spine, is illustrated here [Fig. 4]. The same decorative curl tools are also found on the spines of all five bindings. One roll links them with a much larger group of bindings with the large arms block, described below. It is possible that this whole group was bound in Paris in, or soon after, 1650. Two bindings on which the same arms block within the wreath was used were made in the 1660s in London. One covers Evelyn's own copy of his translation of *Another part of the Mystery of Jesuitism* (London, 1664).[14]

A large number of bindings is decorated with Evelyn's large arms block, also cut by Simon. The imprints of their contents range from 1622 to 1676, and all but one have Evelyn's simple IE monogram on the covers and usually on the spine. Several of the books have been inscribed to show that they were bought in London in 1649 and 1650, or in Venice in 1645, that Evelyn read them at various dates between 1651 and 1680, and that they were catalogued, also sometimes giving the dates.

Although these dates may help to date and therefore to locate these bindings, none are decisive, as Evelyn is likely to have bought most of his books unbound. But he may well have read them and had them catalogued several years after he had them bound. The decorative tools used on the spines of these bindings suggest that a number of them were produced in Paris in the same bindery, *c*.1650-1; for example a copy of Eusebius, Socrates, and Evagrius, *The Ancient Ecclesiasticall Histories* (London, 1650), with Eusebius' *Life of Constantine* (London 1649), catalogued in 1650, possibly soon after being bound, and read in 1655.[15] Five bindings with the same coat of arms, but with different spine tools, were clearly bound in London after 1653 and three of them come from the same bindery.[16]

Naudé had warned not only against too much 'luxe et superfluité' in matters of binding, but also against spending too much money on such frippery: 'as to the binding of Books, there is no need of extraordinary expence; it were better to reserve that money for the purchasing of all the books of the fairest and best editions that are to be found'.[17]

How extravagant was Evelyn? A bill for prices of 'Binding filleted on the

Fig. 4: A binding probably made in Paris for John Evelyn, *c.*1650:
H. Hammond, *The Christians Obligations to Peace and Charity*, London,
1649. Brown marbled calf, tooled in gold with fillets, Evelyn's oval arms
block within a large wreath, as well as his griffin crest and his simple
monogram. 197 × 145 × 24 mm (British Library, Eve.a.125).

Edge gilded & Titld on the back' – alas undated – indicates that for his simpler bindings Evelyn paid between one shilling and sixpence and eight shillings, no doubt depending on the size of the book. A quick comparison with trade prices charged in London by the bookbinders in 1646, 1669, 1695, and 1760 for 'edges and fillets' for comparable books shows that Evelyn paid well above trade prices, even if we take into account that a private collector would be charged more than a bookseller, but that he also got more decoration for his money,[18] a conclusion, as we have seen, borne out by the bindings themselves. As far as his presentation and special bindings were concerned, Naudé would not have approved.

NOTES

1 This is an abbreviated version of a paper given at the British Library on 17 September 2001. For a fuller version, see M. M. Foot, 'An Englishman in Paris: John Evelyn and his Bookbindings', in *Festschrift for Michel Wittock* (Brussels, forthcoming).

2 Gabriel Naudeus, *Instructions Concerning Erecting of a Library ... Interpreted by Jo. Evelyn, Esquire* (London: for G. Bedle and T. Collins, and J. Crook, 1661), pp. 61-2.

3 Now in the Houghton Library, Harvard University; see Geoffrey Keynes, *John Evelyn; a Study in Bibliophily with a Bibliography of his Writings*, 2nd edn (Oxford: Clarendon Press, 1968), p. 250, pl. 14.

4 BL Eve.A.131. I am most grateful to Giles Mandelbrote for letting me work in the stacks of the British Library in order to find examples for this paper.

5 BL Eve.A.2. See G. D. Hobson, *Les reliures à la fanfare: Le problème de l's fermé* (Amsterdam, 1970), pp. 105-6.

6 BL Eve.A.48. See also Keynes, *John Evelyn*, p. 291, no. 182.

7 Keynes, *John Evelyn*, pp. 22-3.

8 Ibid., p. 23.

9 BL Add. MS 78639.

10 BL Eve.A.105.

11 The English binding is on BL Add. MS 78372; the two likely French ones, Add. MS 78371 and C.69.a.10.

12 BL Eve.A.158 and Eve.A.116.

13 BL Eve. A.125-129.

14 BL Eve.A.34. Keynes, *John Evelyn*, pp. 124-8, no. 39.

15 BL Eve.B.11. Other bindings from this shop are at Eve.B.3, Eve.B.6, Eve.B.15, Eve.B.16, Eve.B.18, Eve.B.29, Eve.B.30, Eve.B.42, Eve.B.49, and Eve.B.54.

16 BL Eve.A.138, Eve.C.15, Eve.C.19, Eve.C.20, and Eve.C.24 (Eve.C.15, 19, and 24 are from the same bindery).

17 Naudeus, *Instructions*, pp. 83-4.

18 The bill is in BL Add. MS 78639. For comparable prices see M. M. Foot, 'Some Bookbinders' Price Lists of the Seventeenth and Eighteenth Centuries', in M. M. Foot, *Studies in the History of Bookbinding* (Aldershot: Scolar, 1993), pp. 15-67.

JOHN EVELYN AND HIS BOOKS

GILES MANDELBROTE

ON 13 July 1978 the auctioneer's gavel fell on the last lot – lot 1737 – of the Evelyn Library.[1] The sales at Christie's, beginning in the summer of 1977, marked the final stage of a long process of dispersal of John Evelyn's books – a process which had begun in his own lifetime and gathered momentum in the nineteenth century. Books from Evelyn's library may now be found in institutional and private libraries across the world and they continue to appear regularly in the antiquarian book trade. The largest fragment of the library, however, is now in the British Library, thanks to determined efforts made at the sale.[2] At present there are some 290 books at the 'Eve.' pressmark, most of them bought at the Christie's sale – though additions continue to be made as the opportunity arises – and mostly chosen either for their bindings or because they contain extensive annotation in Evelyn's hand.

Evelyn deplored the dispersal of scholarly libraries by auction, which had become common in England during his own lifetime. In a long and celebrated letter to Samuel Pepys, encouraging him in his collecting, Evelyn complained of libraries being torn limb from limb, and praised his friend's intention to

secure what (with [so much] Cost and Industrie) you have Collected, from the sad dispersions, many noble Libraries [and Cabinets] have [suffered] in these late times: One Auction [I may call it diminution] of a day or two, having scatter'd what has ben gathering many [years]. Hence proceedes it, that we are in England so defective of good Libraries among the Nobilitie and [in our] greatest Townes: Paris alone, I am perswaded, being able to shew [more than all the three nations of] Great Britain.[3]

The reference to Paris is significant: like many other royalist gentlemen of his generation, Evelyn's cultural and intellectual expectations had been transformed by the experience of continental exile during the civil wars.[4]

Leaving England in 1643, Evelyn spent most of the next decade in France and Italy – notably in Rome, in Padua where he studied medicine, and most of all in Paris, where he kept company with fellow royalist exiles and married the daughter of Charles I's ambassador, Sir Richard Browne. Evelyn's own account of his travels reveals the young man as an enthusiastic student of languages, classical scholarship, and antiquities, and a keen observer of foreign customs, art and architecture, and of natural phenomena. His diary also records his interest in foreign libraries, such as the Vatican Library (among others in Italy) and Cardinal Mazarin's library in Paris, following the 'rude dispersion' of which – to use Evelyn's own phrase – he was later able to make acquisitions for himself.[5]

Paris in the mid-seventeenth century was far ahead of London in terms of bibliographical connoisseurship and the appreciation of books for their rarity, binding, and condition. It was here that Evelyn became a bibliophile and book collector, under the guidance of his father-in-law. Both men commissioned elaborate gold-tooled bindings incorporating their initials and arms. It was here too that scholars and collectors were taking an interest in the history of printing and in the classification of knowledge.[6] Evelyn later published translations of several French works, on gardens, architecture, painting, and – most significantly – the treatise by Gabriel Naudé, Mazarin's librarian, entitled *Instructions Concerning Erecting of a Library* (1661), on the formation and systematic organization of libraries.

In 1652 Evelyn returned to England and settled at Sayes Court, his wife's family house at Deptford. He managed his estates, cultivated his gardens and, after the Restoration, had a moderately successful career as an administrator, courtier, and public servant. Right up until his death in 1706, much of his energy went into intellectual pursuits. As a founder-member of the Royal Society and a frequent attender at its meetings, Evelyn was at the centre of intellectual life in Restoration England. He was also the author of numerous books, published and unpublished, on a very wide range of subjects: from tracts on environmental pollution to devotional works, histories of engraving and numismatics, works on economic theory and, especially, treatises on forestry and horticulture.[7]

The two works for which Evelyn is most famous both reveal something of the character of the man. *Sylva* contains much practical advice about growing trees, but presents it in the form of a large and expensive folio, wrapped up with nostalgic classical quotations about rustic life and discourses in the style of Sir Thomas Browne: not a book for someone who wants to get his hands dirty. Evelyn's diary is that of an observer, rather than a participant: deeply religious and highly principled, but also over-cautious and aloof, concerned to do and to be seen to be doing the right thing, and – as Samuel Pepys noticed – with a tendency to conceitedness. What still brings the diary to life is Evelyn's irrepressible curiosity, his fascination with detail, and his enthusiasm for learning: all of these qualities are also abundantly evident in the annotations which he made in his books.[8]

Evelyn's library catalogue, dating from about 1687, has yet to be properly studied.[9] It records nearly four thousand printed books and over eight

hundred pamphlets, arranged by subject and indexed by author. There
are almost a thousand theological titles, some eight hundred and fifty works
on historical subjects, and large sections devoted to poetry and drama,
philology, law, grammar, rhetoric, and logic, mathematics and music, medicine, philosophy, and politics, together with a special subject category (163
titles) of 'Historiæ Materiarum & Oeconom: Rei Rustici Mechanologici,
&c.'.[10] This was a very large collection for its time: larger, for instance, than
the library of Samuel Pepys or John Locke, or of Robert Boyle or Robert
Hooke, who each owned about three thousand or three thousand five
hundred books.[11]

This total of nearly five thousand titles, however, probably represents a
high-water mark for the library, which was in a state of flux in the latter years
of Evelyn's life. The move from Sayes Court to smaller library accommodation at Wotton, in 1694, and the arrival of his son's books following
John Evelyn junior's death in 1699, both triggered substantial disposals.
This was wholly in keeping with Evelyn's recommendation to his grandson
that 'most of the trifling Books' in a library 'should be weeded out to give
place to better till it were thro'ly purged'.[12]

This stern advice is characteristic of Evelyn's seriousness about the library
as a whole. The books were there for edification and instruction and
devotion, to support serious study and writing, not for entertainment –
although Evelyn would doubtless have said that the pursuit of knowledge
and of curiosity was (among other things) the highest form of amusement.
At the same time, Evelyn clearly took pleasure in the aesthetic aspect of
his library: he liked to own grand well-produced books and those with
illustrations; this prevents his selection of books from seeming too severe.

The first page of the main section of Evelyn's library catalogue, the
beginning of the subject sequences, lists theological works[13] [Fig. 1]. Evelyn
owned not one but a range of Bibles, from Brian Walton's massive Polyglot
edition in six folio volumes (1657) to a duodecimo Vulgate. As well as
English translations, there are copies of Italian, Spanish, and French Calvinist
versions, and a Lutheran Bible in English. The selection of New Testaments
is even stronger: there are some twelve editions, in Greek, Latin, Italian, and
English, in a range of formats, with the commentaries of Erasmus, Beza,
Stephanus, and others. This is perhaps still not quite the density of editions
that one would expect in the library of a serious scholar of biblical texts, but
it is certainly a good collection for following the work of such scholars – and
this is the pattern with much of Evelyn's library.

The provisional nature of Evelyn's catalogues is revealed, as Guy de la
Bédoyère has suggested, by his pencil inscription at the top of this page,
'Such only as have a black-lead line dash'd thro them are transcribd into the
faire Catalogue.'[14] The books, however, are described carefully and identified

73

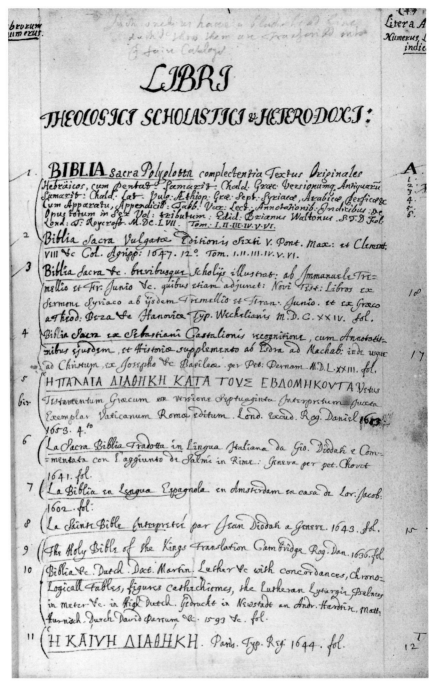

Fig. 1: Evelyn's own record of his collection of Bibles, from his library
catalogue (*c.* 1687), headed with his note referring to a 'faire Catalogue'
(British Library, Add. MS 78632, fol. 15[r]).

by place of publication, date, and format. The set of Walton's Polyglot recorded here itself fell victim to one of Evelyn's purges and was donated by him in 1701 to the parish library which had just been set up by Andrew Cranston, vicar of Reigate in Surrey, where it may still be found.[15]

To take another example, the section of the 1687 catalogue relating to philosophy contains a number of recent editions, mostly printed in Paris, of classical philosophical texts, especially works by Seneca, together with a good range of works by Descartes.[16] One of the more noticeable characteristics of Evelyn's library is evident here. This is a modern library. Unlike some of his book-collecting contemporaries, Evelyn seems to have had little antiquarian interest in books or manuscripts. There are no fifteenth-century editions and relatively few of the sixteenth century. He would have had many opportunities to buy older editions of ancient texts, for instance, but on the whole he seems to have preferred to buy books new rather than secondhand. This perhaps also reflects another feature of the library: with the exception of the special section on horticulture and husbandry, there are few real surprises. Evelyn was interested in his own time and in his contemporaries: he owned many controversial pamphlets, for example, and he followed intellectual fashion, buying books as they came out.

Turning to what has survived the depredations of Evelyn himself, and of William Upcott and others, the four-volume Christie's sale catalogue provides a good overview of a similarly wide-ranging, but much smaller residue: only about 850 lots (mostly single items) are firmly identified, on the evidence of press-marks and annotations, as having belonged to John Evelyn or Sir Richard Browne rather than to later members of the family. The 290 or so books now in the British Library constitute a small sample, which may not be fully representative of the depth and breadth of Evelyn's collection in particular subject areas, but provides plenty of evidence nonetheless of how and why Evelyn annotated his books, how he read them and what he considered important about them.

The first type of information offered by Evelyn's annotations relates to provenance: where, when, and how he acquired his books. His note, dated 1647, on the flyleaf of a copy of Grotius' *La Verité de la Religion Chrestienne* (Paris, [*c.* 1640]), records an early gift to Evelyn while in Paris from his friend and fellow book collector, Sir Richard Browne, who was perhaps not yet his father-in-law (Evelyn married his daughter in June of the same year). A second inscription, also in Evelyn's hand, is the personal motto he adopted and frequently wrote in his books: 'Omnia Explorate, Meliora Retinete', which was derived from I Thessalonians, verse 21: 'Prove all things: hold fast that which is good'[17] [Fig. 2].

The earliest examples of dated inscriptions go back to Evelyn's schooldays: a copy of Thomas Wilson's *The Art of Rhetorique* (1585) is signed and dated

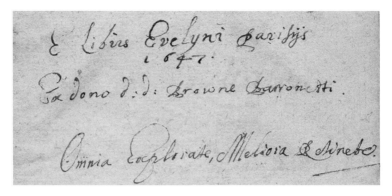

Fig. 2: Flyleaf inscription by Evelyn, recording a gift from
Sir Richard Browne, with Evelyn's motto (British Library, Eve.a.70).

1634.[18] There are also inscriptions in books acquired while he was a student
at Oxford, by which time he was experimenting with calligraphy and red
ink.[19] Of particular interest are those which enable us to follow him on his
travels: there are books bought in Paris in 1643, in Rome in 1644, in Venice
in 1645, and in London in 1649.[20] There are numerous inscriptions from his
time in Paris, but later in life, as he acquired more and more books, Evelyn
became less careful to record details of this sort – with the notable exception
of those books he received as gifts, especially from their authors, in which he
continued to note the donation assiduously.

The presentation copies in Evelyn's library form a remarkably high
proportion of the collection as a whole and relate to every field of study.
The physician and antiquary Walter Charleton gave Evelyn a copy of his
translation of Plato's *Apology of Socrates* (1675), in which Evelyn has carefully
recorded the donation in Latin and then, rather pedantically, has corrected
his own inscription describing Charleton as 'Authoris' to 'Interpretis'[21]
[Fig. 3]. Other examples include Thomas Smith's *De Græcæ Ecclesiæ hodierno
statu epistola* (Oxford, 1676), presented to Evelyn by the book's dedicatee,
Sir Joseph Williamson, the Principal Secretary of State, and a presentation
copy from the educational and agricultural theorist Samuel Hartlib of his
Legacy of Husbandry (3rd edition, 1655).[22] The Anglican divine who perhaps
had most influence on Evelyn's strictly regulated spiritual life, Jeremy Taylor,
gave him a copy of his *A Collection of offices or Forms of Prayer* (1658).[23] Most
striking for their sheer quantity among Evelyn's books are presentation
copies of no fewer than ten different works by Robert Boyle, whose aristocratic background, personal piety, and skill in experimental science made him
a particular object of admiration. They are each inscribed with a formula such
as that used in Evelyn's copy of *New Experiments and Observations Touching
Cold* (1665) – 'ex dono Authoris illustriss[imi]'[24] [Fig. 4].

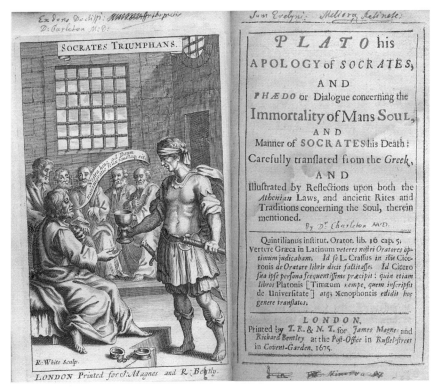

Fig. 3: Evelyn's note records that this copy was presented to him by the
translator, Walter Charleton (British Library, Eve.a.68).

There are two things to notice about these presentation copies. The first
is that they help to locate Evelyn within a social and intellectual network. The
gift of books was one feature of a reciprocal process in which deference,
patronage, and the exchange of information all played a part. The second
observation to be made is that all the presentation inscriptions are in Evelyn's
hand. This is unusual and perhaps it is simply characteristic of Evelyn's desire
to record, and of his sense of honour and obligation, but it may well reveal
a somewhat tiresome persistence in seeking out such opportunities.

Evelyn took very seriously the business of presenting copies of his own
published writings. A copy of his *Publick Employment and an Active Life
Prefer'd to Solitude* (1667), now in the British Library, is in a gilt presentation
binding and inscribed (possibly by a bookseller's clerk) 'Mr Boyle'.[25] Among
the Evelyn manuscripts are carefully compiled lists of the intended recipients
of his various works, sometimes stipulating special bindings for the most
eminent of them; Evelyn's correspondence with the bookseller Benjamin
Tooke concerning the publication of *Numismata* (1697) dwells on this
theme.[26] In his diary entry for 28 October 1664, he recorded with con-

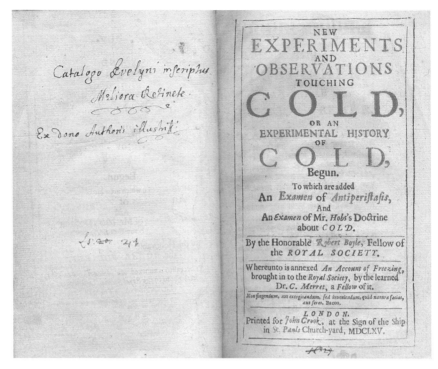

Fig. 4: One of several works by Robert Boyle given by the author to Evelyn, with an inscription in Evelyn's hand (British Library, Eve.a.76).

siderable satisfaction one occasion when his efforts to impress by this means had paid off: 'Being casualy in the Privy Gallery at *White-hall*, his Majestie gave me thanks (before divers Lords & noble men) for my Book of *Architecture* & *Sylva* againe: That they were the best designd & usefull ... the best printed & designd ... that he had seene.'[27] For Evelyn, one of the most compelling reasons for publishing a book was to be able to give it away.

Annotated copies of Evelyn's own works form perhaps the most interesting group of all. Several of them have been marked up with self-criticisms, corrections, and additions intended for insertion into new editions. One example is the English translation of Roland Fréart's *An Idea of the Perfection of Painting* (1668): Evelyn's manuscript note at the end of the printed preface reads: 'I have too literaly follow'd this preface which is in the original itselfe scarse sense in some places.' Evelyn's own copy of his history of engraving, *Sculptura* (1662), is annotated 'I ever intended a second & much improv'd Edition of this Historie'. On the endpapers at the back is a long note listing references to catalogues of French print collections and other material which should be included 'in Revising this History of mine'.[28]

78

The margins of Evelyn's copy of his own *A Philosophical Discourse of Earth* (1676) are likewise filled with addenda, mostly relating to soil preparation or, as in the page illustrated, to the planting of seeds[29] [Fig. 5]. This particular copy may well have been used by the printer of the second edition of 1678, in which most of these notes have been incorporated word for word. A copy of the third edition of *Sylva* (1679), which came to the British Library with the Evelyn archive in 1995, is inscribed 'This Book Belongs to Says-Court, Gardens &c.' and contains numerous additions and corrections by Evelyn in advance of the fourth edition, which was not published until 1706.[30] Perhaps the most scathing example – though there are many to choose from – of Evelyn's comments on the quality of production of his own publications is to be found in one of his copies of his translation of the first book of Lucretius' *De Rerum Natura* (1656). 'Never,' wrote Evelyn, 'was book so abominably misus'd by printer, never Copy so negligently surveied by one who undertooke to looke over the proofes with all exactnesse & care. ... This good yet I receiv'd by it, that publishing it vainely, its ill Successe at the printers discourag'd me from troubling the world with the rest.' The draft of Evelyn's translation of Books 3-6 languished unpublished among his manuscripts for more than three centuries.[31]

What of Evelyn's notes in the rest of his books? A range of different types of annotation may be identified. In the first place, in addition to Evelyn's motto, there may well be a note that the book has been entered in his library catalogue, 'Catalogo Evelini inscriptus', and there are usually press-marks. Evelyn's system of press-marks is as yet not fully understood: several different systems were in use at different times and there is plenty of evidence of press-marks being changed. The reality, however, seems to have fallen far short of the elaborate idealized system, employing the names of Roman deities, emperors, and so on to represent subject categories, which Evelyn devised and which may be found among his papers.[32] A relatively unusual feature are the occasional notes by Evelyn which are simply intended to help the physical articulation of his books. To give just one instance, where Evelyn's copy has been misbound, successive directions in his hand invite the reader to 'turn 2 Leaves forward' and then to 'Turn 2 Leaves back'.[33]

A commonly recurring annotation is a note at the end, 'Perlegi', to indicate that Evelyn has read all the way through, sometimes accompanied by a date, or by notes which may indicate that parts of the text have been transcribed into a commonplace book. There are three large volumes of such compendia among the Evelyn manuscripts, for which Evelyn devised an elaborate method of arrangement and subject indexing.[34] In some instances these make it possible to reconstruct Evelyn's reading and the extracts he made, book by book. Once again, however, it seems that Evelyn's system-atizing may have been over-ambitious: two of the three volumes contain

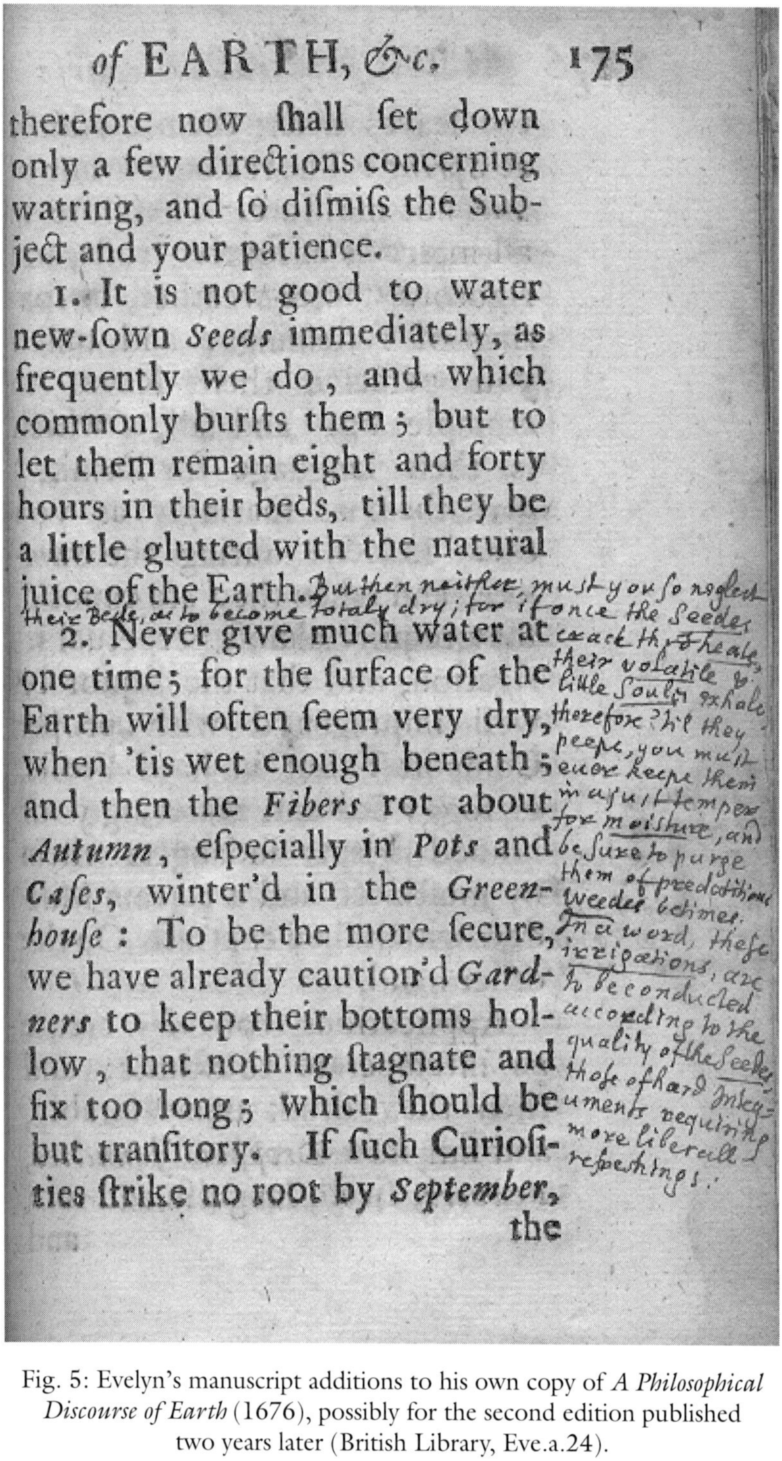

of EARTH, &c. 175

therefore now shall set down
only a few directions concerning
watring, and so dismiss the Subject and your patience.

 1. It is not good to water
new-sown *Seeds* immediately, as
frequently we do, and which
commonly bursts them; but to
let them remain eight and forty
hours in their beds, till they be
a little glutted with the natural
juice of the Earth. *But then neither, must you so neglect their Beds, as to become totaly dry; for if once the Seedes*

 2. Never give much water at *crack they theale their volatile & little Soules exhale,*
one time; for the surface of the
Earth will often seem very dry, *therefore that they*
when 'tis wet enough beneath; *people, you must ever keepe them*
and then the *Fibers* rot about *in a just temper*
Autumn, especially in *Pots* and *for moisture, and be sure to purge them of predations,*
Cases, winter'd in the *Green-* *weeded betimes.*
house: To be the more secure, *In a word, these*
we have already caution'd *Gard-* *irrigations, are*
ners to keep their bottoms hol- *to be conducted*
low, that nothing stagnate and *according to the quality of the Seedes,*
fix too long; which should be *those of hard integuments requiring*
but transitory. If such Curiosi- *more liberall*
ties strike no root by *September*, *refreshings:*
                              the

Fig. 5: Evelyn's manuscript additions to his own copy of *A Philosophical Discourse of Earth* (1676), possibly for the second edition published two years later (British Library, Eve.a.24).

more blank leaves than commonplaces and it appears that many of Evelyn's notes were never written up from bundles of loose sheets, or from the books themselves, into a finished form.[35] The Evelyn manuscripts also include volumes of less formally arranged notes, such as the 'Adversaria Historical, Physical, Mathematical, Mechanicall, &c promiscuously set downe as they Occur in reading, or Casual Discourse', while a fragment collected by William Upcott refers to 'Excerp[t]s & Collections, casualy gather'd out of several Authors &c, and intended to have be[e]n transcrib'd into Adversaria', and mentions material intended for insertion into new editions of *Sylva* and *Numismata*.[36] As yet, relatively few entries in the commonplace books themselves have been found to correspond to the annotated books now in the British Library; surprisingly often they relate instead to another edition of the same text. It may be possible in time, however, to trace each stage of the process of Evelyn's reading and marking of books, through extracts in the commonplace books and notes, and into print again in his own publications.

'A Substantiall and Learned digest of *Common-Places*,' Evelyn wrote, quoting Francis Bacon, 'is a solid, and a good aide to memory: And, because it is a counterfeit thing in knowledge, to be forward and pregnant, unless you be withall deep and full; I hold that the dilligence, and paines in collecting Common-places, is of greate use, and certainety in stud[y]ing.'[37] Many of the annotations in Evelyn's books indicate approved passages suitable for extracting, or they act as aids to memory, to help him find his way around the text. The printed books acted as an adjunct to the volumes of common-places. Thomas Smith's *De Græca Ecclesia* (Oxford, 1676), for example, contains a list of 'Loci laudabiles', with page numbers, typically on the blank leaves at the end of the volume; sometimes these notes are also keyed to particular themes or to the titles of works which Evelyn was revising[38] [Fig. 6]. Evelyn often underlined passages of text in pencil and he employed a variety of marginal marks: most often vertical lines, but also pointing fingers, paraph marks, hash marks, and asterisks; from time to time he used pencil, ink, and red crayon. In some instances, notes have been written over or amended in different colours, providing evidence that he returned to his books and re-read them[39] [Figs 7, 8]. The range of marks used by Evelyn probably reflects personal and individual choice, rather than reference to a more widely recognized set of conventions, although there is some evidence of particular marks being deployed in a consistent way.[40] A trefoil symbol, for instance, seems to have been mainly reserved for bibliographical references, possibly to indicate items that Evelyn particularly wanted for his own library. The illustration shows it against a list of some of the works of William Tyndale[41] [Fig. 9]; these symbols can also be found pencilled in Evelyn's copy of the sale catalogue of the library of Jean de Cordes (Paris, 1643),

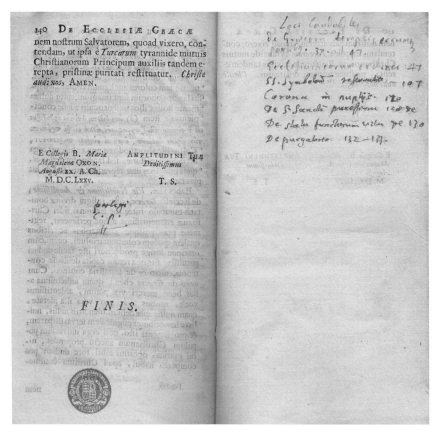

Fig. 6: Evelyn's characteristic 'perlegi' and index of 'Loci laudabiles'
at the end of Thomas Smith, *De Græca Ecclesia* (Oxford, 1676)
(British Library, Eve.a.69).

where a note in his hand explains that the marginal marks are intended to indicate the most essential works and best editions for a learned library.[42] Other annotations are bibliographical in a different sense, cross-referring to other items in Evelyn's library.[43]

Evelyn's view of his library was characteristically self-conscious: he seems, on one level, to have thought of it as a repository of truth and learning for posterity; sometimes his annotations perform the function of putting things on record or of setting the record straight. From time to time he makes attributions of authorship, as, for instance, when he notes in the margin of John Worlidge's *Vinetum Britannicum* (1676) that the passages translated from Rapin are the work of his son, John Evelyn junior, or when he remarks that John Rose's *The English Vineyard Vindicated* (1666) was really 'written by me, & publish'd in his name, from many observations of his'.[44] His notes

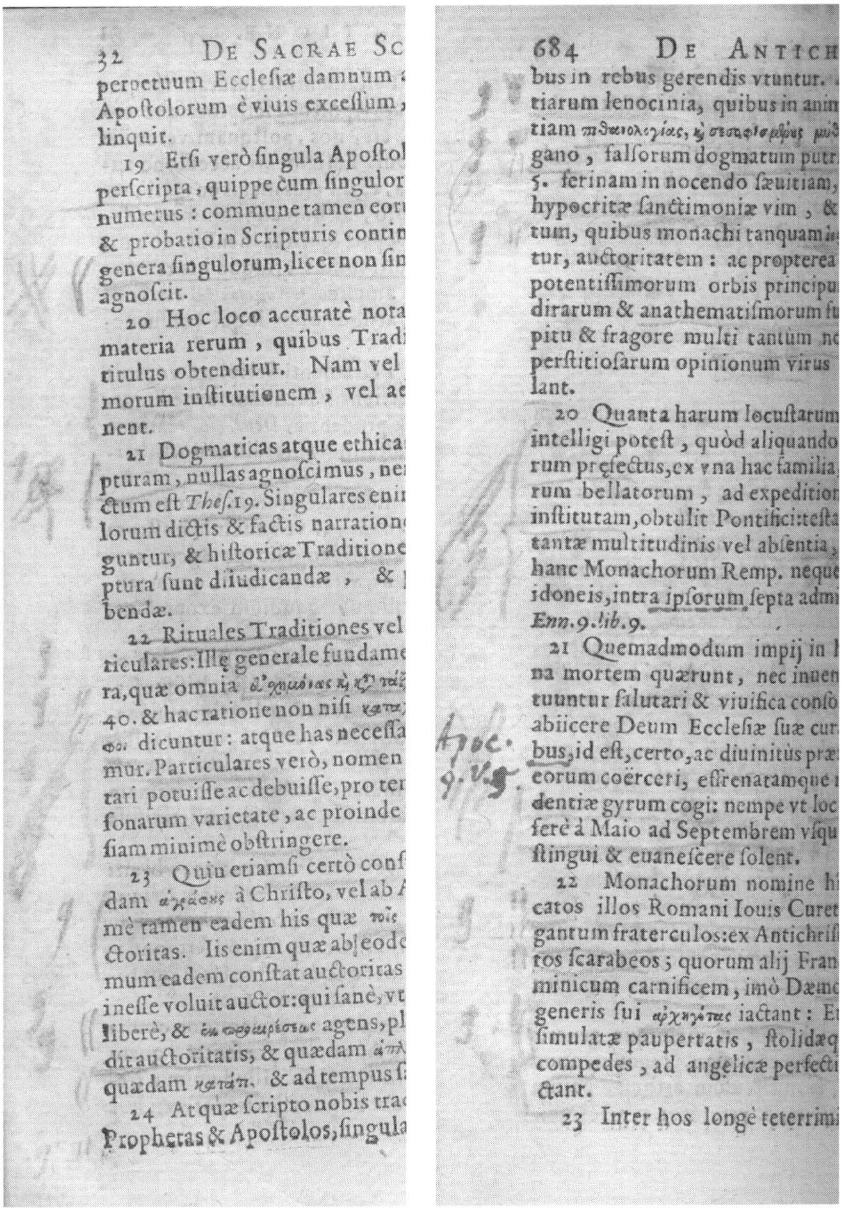

32   DE SACRAE SC

perpetuum Ecclesiæ damnum
Apostolorum è viuis excessum,
linquit.

19. Etsi verò singula Apostol
perscripta, quippe cum singulor
numerus: commune tamen eor
& probatio in Scripturis contin
genera singulorum, licet non fin
agnoscit.

20 Hoc loco accuratè nota
materia rerum, quibus Tradi
titulus obtenditur. Nam vel
morum institutionem, vel ae
nent.

21 Dogmaticas atque ethica
pturam, nullas agnoscimus, nei
ctum est *Thes.*19. Singulares enii
lorum dictis & factis narratione
guntur, & historicæ Traditione
ptura sunt diiudicandæ, & i
bendæ.

22 Rituales Traditiones vel
ticulares: Illę generale fundame
ra, quæ omnia à θεολογίας κỳ ἢ τῆς
40. & hac ratione non nisi κατα;
ὲσι. dicuntur: atque has necessa
mur. Particulares verò, nomen
tari potuisse ac debuisse, pro ter
sonarum varietate, ac proinde
siam minimè obstringere.

23 Quin etiamsi certò conf
dam ἀγραφες à Christo, vel ab /
me tamen eadem his quæ τοις
ctoritas. Iis enim quæ ab eode
mum eadem constat auctoritas
inesse voluit auctor: qui sanè, vt
liberè, & ἐκ προαιρεσεως agens, pl
dit auctoritatis, & quædam ἀπ
quædam κατα. & ad tempus f
24 At quæ scripto nobis trad
Prophetas & Apostolos, singula

---

684   DE ANTICH

bus in rebus gerendis vtuntur.
tiarum lenocinia, quibus in anin
tiam προθεολογίας, κỳ σοφιρισμοι μὸ
gano, falsorum dogmatum putr
5. ferinam in nocendo sæuitiam,
hypocritæ sanctimoniæ vim, &
tum, quibus monachi tanquam in
tur, auctoritatem: ac propterea
potentissimorum orbis principu
dirarum & anathematismorum f
pitu & fragore multi tantùm nc
perstitiosarum opinionum virus
lant.

20 Quanta harum locustarum
intelligi potest, quòd aliquando
rum præfectus, ex vna hac familia
rum bellatorum, ad expeditio
institutam, obtulit Pontifici: testa
tantæ multitudinis vel absentia,
hanc Monachorum Remp. neque
idoneis, intra ipsorum septa adm
Enn.9.lib.9.

21 Quemadmodum impij in l
na mortem quærunt, nec inuen
tuuntur salutari & viuifica conso
abiicere Deum Ecclesiæ suæ cur
bus, id est, certo, ac diuinitus præ
eorum coërceri, effrenaramque i
dentiæ gyrum cogi: nempe vt loc
ferè à Maio ad Septembrem vsqu
stingui & euanescere solent.

22 Monachorum nomine hi
catos illos Romani Iouis Curet
gantum fraterculos: ex Antichrist
tos scarabeos; quorum alij Fran
minicum carnificem, imò Dæmc
generis sui ἀρχηγετας iactant: Et
simulatæ paupertatis, stolidæq
compedes, ad angelicæ perfecti
ctant.

23 Inter hos longè teterrim

Figs 7 & 8: Evelyn's extensive repertory of marginal marks, in ink and pencil:
two pages from Daniel Tilenus, *Syntagmatis Tripertiti Disputationum
Theologicarum in Academia Sedanensi habitarum* (Geneva, 1622)
(British Library, Eve.a.20).

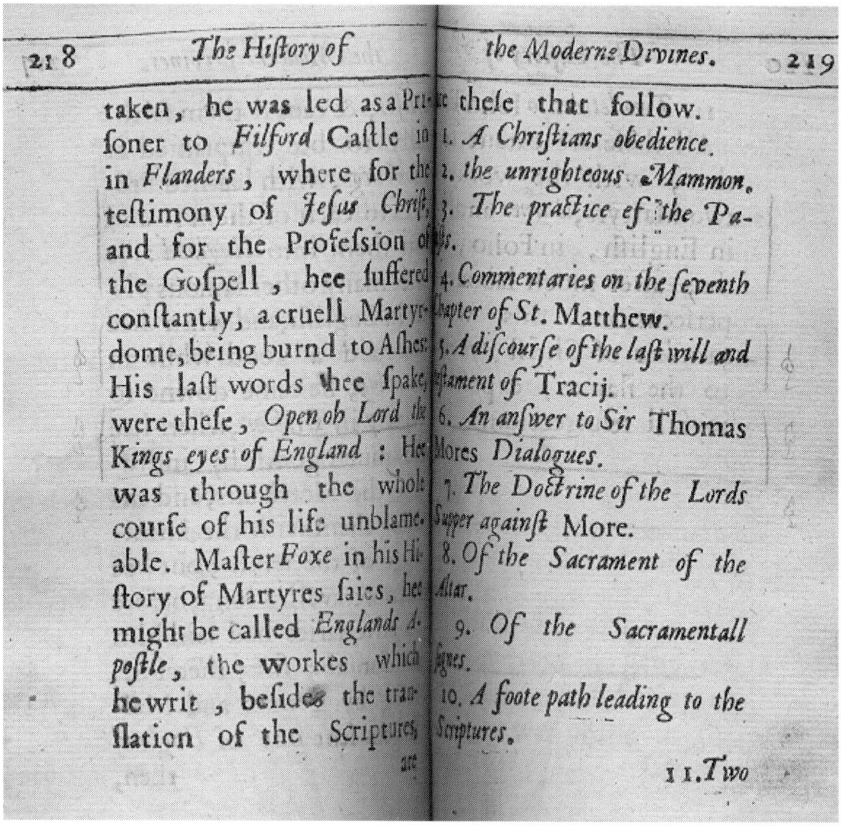

The following is the facsimile text visible in the figure:

218 *The Hiſtory of*

taken, he was led as a Pri-
ſoner to *Filford* Caſtle in
in *Flanders*, where for the
teſtimony of *Jeſus Chriſt*,
and for the Profeſsion of
the Goſpell, hee ſuffered
conſtantly, a cruell Martyr-
dome, being burnd to Aſhes
His laſt words thee ſpake
were theſe, *Open ob Lord the*
Kings eyes of England : He
was through the whole
courſe of his life unblame-
able. Maſter *Foxe* in his Hiſtory of Martyres ſaies, hee
might be called *Englands A-*
poſtle, the workes which
he writ, beſides the tran-
ſlation of the Scriptures,
are

the Moderne Divines. 219

theſe that follow.
1. *A Chriſtians obedience*
2. *the unrighteous Mammon.*
3. *The practice of the Pa-*
ſtor.
4. *Commentaries on the ſeventh*
chapter of St. Matthew.
5. *A diſcourſe of the laſt will and*
teſtament of Tracij.
6. *An anſwer to Sir* Thomas
Mores Dialogues.
7. *The Doctrine of the* Lords
Supper againſt More.
8. *Of the Sacrament of the*
Altar.
9. *Of the Sacramentall*
ſignes.
10. *A foote path leading to the*
Scriptures.
11. *Two*

Fig. 9: Evelyn's marking of bibliographical references, in a list of works
by William Tyndale (British Library, Eve.a.13).

in works dealing with the history of recent events, particularly the Civil War, are especially concerned to correct errors and misinterpretations and often adopt a somewhat petulant tone. *The Secret History of the Reigns of King Charles II and King James II* (1690), for example, is inscribed on the title-page: 'full of malicious mistakes'[45] [Fig. 10]. Evelyn also sometimes quarrels in the margins with the printed text, as when he responds to Alexander Henderson's statement that 'Nor could I ever heare a reason, why a necessary Defensive Warre against unjust Violence is unlawfull' with the sharp retort 'Had y[o]u well read Tertullian you might' [Fig. 11].[46]

An interesting example of Evelyn's desire to rewrite history may be seen among those of his books which mention Colonel Herbert Morley, Lieutenant of the Tower and one of the commissioners for the government of the army, in the confused period leading up to the Restoration. Evelyn had been at school with Morley and late in 1659 he tried unsuccessfully to persuade him to stage a coup in the King's favour. This was the one occasion

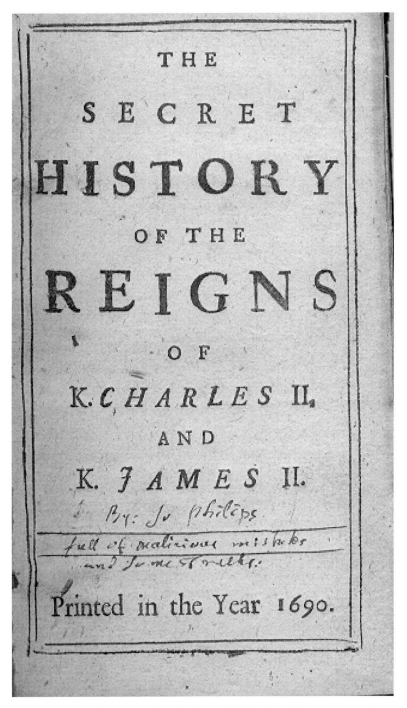

THE

SECRET

HISTORY

OF THE

REIGNS

OF

K. CHARLES II,

AND

K. JAMES II.

By: Sr philips.

full of malicious mistakes
and some truths.

Printed in the Year 1690.

Fig. 10: Evelyn warns that this book is 'full of malicious mistakes'
(British Library, Eve.a.10).

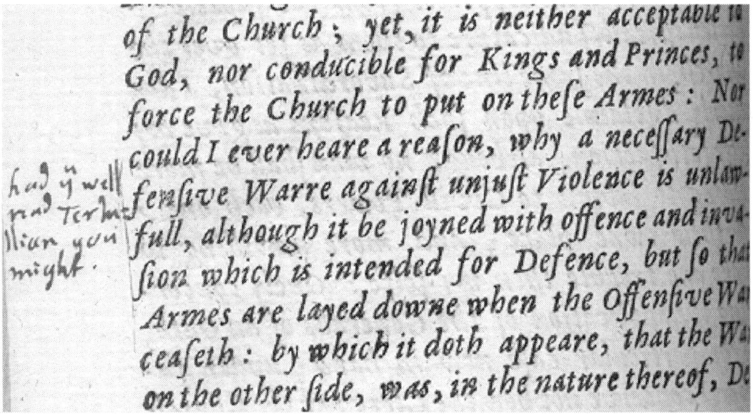
of the Church; yet, it is neither acceptable to
God, nor conducible for Kings and Princes, to
force the Church to put on these Armes: Nor
could I ever heare a reason, why a necessary Defensive Warre against unjust Violence is unlawfull, although it be joyned with offence and invasion which is intended for Defence, but so that
Armes are layed downe when the Offensive Wa
ceaseth: by which it doth appeare, that the Wa
on the other side, was, in the nature thereof, D

Fig. 11: Evelyn takes issue with Alexander Henderson (British Library, Eve.a.39).

when Evelyn's actions might have helped to change the course of English history and he was very sensitive about how his role was portrayed. The margins of his copy of Baker's *Chronicle* (1665) and of Hobbes's *History of the Civil Wars* (1679) are covered with their owner's indignant protests.[47] The critical dialogue with the text has become a long diatribe about his school friend's missed opportunity.

My penultimate group of examples can serve only as a token of a much larger category: annotations that reflect Evelyn's curiosity, particularly about the natural world, and show him (as a good Baconian) making comparisons with his personal experience, as well as trying to accumulate material that might be useful to his own projects. The endpapers of Hartlib's *Legacy of Husbandry*, for instance, contain an extensive index, which Evelyn appears to have compiled in the course of several readings of the text, to judge from the different colours of the annotations. The references to 'phesants, vineyards, silkworm, dung', etc., clearly all of relevance to Evelyn's work on horticulture and husbandry, are listed here with their page numbers.[48] On a spare leaf at the end of John Smith's *The Art of Painting in Oyl* (second edition; London, 1687), Evelyn favourably compares chapter eighteen of the first edition with chapter seventeen in this and goes on to describe his own experiments in waterproofing barrels to hold beer or wine [Fig. 12]. The next two illustrations both come from Evelyn's heavily annotated set of the *Philosophical Transactions* of the Royal Society and relate to John Houghton's discourse on coffee (read to the Royal Society in 1699) – Evelyn was fascinated by anything that smacked of the exotic. Here he adds his personal reminiscence of the introduction of coffee-drinking into England: 'It is now above 60 yeares since I saw Nathaniel Konopius, a Gretian ...

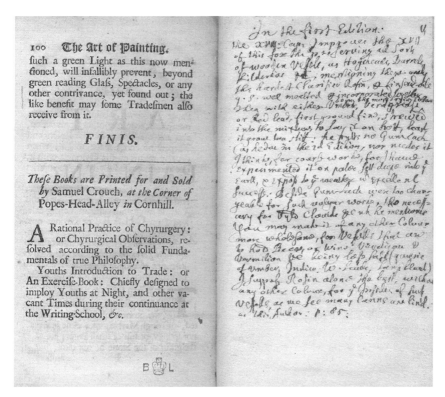

Fig. 12: Evelyn makes comparisons with a previous edition of John Smith,
The Art of Painting in Oyl, and describes his own experiments
(British Library, Eve.a.32).

drinke it frequently in Ball[iol] Coll[ege], Oxon.' He notes also that Houghton had proposed to increase the consumption of tobacco in England by persuading the Queen to take up smoking, an example which all the women of the kingdom would follow[49] [Figs 13, 14].

There is one category of books from Evelyn's library which is even more heavily annotated than those relating to his particular areas of interest in history or natural philosophy: examples of his devotional and theological preoccupations are to be found throughout his collection. The title-page of Evelyn's family Bible (London, 1589), for instance, is covered in detailed notes about the history of the printing and translation of the Geneva version[50] [Fig. 15]. Another printed Bible, in two folio volumes (Cambridge, 1638), with extensive annotations by Evelyn, relating especially to the Garden of Eden, is among the Evelyn manuscripts.[51] In discussions of church discipline too, Evelyn's marginal interjections are sometimes lively details drawn from his own experience. In the margin of Jeremy Taylor's *A Collection of Offices or Forms of Prayer* (1658), for instance, he remarks

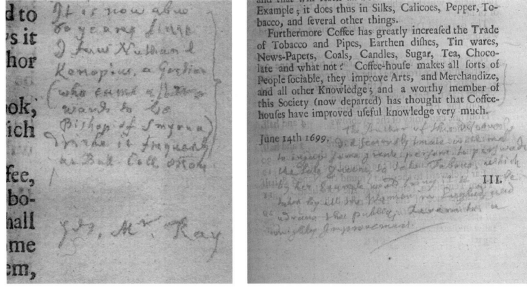

Figs 13 & 14: Evelyn's recollections, written in his copy of *Philosophical Transactions*, about the beginning of coffee-drinking in England and a scheme to popularize smoking (British Library, Eve.a.149).

on the practice of Presbyterian congregations of sitting with their hats on at the reading of the Psalms[52] [Fig. 16]. Several volumes in Evelyn's library attest to his strong sense of religious duty as the head of a household, and his commitment to private and family worship and confessional forms of prayer. On one of the endpapers of his copy of Simon Patrick's *The Christian Sacrifice* (second edition; London, 1672), he has written out a sort of preparatory count-down to the Holy Sacrament, with references for the use of the book at every stage, even 'In the *Church*, if you have time & opportunity'. On the facing page are references to passages 'profitable to be read to servants when you find them remisse in preparing them-selves'[52] [Fig. 17]. We should not forget that religious works comprised the largest single category in Evelyn's library catalogue.

The main Evelyn archive came to the British Library only in 1995, but it should be clear from these examples that the Library had in fact already acquired quite a few Evelyn manuscripts in 1977 and 1978. At the time of the Christie's sales, a correspondent in *The Times* suggested that it was important merely to preserve a record of what Evelyn's library had contained, since other copies of most of the books were readily available.[54] It is inconceivable that such a view could be seriously expressed today. The intervening years have seen a remarkable growth of interest in the types of historical evidence to be found uniquely in individual copies of printed

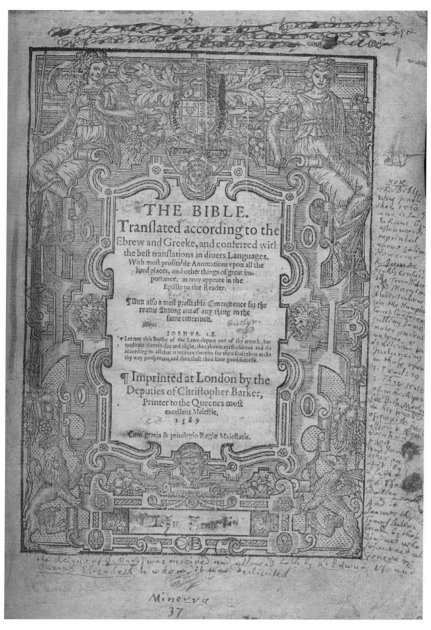

Fig. 15: Title-page of Evelyn's family Bible, with his notes about the
history of the printing and translation of the Geneva version
(British Library, Eve.a.122).

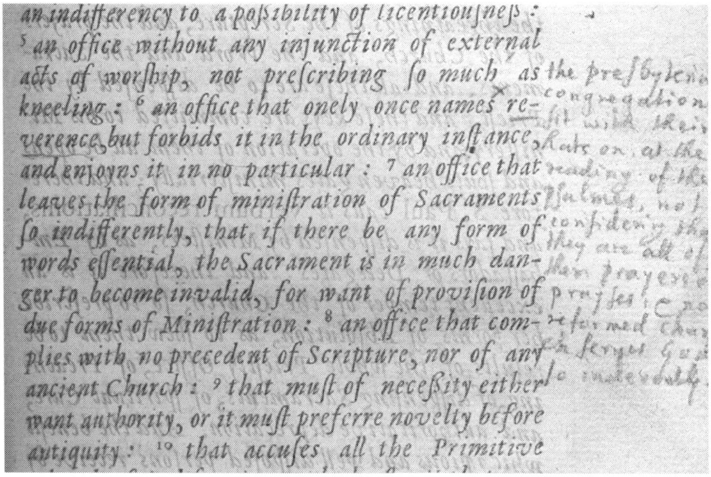
an indifferency to a poſsibility of licentiouſneſs:
5 an office without any injunction of external
acts of worſhip, not preſcribing ſo much as
kneeling: 6 an office that onely once names reverence, but forbids it in the ordinary inſtance,
and enjoyns it in no particular: 7 an office that
leaves the form of miniſtration of Sacraments
ſo indifferently, that if there be any form of
words eſſential, the Sacrament is in much danger to become invalid, for want of proviſion of
due forms of Miniſtration: 8 an office that com-
plies with no precedent of Scripture, nor of any
ancient Church: 9 that muſt of neceſsity either
want authority, or it muſt preferre novelty before
antiquity: 10 that accuſes all the Primitive

Fig. 16: A marginal note in Jeremy Taylor, *A Collection of Offices or Forms of Prayer* (1658), recording Evelyn's observations about the behaviour of Presbyterians in church (British Library, Eve.a.56).

books – and increasing attention paid to the business of describing them. Annotations of all kinds – not only the autographs of famous people or the notes of celebrated scholars or collectors (which have always been appreciated) – are now seen to provide important evidence of ownership and use, broadly defined; a recent editorial in *The Book Collector* went so far as to liken an *un*annotated book to an uninhabited island.[55] Historical case studies have begun to tease out the combination of skills most valued by early modern readers, characterized as 'critical reading, skilful annotation, and active appropriation'.[56] Much work remains to be done, however, not only on early modern theories of how and what one should read, and on the uses and products of that reading, but also on the practices which link the two.

For Evelyn, of course, his manuscripts, working papers, and printed books were interconnected parts of his library and all grist to the same mill. Now that his annotated printed books can be put side by side with the commonplace books and notes, with Evelyn's library catalogue, his published and unpublished works, and his correspondence, it is possible to begin to reconstruct his methods of study, devotion, and work. The annotated books themselves contain much material that cannot be found elsewhere. Admittedly they form only a small proportion of the whole library, and it is possible to find among them a few examples where the annotations peter out after the first few pages.[57] Taken together, however, they provide overwhelming evidence of intensive and thoughtful reading and re-reading. John Evelyn's books certainly wore fine bindings, but their purpose was much more than mere show.

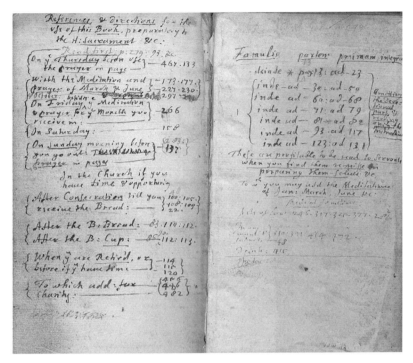

Fig. 17: Evelyn's notes concerning religious preparation, both for servants and for his own family, on the endpapers of his copy of Simon Patrick, *The Christian Sacrifice* (1672) (British Library, Eve.a.23).

NOTES

I should like to thank my colleague Dr Frances Harris for her generosity in sharing her wide-ranging knowledge of the Evelyn Papers.

1 *The Evelyn Library* (London: Christie's, 4 parts, 22 June 1977 to 13 July 1978); *The Evelyn Family Library* (London: Christie's, 12 Oct. 1977). A later sale at Christie's, 8 Nov. 1978, contained a further 86 lots, including items previously bought in. For earlier dispersals, see Michael Hunter, 'The British Library and the Library of John Evelyn', in Theodore Hofmann et al., *John Evelyn in the British Library* (London: British Library, 1995), pp. 82-102.

2 A full account of these efforts, with a useful list of the books purchased, is given in the articles by Nicolas Barker and Michael Hunter in *John Evelyn in the British Library*, pp. 74-102.

3 Evelyn to Pepys, 26 Aug. 1689; Pforzheimer MS 351, cited with some text restored from Evelyn's letterbook and a scribal copy: *Particular Friends: the correspondence of Samuel Pepys and John Evelyn*, ed. by Guy de la Bédoyère (Woodbridge: Boydell, 1997), p. 198. For some auction catalogues owned by John Evelyn junior, see John Bidwell, 'Book-sale Catalogues from the Evelyn Library, 1682-92', in *Fine Books and Book Collecting*, ed. by Christopher de Hamel & Richard A. Linenthal (Leamington Spa: James Hall, 1981), 62-4; cf.

T. A. Birrell, 'Books and Buyers in Seventeenth-century English Auction Sales', in *Under the Hammer: Book Auctions since the Seventeenth Century*, ed. by Robin Myers, Michael Harris, & Giles Mandelbrote (London & New Castle, DE: British Library & Oak Knoll Press, 2001), 51-64, at p. 62.

4 For other book collectors in exile see, for example, A. I. Doyle, 'John Cosin (1595-1672) as a Library Maker', *Book Collector*, 40 (1991), 335-57; Naomi Linnell, 'Michael Honywood and Lincoln Cathedral Library', *The Library*, 6th ser., 5 (1983), 126-39; Marika Keblusek, 'Boeken in ballingschap. De betekenis van de bibliotheek van Michael Honywood voor de royalistische gemeenschap in de Republiek (1643-1660)', *Jaarboek voor Nederlandse Boekgeschiedenis*, 2 (1995), 153-74.

5 *The Evelyn Library*, pt I, lot 32 and plate 3; one of Mazarin's books now in the British Library is Eve.c.21: Jacques Besson, *Teatro de los Instrumentos y figuras matematicas y mecanicas* (Lyon, 1602).

6 Jean Viardot, 'Livres rares et pratiques bibliophiliques', in *Histoire de l'édition française*, ed. by Henri-Jean Martin & Roger Chartier, II, *Le livre triomphant, 1660-1830* (Paris: Promodis, 1984), 447-67; id., 'Naissance de la bibliophilie: les cabinets de livres rares', in *Histoire des bibliothèques françaises*, II, *Les bibliothèques sous l'Ancien Régime, 1530-1789*, ed. by Claude Jolly (Paris: Promodis, 1988), 268-89; Pierre Gasnault, 'Les collections et leurs enrichissements', ibid., 334-51. For the market in antiquarian books in seventeenth-century Paris, see also my comments in *Les ventes de livres et leurs catalogues*, ed. by Annie Charon & Élisabeth Parinet (Paris: École des chartes, 2000), 49-76.

7 See Geoffrey Keynes, *John Evelyn: a Study in Bibliophily with a Bibliography of his Writings*, 2nd edn (Oxford: Clarendon Press, 1968).

8 For further remarks on Evelyn's character, see Evelyn *Diary*, I, *38-43*.

9 Now BL Add. MS 78632. For Evelyn's catalogues, see Keynes, pp. 13-17, and Guy de la Bédoyère, 'John Evelyn's Library Catalogue', *Book Collector*, 43 (1994), 529-48.

10 BL Add. MS 78632, fols 100^r-103^v, printed by Keynes, pp. 295-303.

11 For more references to the libraries of some of Evelyn's contemporaries, see my survey, 'Scientific Books and their Owners', in *Scientific Books, Libraries, and Collectors*, 4th edn, ed. by Andrew Hunter (Aldershot: Ashgate, 2000), 333-66.

12 John Evelyn, *Memoires for my Grand-son*, ed. by Geoffrey Keynes (London: Nonesuch Press, 1926), p. 51.

13 BL Add. MS 78632, fols 15 ff.

14 'John Evelyn's Library Catalogue', p. 537 (mistranscribing this sentence) and p. 545, plate 7.

15 Cranston Library, Reigate, Register of Benefactors, f. 11, 1 Sept. 1701.

16 BL Add. MS 78632, fols 89^r-94^v.

17 Eve.a.70. For Evelyn's mottoes, see Keynes, pp. 11-12.

18 Eve.a.59(1).

19 For example, Eve.a.4: Samuel Smith, *Aditus ad logicam*, 5th edn (Oxford, 1634), inscribed in red ink 'Balliol College, 1637'.

20 See, for example, Evelyn's copy of J. H. Pflaumern, *Mercurius Italicus* (Lyon, 1628), purchased in Rome on 14 Nov. 1644, and read *en route* to Geneva, 1646: BL C.97.a.22.

21 Eve.a.68.

22 Eve.a.69; Eve.a.78.

23 Eve.a.56.

24 Eve.a.76. All ten of the works by Boyle listed in *John Evelyn in the British Library*, pp. 92-3, are presentation copies.

25 Eve.a.15. For details of other presentation copies of works by Evelyn, see Keynes.

26 BL Add. MS 78314(3): Benjamin Tooke to John Evelyn, 11 Jan. 1698, with a list of 34 recipients of presentation copies in various bindings.

27 Evelyn, *Diary*, IV, 386-7.

28 Eve.a.16; Eve.a.19.

29 Eve.a.24.

30 BL Add. MS 78348.

31 BL Add. MS 78353 (title-page verso). See Michael M. Repetzki, *John Evelyn's Translation of Lucretius Carus* De rerum natura, Münsteraner Monographien zur englischen Literatur 22 (Frankfurt am Main: Peter Lang, 2000). Cf. Eve.a.168, another copy with manuscript corrections by Evelyn.

32 Cf. Keynes, pp. 13-17, and la Bédoyère, 'John Evelyn's Library Catalogue'.

33 Eve.a.32: John Smith, *The Art of Painting in Oyl*, 2nd edn (1687).

34 BL Add. MSS 78328-30, with index volume Add. MS 78331.

35 BL Add. MS 78328 begins with a list of 179 theological and 207 historical and philological books which have been read and commonplaced, but the process of transferring the commonplaced passages appears to have been completed for only 92 and 101 works in these respective categories.

36 BL Add. MSS 78332-3; BL Add. MS 15950, fol. 80.

37 BL Add. MS 78329, fol. 1ᵛ, slightly paraphrasing Francis Bacon, *Of The Advancement and Proficience of Learning* (London, 1640), p. 254.

38 Eve.a.69; for other examples, see Eve.a.44 (notes for *Sylva*); Eve.a.67; Eve.a.77 (notes on 'Hortus'); Eve.a.155 (notes on 'Friendship'); Eve.c.24 (notes on 'Arbor' and 'Hortus').

39 For a copy heavily annotated with all these features, see Eve.a.20: Daniel Tilenus, *Syntagmatis Tripertiti Disputationum Theologicarum in Academia Sedanensi habitarum* (Geneva, 1622).

40 The extensive early modern literature on the practice of making commonplace books, while prescribing in considerable detail how these should be constructed, is astonishingly silent on the question of exactly how a reader should mark passages of text to be extracted. For an excellent account of this literature, see Peter Beal, 'Notions in Garrison: the Seventeenth-Century Commonplace Book', in *New Ways of Looking at Old Texts*, ed. by W. Speed Hill, Medieval & Renaissance Texts & Studies, 107 (Binghamton, New York, 1993), 131-47, and Earle Havens, *Commonplace Books* (New Haven: Beinecke Rare Book & Manuscript Library, 2001). For examples of some other elaborate vocabularies of marginal marks, see Roger Stoddard, *Marks in Books, Illustrated and Explained* (Cambridge, Mass.: Houghton Library, 1985), no. 52, and G. R. Rose, 'The Libraries of Bacon and Ben Jonson: How They Marked Their Books', *Baconiana*, XXVII, no. 107 (April, 1943), 57-9; Harold S. Wilson, 'Gabriel Harvey's Method of Annotating his Books', *Harvard Library Bulletin*, II, no. 3 (autumn 1948), 344-61; G. G. Meynell, 'John Locke's Method of Commonplacing, as Seen in his Drafts and his Medical Notebooks', *The Seventeenth Century*, VIII, no. 2 (autumn 1993), 245-67.

41 Eve.a.13: Jacob Verheiden & Henry Holland, *The History of the Moderne Protestant Divines* (London, 1637), pp. 218-19.

42 Eve.a.103: *Bibliothecæ Cordesianæ Catalogus* (Paris, 1643), fol. 12ᵛ.

43 See, for example, annotations in Eve.a.78: *Samuel Hartlib his Legacy of Husbandry*, 3rd edn (London, 1655), and Eve.a.47: John Worlidge, *Vinetum Britannicum* (London, 1676).

44 Eve.a.47; Evelyn's comments about the authorship of *The English Vineyard Vindicated* appear in the margin of his copy of *Philosophical Transactions*, no. 15 (18 July 1666), p. 262, where the work was reviewed: Eve.a.149.

45 Eve.a.10: [John Phillips?], *The Secret History of the Reigns of K. Charles II and K. James II* (London, 1690).

46 Eve.a.39: *The Papers Which passed at New-castle betwixt His Sacred Majestie and Mr Al: Henderson: Concerning the Change of Church-Government* (London, 1649), p. 34.

47 Sir Richard Baker, *A Chronicle of the Kings of England ... with a Continuation* [by Edward Phillips] *... to the Coronation of His Sacred Majesty King Charles the Second* (London, 1665): Evelyn's copy is now Huntington Library RB 33556 (purchased 1922); his copy of Thomas Hobbes, *The History of the Civil Wars of England*, 2nd edn (London, 1679) is Eve.a.14. Cf. Evelyn's notes in BL Add. MS 78393. For the background and a full discussion, see E. S. de Beer, 'Evelyn and Colonel Herbert Morley in 1659 and 1660', *Sussex Archaeological Collections*, 78 (1937), 177-83, and Arthur H. Nethercot, 'John Evelyn and Colonel Herbert Morley in 1659-60' (subsequently corrected to 'New Marginalia by John Evelyn on Morley, Monck and the Restoration'), *Huntington Library Quarterly*, 1 (1937-8), 439-46.

48 Eve.a.78.

49 Eve.a.149: *Philosophical Transactions*, no. 256 (Sept. 1699), 313, 317.

50 Eve.a.122.

51 BL Add. MSS 78360-1; see especially Evelyn's notes on the Book of Genesis.

52 Eve.a.56.

53 Eve.a.23.

54 *John Evelyn in the British Library*, p. 87.

55 *Book Collector*, 47 (1998), 161. For some other recent examples of interest in this field, see *The Rosenthal Collection of Printed Books with Manuscript Annotations* (New Haven: Beinecke Rare Book and Manuscript Library, 1997); *Papers of the Bibliographical Society of America*, 91:4 (Dec. 1997); *Le Livre annoté (Revue de la Bibliothèque Nationale de France*, 2 (1999); Kevin Sharpe, *Reading Revolutions: the Politics of Reading in Early Modern England* (New Haven & London: Yale University Press, 2000); *The Reader Revealed*, ed. by Sabrina Alcorn Baron (Washington, DC: Folger Shakespeare Library, 2001); Anthony Grafton, 'Joseph Scaliger as a Reader', in *Old Books, New Learning*, ed. by Robert G. Babcock & Lee Patterson, *Yale University Library Gazette*, occasional supplement 4 (New Haven: Beinecke Rare Book & Manuscript Library, 2001), 152-77; William H. Sherman, 'What Did Renaissance Readers Write in their Books?', in *Books and Readers in Early Modern England*, ed. by Jennifer Andersen & Elizabeth Sauer (Philadelphia: University of Pennsylvania Press, 2002), 119-37.

56 Lisa Jardine & Anthony Grafton, '"Studied for Action": How Gabriel Harvey Read his Livy', *Past & Present*, 129 (Nov. 1990), 30-78, at p. 76.

57 For an early example, see Eve.a.158: Tommaso Campanella, *Atheismus Triumphatus* [etc.] (Paris, 1636), purchased in Paris in 1643.

JOHN EVELYN AND THE PRINT

ANTONY GRIFFITHS

JOHN EVELYN relates to the art of printmaking in three distinct ways. The first is the most familiar, and presents Evelyn as the author of *Sculptura*, published in 1662, which has the distinction of being the first monograph about prints and printmaking published in any language. This is a book that has been more often cited than read; it not easy to get through it from beginning to end. Less familiar is Evelyn as a practising printmaker; a certain amount has been written about this in recent years, but it is still a little-known aspect of his work. Lastly, and so far almost completely unstudied, is Evelyn as a collector of prints. I shall take each of these aspects in turn, and shall treat them in the order in which Evelyn himself came to them, which is the reverse order to the one given above.

Perhaps I might begin my remarks on Evelyn's collection by a personal reminiscence. I joined the Department of Prints and Drawings in the British Museum in July 1976. So I had been there less than a year when the first of the many heritage crises that mark a modern museum man's career hit me – the sale of Evelyn's collection in the summer of 1977. To be entirely honest, it never hit me, because I barely knew that it was happening. The huge fuss about the sale of the library that led to the British Library's making so many important purchases at the sales had passed the British Museum by, and there was no concern that reached me that the prints and drawings were being sold. The situation was not helped by the fact that Christie's made a mess of the disposal, and scattered the prints and drawings through at least five different sales with minimal catalogue descriptions.[1] I remember as a neo-phyte looking through the bundles the day before one of the sales in a bemused way. I remember in particular a single lot with dozens of views of Rome, many of which had extensive annotations in pen and ink on them by Evelyn himself. I remember thinking that these must be rather important and wondering why no one seemed to be paying any attention to them. I now realize why this was so. In those days there was no interest in provenance (there still is not much in the print world), and the print trade regarded all these prints as damaged goods. Bundles of this kind were at that time bought up by Italian print dealers, and the restoration shops of the via del Babuino would have been busy for weeks afterwards bleaching off all traces of the writing and adding colouring. These prints will now be in highly decorated mounts and pretentious frames, and there will be no possibility of linking them with Evelyn.

The Christie's catalogues therefore remain the only hope of finding what was sold in 1977. The most valuable single print was an etched *Pietà* by Jacques Bellange, which was annotated by Evelyn with the statement that he purchased it in Rome in 1645 – that is only about thirty years after the plate was made. This was bought by the London dealer Dr Frederick Mulder, who tells me that he no longer has a record of to whom he sold it.[2] The most important drawing was of the famous frieze on the Arch of Titus showing the Emperor's triumph after the capture of Jerusalem.[3] This was commissioned by Evelyn from the young Carlo Maratti, and the whole episode is fully described in Evelyn's correspondence. He commissioned it because he thought that the prints available of the frieze were inaccurate. His paricular concern was that it corroborated the account of the capture of Jerusalem given in the Bible and thus helped prove the truth of Holy Scripture. This is a historic item on many counts, not least in being the earliest documented drawing by Maratti, and by good fortune, when it reappeared on the market in 1992, the British Museum was able to buy it with the help of the National Art Collections Fund.[4]

I initially assumed that the entire Evelyn print collection was in the 1977 sales, and that the whole could therefore be reconstructed from the 1977 catalogues, but this is certainly wrong. Much had been dispersed beforehand. An impression of Pierre Lombart's engraved portrait of Oliver Cromwell after Robert Walker of 1651/3, in the British Museum, was lifted for exhibition in 1998, and Evelyn's bold signature emerged on the verso[5] [Fig. 1]. This impression was bequeathed to the British Museum by the Rev. C. M. Cracherode in 1799, and this gives the earliest date that I yet have for the dispersal of the collection. So the key document for understanding the collection is not the 1977 auction catalogue, but Evelyn's own catalogue which is to be found on three pages towards the end of his 1687 library catalogue, after the printed books and maps, but before the manuscripts. It is here transcribed in an appendix[6] [Fig. 2].

The prints were pasted into books, numbered from A to Y, and the text gives a generalized description of each book as a whole. The volumes were arranged by subject, and most cover topography, portraits, costume, architecture, and antiquities. The exceptions were a volume of drawings and a single volume of prints by Callot, della Bella, Silvestre, Perelle, and Hollar. Some volumes, particularly the smaller ones that are listed from O to Y, contained uniform sets of prints, rather than groups assembled by Evelyn himself. Some of them would today be regarded as books, most notably

Fig 1: Verso of Pierre Lombart's engraving of *Cromwell with a Page*, after Robert Walker, showing Evelyn's signature (British Museum).

Evelyn's own *Sculptura*, which is coupled with Faithorne's *Art of Graving and Etching* as W and X. Invaluable though these descriptions are, they describe only classes of subject, and give no indication of exactly which prints Evelyn owned. More helpful is the section on page 199 titled 'Icones', listing the prints which were too large to go into the albums and so were kept rolled. There are eighteen of these, and the descriptions are full enough for almost all to be identified, even though none of them appeared in the 1977 sales. The assumption must be that the rolled prints, not being protected by the covers of albums, soon became damaged, and were thrown out at an early stage.

Alongside each volume on the pages of Evelyn's catalogue is a sign of a type that he used for his library classification. It is always the same sign, the alchemical sign for mercury, which evidently stood for the print section. This raises the possibility that it might help us identify stray prints that once belonged to him. Richard Godfrey and Robert Harding recently found an impression of another engraving by Pierre Lombart, this one being after a self-portrait by Robert Walker of *circa* 1653/4;[7] above the head, within the oval of the surround, is Evelyn's sign, which must be tantamount to proof that this once belonged to him [Fig. 3]. On the verso is an annotation, 'Pray lay this up for me', and it would presumably have been placed in album G, 'A collection of effigies, portraicture and heads'. There must be more such marks waiting to be found.

The earliest date of acquisition that I have yet recorded is on a set of cartouches by Collignon after della Bella, which was purchased at the 1977 sale by Paul Grinke. The first plate was inscribed 'Coll.Evelynus Parisiis 1643', and was followed by a number 198 and Evelyn's motto, 'Omnia explorate, meliora retinete', which is rather suitable for a print collector[8] [Fig. 4]. This puts him among the earliest known British print collectors. I stress 'known' for there was an active print trade in London in these years, and the dealers must have been selling to others besides Evelyn. Evelyn mentions in a letter to Pepys that Robert Peake used to have the best stock

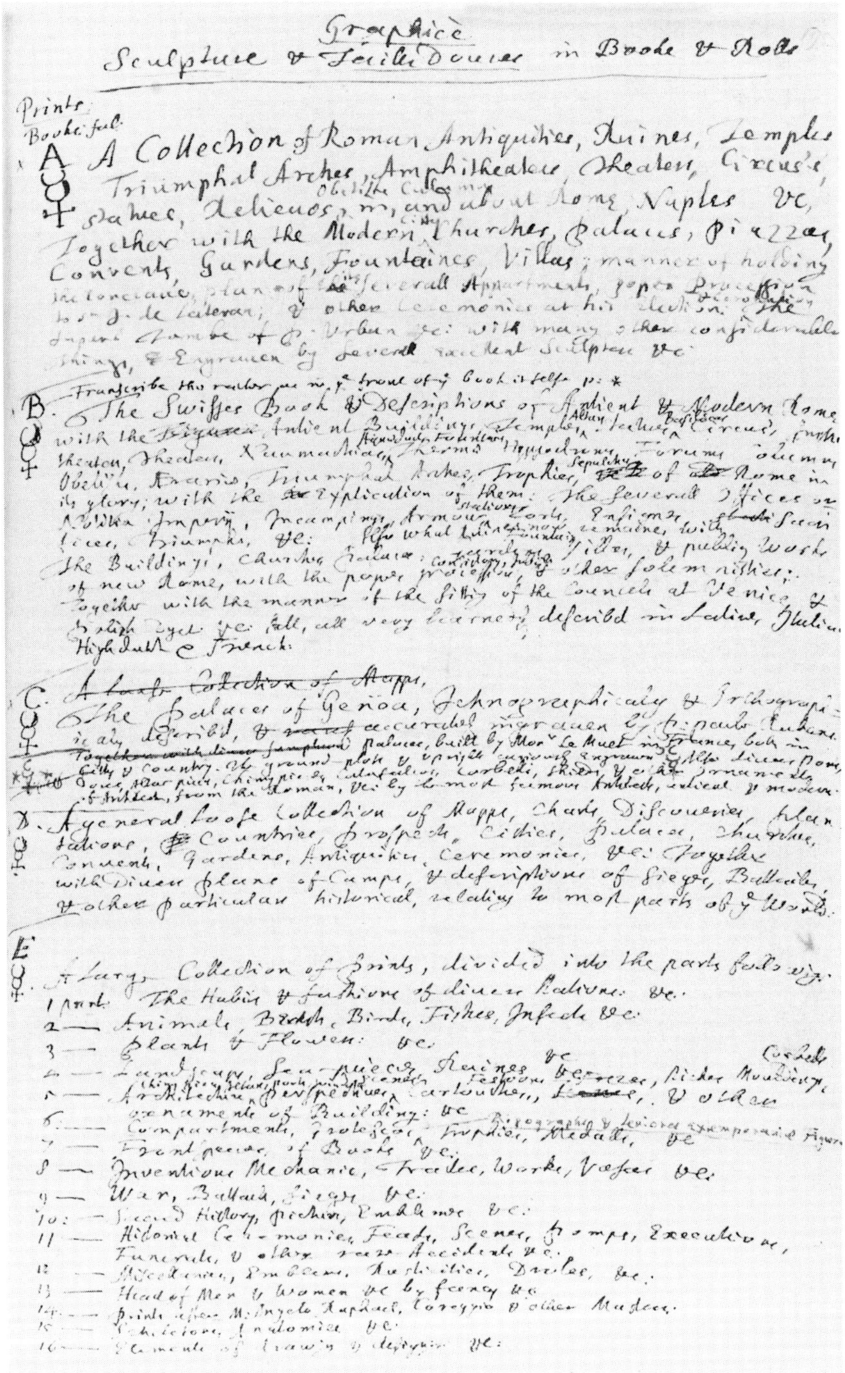

Fig. 2: Folio 195 of Evelyn's Library Catalogue of 1687
(British Library, Add. MS 78632).

Fig. 3: Detail, showing the symbol of mercury, on an impression of
Pierre Lombart's engraving after a self-portrait by Robert Walker
(Private Collection).

in London; and we know that he bought Hollars in the 1640s directly from
the artist or his wholesale agent Hendrick van der Borcht.[9]

If his collecting zeal began with his departure on his Grand Tour in
November 1643, it was at its peak during his years of exile in Paris between
1649 and 1652. His diary contains references to visits he made to Stefano
della Bella (then living in France) and to Perelle, the landscape etcher. His

Fig. 4: Title plate of Evelyn's set of Collignon's *Recueil de douze cartouches* after Stefano della Bella (reproduced from Paul Grinke, catalogue 15, p. 11).

relations with the great French portrait engraver Robert Nanteuil were very close, for he commissioned from him the well-known engraved portrait, after a drawing made 'ad vivum' by Nanteuil himself.[10] The engraving is found in two states, before and with letter, the point of this being that collectors knew that proofs before the engraved lettering was added to the plate had to be the earliest and so best impressions. This sophistication shows the level of connoisseurship that Evelyn had already reached. The copper plate remained Evelyn's property, and was still at Wotton in 1818, though it has not been seen more recently. Nanteuil later presented him with the original drawing from which the engraving had been made, and this led to further commissions for drawn portraits of Evelyn's wife and parents-in-law, Sir Richard and Lady Browne. Documents relating to this remain in the Evelyn papers; others escaped long ago as the archive fell victim to autograph collectors. One that is in the Lugt collection in Paris has not to the best of my knowledge been published. It is dated 20 November 1650, and contains a request from Nanteuil for payment of four pistols for the portrait drawings he had made for Evelyn.[11] Another French engraver with whom Evelyn corresponded was Abraham Bosse.[12]

Evelyn's interest in collecting and commissioning prints led him directly into making prints himself. Many seventeenth-century amateurs made etchings, among them Louis XIV and Prince Rupert, and some knowledge of the principles of etching was seen as part of a noble education at the time. Evelyn's plates are modest though far from incompetent, but what sets them apart from other amateur etchings is the fact that they were not, as one would expect from a man of his standing, merely distributed privately as gifts to a few friends and relations, but were published and sold on the open market. This curious episode was confined to one year only, 1649, and much remains obscure about it.[13]

Evelyn's first prints form a set of five quite large (about seven inches across) imaginary landscapes. They were made in London between March and June, and were dedicated on the title-plate to Lady Isabella Thynne. She was a prominent lady at the court of Charles I in Oxford, and the daughter of Henry Rich, Earl of Holland, who had been beheaded by the Roundheads a few months earlier in 1649. So Evelyn's dedication was not intended to ingratiate him with the new government, to which we know from his writings that he was bitterly hostile. The title-plate also bears the name of the publisher Thomas Rowlett. He was by far the most remarkable print publisher in London during the entire seventeenth century.[14] He was active for only a few years between 1645 and 1649, when he published an extraordinary group of new plates by William Faithorne, Josiah English, Isaac de Caus, Francis Clein, and Edward Pearce. Exceptionally for a London print publisher of the period, his inventory of plates did not contain a single one purchased from an earlier publisher. Rowlett had been apprenticed to the largest print dealer and publisher in London before the civil war, Robert Peake, a man whose loyalty to the Stuart cause had been demonstrated in his production of biblical illustrations to the delight of Archbishop Laud and the fury of William Prynne,[15] and later by his command of a troop of soldiers in the Civil War. It was his heroic defence of Basing House in the long siege that earned him a knighthood, and such enmity from the Roundheads that he had to go into exile.

It was Rowlett who took his place and tried to get Peake's publishing and printselling business, which had been closed at the beginning of the war, back into action. The need was desperate. All of these artists' lives were blighted by the execution of Charles and the complete stop it put to any hope of a restoration; all were unemployed and many were penniless. Some had fought in the war – a relative of Rowlett and the engraver Faithorne had actually been part of Peake's troop at Basing House. The rest had been ruined by the disappearance of the patrons in the Stuart court on whom they had relied. The greatest of them all, the painter William Dobson, after whom Faithorne engraved a number of plates for Rowlett, died in abject poverty in the course of 1649. A living had to be found for the rest. It was in these exceptional circumstances that Evelyn joined the team, and made a set of plates for Rowlett to publish [Fig. 5]. I would even hazard a guess that Evelyn was one of Rowlett's financial backers. Who taught Evelyn how to etch is not known; but it could have been any one of this group. Rowlett's

Fig. 5: Title plate of Evelyn's set of imaginary landscapes dedicated to
Lady Isabella Thynne with the address of the publisher Thomas Rowlett
(British Museum).

venture failed, and by 1651 at the latest all his plates had been sold on to
another publisher, Thomas Hinde. Evelyn's set was probably the last prints
he published. The causes of his failure are not documented, but can easily be
guessed, for who was left in London who wanted to buy the kind of prints
that Rowlett was producing?

But Evelyn did not stop here, and this makes his output all the more
interesting. For someone of his practical turn of mind, making idealized
landscapes must have come to seem insufficiently useful. In his diary for
20 June 1649 he wrote: 'I went to Putney and other places of the Thames
to take prospects in crayon, to carry into France, where I thought to have
them engraved.' One such view of Putney was actually made. Evelyn's
etching of it was recorded by Walpole and seen by Bray, though I have
never found an impression myself, nor do the drawings survive. Why he
never made his set of English views – a subject of public utility that he
recommended to his reader in *Sculptura* – remains unclear. Perhaps it
seemed less useful once he had reached France; perhaps he had simply lost
the drawings.

Whatever the reason, the chief product of the months in Paris between

Fig. 6: *Tres tabernae*, from Evelyn's set of etchings of scenes on the
route from Rome to Naples (British Museum).

August and December 1649 was a set of six smaller plates with views of
places lying on the road between Rome and Naples. The subjects show
a view of Naples from Vesuvius; the crater of Vesuvius; the twin peaks of
Vesuvius; Cape Terracina; and the Tres Tabernae, with a reference to Acts 28
that shows that his interest in proving biblical authority was ever present
[Fig. 6]. These were based on drawings he had made on his Grand Tour in
1645, and the title-plate bears a dedication to Thomas Henshaw, his companion on that voyage. One of the original drawings survives in the British
Museum.

But he had not lost his concern to bring his prints before a wide public,
for the title-plate, besides its dedication, bears in tiny letters at the bottom
the name of the publisher, 'R.Hoare excud' [Fig. 7]. The name of R. Hoare
is otherwise unknown in the annals of the print trade, and he must be
identified with Richard Hoare, Evelyn's one-eyed private secretary, whose
beautiful italic handwriting is such a delight to readers of the archive after
the abominable scrawl of Evelyn himself and many of his correspondents.
How poor Hoare, who knew nothing about the print trade, was supposed

Fig. 7: Title plate of the set of etchings of scenes on the route from Rome
to Naples, with the dedication to Thomas Henshaw and the name of
the publisher Richard Hoare (British Museum).

to publish and distribute impressions of Evelyn's prints, defeats me and
evidently defeated him, for we hear no more about the plates after 1649, and
the prints remain extraordinary rarities. I have seen no other set beside the
one in the British Museum, though three more sets are recorded in the older
literature.

There is one later moment in 1653 when Evelyn's thoughts again turned
to printmaking. There is an etching of Wotton which seems to belong to this
year [Fig. 8],[16] and Frances Harris has given me a transcription of a passage
in a letter from Deptford of 23 January 1654 to his father-in-law Sir Richard
Browne, which reads: 'I am exceedingly rejoyced to find that my little
designes heere have pleased you as I find they have by the foote of your letter,
in those most excellent verses, which I entend to engrave on a plate designed
with this epigraph: *Nob. viro D.D.R.B. Equiti aurato et Baronetto ... Hunc
Tamesis spectissimi Fluvii prospectum quem a Ripa Haeredituriae eius Terrae
et Nativitatis loci in Agro Deptfordiae manu sua propria delineavit et in Aere
excusit J.E. Gener. eius Amantiss. observantiae ...* but of this more hereafter.'[17]

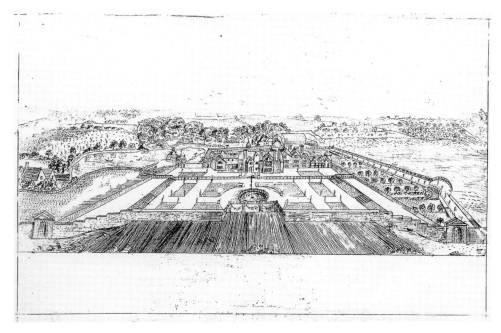

Fig. 8: Evelyn's etched view of Wotton, *c.*1653 (British Museum).

She remarks that the wording on the inscription is very close to the one on the well-known manuscript plan of the garden at Sayes Court of a similar date, and that the plan itself is very precisely drawn as if with engraving in mind.[18] But the print seems never to have been etched, for no impression of it has ever been seen.

Evelyn's years in Paris mark the high-water mark of his interest in print collecting and making. A letter to him from Hoare in July 1650 talks about ordering the prints into a 'Great Book', but warns that it is not large enough to hold half of them.[19] So the arrangement in many volumes that is described in the 1687 catalogue must post-date this.

Evelyn made a deliberate decision to stop collecting shortly after 1655. In a letter to Dr William Lloyd, the Bishop of Coventry and Lichfield, written on 5 February 1695, and of which I owe my knowledge to the kindness of Douglas Chambers, Evelyn gave an account of the course of his collecting: 'I do acknowledge that … I have heretofore been a sedulous collector of whatever prints of that nature I could meete with [he is talking about prints of antiquities]; especially whilst I was at Rome and abroad. But as it is now near fourty yeares past since I made any considerable addition to them', he explains that his knowledge of what has been produced since is very incomplete. He continues:

Nor was I onely curious of antiquities, but of all modern edifices, gardens, fountaines, prospects of cities, countries, sieges, battels, triumphs, publique and famous solemnities, sports, executions, cavalcades; the effigies and portraits of greate persons; habits, machines, inventions, emblems, devises, animals, pictures, charts and maps innumerable, which I ranged in several classes. But as it took up a great-deale of time and no little mony; and that the thirst of still augmenting grew upon me, I at last gave it over, contenting my selfe with a competent number, and very seldome since enquiring after more of any sort, excepting some which my son brought me out of France of the pompous buildings, palaces and other new things don by the present monarch. It is, I confesse my Lord, a very tempting diversion, so many rare sculptors every day setting out something or other remarkable of those kinds. But *est modus in rebus.*[20]

If Evelyn renounced print collecting soon after 1655, this seems to have been at precisely the time that he began working on *Sculptura*, which he once refers to as having been written in 1657. And we must now turn our attention to this book. Among print historians of the nineteenth and twentieth centuries, it has had a very bad reception. An example is Francis Douce, who in 1833 stated that *Sculptura* is 'the only one of his works that does him no credit, and which is a meagre and extremely inaccurate compilation'.[21] Even C. F. Bell, who published a new edition of the text in 1906, could not muster more enthusiasm than to conclude his introduction with the words, 'It is impossible, however, to deny that as an attempt to bring art criticism within the sphere of natural philosophy ... *Sculptura* takes a certain place in the history of English thought which the actual contents of the volume itself might scarcely seem to warrant.'

Those who have paid any attention to *Sculptura* in recent decades have usually concentrated on its place in Evelyn's proposed 'History of Arts liberal and mechanick' which he placed before the Royal Society in 1661. Within this eight-part scheme, category 7 headed 'Curious', included the arts of painting, sculpture, and engraving, with various sub-divisions. But rather than add to the discussion of the scheme, I would prefer to concentrate on *Sculptura* itself, since it is quite possible that Evelyn the print collector began it for its own sake, and only subsequently enlarged his ambitions to include it in a more general history of trades.

The first important point to notice is that it is only half a book. Evelyn originally intended to accompany it with a translation of Abraham Bosse's 1645 *Traité des manières de graver en taille douce sur l'airain*. He abandoned this idea only when he found that William Faithorne had himself produced such a translation.[22] Nevertheless the two books both came out in 1662, and were seen by Evelyn himself as companion volumes. He shelved them together in his print library; others went further and bound the two books together. In this context Evelyn's chapters look less unbalanced than they do if seen by themselves. The first is on the technical terms used for sculpture in antiquity; the second and third on its history in those years; and so it is only with chapter four (which takes up nearly half the book) that he reaches the invention of printmaking, and gives a breathless list of its greatest masters. The fifth chapter is devoted to drawing: 'Of drawing and designe previous to the art of chalcography, and of the use of pictures in order to the education of children', and the final chapter, which is only four pages long, is devoted to the newly invented art of mezzotint.

We can see why modern print historians, quarrying the text for information that they could find nowhere else, have given up in disgust. Even the section on mezzotint, written within a few years of the invention of the medium, and hence of enormous potential, proves disappointing because Evelyn reveals almost nothing of the technique or its history. We now know that this was not his fault, for Prince Rupert would not give his permission for anything of any use to be published.[23] And the oddity of suddenly finding a few pages on mezzotint in his book disappears if we realise that this is really a supplement to Faithorne's text, and not strictly part of Evelyn's argument.

If we look again at the text from the perspective of Evelyn and his day, and not from our own, it becomes much easier to understand and appreciate. All the lists of engravers and works that Douce found so useless and inaccurate were not regurgitating what could be found in any book. They were a first attempt at trying to write the history of a subject that had scarcely been treated before. Evelyn's is the first monograph on the history of printmaking in any language. Previous writers had put chapters on individual printmakers and schools into more general books, such as Vasari's 'Lives', but Evelyn does not seem to have made much use of them. His text was rather constructed bottom up, from the works that he had in his collection or had seen elsewhere, and what they told him. Of course in this way he made hundreds of mistakes; but equally he recorded a lot of detailed information that had never found its way into print before. To a collector in 1662 his text must have been invaluable; but its period of use was brief, and by the turn of the century it had been replaced by much better texts by French writers such as Roger de Piles.

That the book was much appreciated by his contemporaries can be seen from various letters in which Evelyn talks about the pressure he was being put under to produce a revised and corrected new edition. The key passage is in a letter of February 1686 to Dr Godolphin, the provost of Eton. In it he talks about preparing his book on medals, and continues:

While I was about this (and indeed often and long before), I had been importuned to make a second edition of my Chalcography (now grown very scarce), and to bring it from 1662, where I left off, to this time, there having since that been so great an improvement of sculpture. This being a task I had no inclination for (having of a long time given over collections of that sort) I thought yet of gratifying them in some manner with an ex-chapter in my discourse of medals, where I speak of the effigies of famous persons and the use which may be derived of such a collection.[24]

This explains why there was no second edition of *Sculptura*, and why we find the curious section on prints in his history of medals, *Numismata*, of 1697.

But by this time Evelyn no longer played a part in the contemporary print scene. I know of no dedication of a print to him after the 1650s. In the 1695 letter to Dr Lloyd quoted above, he makes the startling admission: 'I am not acquainted with any one print seller, yet there being now more than ten for one of that trade than when I was a young gatherer.' His authorship of the standard textbook meant that he had to field enquiries from aspirant collectors such as Lloyd and Samuel Pepys, to which he responded as best he could, by giving long and (to the modern reader) tedious lists of what should be included.[25] He admitted candidly that his information was long out of date, but excused himself ingeniously by saying that the antiquities portrayed could only have become more damaged over the years, and so the earlier prints of them must necessarily be the better.

In conclusion, I would like briefly to consider why Evelyn was interested in prints. As we have seen from the arrangement of his collection, his interest was primarily in their subject-matter. As an intelligent student of antiquity in Paris and Rome, he realised that there was a huge amount of visual infor-mation in them that no text could supply, and as a devout Christian he used them as an aid to his study of the Bible. But he soon became seduced by the aesthetic qualities of the art of the print, and, although he seems never to have been much interested in prints as documents of the history of painting, he did begin to collect prints by some of his contemporaries as examples of their work rather than purely for their subject-matter. His acquaintance with engravers, and the extraordinary circumstances of the aftermath of the Civil War, led him very briefly into becoming a printmaker himself. But his increasingly public concerns in the later 1650s led him to renounce the private hobby of print collecting, and one way to read *Sculptura* is as a form of exorcism. By draining himself dry of everything that he knew about prints, he could put them behind him, and start afresh on new paths such as his translations of Naudé and Fréart, and his books on trees and gardening.

[From the annotation to album B, it can be deduced that this listing more or less corresponds to lists written inside the albums themselves; capitalization and punctuation have been modified in the interests of clarity].

Graphice: Sculpture & taille douces in books and rolls
Prints: Books fol.

A A collection of Roman antiquities, ruines, temples, triumphal arches, amphitheaters, theaters, circus's, statues, rilievos, obelisks, columns in and about Rome, Naples etc. together with the modern citty, churches, palaces, piazzas, convents, gardens, fountaines, villas; manner of holding the conclave, plans of its severall appartments, Pope's procession to St J. de Lateran; & other ceremonies at his election & coronation; the superb tombe of P. Urban &c; with many other considerable things, engraven by severall excellent sculptors &c

B (transcribe this rather in the front of the book itself p:*)
The Swisses book & descriptions of ancient & modern Rome with the antient buildings, temples, altars, statues, basilicas, circus's, arches, amphitheaters, theaters, naumachias, aqueducts, fountains, thermae, hippodromes, forums, columns, obelisks, granaries (?), triumphal arches, trophies, sepulchres of Rome in its glory; with the explication of them; the severall offices or Notitia Imperii, incampings, armour, stations, lords, ensignes, sacrifices, triumphs &c. Also what ruines now remaine with the buildings, churches, palaces, gardens, fountains, villas, & public works of new Rome, with the Pope's processions, consistory, jubilee, & other solemnities; together with the manner of the sitting of the Councels at Venice & Polish Dyet &c. All very learnedly describ'd in Latine, Italian, High Dutch & French.

C The Palaces of Genoa, ichnographicaly & orthographicaly describ'd & accurately ingraven by P. Paulo Rubens. Together with divers sumptuous palaces built by Mons Le Muet in France, both in citty & country, the ground-plots & uprights curiously engraven. Also divers dores, altarpieces, chimnypieces, catafalques, corbels, shields, & other ornaments of architecture, from the Roman, &c by the most famous architects antient & modern.

D A general loose collection of mapps, charts, discoveries, plantations, countries, prospects, citties, palaces, churches, convents, gardens, antiquities, ceremonies, &c together with divers plans of camps & descriptions of sieges, battailes & other particulars historical, relating to most parts of the world.

E A large collection of prints divided into the parts following:
1 part. The habits & fashions of divers nations &c
2 part. Animals, beasts, birds, fishes, insects, &c
3 part. Plants & flowers &c
4 part. Landscape, sea-pieces, ruines, &c
5 part. Architecture, chimnypieces, ports, windows, perspective scenes,

cartouches, festoons, frezes, riche mouldings, corbells, & other ornaments of building &c

6 part. Compartments, grotescos, risographs & leviores extemporariae figurae, trophies, medalls &c

7 part. Frontispieces of books &c

8 part. Inventions mechanic, trades, works, vases &c

9 part. War, battails, sieges &c

10 part. Sacred history, picture, emblemes &c

11 part. Historical ceremonies, feasts, scenes, pomps, executions, funerals & other rare accidents &c

12 part. Miscellanies, emblems, rusticities, droles &c

13 part. Heads of men & women &c by fancy &c

14 part. Prints after M.Angelo, Raphael, Coreggio & other masters

15 part. Scheletons, anatomies &c

16 part. Elements of drawing & designing &c

F A collection of prints, the intire works of Callot, de la Bella, Israel Sylvestre, Perelle, Win.Hollar &c containing innumerable sculps & draughts of countries, landscape, citties, churches, convents, palaces, magnificent buildings, great houses, gardens, battells, solemnities, pomps, fairs & other historical pieces sacred & profane, designed from the Arundelean collection & others, & of the most renowned painters & masters; elements of design; portraicts; various <?> habits of people, masks, scenes, funerals, kirmasses, perspectives, pieces of architecture, vases, ruines, ships, beasts, birds, fishes, insects, & other varieties of the world, all design'd from the nature & things themselves.

G A collection of the effigies, portraiture & heads of Emperors, Kings, Queenes, princes, noblemen, ladys, & persons of quality; generals & greater captains, popes, cardinals, bishops, eminent divines, ambassadors, politicians, judges, lawyers, historians, philosophers, mathematicians, physicians, poets, painters, musicians, mechanicians, & other famous persons, benefactors, notables of either sex &c

H

1 Icones et segmata illustrium e marmore tabularum quae Romae adhuc extant &c a Franc. Perrier delineata et ad antiquam formam lapidis exemplaribus passim collapsae restitutae. Paris MDCXLV. Also the antient statues of Rome delineated & graven by the same Perrier, Paris MDCXXXVIII. Also

2 [the title of the book by Onofrio Panvinio repeated under L below, crossed out]

I – Sacrae Historiae acta a Raphaele Urbin in Vaticanis Xystis ad picturae miraculum expressa. Nichol. Chapron Gallus a se delineata et incisa. Romae MDCXXXXIX

– Imagines Aceorum ac Praeliorum Veteris Testamenti &c ab Antonio Tempesta delineatae et sculptae. Romae 1613

– Historia di Gierusaleme liberato del Torquato Tasso. Invent. desig. & sculpiti da Antonio Tempesta

K The storie of Psyche & Cupid &c design'd & ingraven by Villamena. Romae

L A collection of Roman antiquities of old and Modern Rome. Temples, sacrifices, & sacred vessels, aquaducts, arches, trophies, sepulchres, statues, obelisks, columns, amphiteatres, theatres, naumachia, circus, thermae, the port at Ostia, Neros garden, marriages, bassorilieve of the Rape of Proserpine, Meleager, Bacchanalias &c, more especially the triumphs of L.Paulus de Rege Macedonum per se capto; P.Africanus Aemilianus de Carthaginibus excisis. C.N.Pompeius Mag. ex oriente Julius <?> Vespasianus Traianus & other Roman emperors triumphs taken from antient marbles, medalls, books & other antient monuments accurately described by Onuphrii Panvini Veronensis inventoris opera et aeneis formis edita Romae MDCXVIII. Together with: the collection of Phil. Tomassinus ex antiquis cameorum et gemmae delineata, ab Enea Vico Parme incisae.

Also: Tabuale Isiacae Pignorii, with severall other Aegyptian Hieroglyphics &c Prints of modern Rome, Capital, castle at St Angelo, Popes cavalcade, ceremonie of coronation, Jubilee &c and other public solemnities.

M A collection of drawings & designes of severall masters, academies & designes from the life by Carlo Marat. Neapolitano given me by him at Rome 1645, now the most famous painter there. ROLL This was the Pope's chiefe painter since I came from Italy

N Villa Angiana belonging to the Duke of Arichol set forth by Nic. Visscher. Design'd & engraven by Romanus de Hooghe.

Other books in smaller volumes on the shelfe of prints

O Historie of the Bible with old English verses under each print by Peter d'Arundel, the cutts being of Peter Bernard, Lyons 1553.

Also the argument of the new Testament in Dutch verse, the figures rarely cut by one of the petit maisters 1564.

P Icones Historiarum Veteris Testamenti ad vivum expressae auctore Fr. Frellonio; the figures cut by Holbein. Lugdun. 1547

Q Metamorphoseo d'Ovidio figurado et abbreviato in forma d'Epigrammi da M. Gal. Symeoni A Lion 1559

R L'Amour de Cupido et de Psyche prise de la Metamorph. de Luciano Apuleo; curiously engraven by Gaultier 1606

S The argument of Homers Ilias 4o accurately ingraven

T Representation de diverses figures humaines avec leurs mesures prises sur des Antiques qui sont de present a Rome par A.Bosse Paris 1656

V Elemens de portraicture par le sieur de S.Igny

V* Palmas drawing book

W Sculptura, or the Historie of Chalcography &c by J.Evelyn. Lond. 1662

X The art of graving & etching by Ab. Bosse translated by W.Faithorne. Lond. 1662

Y Panoplia omnium illiberalium mechanicarum aut sedentarium artium genera &c Hartman Schoppers authore Francfurti 1568 cum imaginibus omnium artificum &c

ABC 1.2.3 Copy-books

1. Field & Cocker, John de Beauchesne

2. Cocker Pens Triumph Coriose
3. Luca Orpheo
[pp. 199, 200]
Icones &c

– Principes Hollandiae et Zelandiae domini Frisiae … industria Guil. Thybauti repertis &c delineatis: containing a short history of the lives, death[s], names, wives, sepulchres &c. Antwerp 1578

– Portraits, noms, et qualitez des ambassadeurs assemblez tant a Munster qu'a Osnabruk pour le traité et conclusion de la paix générale. 4o Paris 1648

– Portraits of the principal captains & commanders of the imperial Swedish armies during that War in Germany between Gustavus Adolphus & the Emp. Anno 1630, 1632 &c

– Effigies of King James 2nd & his Queen Mary. French K. Lewis 13th on horseback by L'Asne. Wolfgangus Will. Duke of Bavaria 1631 by Delfius after Miereveld: Mons Perefix A Bish. of Paris by Nanteuil (Roll XXV)

– Large Crucifix by Morin. Another by Chereau (Roll XIX)

– A very large cutt of Pharaoh in the Red Sea, a wood cutt of Titian (Roll LXXV)

– Judgement of M. Angelo in the Vatican Chapel. The prophets & sibylls on the frieze there (Roll IV)

– Prospects, landscapes &c
Versailles, Salines in Burgundy <?> van der Meulen desig. & B<?> graver [added 'Chelsea coll. prospect']

– The prophet Osea dauncing & The <?> in the wood, graven by Coninxloyensis (Roll XXXVIII)

– Contention of the 3 goddesses & Paris, graven by Nic. Vinckboen. Adam & Eve in paradese graven by de Bruyn. Golden Age, by Caesar Bassanus &c [added 'Chelsea Colledge'] (Roll LXXVII)

– A portfeuile of rede draughts of landscapes, b[u]ildings, surveys, & other papers drawne by J.Evelyn casualy

– Droles, comoedies, buffoons, severall sorts of drunkard &c, cries of Paris &c v.Roll XVII (Roll XIII)

[p. 198] – Ceremonies & description. Popes cavalcade or procession to St J. de Lateran by Tempest. The cavalcade at the entrance of the Polish Ambass. at Paris, Tempest. Cavalcade of the Grand Signor to S.Sophia &c Dela Bella. (Roll XII)

NOTES

1 The main sales in 1977 were on 14 June (lots 152-68); 29 June (lots 1-126); 6 July (lots 1-20); 12 July (lots 48-51); and 26 July (lots 156-99).
2 29 June 1977, lot 23, and later in Frederick Mulder catalogue 4 (1977), no. 2.
3 6 July 1977, lot 9.
4 Antony Griffiths, 'The Arch of Titus by Carlo Maratti', *The National Art Collections Fund Annual Review* (1992), pp. 35-7.
5 Antony Griffiths with the collaboration of Robert Gerard, *The Print in Stuart Britain 1603-1689* (London: British Museum, 1998), cat. 116.

6 The 1687 catalogue is discussed by Guy de la Bédoyère, 'John Evelyn's Library Catalogue', *The Book Collector*, 43 (1994), 529-48.

7 For the engraving, see *The Print in Stuart Britain*, cat. 118

8 Reproduced in Paul Grinke catalogue 15, no. 20. The significance of the number 198 remains unclear.

9 Robert Harding, 'John Evelyn, Hendrik van der Borcht the Younger, and Wenceslaus Hollar', *Apollo*, 144 (Aug. 1996), 39-44.

10 *The Print in Stuart Britain*, cat. 81.

11 I must here thank Dr Hans Buijs of the Fondation Custodia for his kind help.

12 The Evelyn archive contains two pencil designs for Evelyn's bookplate dated 1652, as well as a letter asking for payment on behalf of himself and Nanteuil: BL Add. MS 78639.

13 Antony Griffiths, 'The Etchings of John Evelyn', in *Art and Patronage at the Caroline Courts: Essays in Honour of Sir Oliver Millar*, ed. by David Howarth (Cambridge: Cambridge University Press, 1993), pp. 51-67. Since this was published a second set of the landscapes published by Rowlett has been found to be in the Rijksmuseum.

14 On Rowlett, see Antony Griffiths, '*The Print in Stuart Britain* Revisited', *Print Quarterly*, 17 (2000), 115-16. This corrects and adds to my earlier writings on Rowlett.

15 George Henderson, 'Bible Illustration in the Age of Laud', *Transactions of the Cambridge Bibliographical Society*, 8 (1982), 178-85.

16 Griffiths, 'The Etchings of John Evelyn', p. 65.

17 BL Add. MS 78221.

18 BL Add. MS 78628 A.

19 BL Add. MS 15948, fol. 53.

20 BL Add. MS 78299: to William Lloyd, 5 Feb. 1695.

21 Francis Douce, *The Dance of Death* (London: Pickering, 1833), p. 234.

22 *Evelyn's Sculptura with the Unpublished Second Part*. ed. by C. F. Bell (Oxford: Clarendon Press, 1906), pp. 149-50.

23 *The Print in Stuart Britain*, p. 194.

24 *Diary of John Evelyn*, ed. H. B. Wheatley, 4 vols (London: Bickers, 1906), IV, 16.

25 These letters are most conveniently collected together by Howard C. Levis, *Extracts from the Diaries and Correspondence of John Evelyn and Samuel Pepys Relating to Engraving* (London: Ellis, 1915).

SAYES COURT REVISITED

MARK LAIRD

ONE ESPECIALLY COMPELLING PAGE of John Evelyn's diary is reproduced in the de Beer edition.[1] The year is 1658. We find Evelyn resident at Sayes Court long enough to perfect his oval parterre; the orchard has five season's growth, and his grove, though immature, appears part of a garden 'infinitely Sweete & beautifull'.[2] At the top of the page Evelyn writes: '*June 2*. An extraordinary storme of haile & raine, cold season as winter, wind northerly neere 6 moneths.'[3] The following day, in the wake of the storm, something of equal portent occurred outside the garden walls. The entry for the 3 June 1658 begins:

A large *Whale* taken, twixt my Land butting on the *Thames* & *Greenewich*, which drew an infinite Concourse to see it, by water, horse, coach, on foote from *Lond*, & all parts: It appeared first below *Greenewich* at low-water, for at high water, it would have destroyed all the boates: but lying now in shallow water, incompassd with boates, after a long Conflict it was killed with the harping yrons, & struck in the head, out of which spouted blood & water, by two tunnells like Smoake from a chimny: & after an horrid grone it ran quite on shore & died.[4]

He attempted a sketch and gave the following description of its features:

The length was 58 foote: 16 in height, black skin'd like Coach-leather, very small eyes, greate taile, small finns & but 2: a piked snout, & a mouth so wide & divers men might have stood upright in it: No teeth at all, but sucked the slime onely as thro a grate made of that bone which we call Whale bone: The throate <yet> so narrow, as would not have admitted the least of fishes: The extreames of the *Cetaceous* bones hang downewards, from the Upper <jaw>, & was hairy towards the Ends, & bottome withinside: all of it prodigious, but in nothing more wonderfull then that an Animal of so greate a bulk, should be nourished onely by slime, thro' those grates:[5]

Peter Mundy's drawing shows an Atlantic right whale [Fig. 1]; and his account concludes – mistakenly – that it was young 'by the smallnesse and shortnesse of the said fynnes'.[6] John Dryden saw its arrival as a portent of Cromwell's death.[7] For us today, however, it is a thoroughly troubling image, not least because it materializes so close to the Elysium John Evelyn had constructed on the banks of the Thames [Fig. 2].

When I first attempted to visualize John Evelyn's garden at Sayes Court,

115

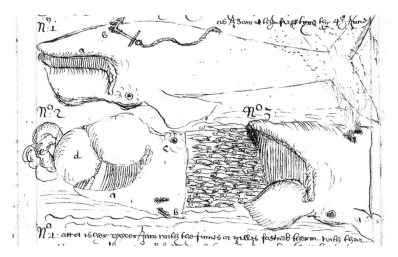

Fig. 1: 'Whale in the Thames, June 1658', from Peter Mundy's *Travels*
(Bodleian Library, Oxford, MS Rawl.A.315).

I was preoccupied with stylistic provenance and various linkages to the early formulation of the *Elysium Britannicum*.[8] The oval parterre, which was based on Pierre Morin's garden in Paris, appeared to me a complex fusion of French prototypes. Likewise the grove reflected the Italian *bosco* and French *bosquet*; indeed, the laurels, pines, and olives of the Villa Borghese in Rome inspired the image of a 'Ver Perpetuum' of alaternus, bays, laurel, and citrus fruit in deepest Deptford. Lastly, the coronary or flower garden suggested precedents in antiquity. My picture of formal equilibrium was unsettled only by a brief reflection on how weather might have affected a yearly change of anemones and tulips.

When I now try to visualize Sayes Court I see an environment of chaos as much as stasis. The ominous weather and stranded whale invade the frame. I am looking, for example, at Johannes Vorsterman's painting of Greenwich [Fig. 3]; and imagining somewhere close to the docked boats near Sayes Court that scene of slaughter, dark blood spurting like smoke from a chimney. Vorsterman's heavenly clouds and golden evening light turn into an approaching storm, cold winds suddenly gusting from Hampstead; then transform themselves still further into that 'Hellish and dismall Cloud of SEA-COALE'[9] issuing from the city. As Evelyn wrote in *Fumifugium*, it diffuses and spreads, becoming an:

Avernus to *Fowl*, and kills our *Bees* and *Flowers* abroad, suffering nothing in our Gardens to bud, display themselves, or ripen; so as our *Anemonies* and many other choycest Flowers, will by no Industry be made to blow in *London*, or the Precincts of it, unless they be raised on a *Hot-bed*, and governed with extraordinary Artifice to accellerate their springing; imparting a bitter and ungrateful Tast to those few

Fig. 2: 'View of the Dock Yard at Deptford taken from the opposite
Side of the Thames' (British Library, King's MS 43, fols 65ᵛ-66ʳ).

wretched *Fruits*, which never arriving to their desired maturity, seem, like the *Apples*
of *Sodome*, to fall even to dust, when they are but touched.[10]

Even the elm avenue in the foreground, a perfect symbol of orderly planting,
begins to look less majestic or absolute when I discover that His Majesty's
gardeners were stealing some of the trees from Sayes Court – 'at least 40 of
my very best', grumbled Evelyn in a letter.[11]

   Rather than revisiting Sayes Court in purely formal and horticultural
terms, it seems to me more interesting to reconstruct aspects of the human-
biological life in and around the garden, especially in the final decade of
family residence – 1684 to 1694. The discovery, while the Evelyn archive
was being catalogued at the British Library, of a further design for the garden
by Evelyn himself, dated February 1685, provides a convenient point of
departure [Fig. 4]. In the wake of a devastating winter, the plan was devised
for replanting the area formerly occupied by the parterre and part of the
orchard (compare Fig. 9). It helps strengthen our sense of how the garden
evolved from the 1650s to the layout shown on two plans of the 1690s[12]
[Fig. 5]; and it allows us to meditate on the idea of the formal garden as
dynamic rather than static, shaped by contingency as much as by design.

   On 3 June 1685 Mary Evelyn wrote to a friend: 'Mr Evelyn makes the
Garden his buisnesse and delight[.] It now gros towards finishing and dos
answer expectation very well being finer than ever, for the future I hope it
will be lesse expensive.'[13] Following the first plantings of 1653, John Evelyn
had always been in the practice of refining his garden at Sayes Court. In
1664, for example, the holly hedge – that 'boast of my *Villa*' – was 160 foot
long, 7 foot high and 5 foot thick (according to the entry in *Sylva*); yet by

117

Fig. 3: Johannes Vorsterman (1643-99), *Greenwich from One Tree Hill*
(National Maritime Museum, Greenwich).

1679 it had almost doubled to 300 foot.[14] The alterations in the spring
of 1685, however, amounted to more than just piecemeal additions or
improvements. Indeed, at the age of sixty-four and grieving for his daughter
Mary, who had just died of smallpox that March, he embarked on a major
revision of his private Elysium.

It was the winter of 1683-4 that provided the immediate impulse for
change. The prolonged frosts created an environmental breakdown in the
order and harmony that Evelyn had tried to establish in his 1653 plan of
Sayes Court. This put a new premium on flexibility or improvization – the
essence of gardening as opposed to formal garden design.

The first hint of the ensuing trouble was the entry in his diary of
20 December 1683: 'I went to Deptford, return'd the 22d in very cold &
severe weather: My poore Servant *Humphry Prideaux* being falln sick of the
small-pox some days before.'[15] By 23 December, he recorded, 'This night
died my poore excellent servant of the small pox. ... It was exceedingly
mortal at this time; & the season was unsufferably cold. The Thames frozen,
&c.'[16] On 24 January 1684 the impact of a month of bitter weather was
beginning to tell. Evelyn painted a vivid picture [Fig. 6]:

The Frost still continuing more & more severe, the Thames before London was
planted with bothes in formal streetes, as in a Citty, or Continual faire, all sorts of
Trades & shops furnished, & full of Commodities, even to a Printing presse. ... There
was likewise Bull-baiting, Horse & Coach races, Pupet-plays & interludes, Cookes &
Tipling, & lewder places; so as it seem'd to be a bacchanalia, Triumph or Carnoval
on the Water, whilst it was a severe Judgement upon the Land: the Trees not only

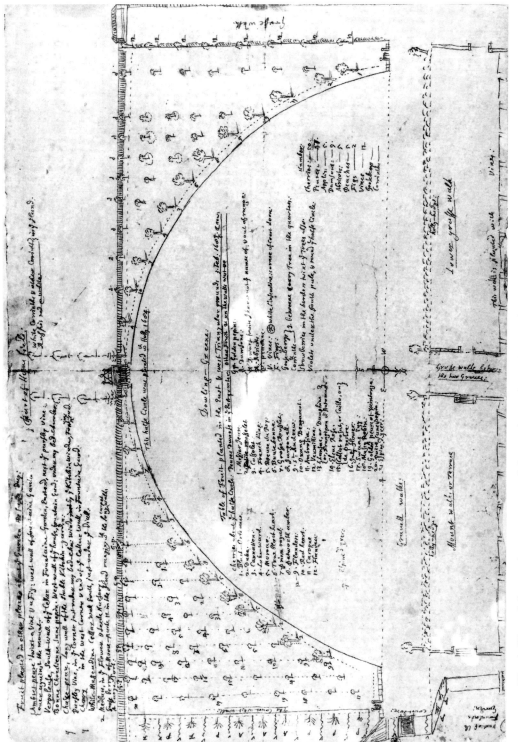

Fig. 4: Plan of the south-west corner of the garden at Sayes Court, showing the changes from the former parterre, by John Evelyn, 3 February 1684/5 (British Library, Add. MS 78628 B).

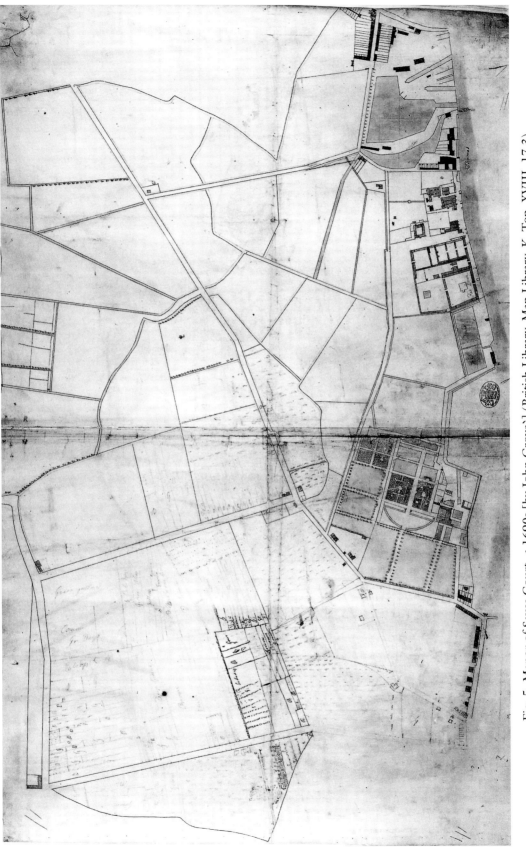

Fig. 5. Manor of Sayes Court, c. 1690s [by John Grove?] (British Library, Map Library, K. Top. XVIII. 17.3).

Fig. 6: Frost fair on the Thames 1683-4, by Abraham Hondius
(Museum of London).

splitting as if lightning-strock. ... The fowle [Fish] & birds, & all our exotique Plants
& Greenes universaly perishing; many Parks of deere destroied. ... London, by reason
of the excessive coldnesse of the aire, hindring the ascent of the smoke, was so filld
with the fuliginous steame of the Sea-Coale, that hardly could one see crosse the
streete, & this filling the lungs with its grosse particles exceedingly obstructed the
breast, so as one could scarce breath.[17]

It was not until 4 February 1684, however, that Evelyn saw the damage in
the garden at first hand. He wrote: 'I went to Says-Court to see how the frost
& rigorous weather had dealt with my Garden, where I found many of the
Greenes & rare plants utterly destroied: The Oranges & Myrtils very sick, the
Rosemary & Lawrell dead to all appearance, but the Cypresse like to indure
it out.'[18]

His record of that winter destruction formed the basis of his report to the
Royal Society:

I fear my cork trees [*Quercus suber* L.] will hardly recover ... my cedars [*Cedrus libani*
A. Rich] I think are lost; the ilex [*Quercus ilex* L.] and scarlet oak [*Quercus coccifera*
L.] not so, the arbutus [*Arbutus unedo* L.] doubtful, and so are bays [*Laurus nobilis*
L.]. ... Among our shrubs, rosemary is entirely lost, and to my great sorrow; because
I had not only beautiful hedges of it, but sufficient to afford me flowers for making a
considerable quantity to hungary water; so universal, I fear, is the destruction of this

121

plant, not only over England but the neighbouring countries more southward, that
we must raise our next hopes from the seed. Atriplex or sea purslane [*Atriplex halimus*
L.], of which I had a hedge, has also perished, and so another of French furzes [*Ulex
europaeus* L.]; the cypresses are most of them destroyed, especially such as were kept
shorn in pyramids. ... The aborescent and other sedums, aloes &c, though housed,
perished with me; but the yucca [*Yucca gloriosa* L.] and opuntia [*Opuntia ficus-indica*
(L.) Miller and/or *O. vulgaris* Miller] escaped; tulips many are lost, and so the
Constantinople narcissus, and such turberosae as were not kept in the chimney
corner, where was continual fire; some anemonies appear but I believe many are
rotted. ... My tortoise ... is found quite dead after having for many years escaped the
severest winter.[19]

This was not, of course, the first time that Evelyn had encountered destructive weather in the garden. The storm of 2 June 1658, just before the whale's
portentous arrival, was followed by another on 30 August. It produced
devastation in the form of a 'tempestious Wind, which threw-downe my
greatest trees at *Says-Court*, & did much mischiefe all *England* over: It
continued all night, till 3 afternoone next day, & was *S. West*, destroying all
our winter fruit.'[20] And a few years later Evelyn jotted down an entry for
17 February 1662 : 'this night, & the next day fell such a storme of Haile,
Thunder & lightning, as never was seene the like in any mans memorie;
especialy the tempest of Wind, being South-west, which subverted besids
huge trees, many houses, innumerable Chimnies, among other that of my
parlor at *Says Court*.'[21] By 20 February 1662 he had 'returned home to
repair my miserably shatt(er)ed house by the late Tempest'.[22]

It would be wrong then to view the events of 1683-4 as a first cataclysm
in the garden; equally misleading, moreover, to take Evelyn's record of
unparalleled weather fluctuations in subsequent years as only the feeble
recollections of an old age afflicted by kidney pains and ague. It had always
been his way to see the vagaries of the weather as a 'judgement' from on
high. Thus on 9 March 1667 he recorded: 'Greate frosts, snow & winds,
prodigious at the vernal æquinox; indeede it had hitherto ben a yeare of
nothing but prodigies in this Nation: Plage, War, fire, raines, Tempest:
Comets.'[23] And a few years later on 30 January 1671; 'we have had a plague,
a Warr, & such a fire, as never was the like in any nation since the overthrow
of *Sodome*, and this very yeare so Wett, Stormy & unseasonable.'[24]

Nevertheless, though he was apt to use hyperbole on all such occasions
and to see portents in black clouds, the weather events of the 1680s and early
1690s certainly justified the extravagant claims of empirical observation.
Even as the harsh winter subsided and Evelyn set about planting in the spring
of 1685, gardening conditions were difficult. On 24 May, for example, he
noted: 'We had hithertoo [not] any raine for many monethes, insomuch as
the Caterpillar had already devoured all the Winter fruite through the whole
land, & even killed severall greate & old trees; such two Winters, & Summers

I had never known.'[25] Only by 28 June did conditions improve: 'We had now plentifull Raine after two yeares excessive drowth, & severe winters'.[26]

What Evelyn would never know was that he was trying to garden at the end of the Little Ice Age. This did not mean that it was universally cold, simply that with cooler temperatures there also came an enhanced variability of the temperature level. As H. H. Lamb puts it: 'The well-known occurrence of very hot summer weather in the two summers of 1665 and 1666, when London experienced its last great epidemic of the plague which ended with the great fire that burnt the city in September 1666, occurred in the middle of the coldest century of the last millennium.'[27] December 1676 was cold enough for the Thames to freeze over, yet the summer of 1676 had been amongst the hottest on record. Overall temperatures in 1695 were enough to reduce the growing season by at least two months, yet there was a run of good harvests from 1685 to 1690.

Cold was, however, clearly the most dominant extreme. Between 1670 and 1700 the long-term average winter temperatures for central England were sufficiently cold to suggest that the normal yearly number of days with snow lying was twenty to thirty days. In one location in southern England that figure rose to 102 days in the winter of 1657-8, making sense of Evelyn's remarks on 2 June 1658 (the day before the whale arrived) that there had been six months of northerly winds. The great winter of 1683-4 was especially remarkable for the recorded fact that in Somerset the ground was frozen to a depth of nearly four feet where it had been snow-free. The implications of these figures for harvests and health are obvious though complicated. The vernal fever that followed the bitter winter of 1658 brought catarrh and feverish distemper and high mortality (although, interestingly, the winter of 1683-4 brought no epidemics). Despite the good harvest years at the end of the 1680s, the yearly number of burials still exceeded births from the 1660s until about 1730.[28]

Of course the contours of mortality, as Mary Dobson points out, followed not just complex meteorological patterns, but also the contours of geographical zones such as the low-lying marshes of south-east England – what she calls the 'sinks of disease, the depths of death'.[29] It is thus possible to place Sayes Court on the Thames in a geographical as well as meteorological matrix of death and disease, just at that moment when Fellows of the Royal Society – Wren, Hooke, Locke, Boyle, and Evelyn – began to develop the rain gauge, thermometers, barometers, the wind recorder, and hygroscope for measuring the weather and the disease-weather relationship.[30] Dobson's olfactory map of south-east England charts the contours in graphic form.[31] Sayes Court lies by the docks at that confluence of London's smoky airs and foul smells with the Thames estuary's bad airs and noxious smells. Confined airs and filthy smells, as well as pestiferous airs and lousy smells, follow the

Thames out of London, trapped between hills that prevented the inhabitants benefiting much from the adjacent upland fresh air [Fig. 7].

It is worth pausing here to review these statistical data against the anecdotal evidence: the entries in his diary for the period of a decade. The impression is of wild variability. If we extend the period to include Evelyn's record of the great storm of 7-8 December 1703, that impression is further consolidated.

When writing the *Elysium Britannicum*, Evelyn had tried to make sense of the weather as a set of conditions that could be predicted in part. Thus, for example, the winds had certain properties, whose causes could be scientifically studied and whose effects were all too familiar to the ordinary gardener. Starting from first principles he stated the general effect of one wind or another, noting that accident or contingency played a role:

The Wind is onely an agitation of the particles of Aire, or rather a flux thereof, caused by the plenty of exhalations, attributed to the external and internal operations of heate upon the *terraqueus* Globe: and imbu'd with the qualities of the vapours through which ... {it} passes; so as the same winds are ... {wholesome} and in-salubrous according to {the variety of} accidents; sometymes wafting cold and nitrous *atomes*, blasts, and medews producing wormes, killing ... nipping ... scorching ... {and} retarding the beauty and maturitie of our flowers and fruite when they seeme to flatter us with the fairest expectations: Especially the ... *Etesian* and anniversary winds spiring from the {North &} *North East* for at the least fourty days about March ... {proceeding} from the *Russian* tracts, where the snows and the yce are not yet dissolv'd: {A}nd the {furious}*prodromi* about *Midsomer* the concussions whereoff leave their markes all the yeare after. ... The South wind is hot and moist, Sulphury, furious and too opening; yet convenient for {drying & preparing the ground} the advancement of vegetable groths.[32]

The east wind was 'one of the most noxious winds to our Gardens (whatever *Virgils* counsell be concerning the site of Vineyards) as frequently blowing so long at the *Spring* that it nipps and dries the flowers and blossums of our choycest fruits'. In contrast there was 'the West and genial *Zephyre*, the most benigne and temperate of all'.[33]

There were various things the gardener could do to deal with the consequences. First he could use instruments to measure or forecast adverse conditions. And second, he could observe the signs. A primitive form of hygroscope [Fig. 8a] is described in the following marginal note of the *Elysium Britannicum*:

Take the stipula or spirall beard of the wild Oak {vine}, or rather ... the cod of a wild Vetch, place it on a style, as in the fig: A.B. So as one extreame may be fix't on a piece of a stick or the like; then put on the other point of it: viz. B. a small ... slip of paper form'd like a magnetic index viz, B.C. placd horizontaly on A. Touch this Oak beard or Vetch with the least ... moisture & 'twill untwist itselfe so as to move the Needle; which when dry will revert the contrary way again.[34]

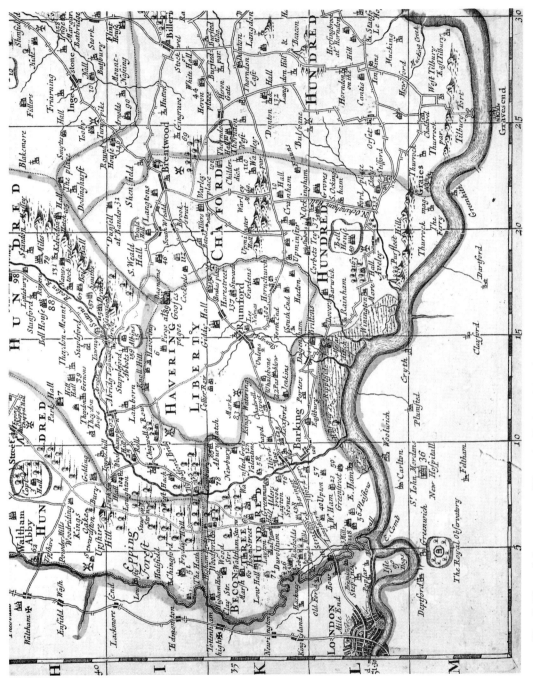

Fig. 7: Plan of the county of Essex by Robert Morden, *c*.1700, detail (Harvard University, Pusey Map Library).

125

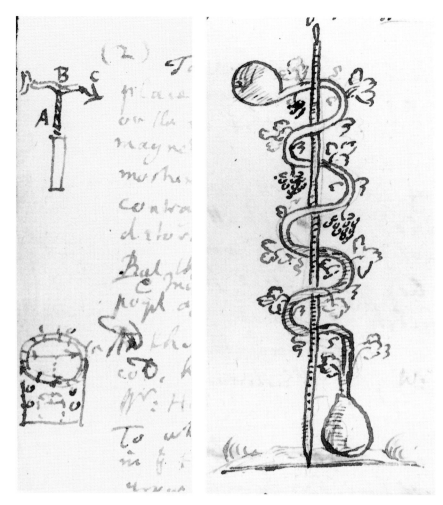

Fig. 8a: John Evelyn: a 'hygroscope', 'to detect the degrees of wett & dry, or any change of Weather', pen and ink drawing from 'Elysium Britannicum' (British Library, Add. MS 78342, fol. 21ᵛ). Fig. 8b: John Evelyn: 'How to contrive a Thermoscope or Weather-Glass for a Garden', pen and ink drawing from 'Elysium Britannicum' (British Library, Add. MS 78342, fol. 189ʳ).

In a later section of the *Elysium Britannicum*, Evelyn wrote instructions on *How to contrive a Thermoscope or whe{a}ther-Glasse for a Garden* [Fig. 8b]. These began: 'Make a *Siphon* or *Tube* of Glasse straight or *Tortuous* like to some winding *Stalke* or *Convolvulus*', and concluded, 'We have severall formes of these Weather-glasses, placed artificially in Rock-worke, the water for better distinction … {tinged} greene.'[35]

Evelyn balanced empirical observation and gardening lore with some respect for the influence of celestial bodies. He claimed in one separate insertion: 'I am no friend to Astrological nicities in these matters: & that generally warme & moist weather is {certainly} the best for all these … operations what ever the Aspect or Signe be'.[36] Yet, at the same time, he acknowledged that, 'as the *Moone* is of all the rest neerest to the *Earth*; so hath she a very greate influence upon the Labours and endeavors of our *Gardiner*, during the intire course of her periodic moneth … for Seedes committed to the Earth at the end or beginning of the *Moone*, produce lusty and goodly plants, those in the full Low & Shrubby.'[37] Thus on 19 February 1653 he followed the astrological and meteorological indicators: 'I planted the *Ortchard* at *Sayes-Court, New Moone, wind West*.'[38] But, as an insurance policy, his '300 fruit trees of the best sorts mingled' were 'warranted for 3 yeares upon a bond of 20 pound'.[39]

Whatever astrological or empirical precautions Evelyn might have observed in 1653, he could scarcely have predicted the course of events some thirty years later. In the winter of 1683-4, it was not so much the orchard that suffered, as the elaborate parterre of continental aspiration [Fig. 9] (and see again Fig. 4). Here the youthful confidence of the ideal plan of the 1650s can be measured against the seasoned revision of February 1685 (a revision that the two surveys of the 1690s suggest was implemented; see Fig. 5).

The major sacrifice to create the half-circle bowling-green and orchards involved the uprooting of the oval garden – Evelyn's 'Morine Garden'. At the centre of that oval garden, the circular parterre had been composed of box broderie combined with twelve flowerbeds. Eight cypress trees had stood as sentinels around a mount with sundial, and an additional twenty-four cypress trees had been used to punctuate every junction of parterre, grass plats, and gravel walks. These cypress cones were victims of the bitter cold, along with hedges of rosemary, sea purslane and French furze or gorse. From every point of view (perhaps including 'economy'), it surely made sense to simplify. At the age of sixty-four, after thirty years of gardening, Evelyn appears to have seen advantage in home-grown as opposed to imported ways. To what extent this reflected a gradual shift in personal taste or in English gardening style remains a matter of conjecture.[40] But Evelyn, in constructing a grand but simple axial layout of lawn, hedgework, and fruit trees, was to turn to the very hardy holly for his new hedging, and to eliminate topiary, broderie, and tender exotics. The predominant fruits were cherries around the half-circle, dwarf pears in the east triangle, golden pippin and damsons along the north-facing wall, and vines along the south-facing wall by the lower grass walk. In the west triangle he could take advantage of existing trees retained from part of the old orchard. We can assume that he still chose a propitious day of zephyr winds and new moon to plant out these trees and vines.

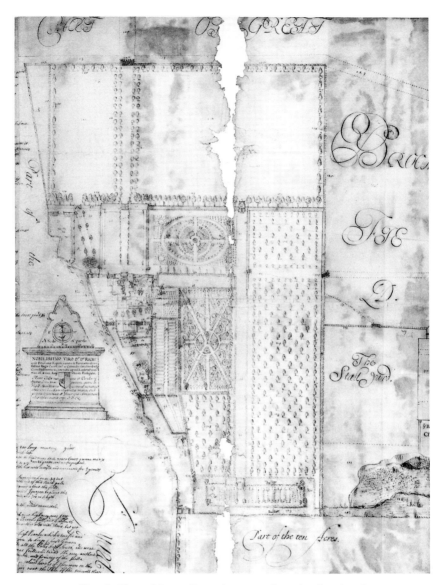

Fig. 9: Plan of Sayes Court house and garden [1653-4]
(British Library, Add. MS 78628 A).

Of course, it was one thing to deal with a cataclysm in the garden; quite another to go on fighting the daily battles against weeds, moles, and other subterfuges. In grasping the drudgery of such diurnal and seasonal encounters in the garden, we might do well to begin with the bowling-green grass. The bowling-green was on the circuit of routine gardening tasks. 'Directions' were written for Jonathan Mosse who was taken on as an apprentice gardener for six years on 24 June 1686. Thus, for example, on any given Monday in the summer, Mosse would rise shortly after sunrise. Evelyn recorded the sun as coming up at 3.51 a.m. in June.[41] He would follow the very practical instructions: 'Early, before the deaw be off in Mowing season, and as his grasse is growne too high (that is, if any daiysie or like appeare) he is to cut the grasse of the greate Court, & roll all the gravell: having rolled also the carpet, the *Saturday* night before, and this Monday evening the upper Terrace & lower.'[42] We can assume then that Sunday was the day off; hence the need to prepare for mowing on the Saturday before sundown. Evelyn recorded the sun as setting at 8.09 p.m. in June.

Rolling a night or two before mowing was to capture the weight of the dew. Each blade of grass, bent over by the roller, would remain prone as long as the dew persisted – perhaps an hour or so after dawn – and the blade of the freshly whetted scythe would find resistance against the dew-heavy blade of grass. In this way, Mosse would proceed to mow the upper and lower terrace near the bowling-green first thing on Tuesday morning. In fact he would only reach the bowling-green itself the following Monday, after the round of the fountain and greenhouse lawns, the grass walks of the groves, the long promenade of over four hundred feet to the island, and what Evelyn called the 'three former crosse grasse walkes'.[43] Once again before the start of that second week, Mosse would need to roll the bowling-green lawn on the Saturday evening. Given the size of that lawn, it would require him to return to the task on two consecutive mornings before the scything was complete. The effect of the regimen was to ensure that every part received regular attention: 'And thus alternatively may all the Grasse & Walkes be rolled, & cut once a fortnight, with ease: that is the grasse every 15 dayes, & the gravell rolled twice every six dayes.'[44]

What the lawns looked like on that momentous day of departure from Sayes Court – 4 May 1694 – is an interesting thought. We know from statistical data that the summer would prove a cold one in central England. But just twelve days before leaving for good for Wotton, he recorded in his diary for 22 April 1694: 'I return'd this Evening home, it being an extraordinary hot season.' There was a 'firy exhalation rising out of the sea in Montgomery-shire ... burning all Straw, hay, Thatch, grasse'.[45] The chances are high that, less than a fortnight later, the grass was rather yellowish than green. After forty years of gardening it would have been a sorry sight: a parched bowling-green in springtime when the apples and pears were in blossom.

Of course there was one device that could offset drought: the foist or watering truck [Fig. 10b: 43]. And, during a dry spell, we may picture Mosse resorting to it at the expense of other tasks. Because it could mimic rain and destroy noxious caterpillars, it was described in the *Elysium Britannicum* in rather charming terms: 'In summ, of all the Gardiners Instruments, this ... is the most elegant, usefull, and Philosophicall.'[46]

If drought was an environmental impact of periodic nature, weeds were a perennial and seasonal curse. One section of the 'Directions' was devoted to 'Weeding, Howing, Rolling, &c' and reads as follows:

Above all, be carefull not to suffer weedes (especially *Nettles, Dendelion, Groundsill,* & all downy-plants) to run up to seede; for they will in a moment infect the whole ground: wherefore, whatever work you neglect, ply weeding at the first peeping of the Spring. Malows, Thistles, Beane-bind, Couch, must be grubb'd up and the ground forked & diligently pick'd.
Whatever you How-up, rake-soone away off the ground, for most weedes will run to seede, and some rootes fasten againe in the ground: ...
Ground, walkes & Carpet grasse is best Rolled after soaking raines: the worme-casts pared off becomes good mould: These Carpet grasse walkes & Greenes, should also be sometimes beaten in moist seasons with a broad Rammer where the grasse rises in Tufts, & the ground uneven.
Mould made of rotted weedes, infects the ground againe where it is used.[47]

Along with watering, mowing, rolling, and weeding, the gardener was expected to deal with whatever conspired to vex him: strong winds knocking down flowers, moles throwing up mole-hills, or birds pecking at blossoms buds. Indeed, it was the first duty of the week to assess damage or trouble. Consequently, Mosse was instructed that, 'The Gardiner should walke aboute the whole Gardens every Monday-morning duely, not omitting the least corner, and so observe what Flowers or Trees & plants want staking, binding and redressing, watering, or are in danger; especialy after greate stormes, & high winds and then immediately to reforme, establish, shade, water &c what he finds amisse, before he go about any other work.'[48]

One section of the 'Directions' is entitled 'Vermine & Diseases'. It introduces all that can afflict the garden and the appropriate remedies. As Keith Thomas points out, the gardener was continually at war with noxious things: 'Every gardener destroyed smaller pests, and it was usual for the gardening-books to contain a calendar like the one drawn up by John Worlidge in 1668: "January: set traps to destroy vermin. February: pick up all the snails you can find, and destroy frogs and their spawn. March: the principal time of the year for the destruction of moles. April: gather up worms and snails. May: kill ivy. June: destroy ants. July: kill ... wasps, flies".'[49] By relating this to the *Kalendarium Hortense* and to the tools

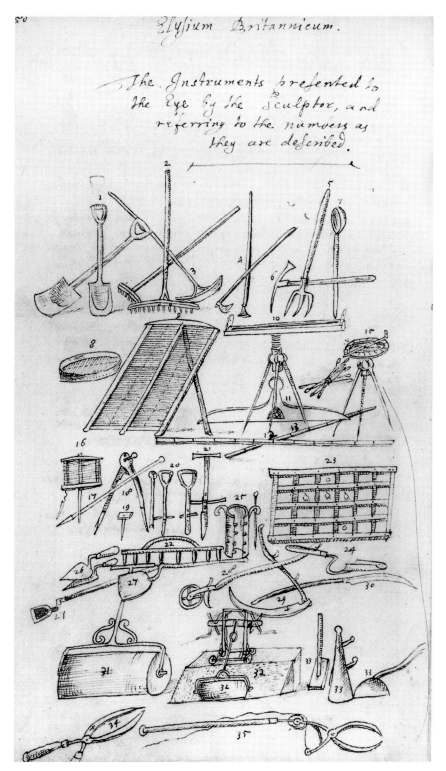

Fig. 10a: John Evelyn: garden tools and implements (nos 1-35),
pen and ink drawing from 'Elysium Britannicum'
(British Library, Add. MS 78342, fol. 57ᵛ).

depicted in the *Elysium Britannicum*, we can picture Mosse in his seasonal roles.

In January, for example, when the sun would rise at 8 a.m. and set at 4.06 p.m., he would be expected to set traps for vermin, notably mice. Field traps could be rather like a modern mouse-trap: 'the wrire springs fastned with threid boiled in oate meale'.[50] Or they might resemble a cage. By 1618, for example, an elaborate 'portcullis' type had come on the market.[51] Or they could be enticed into netting – what Evelyn calls 'Samsons Posts Netts' [Fig. 10b: 67]. Or, indeed, they might be lured near their 'Haunts' by a bait: 'A *Paste* made of course *Honey*, wherein is mingled *Green-glass* beaten, with *Copperas*'.[52]

By March it would be Mosse's duty to eliminate moles. Evelyn's picture of 'Mole-Graines' and tubes is not especially graphic (see Fig. 10b), but a woodcut of 1590 demonstrates a vicious device that looks like a turnstile within the mole tunnel. On pushing through, the mole would be lacerated by sharp blades released by the action. In April Mosse would follow the instructions in *Kalendarium Hortense*: 'Gather up *Worms* and *Snails* after Evening *Showers*.' He would also take preventative action: '*Soot-Ashes*, refuse Sweepings of *Tobacco-Stalks*, made into a fine Powder, or Dust, and strewed half an Inch in thickness at the foot of *Trees*, and now and then renewed, prevents *Pismires* and other crawling *Insects*, from invading the *Fruit*, &c.'[53] The pismire was an ant – so named from the urinous smell of the anthill.

A good deal of effort would be expended from July to autumn in keeping insects and birds away from fruit. An especially flexible tool for dealing with infestations and picking fruit was what Evelyn described as 'A paire of Reachers' (see Fig. 10a).[54] Apart from its use in clipping arbours or tall hedges, this device was practical for reaching 'inaccessible twiggs on which the Caterpillars do fasten their webbs'.[55] The gardener Mosse would thus have cleansed the orchards of caterpillars in the early summer, thereafter converting the tool to pick fruit at the end of the summer. William Lawson in *A New Orchard and Garden* of 1618 wrote that, for harvesting, the fruit picker should have 'a gathering apron like a poake before you, made of purpose, or a wallet hung on a bough, or a basket with a sive bottome or skin bottome, with lathes or splinters under, hung in a rope to pull up and downe'.[56]

Evelyn might view the caterpillar as a 'cursed Devourer', but the butterfly ranked as one of 'the flying flowers of our *Elysium*'.[57] Whether the butterfly was alive or dead it represented the curious and the collectable, as precious as a tulip. Indeed, every insect had a double identity: noxious and despicable, yet wonderful in construction, industry, and power. Take the butterfly's wings, 'whose colours mocks the skill of the painter to imitate';[58] or the spider's web which displays their '{geometricall} Toyles' and 'taught foulers

Fig. 10b: John Evelyn: gardens tools and implements (nos 36-70),
pen and ink drawing from 'Elysium Britannicum'
(British Library, Add. MS 78342, fol. 58ʳ).

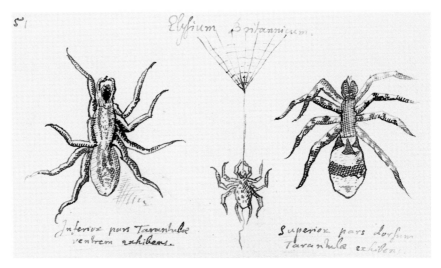

Fig. 11: John Evelyn: tarantula spider, pen and ink drawing from 'Elysium Britannicum' (British Library, Add. MS 78342, fol. 234ᵛ).

both how to make their netts, & to catch with them'[59] [Fig. 11]; or the ant's 'Industry, Justice, love and regimen'.[60] Like a storm or drought, insects could be a judgement. As he concluded in the *Elysium Britannicum*:

{And if we will argue from their worth} He ... that contemplates the Bee, the Silkworme, & the Cochinell, & that which makes our Gummlug, besides ... what others contribute to ... the *dispensatory*, will not despise Insects & ... even these productions of our Gardens. And then for their fortitude & other considerations, How even these despicable things can when ... {Heaven} pleases confound the power of the greatest {potentate}; God himself calls them his Army, & by divers of them he chastiz'd *Pharo* {in *Egypt*} & has since brought them upon other Countrys'.[61]

Birds presented an extreme dilemma resulting from this double identity. Paradise itself had been full of avian choristers, and birds with wings and two legs appeared close to angels and humans. As Evelyn wrote in *Elysium Britannicum*:

But whither this divine Art was taught by birds or Angels, there is nothing certainly more agreable then the chirping of these winged choristers, the cherefull inhabitants of our Gardens and Groves, where if the place or the climat prove so ... unhospitable as ... not to invite their spontaneous frequenting; ... our Elysium cannot be without their company though it be at the price of their liberty: For doubtlesse amongst the ... innumerable ornaments of our Gardens, none is more to be valued then the Volarie, none more divertissant affording so much profet in the contemplation of their nature.[62]

The indigenous winged choristers might be attracted into the garden by planting appropriate fruit and shrubs. Thus, for example, in the 1650s plan the evergreen thicket to the east of the parterre was for 'Birds private walkes, shades and Cabinetts'.[63] Whether the same licence was extended to the same birds in hopping into the two 'Cantons' on the opposite side remains doubtful. This was furnished with raspberries, strawberries, currants, and cherries. Evelyn might write that orchards 'harbour a constant aviary of sweet singers, which are here retained without the charge or violence of the *Italian* Wiers'. But his gardener was probably less charitable when it came to protecting fruit for the table.

In the original design for Sayes Court, Evelyn located his wire aviary in the private garden close to the house. This must have been a small enclosure rather than the volerie of princes or kings. The two types he described in *Elysium Britannicum* as:

An Aviary of 60 foote long, 15 broade & 30 high will be sufficient to hold 500 smale Birds together with … a competent number of Turtles [turtle doves], Quailes, Partridg & Pheasant. … And … if an Aviary of these dimensions do neither camport with every mans occasion, cages of 20 & 30 foote in length will hold birds enough to make the Welkin ring with their musique, for it is incredible to believe {what} a concert 50 or 60 birds will produce, being well sorted & chosen.[64]

Any such exotica might be seen as akin to pets, worthy of compassion that was not extended to their predating cousins. On 9 February 1665, for example, in describing birds at St James's Park, Evelyn mentioned '2 Balearian *Cranes*, one of which having had one of his leggs broken and cut off above the knee, had a wodden or boxen leg & thigh with a joynt for the (knee) so accurately made, that the poore creature could walke with it, & use it as well as if it had ben natural: It was made by a souldier.'[65]

A bird in a cage might receive the tender care of the 'sick and wounded'; but a bird outside a cage was a potential enemy. The inescapable fact was that 'winged choristers', along with vermin and insects, could destroy fruit and crops. Hence, among the tools of the gardener, there were various devices to either scare birds or destroy them. Number 62 in Evelyn's list was the rather quaint 'Scarr-Crows and *Terriculamenta* t'afright the birds, made … {with} horse bells, hanging upon a string which having feathers fastned crosseways 'twixt every bell, sett them a ringing and trembling being plaied upon by the least breath of aire or wind' (see Fig. 10b).[66] Hand and wind clappers might be used for the same purpose. But less appealing were the 'Samsons Posts Netts' in which birds, once meshed, might struggle and thrash in prolonged death throes.

The farmer and the gardener were part of a merciless campaign to rid the air of birds in every parish. As Keith Thomas writes:

In early Tudor times the campaign was placed on a statutory basis. An Act of Parliament in 1533 required parishes to equip themselves with nets in which to catch rooks, choughs and crows. In 1566 another authorized churchwardens to raise funds

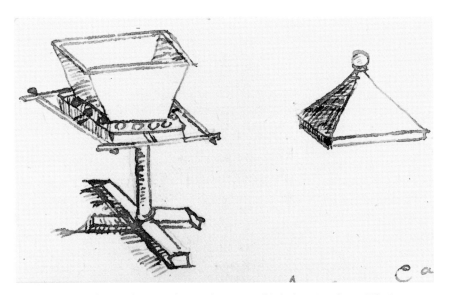

Fig. 12: John Evelyn: seed trough, pen and ink drawing from 'Elysium Britannicum'. The trough was 'contrived that the seede may fall into them as fast as they eate it: which it will do if the box containing it be made in fashion of a Mill-hopper' (British Library, Add. MS 78342, fol. 192).

to pay so much a head to all those who brought in corpses of foxes, polecats, weasels, stoats, otters, hedgehogs, rats, mice, moles, hawks, buzzards, ospreys, jays, ravens, even kingfishers. ... In later Stuart times the campaign turned against kites and ravens because they were a menace to poultry and agriculture; hitherto they had been protected as indispensable scavengers, but they became more vulnerable when urban authorities took to cleaning the streets and selling the manure to farmers. Also harried were the jays and bullfinches who nipped the buds off the fruit trees. ... As surviving parochial records show, the destruction effected under these Acts of Parliament was colossal, particularly from the later seventeenth century, when guns were increasingly used to shoot birds on the wing. At Tenterden, Kent, for example, they killed over 2,000 jays in the 1680s.[67]

We can see the gardener Jonathan Mosse then as caught in a vicious battle within the 'Elysium' of Sayes Court. He was at war with moles, mice, insects, and birds. Doubtless he knew which of the spontaneous visitors to feed in the winter along with exotic birds and pets [Fig. 12]. However, when it came down to it, he must have resorted to many cruel practices to protect the winter fruit for the table. Evelyn's innocent diet of salads could not preclude the killing of animals.

Here it is interesting to reconstruct the daily routine of gathering produce. Evelyn required Mosse to communicate on a regular basis with the cook, the housekeeper, and Mrs Evelyn herself. Enriching the diet was a consideration – a regimen elaborately detailed in *Acetaria*. Even within his gardener's manual, Evelyn included a specific directive:

The Gardner, is every night to aske what Rootes, sallading, garnishing, &c will be used the next day, which he is accordingly to bring to the Cook in the morning; and therefore from time to time to informe her what garden provision & fruite is ripe and in season to be spent.
He is also to Gather, & bring in to the House-Keeper all such Fruit of Apples, peares, quinces, Cherrys, Grapes, peaches, Abricots, Mulberies, strawberry, Rasberies, Corinths, Cornelians, Nutts, Plums, & generally all sort of Fruite, as the seasone ripens them, gathering all the windfalls by themselves: That they may be immediately spent, or reserved in the Fruite & store-house.[68]

There was a prohibition on selling or giving away produce, unless the Evelyns permitted it when a surplus arose. That surplus depended again on the weather and the seasons.

Evelyn's interest in '*Health* and *Long Life*, and the Wholesomeness of the Herby-Diet'[69] has been discussed elsewhere, notably in Graham Parry's essay 'John Evelyn as Hortulan Saint',[70] and in a wider context by John Prest and Keith Thomas. The emphasis on fruit at Sayes Court is especially interesting. John Prest points out, for example: 'On the whole then, the animals did not benefit much from seventeenth-century concepts of an innocent diet. The appetite was too strong to be denied, and what happened was not that men abandoned meat, but that they consciously added fruit to their foodstuffs.'[71] Certainly, Evelyn's diary reflects a relish in fish and meats that continued into later life. As just one example, on a visit to Lady Clarendon's Swallowfield on 22 October 1685, he wrote: 'We had Carps & Pike &c of size fit for the table of a Prince, every meale, & what added to the delight, the seeing hundreds taken in the drag, out of which the Cooke standing by, we pointed what we had most mind to, & had Carps every meale, that had be worth at London twenty shill a piece.'[72]

In *Acetaria*, the arguments are not solely concerned with the merits of 'the Herby-Diet', but also with what makes for good food. This is especially vital to 'those who dwell in the Middle and Skirts of vast and crowded Cities, inviron'd with rotten Dung, loathsome and common Ley stalls '.[73] Bad feed produces bad food. By contrast, good practices are rewarded by good taste, 'most powerfully in *Fowl*, from such as are nourish'd with Corn, sweet and dry Food'.[74] Here the issue of cruelty surfaces as an aspect of purity and innocence; and more broadly elsewhere as a matter of ethics. Just as today, there is an arbitrary line to draw somewhere. Compare, for example, Evelyn's reactions on two occasions. First, on March 15 1665, he observed: 'It was now Lent: Afternoone at our *Society*, where was tried some of the Poysons sent from the King of *Macassar* out of *E. India*, so famous for its suddaine operation: we gave it a wounded dog, but it did not succeede.'[75] Then second, on 10 October 1667, he commented: 'To *Lond*: dined with the *Swedish Resident*: where was a disection of a dog, the poore curr, kept long alive after the *Thorax* was open, by blowing with bellows into his lungs, &

that long after his heart was out, & the lungs both gashed & pierced, his eyes quick all the while: This was an experiment of more cruelty than pleased me.'[76]

A dog might die by poison or through vivisection. A mouse might chew bait laced with glass. A whale could get stranded and harpooned between Greenwich and Deptford. Mary would die of smallpox brought from London. The tortoise and many cypress trees would succumb to the cold. As Evelyn reshaped his garden at Sayes Court in the summer of 1685, a brief period of benign weather gave him a respite. At the end of June came plentiful rain; the winter that followed was especially mild. Nevertheless, with two bitter winters fresh in his memory, and the loss of his daughter still acute, the viewing of an orangery at Chelsea Physic Garden on the Thames must have offered a glimpse of an Elysium protected from the vagaries of life. It sheltered plants that could cure even the agues of the Thames estuary. He wrote on 6 August that year:

I went to Lond: next day to see Mr. Wats, keeper of the Apothecaries Garden of simples at Chelsey: where there is a collection of innumerable rarities of that sort: Particularly, besids many rare annuals the Tree bearing the Jesuits bark, which had don such cures in quartans: & what was very ingenious the subterranean heate, conveyed by a stove under the Conservatory, which was all Vaulted with brick; so as he leaves the doores & windowes open in the hard(e)st frosts, secluding onely the snow &c.[77]

Given the weather at the end of the Little Ice Age, this must have appeared wondrous. As Douglas Chambers points out, here was a 'possibility of realizing the dream of seventeenth-century botanists and horticulturists – of re-creating Eden in England'.[78]

In this sense, and despite the mortifying experience of repeated devastation and loss, Evelyn seems to have remained perennially hopeful of the garden's redemptive powers. Spring bulbs in particular were like a resurrection from the dead after the 'last cruell Winter'. Indeed on 9 December 1693, only a short time before moving to his brother's estate of Wotton, he was still receiving a delivery of plants from Henry Wise of the Brompton Park nursery. It included '50 roots of the Royall Parrott Tulips and 100 Roots of Ranunculoes which were received not long since from Flanders'.[79] Whether he continued to try anemones is another matter. As he had explained in the *Elysium Britannicum*: 'No plant, nor flower delights more in a sweet warme delicate aire then the Anemone, which you may see by the ill blowing of these flowers ... in and neere London where every thing is smutted & the aire spoild with the smoake of sea coale.'[80]

Back in 1661 he had believed in the melioration of London's air through hedges of sweet brier, honeysuckles, jasmine, mock-orange, and roses, and through acres of beans and peas. He wrote how an act of Parliament was required to place industry behind the 'Mountain' at Greenwich – a noble attempt at statutory regulation that failed, as the timely re-printing of *Fumifugium* in 1772 underscores. His solutions might seem quaint (albeit insightful) to the modern mind, familiar with a depleted ozone layer or vast polluted oceans, and distanced moreover from the use of perfumes and aromatic herbs in times of plague. Yet, given the extreme weather patterns that have come with Global Warming, and given the judgements of 'Mad-Cow Disease' and 'Foot-and-Mouth' in the wet and gloomy winter of 2001, his concerns for a better environment, clean air and good animal-feed, moderate consumption, and a 'more wholsome and temperate' diet without cruelty to animals all strike a familiar note.

If there were limits to scientific ingenuity in creating artificial environ-ments and if governmental inertia failed to make decrees that would regulate environment, one stratagem remained effective in preserving the miracles of nature. In the garden the caterpillar was the gardener's enemy, while the butterfly was a 'flying flower'. In contrast, within the collector's cabinet and pages of a florilegium, all insects – noxious or otherwise – were welcome. When Evelyn visited Pierre Morin's garden in Paris in April 1644, he recorded how the insects, especially butterflies, were prepared 'that no corruption invading them he keepes in drawers, so plac'd that they present you with a most surprizing and delighfull tapissry'.[81]

Over the decade when Evelyn was reshaping his Elysium on the Thames, he took himself to see other such collections. Thus, for example, on 16 December 1686 he recorded in his diary:

I carried the Countesse of Sunderland to see the rarities of one Mr. Charleton at the Middle Temple, who shewed us such a Collection of Miniatures, Drawings, Shells, Insects, Medailes, & natural things, Animals whereoff divers were kept in glasses of Sp: of wine, I think an hundred, besids, Minerals, precious stones, vessels & curriosities in Amber, Achat, chrystal &c: as I had never in all my Travells abroad seene any either of private Gent: or Princes exceed it; all being very perfect & rare in their kind, espec(i)aly his booke of Birds, Fish: flowers, shells &c drawn & miniatured to the life, he told us that one book stood him in 300 pounds; it was painted by that excellent workeman whom the late Gastion duke of Orleans emploied [Nicolas Robert?]: This Gent:'s whole Collection (gathered by himselfe travelling most parte of Europe) is estimated at 8000 pounds: He seem'd a Modest and obliging person.[82]

He returned again on 11 March 1690 and 30 December 1691. Of particular interest to us was the visit to another Elysium on the Thames: Henry Compton's Fulham garden on the opposite side of London. The entry for 1 August 1682 reads: '& thence to *Fulham* to visite the *Bish*: of *London*, & review againe the additions which *Mr. Marshall* had made of his curious booke of flowers in miniature, and Collection of Insecta'.[83] Thanks to the recent publication of Prudence Leith-Ross's superb book *The Florilegium of*

Fig. 13: Marbled rose; Silk-vine; False acacia; Scarlet Turk's cap lily; Mullein moth larva; Sad dame's violet, from the Florilegium of Alexander Marshal (Royal Collection).

Alexander Marshal at Windsor Castle,[84] we can picture the biological world that existed in the minds of Evelyn's contemporaries, and sometimes also – albeit fleetingly and sporadically – in those garden pockets along the Thames

The garden was, in this sense, a fugitive ideal world. As Evelyn put it in the opening pages of the *Elysium Britannicum*: 'So that to define a Garden now, is to pronounce it *Inter Solatia humana purissimum*. A place of all terrestriall enjoyments the most resembling *Heaven*, and the best representation of our lost felicitie. It is the common Terme and the pit from whenc we were dug; We all came out of this parsly bed.'[85] Amid the felicity, any number of 'judgements' might suddenly materialize like a whale out of the Atlantic. In his Deptford Elysium, winged choristers were snared in 'Samson Posts Netts'; raging storms, putrid air, disease, and destruction breached the garden walls. And so within that ideal place, prone to decay from inside and decimation from outside, the orangery was the closest to a terrestrial paradise: a place of perennial verdure and miraculous cures. Safest of all from corruption was a collection of miniatures that could defy the smoke, the storms, the pestilence, death, and time itself. Anemones would flourish in the clean air of vellum; and fruit would ripen without the acrid taste of sea-coal smoke. Even petals might fall without flowers fading. And here at last, in peace and harmony, the mullein moth larva might crawl on a turk's cap, near a sad dame's violet, without damaging the moth mulleins and winter fruit of adjoining pages [Fig. 13].

NOTES

1 Evelyn, *Diary*, III, opp. 215.
2 Prudence Leith-Ross, 'The Garden of John Evelyn at Deptford', *Garden History*, 25 (1997), 145-6. The letter is from July 1658 and refers to 'the ravage of this winter upon my nursery'.
3 Evelyn, *Diary*, III, 214.
4 Ibid., 214-15.
5 Ibid., 215.
6 See *The Travels of Peter Mundy in Europe and Asia, 1608-1667*, ed. by R. C. Temple & L. M. Anstey, Hakluyt Society, V (1936), 95-6. See also *The Proceedings of the Linnean Society* (10 Jan. 1935), pp. 35-7, in which F. C. Fraser first identified the whale as an adult Atlantic Right Whale, *Balaena glacialis*. He commented that the drawing no. 2 depicts the tongue 'in an inflated and extended condition as commonly seen in decomposed Cetacea. This could easily have happened between Mundy's first and second visits to the carcass'; and that drawing no. 3 is inaccurate as regards feeding off a shoal of fish, but Mundy's description of the feeding mechanism is correct and perhaps one of the first true accounts.
   Judy Chupasko, Curatorial Associate at the Mammal Department of the Harvard Museum of Comparative Zoology, kindly confirmed that the drawing is of a great right whale, now *Eubalaena glacialis*. Peter Mundy seems to have misjudged the age, since 58 feet would make this creature close to the maximum adult length of 60 feet. Since the right whale spends much of its time in shallow coastal waters, it rarely ends up stranded; hence the storm of June 1658 may account for the Greenwich stranding. The original number of right whales in the world has been estimated at 100,000 to 300,000. However, the species has now become one of the rarest of large mammals; the total world population may be as low as 3000-2000. The eastern north Atlantic population is virtually extinct, and according to several recent authorities the present population in the western North Atlantic is only around 200-350; see *Walker's Mammals of the World*, 6th edn, ed. by Ronald M. Nowak (Baltimore & London: Johns Hopkins University Press, 1999), II, 963-8; and Lyall Watson, *Sea Guide to Whales of the World* (New York: E. P. Dutton, 1981), pp. 68-70. In Toronto's *The Globe and Mail*, 26 Feb. 2002, p. A13, a report of the birth of at least fifteen North Atlantic right whales off the coast of Florida raises some hope that the endangered species may rebound after the decline of the 1990s.
7 Evelyn, *Diary*, III, 215, n. 3, citing John Dryden, *A Poem upon the Death of His Late Highness, Oliver Lord Protector* (London, 1659), Stanza XXXV: 'But first, the Ocean, as a Tribute sent/That Giant-Prince of all her Watry Herd;/And th'Isle, when her protecting *Genius* went, Upon his Obsequies loud Sighs conferr'd.'

8 See Mark Laird, 'Parterre, Grove, and Flower Garden: European Horticulture and Planting Design in John Evelyn's Time', in *John Evelyn's 'Elysium Britannicum' and European Gardening*, ed. by Therese O'Malley & Joachim Wolschke-Bulmahn (Washington, D.C.: Dumbarton Oaks, 1998), pp. 171-219.

9 John Evelyn, *Fumifugium: or, The Inconvenience of the Aer, and Smoake of London Dissipated* (London, 1661; repr. 1772), p. 18.

10 Ibid., pp. 20-1.

11 BL Add. MS 78219: Evelyn to Sir Richard Browne, 22 Dec. 1665, quoted in Leith-Ross, 'The Garden of John Evelyn' (see n. 2 above), 146.

12 These were first published in Laird, 'Parterre, Grove, and Flower Garden', p. 218. The 1685 plan (now BL Add. MS 78628 B) was found in a folder of Wotton drawings and identified on internal evidence as Sayes Court.

13 BL Add. MS 78539: to Ralph Bohun, 3 June 1685, quoted in Leith-Ross, 'The Garden of John Evelyn', 147.

14 Leith-Ross, 'The Garden of John Evelyn', 146, comparing the 1664, 1679, and 1706 editions of *Sylva*.

15 Evelyn, *Diary*, IV, 357.

16 Ibid.

17 Ibid., 361-3.

18 Ibid., 364-5.

19 *Philosophical Transactions of the Royal Society*, no. 158 (1684), p. 559, with the addition of some modern botanical names for clarification.

20 Evelyn, *Diary*, III, 220.

21 Ibid., 316.

22 Ibid., 316-17.

23 Ibid., 477.

24 Ibid., 569. The ability to interpret portents in weather was obviously increased in hindsight, when Evelyn was revising his diary. The reliability of his meteorological observations is, however, largely borne out by other contemporary accounts which de Beer includes in his editorial notes.

25 Evelyn, *Diary*, IV, 446.

26 Ibid., 450.

27 H. H. Lamb, *Climate, History and the Modern World* (London & New York: Routledge, 1995), p. 229.

28 These figures are extracted from ibid., pp. 228-32, and with reference to Mary Dobson's book cited below.

29 Mary Dobson, *Contours of Death and Disease in Early Modern England* (Cambridge: Cambridge University Press, 1997), p. 2.

30 Ibid., p. 19. See also Richard Hamblyn, *The Invention of Clouds: How an Amateur Meteorologist Forged the Language of the Skies* (New York: Farrar, Strauss & Giroux, 2001), esp. p. 43 (Descartes's work on clouds, and the development of the thermometer and barometer), and pp. 12-34 (Robert Hooke's engagement with 'A Method for Making a History of the Weather', 1665).

31 Ibid., p. 14.

32 John Evelyn, *Elysium Britannicum or The Royal Gardens*, ed. by John Ingram (Philadelphia: University of Pennsylvania Press, 2001), pp. 45-6.

33 Ibid., p. 46.

34 Ibid., p. 47.

35 Ibid., p. 251.

36 Ibid., p. 56
37 Ibid., p. 57.
38 Evelyn, *Diary*, III, 81.
39 BL Add. MS 78628 A: plan of Sayes Court, [1653?], key no. 118.
40 See my discussion of the shift from the plan of the 1650s to the 1690s layout in Laird, 'Parterre, Grove, and Flower Garden', 215-19.
41 John Evelyn, *Kalendarium Hortense*, incorporated into *Silva*, 4th edn (London, 1706), p. 243: entry for June.
42 John Evelyn, *Directions for the Gardiner at Says-Court But which may be of Use for Other Gardens*, ed. by Geoffrey Keynes (Oxford: Nonesuch Press, 1938), p. 96.
43 Ibid., p. 97.
44 Ibid., p. 98.
45 Evelyn, *Diary*, V, 174.
46 Evelyn, *Elysium Britannicum*, p. 89.
47 Evelyn, *Directions for the Gardiner*, pp. 80-1.
48 Ibid., p. 96.
49 Keith Thomas, *Man and the Natural World: Changing Attitudes in England 1500-1800* (London: Allen Lane, 1983), pp. 274-5.
50 Evelyn, *Elysium Britannicum*, p. 92.
51 See Anthony Huxley, *An Illustrated History of Gardening* (London: Papermac, 1983), p. 173.
52 Evelyn, *Kalendarium Hortense*, p. 224: entry for January. See also *Directions for the Gardiner*, pp. 82-3
53 Evelyn, *Kalendarium Hortense*, pp. 233-4: entry for April.
54 Evelyn, *Elysium Britannicum*, p. 97, with description under no. 35.
55 Ibid., p. 97.
56 Quoted from Huxley, *Illustrated History*, p. 124.
57 Evelyn, *Elysium Britannicum*, p. 299.
58 Ibid., p. 299.
59 Ibid., p. 301.
60 Ibid., p. 307.
61 Ibid., pp. 311-12
62 Ibid., p. 254.
63 BL Add. MS 78628 A: plan of Sayes Court, [1653?], key no. 37.
64 Evelyn, *Elysium Britannicum*, pp. 254-5.
65 Evelyn, *Diary*, III, 399.
66 Evelyn, *Elysium Britannicum*, p. 92.
67 Thomas, *Man and the Natural World* (see n. 49 above), pp. 273-4.
68 Evelyn, *Directions for the Gardiner*, pp. 99-100.
69 John Evelyn, *Acetaria: A Discourse of Sallets* (London: B. Tooke, 1699), p. 137.
70 See Graham Parry, 'John Evelyn as Hortulan Saint', in *Culture and Culitvation in Early Modern England*, ed. by Michael Leslie & Timothy Raylor (Leicester: Leicester University Press, 1992), pp. 130-50.
71 John Prest, *The Garden of Eden: The Botanic Garden and the Re-Creation of Paradise* (New Haven & London: Yale University Press, 1981), p. 75.
72 Evelyn, *Diary*, IV, 481-2.
73 Evelyn, *Acetaria*, p. 132.
74 Ibid., p. 134.
75 Evelyn, *Diary*, III, 403.

76 Ibid., 497-8. For the implications of such observations and a comprehensive account of attitudes to animals, see Thomas, *Man and the Natural World*, esp. pp. 143-91.

77 Evelyn, *Diary*, IV, 462.

78 See Douglas Chambers's valuable discussion of the environmental, technical, and horticultural context in 'John Evelyn and the Invention of the Heated Greenhouse', *Garden History*, 20 (1992), 201-5.

79 BL Add. MS 78318: Wise to Evelyn, 9 Dec. 1693, quoted in Leith-Ross, 'The Garden of John Evelyn', 148.

80 Evelyn, *Elysium Britannicum*, pp. 451-2.

81 Evelyn, *Diary*, II, 133.

82 Ibid., IV, 531-2.

83 Ibid., 289.

84 Prudence Leith-Ross, *The Florilegium of Alexander Marshal at Windsor Castle* (London: Royal Collection Enterprises, 2000).

85 Evelyn, *Elysium Britannicum*, p. 31.

'A SUBLIME AND NOBLE SERVICE'

John Evelyn and the Church of England

JOHN SPURR

WHY was John Evelyn an Anglican? In many ways this is an artificial, even absurd, question; his status and his time, his family and his connections, all naturally inclined him to be a conforming member of the Church of England: but it was a question that Evelyn himself repeatedly raised. 'I am neither Puritan, Presbyter, nor Independent, that have scribbled this large letter,' he wrote to his cousin Thomas Keightley in 1651. 'You partly know what my Education hath bin; and how freely I have lived from compulsion, though I have wrestled with infinite temptations, enjoyed much Liberty, frequent in doubts, and reluctances as to matters of Conscience; and really, Cousin, it seemed ever to me a thing unreasonable that men should so diligently weigh their Gold, and take up their Religion on Trust.'[1] Elsewhere Evelyn asserted that he had 'bin none of the least conversant and curious in the search' for religious satisfaction from both people and books, and he exhorted his grandson to the study of theology, 'the most necessary and sublime' of all studies, so 'that you may be able to give an Account of your Faith, & Choise of your Religion, upon principles, solid and rational, and not because it is your countrys profession, onely'.[2] This was what Evelyn had done: he had decided for himself in matters of religion; and since, as he liked to remark, reason is reason wherever it is found, the Church of England would command his allegiance whatever her outward fortunes. The principles, 'solid and rational', which swayed Evelyn were the familiar ones offered by the seventeenth-century Church of England and its supporters. That church 'is certainly of all the Christian Professions on the Earth, the most Primitive, Apostolical, & Excellent'; it teaches the truths of primitive Christianity, recognizes the authority of scripture and respects patristic tradition, but simultaneously allows a real role to individual reason.[3] The Anglican church steers a via media between superstition and idolatry on one side and squalor and indecency on the other: 'I found in her alone the *Golden Meane*, neither too streite, nor too wide, but of just dimensions and admirable ... constitution,' as Evelyn told James Hamilton in 1671.[4]

Yet the Church of England had more to recommend it than this much prized 'reverent mediocrity'. To many the Church also had an emotional and spiritual appeal: in John Evelyn's words, 'the Religion of the Ch[urch] of England is a Sublime & noble Service, comely, and adequat to the glorious Object'.[5] These fine ringing phrases challenge us to understand what it was that Evelyn so valued in the Church of England. Does 'a sublime and noble service' hint at one of the Church's more ineffable qualities, its strange combination of different measures of sanctity, antiquity, and suffering? The word 'sublime', especially conjoined with 'the glorious Object', may evoke Evelyn's concern with the transcendent, a trait which has been more remarked upon of late in his writings about gardens and groves than in his more overtly religious works. Yet 'if there be an heaven upon Earth', for Evelyn, 'it is at the Holy Assembly & Action [of the holy communion] devoutly celebrated'.[6] Personal union with God was at the heart of Evelyn's piety. Out of his 'infinite goodness' God 're-news the opportunities of our re-union with him' in the holy communion which 'is the highest and most glorious Instance of it, that we are capable of on this side [of] heaven'.[7] A regular and fervent communicant throughout his life, Evelyn often exceeded his own ideal of monthly reception of the sacrament. The 'noble service' that Evelyn mentions is, of course, that of all Christians towards God: a dual obligation to offer worship to the creator and to live in accordance with God's revealed will. Introspective and pious, John Evelyn made a conscious decision to serve God in and through the Church of England. It is no easy matter to plumb the depths of anyone's religious life, but Evelyn has left more evidence than most. This at least allows us to begin by exploring two of his major preoccupations, preaching, and prayer, before tracing the evolution of his commitment to the English church.

Readers of Evelyn's diary will already know that his most obvious religious 'service' was his attendance at sermons. Page after page contains notes of sermons he has heard. Not that all readers are impressed; one complains that 'his diary becomes increasingly cluttered up with elaborate and tedious accounts of sermons, interspersed, as old age makes him drowsy, with apologies to the Creator for falling asleep'.[8] At Deptford Evelyn carefully attended to the two sermons preached in his parish church each Sunday, and when away from home he dropped in to hear a sermon wherever and whenever the opportunity presented itself. In the summer of 1674, for example, he and Samuel Pepys attended the court's Saturday night revels at Windsor and did not return to London until 3 a.m. on Sunday morning, but Evelyn was up early to hear the preacher at St Martins-in-the-Fields and 'the very same sermon, by the same preacher, I happn'd to heare againe at St Jamess [Palace] this Afternoon'.[9] It was not unusual for Evelyn to turn up at church without knowing whom or what he would hear from the pulpit, especially in the 1650s when 'a stranger' in the parish church might well preach 'somewhat mysteriously about predestination, & such high points', or even be an 'enthusiast', a rude mechanic, or a former trooper – although on such occasions Evelyn might turn a deaf ear and simply note, 'I minded him little.'[10] He certainly sought out preachers whom he respected. In April 1655 he walked to London 'on purpose to heare that excellent preacher Dr Jeremy Taylor on 14 Matt. 17'; and in March 1673 he set out for London 'to solemnize the Passion Week & heare the excellent Preaching which there constantly is by the most eminent Bish[ops] & Divines of the Nation, during lent'.[11]

In his diary Evelyn was generous with his praise and his condemnation of what he heard from the pulpit. Dr Tenison, for instance, gave 'an incomparable discourse perswading to the Love of God' and Dr Richard Owen preached 'a profitable and pathetic discourse'.[12] 'Excellent' and 'incomparable' figure prominently in Evelyn's lexicon of praise, but 'pathetic', in the sense of arousing pathos, was perhaps the highest compliment: William Lloyd, for one, was judged to have described the crucifixion 'with exceeding patheticalnesse'.[13] On the other hand, a curate's efforts could be dismissed as 'but weakely perform'd' or as pretentious; meanwhile an older divine might be castigated for preaching 'floridly, like a young preacher'.[14] In most cases, Evelyn's are the only opinions to survive on these particular performances. The diary entries are succinct, usually recording the preacher, his text, the gist of his text or sermon in a phrase, and a pithy judgement; for example, 'Dr White, Bishop of Peterborow on 26 Matt. 29. Submission to the will of God on all Accidents, and at all times, a very eloquent style etc.'[15] Yet attentive readers of the de Beer edition of the diary will have noticed that many such sermon reports are accompanied by injunctions to 'see your notes'. This was Evelyn's system of cross-referencing to the longer notes that he made on sermons. And we can follow the cross-reference because some of these notes survive in the Evelyn archive.

This manuscript is a bound folio volume of almost three hundred pages which contains substantial notes on sermons that Evelyn heard between 1650 and 1687. The calligraphic title-page offers a flourish of Greek and then the title 'A brief Accoumpt of divers Sermons recollected at my after Retirements, and begun Anno Dom[in]i MDCL'. Transcribed from other notes, these entries are written in the hands of Evelyn and amanuenses, vary in formality and length between a few hundred and a few thousand words, and in almost every case give the date, the place, the preacher, and his text. I estimate that there are entries on more than three hundred sermons.[16] These sermon notes are a wonderful adjunct to the record of the diary and confirm what we learn from that and other sources about preaching practice and the tenor of contemporary Anglicanism. For example, Evelyn's diary records that on 17 July 1670 his friend Dr Breton preached at Deptford 'that the whole duty of man consisted in Justice, mercy, humility', which sounds like a rather vacuous recommendation of moral duties and which might therefore only deepen the misgivings of those who suspect that the Restoration church had abandoned any meaningful Protestant soteriology. But the manuscript notes explain that these duties are what a man can and should do, but 'he cannot be a true convert, or a regenerate person of himself; tis by a supernatural Grace; yet we can pray for it, seeke it, & cooperate towards it, & so may not charge God foolishly, as the author of sinn'.[17]

Interpreting Evelyn's sermon notes is not without its difficulties. Evelyn honestly described them as 'Sermons recollected at my after Retirements' and wrote of his need 'to recall, and digest what I had heard'. The final notes vary in their 'distance' from what was actually said in the pulpit, and the preachers, although named, are subsumed within the prose summary of their sermon; there is virtually no praise or evaluation of the performance here. Presumably it was rare for a preacher to hit the 'pathetical' heights that might transport Evelyn and turn a sermon into a 'sublime' experience, but it is possible that Evelyn drew spiritual sustenance from 'digesting' the sermon in the privacy of the study and penning his own version. In several cases these sermon notes indicate that Evelyn had internalized the message, made it his own, and was now offering a free translation. Let me illustrate the point. In his diary for 27 October 1672 Evelyn extolled Robert Frampton as 'not onely a very pious & holy man, but excellent in the Pulpet; for the moving affections'. The sermon note for the same occasion gives nothing away about the preacher, but it discusses the text, Psalm 29.6: 'by walking here (& in most scriptures) is meant the whole conversation of man, the imaginations in his heart, as well as the actions of his hands, the bent & ayme of his studies, the politic contrivances of his braine, the crafty circumventions of his designes, the Covetous, Ambitious, Revengefull passions & affections of luxurious & sensual men'.[18] This is a seamless account, there are no ragged edges, almost no reference to the sermon's prior existence as a pulpit discourse; there is a pleasure in the language, the cadences roll off the tongue: perhaps, then, we should ask ourselves whether in this fully formed piece of prose we are reading the words of Robert Frampton or those of that indefatigable author of devotional works, that pious lay Anglican, John Evelyn?

That John Evelyn composed devotional works is well known, not least because such writings played a role in his intriguing relationship with Margaret Blagge. His self-consciousness as a devotional writer is evident from the scribal publication of several of these works (even if intended solely for her), and from his hope that some of his 'Private Devotions and Offices' would be printed.[19] While other gentlemen also composed and indeed published their own 'meditations', 'devotions', or scriptural 'paraphrases', it is rare for a seventeenth-century individual's spiritual life and devotional regime to be recorded in the kind of detail afforded by Evelyn's diary and archive. Much is already being discovered by scholars about the spirituality of Evelyn and of his family and friends.[20]

The prayers, hymns, confessions, ejaculations, meditations, psalms, and lessons which are to be found among Evelyn's papers were artfully woven together from scripture verses – line by line in many cases, ranging widely across different books of scripture – or they were more original compositions, inspired by the example of Anglican clergymen, particularly Simon Patrick and Jeremy Taylor. Evelyn composed his own versions of religious services, tying them to special seasons, the New Year or Lent, or to significant events, such as reception of the holy sacrament. In one manual, entitled 'The Wedding Garment', he provided a regime of self-examination and spiritual preparation which in every detail follows the many contemporary Anglican manuals for a 'worthy reception' of the sacrament.[21] Evelyn's devotional compositions match the mid-seventeenth-century ideal of 'prayer book piety'. We should perhaps note in passing that this was an ideal which was common to churchmen of many different generations, experiences, and theological alignments; thus in the spiritual field Evelyn could read, recommend, and emulate Anglican authors as diverse as Andrewes, Featley, Hammond, Pearson, Wilkins, Taylor, and Patrick.

The private or 'closet devotion' so strenuously advocated by the Church of England, and so close to John Evelyn's heart, taught its practitioners to dovetail private and public worship, to use the church's fasts, festivals, and sacraments as prompts for what went on in the privacy of the individual's chamber, and it trained the Christian in techniques of meditation and prayer so that he or she could eventually fly free of the phraseology of the clerical authors and find their own words and material for devotional purposes. Evelyn expected the Prayer Book to form a part of the devotional repertoire of private worship, but hoped that it would inspire rather than confine spirituality. He advised his daughter to read from a devotional book 'sometimes a part of some Meditation or Office of the Day' (meaning the Prayer Book) and then to offer prayer 'conceived sometimes by your selfe, as you find your Spirit tender & disposed, or else out of some devout Book'.[22] How Evelyn himself might have encountered the numinous can perhaps be appreciated from a letter to his son, John, on the eve of his first communion at Easter 1673:

Above all I conjure you that you be curious to observe the seacret breathings & motions of Gods holy spirit; that you do not in the least suppresse them, but give them your immediate furtherance whether they incite in you any pious thoughts, or checq any ill suggestions: It is a loving, tender & delicate Spirit. O make him yours

149

by all possible indearements, it will keepe your heart soft, and accompanie you with powerfull and mighty operations.[23]

This numinous piety was central to Evelyn's religion and to that of many other Anglican lay people and clergy. The operation of the holy spirit was never divorced from its Protestant context; it was neither allowed to degenerate into 'enthusiasm' nor to ascend to mysticism: it took its place in a practical and, at times, even visceral life of prayer. Evelyn's worthy communicant, for example, is instructed to 'contemplat on the passion of your most deare Lord, now represented in the Sacrament, imagining you see (as the Bread is consecrated & broaken & wine powred out) him bloodily extended & nayled to the Crosse'; Evelyn's prayers for the feast of the circumcision are even more sanguinary in their emphasis on 'Baptism the Type of this bloody Rite'.[24] Prayer of this kind was a vital component of a holy life, and a holy life was paramount. As he told his daughter, 'all our Reading & praying signifies nothing without the improvement of our lives, subduing passions, & increasing in all manner of heavenly Graces'.[25]

John Evelyn trusted in the efficacy of this 'holy living'. He consoled Lady Berkeley on the death of a child that 'holiness & a religious life' would lead to the reunion of all families – a poignant hope from a man so cruelly robbed of his own children.[26] He reminded his adolescent son that 'you are now entering upon the stage, that God is the Spectator, judge & rewarder of all your Actions'. But a holy life was more than the voluntary choice of a free agent: 'you are to looke upon your selfe as the purchase of the blood of the incarnate Jesus, that you are no more your owne, but his who so dearely bought you'.[27] In his own devotional life, Evelyn, who described himself as a member of the Reformed Protestant Church of England, instinctively shied away from vulgar misunderstandings of justification by faith alone and unhesitatingly recognized the human effort in the process of salvation. 'How shall I pleade thy Sacrifice, without an Oblation of something which Thou maist accept'? Evelyn asked of his Redeemer. 'The broken & the contrite Heart is that which Thou hast declar'd Thou wilt not reject [In margin: Psalm 51] – Here it is, Lord! Here it is, blessed be Thy mercy! Ah, receive it then; for it is from Thee alone, To Thee therefore I offer it, with a stedfast & resolute purpose to become more holy, & to serve Thee better.'[28]

It has been said that the 1650s were Evelyn's 'most formative and fertile' years.[29] Everything seems to have a beginning here – the book-collecting, the gardening, the obsessive writing which laid the foundations for most of his published and unpublished works, and indeed the Anglican piety. It was, incidentally, no less crucial a decade in the self-fashioning of the Church of England. A starting point must be Evelyn's decision to return to England: in December 1651 he wrote to his uncle that he was resigned to the loss of his education and ready to abandon hopes of public life if he could but attain 'repose … the thing in this world I so greatly ayme at'; 'A Friend, a Booke, and a Garden shall for the future perfectly subscribe my utmost designes'. But he feared 'the vertiginous condition of our poor Country' rendered it unsuited to the 'sons of peace'.[30] Two months later his cousin John Stephens could only welcome him back to 'this soe troubled and confused a countrey' with the confession 'that here is little that can invite you to a settlement; much to dissuade you from it', but at least he understood the dangers.[31] So why did Evelyn return if circumstances were so unpropitious?

Practical reasons – the need to establish an estate and provide for his wife and anticipated children – played their part, but so too did his hunger for 'a settled life', for that 'repose' in which he could embark upon more systematic study and work.[32] And beyond this, too, I sense an urge to come home in a spiritual sense, to come home not just to England but to the Church of England. Later Evelyn would claim that he had been an inquirer into religion for fifteen years, presumably from 1635 to 1650, before finding a safe haven in the Church of England. He first found that harbour at Paris in Sir Richard Browne's chapel where he encountered John Cosin and John Earle. Here intellectual conviction had been achieved. As Evelyn and Cosin told the Catholic convert Keightley in Paris in 1651, the Church of England was an autonomous church founded on the two testaments, three creeds, four general councils, and the first thousand years of the Christian church: the English church accepted the ideal of confession and acknowledged a spiritual real presence at the eucharist; it was the Church of Rome which erred in appropriating the label of Catholic to itself and denouncing other churches as schismatic. In support of his case Evelyn deployed not only Anglican apologists of the early seventeenth century such as Andrewes, Grotius, Prideaux, Laud, and White, but also divines of the current generation, like Taylor and Thorndike and of course Cosin himself. In short, Evelyn was present as the Church of England put the finishing touches to its ecclesiological understanding of itself as an autonomous Catholic church.[33]

But Evelyn's heart as well as his mind had been captured. In Paris Earle moved him to tears with his 'passionate' sermons, Richard Steward reassured him 'that God would certainly avenge his *Saints*, however deferr'd', and John Cosin's regular and wide-ranging sermons so impressed him that he recorded more than thirty of them in little over a year.[34] Cosin was convinced that for all the 'violent Stormes' the Church of England 'beares upon her more signally then any other, that I know does, the Marks of Christ, which when all is done will be our greatest glory'.[35] Identifying himself with the English church as it was portrayed to him, Evelyn naturally felt compelled to serve the church in its hour of need. Although he had no desire to be a martyr and made careful inquiries about his likely safety, he did feel a need to do more than witness for the Church of England in a Parisian chapel. Hence his return and within weeks his report to Cosin in Paris that there was 'Confusion in Religion' and 'Intemperance in Life' in England, but more cheeringly that he could 'number so many times 7000 that make more esteeme of their knees & their souls together, then to bow them downe to Baal'.[36] For the moment at least, the Anglican church and community still stood.

Evelyn was drawn to be a 'sufferer' for the church, to relish its *sub rosa* worship and gain strength from its position 'under the cross'. He habitually referred to the Interregnum as 'the great persecution' of the Church of England and used the language of the Early Church to describe how the English church was 'now in the Dens and Caves of the Earth' or 'the poore Church of England [was] breathing as it were her last'.[37] He returned with a letter of introduction from Earle to Henry Hammond, the doyen of royalist Anglican theologians, and with good connections to several other Anglican divines.[38] Evelyn lionized Jeremy Taylor, treating him as a spiritual guide, and praising his fortitude under persecution: 'Tis true vallor to dare to be undon,' he told the divine; you preach 'to us as effectively in your Chaines, as in the Chaire, in the Prison as in the Pulpit'.[39] In return Taylor observed of Evelyn's developing spirituality, 'I perceive your relish and gust of the things of the world goes off continually, so you will be invested with new capacities, and entertained with new appetites, for in religion every new degree of love is a new appetite.'[40] Not content to nurture his own piety in private Evelyn attended the semi-clandestine Book of Common Prayer services at St Gregory's by St Paul's, at St Mary Magdalen, Old Fish St, at George Wild's lodgings in Fleet Street, and at Exeter House chapel in the Strand. At Sayes Court he secured Richard Owen the sequestered minister of Eltham to read Prayer Book services of baptism and churching and to celebrate the eucharist.[41] Preaching to the Evelyn household, Owen instructed them that even in the Church of England's 'present diminution we should not faint, or despond, but reinforce our devotions to God'.[42]

In 1655 the Cromwellian authorities threatened to stamp out the last freedoms of Anglicans: we are preparing to bid farewell to 'God's service in this Citty or anywhere else in publique,' wrote Evelyn. He was perturbed but not despairing: 'Where shall we now receive the Viaticum with safety? How shall we be baptis'd?' he asked Taylor. 'The Comfort is, The Captivity had no Temple, no Altar, no King. But did they not observe the Passover, nor Circumcise, had they no priests & prophets amongst them?'[43] The lower the Church's fortunes sank, the more confident Evelyn was that it was the true church. This was a pronounced characteristic of his response to friends and acquaintances who went over to Rome, men like John Cosin, son of Bishop Cosin, whose motives were 'youth, discontent, Impatience, successe, men of unconstant braines, fierce biggotishness, and superficial Catechisme'.[44] He addressed his convert cousin Keightley with a splendid mixture of bravado, learning, and piety:

I heare you scandalized at the present calamity, and fate of our Church. I beseech you looke back upon the whole Eastern-Empire; the perpetual flux and period of all sublunary things; judg you of the truth of a Religion because it flourishes? Turne Musselman; suspect you the persecuted? renounc Christianity. Those that will live piously must suffer for it. The Church of the Jewes was once without Temple, without priest, without Altar, & without Sacrifice, and yet as deare to God as ever: was not the woman banished in to the Wildernesse, whilst the Dragon sought to devoure her production? Cousen, deceive not your selfe; there are yet seaven tymes seaven thousand which never bowed the knee to that Idol amongst us; nor is there yet so little life left in the Church of England, as that she should despaire of her recovery though if it should so please God to afflict her farther; the sufferings of this life (you know) are not worthy to be mentioned for the exceeding reward of the perseverant and in that weight of Glory which shall one day be revealed.[45]

Note the themes and the phrases that we have heard so often before, and the utter conviction that 'those that will live piously must suffer for it'.

This was not, however, the whole picture. John Evelyn's religious experience in Interregnum England was rather broader than he sometimes recognized. A Protestant Englishman, a bible-reading, plain practical Christian, first formed by godly Sussex and by Balliol, a man whose religious and moral values were solid and conventional, Evelyn practised his own teaching of patient submission to the often hard personal and national lessons delivered by God. He was open-minded enough to value good advice or doctrine whatever its source. So he had no qualms in recording that a 'stranger' preached at Deptford in September 1655, 'clearing the point of predestination, that God did not cause, but permit sin, for the punition of the sinner, by withholding his Grace; That Men and Satan were the cheife Instruments of hardning their owne hearts; & that final Impenitency onely, was the Sinn against the Holy Spirit, and so irremissible'.[46] And although he was uncertain whether his own vicar, Mr Mallory, was a Presbyterian or an Independent, he appreciated the good sense of his preaching that the only way to 'procure an interest in Christ … is … by faith, and universal obedience'. Later, in the diary, he admitted that Mallory 'ordinarily preachd sound doctrine, & was a peaceable man'.[47]

Intentionally or not, Evelyn sometimes muddied the water around religion in the 1650s. He portrayed himself as hearing royalist Anglican sermons only 'by stealth & connivance sometimes in churches, somtimes in privat chambers till his Majestie returne', and he stated that the pulpits were full of 'Independents and fanatics'.[48] Neither of these claims is true. Careful reading of the diary and a simple perusal of the sermon notes show that in the 1650s Evelyn heard preachers of many denominations. Indeed he did not encounter a 'phanatical' preacher at all until December 1653 – almost two years after his return to England. He heard 'Anglican' preachers with little difficulty. Perhaps more important is that the sermons he heard, whether 'Anglican' or non-aligned, tended to have a strong emphasis on practical Christianity. Evelyn was well aware of the spiritual dangers that accompanied too much reliance on either the free unmerited grace of God or the efforts of unregenerate human beings. What he wanted and what he heard in sermon after sermon from all quarters during the 1650s was a far more balanced message. He was a witness to a tidal change in English religious teaching: the preaching he heard in the 1650s was high-minded, morally earnest, indisputably Protestant, but no longer obsessed with the soteriological speculations of Calvinists or their opponents; practical Christianity of this kind was to be the prevailing spirit of the restored Church of England.

The liturgical and sacramental service of God outside the Church of England is a complex question. Evelyn clearly preferred the Book of Common Prayer to other liturgies: he tried unsuccessfully to keep 'my Eares incontaminate from their new fangled service', presumably a reference to worship constructed under the guidance of the *Directory*.[49] His description of saying farewell to the public service of God when the Prayer Book was being suppressed in 1655 implies that he did not believe God was properly served by other forms of worship. Yet this can hardly be the case. He owned and read Anglican works like Jeremy Taylor's *Collection of Offices* and must have known that many ministers conducted worship according to scriptural and Anglican models. The same is true of the sacrament of communion. The prospect of communion in the Anglican rite drew him to London, but he was prepared to receive the sacrament in other settings. As he complained, the sacrament was rarely celebrated anywhere in the 1650s; when a communion was celebrated at Deptford, Evelyn readily received even though this was not a Prayer Book service.[50] Perhaps a sacrament celebrated with fellow Anglicans according to the Prayer Book was the deepest expression of Anglican communion and identity, but any sacrament decently celebrated was a personal opportunity for union with God. As he had told his cousin, the church of the Jews had once been without Temple, priest, altar, or sacrifice, yet it was still dear to God and had survived in the hearts and devotions of individuals. In brief, Evelyn's Anglicanism permitted him to participate in the diverse parish religion of the 1650s and also allowed him to define 'Anglicanism' as a quality which he possessed irrespective of the outward status of the Church of England.

Evelyn's enviable ability to make the best of his situation is evident in other ways. In the same years that he bewailed 'the sad and deplorable catastrophe of our calamitous Country' and church, Evelyn was also buying land, paying visits, reading Machiavelli, Grotius, and Bacon, playing the connoisseur and artist, and penning playful appreciations of 'the evening circle [at Wotton], the onely sceane of ingenious divertisement, from where some Boccatian witt might furnish a better Decameron'.[51] He could not refrain from attempts to improve English taste and culture; he could not help himself from preaching to his countrymen about architecture and art. According to William Rand, his 'sprightly curiousity left nothing unreacht into, in the vast all-comprehending Dominions of Nature and Art'. So instead of the pious Anglican, we could just as easily focus upon 'the virtuoso in quest of a role', as Michael Hunter has described him: Evelyn the guilt-ridden translator of Lucretius and subsequently the author of a history of religion. Or Evelyn the gardener and proponent of a British Elysium. Or Evelyn the natural philosopher. For with Sayes Court his 'Tusculum', and the *Georgics* to hand, Evelyn's classical and humanist heritage offered him other routes besides Christianity to virtue, meditation, and contemplation of the transcendent.[52] These different facets of John Evelyn are not to be explained away: although they might jar, they were genuine. The winter of 1659-60, for instance, that extraordinary moment in the nation's history, also saw John Evelyn being torn in different directions. As the world collapsed about him, he took to his knees with Peter Gunning's Anglican congregation at their special Friday fasts to solicit divine forgiveness and protection. Yet at the same time he was busy writing the propaganda pamphlet *An Apology for the Royal Party* and wooing the Lieutenant of the Tower to join the royalist cause. Meanwhile the 'barbarous inundations, which the dissoluteness of this fatall conjunction universally menaces' also prompted him to discuss the creation of a philosophical college or 'monasticall society' with Boyle, Browne, and Hartlib.[53] All this is the frenetic activity of a man eager, nay desperate, to contribute, to play his part in public affairs, and his chance finally arrived with the restoration of the monarchy.

The question in 1660 was where to contribute? Evelyn had no interest in the 'splended things of the World', in power or wealth, he told Taylor, 'not because I have no ambitions to serve: but because I have too many'. Later in life he ruefully admitted that 'I have the vanity sometimes to think what I would do if I were a great man'.[54] He especially hoped that the government would 'make use of me in anything which relates to the church, though in my secular station'.[55] Although he never became a great man, Evelyn made his mark as a writer and translator, a leading light of the Royal Society, an effective Commissioner for Sick and Wounded Seamen in two Dutch wars, and a member of the Council of Trade and Plantation. His service of the

Church of England was less public: he certainly was not cut out to be a party man, not for him a role as lobby fodder for Archbishop Sheldon in the Cavalier Parliament; indeed, despite warm relations with politicians like Clarendon and Ossory and with leading churchmen, Evelyn does not seem to have been particularly close to Sheldon.[56] His bookish and introspective temperament ensured that he would never be a courtier – in fact he was deeply critical of the court's debauchery – but he was able to nurture a coterie of devout Christianity on the court's fringes in the 1670s. Meanwhile time and preferment to distant bishoprics were taking their toll of those Anglican luminaries who had so dazzled Evelyn in the 1650s, and new stars were rising in the pulpits of London. So although he took his son to Bishop Gunning for instruction before his first communion, Evelyn himself sought counsel and gained inspiration from the rising generation of divines.[57] As he hobnobbed with bishops, attended church and the Royal Society, waited upon the King and great men, Evelyn undoubtedly passed as an exemplar of Anglican godliness. In his letters, and presumably in his conversation, he castigated the rising tide of profanity and immorality and pointed to the unmistakable signs of divine anger: 'the late Chastisements of Pestilence, Fire or Sword which as yet (tho' greate, very greate) have been but gentle reprofes, considering our prodigious Ingratitude? Where is our Reformation in one point? After all the powerfull preaching, Sacred Ordinances, & a milion of distinguishing favours accumulated on us?'[58]

On the great religious questions of the day, Evelyn was impeccably Anglican and conventional. He lamented the 'prodigious liberty, and Barbarisme' which allowed the Baptists to 'swarme' in Cromwellian England and warned against the 'factious spirits' who disrupted Deptford parish in the 1670s.[59] With the benefit of a decade's hindsight, he judged the 1672 Declaration of Indulgence as detrimental to the Church of England: 'to let go the reines in this manner, & then to imagine they could take them up again as easily, was a false politique, & greatly destructive'. He regarded the bishops as partly to blame – 'they were then remisse, & covetous after advantages of another kind' – and he would only have conceded 'some relaxations … discreetely limited'.[60] This was still his position at the Revolution of 1688 when he was only willing to extend 'Indulgence to all sober dissenters; Socinians, Independents, & Quakers (in my owne Judgment) to be excepted: I am sure the first are scarsly Christian, & the latter of publique danger & unaccountable'.[61] Socinians were regarded as the tip of a 'rationalist' threat to revealed religion in Restoration England. Alarmed by a translation of Richard Simon's *Histoire Critique*, Evelyn appealed to Bishop Fell of Oxford for help in combating the 'fatal mischiefe this piece is like to Create'. Whether Simon is a papist, Socinian, or theist is unclear, 'but this is evident, that as for the H[oly] Scriptures, one may make what one will of them for him: He tells the World we can establish no Doctrine or principles upon them, and then, are not we of the Reform'd Religion in a blessed Condition? For the love of God, let our Universities (my Lord) no longer remain thus silent; It is the Cause of God, and of our Church'. Evelyn appreciated that Stillingfleet and Wilkins had confuted 'our modern Atheists', 'but as these start new & later Notions, or Rally & reinforce the Scatterd Enemie, we should I think march as often out to meete & outnumber them for the Men of this Curious & nice age, do not Consider what has been said or Written formerly, but expect something fresh'.[62] This is Evelyn's characteristic note, chivvying the Church of England's clergymen to pick up the cudgels and take the fight to the enemy, and above all to refute the claims of Roman Catholicism.

Evelyn was preoccupied by Catholicism, perhaps because he was more familiar with it than many of his contemporaries thanks to his years in Europe and his many Catholic friends and even patrons. He was indulgent towards his Catholic friends as individuals, having 'a very greate Charity for all who sincerely adore the blessed Jesus our comon and deare Saviour'.[63] Not that this prevented him from bombarding them with lengthy and learned letters full of the theological and historical case against Rome. He was irritated by the revival of old canards like the Nags Head ordination and he railed to the Countess of Clarendon against Nicholas Sanders' 'acursed lying Booke (the worst & the falsest that was ever written)'.[64] So proud was Evelyn of his part in the 1651 Paris 'conference' with Keightley on the relative merits of the churches of Rome and England that he had it professionally transcribed.[65] When Pepys showed him the 'strong box papers' which supposedly showed that Charles II had been a convinced Roman Catholic, Evelyn was dismissive of the Catholic arguments as 'without any force or reason, and a thousand times confuted'. But a few days later he sought to bolster Pepys by recommending one of Pierre Jurieu's weighty books as a handy 'Magazin' of anti-Catholic arguments.[66]

Evelyn was prepared to take a public stand. 'Tho' I am not a profess'd Divine, but a poore Christian & a Country Man,' he told Christopher Davenport the Franciscan, he was ready to take up his pen 'to assert a Truth which is very obvious'.[67] His translation at Clarendon's request of two Jansenist tracts as *The Mystery of Jesuitism* (1664) exposed, in Thomas Barlow's words, 'the prodigious villainies and atheism of the Jesuits, who really are the wild fanatics of the Romish faction'.[68] Two years later, John Tillotson's *Rule of Faith* capped his anti-Catholic work: 'never in my life did I see a thing more illustrated, more convincing, unless men will be blind because they will be so'.[69] But this was a war without end. In 1668 Evelyn debated with Davenport at Sayes Court and in 1671 he composed a long letter to Fr Patrick McGinn, whom he knew through Lord Treasurer

Clifford.[70] He sought and gained help from across the Church of England: the Calvinist Thomas Barlow sent 'a just Treatise, so full, so convincing, so accomplished, & to leave nothing to doubt or aske of'; but younger men like Stillingfleet and Tillotson also aided him.[71] As Evelyn remarked to Durel in 1672, all the arguments had long been exhausted, but the Church of England must keep fighting the Popish Hydra, our 'former weapons, for substance, improv'd or modified as the constitution and humor of the time, & conversation of men varie'.[72]

Popery was an urgent issue because it was the religion of James, Duke of York. On James's accession to the throne, Evelyn as a good royalist tried to suppress his anxiety for the Church of England. But when his own connections with Clarendon carried him into office as a Commissioner for the Privy Seal, Evelyn was soon on the horns of a dilemma. He missed meetings and appealed to Godolphin for help when asked to affix the seal to 'such particulars & Indulgences as concerne Religious matters etc inconsistent with our Oaths & statutes still in force'.[73] When James II changed political tack and Evelyn and other Anglicans lost office in 1687 they gave vent to their feelings by thronging to the Lent sermon at Whitehall to hear Thomas Ken exhort the people to persevere in the Church of England and prophesy 'that whatsoever it suffer'd, it should after a short trial Emerge to the confusion of her Adversaries, & the glory of God'.[74] Evelyn and the Church of England had been through this before. In their view the church was beleaguered in the later 1680s as it had been in the 1650s. The sermons that Evelyn heard were once again all about the afflictions of the church and the need to embrace suffering and trust in providence. As always, he was confident that the doctrine of the Church of England would 'never be extinguish'd, but remaine Visible, though not Eminent, to the consummation of the World'.[75]

As affairs moved to a crisis in 1688, Evelyn was active in defence of the church, visiting the seven bishops in the Tower and writing on 10 October to warn Sancroft of the dangers of Jesuit trickery: 'whosoever threatens to Invade or come against us, to the prejudice of that church, in Gods name, be they Dutch or Irish, let us heartily pray and fight against them'.[76] Evelyn could never pass up a chance to offer advice. In a suspicious-looking copy-letter dated '4 November 1688' which purports to be a response to an inquiry about English opinion on William of Orange, Evelyn expressed a preference for a Protestant regency, a 1689-style restriction on Catholicism in the royal family, and a system of regulating named itinerant Catholic priests. This disparate shopping-list of improvements and reforms, so typical of Evelyn's other flights of fancy, also included 'Indulgence to all sober dissenters'.[77] Meanwhile Evelyn's son John had, with his father's apparent blessing, joined William's camp and sent his father a narrative of his 'martial exploits', and what Evelyn described as 'the favourable Accesse you had to the Hero'. There was nothing sinister in this, and Evelyn remained a loyal royalist and Anglican while confident and grateful that 'poperie will be universaly declining'.[78] Over the winter of 1688-9 he visited Sancroft and suggested minor administrative improvements in the church, but could only watch as the Church of England drifted rudderless towards the rocks of the new Oaths of Allegiance and the Toleration Act. Everyone knew what the effects would be and Evelyn duly recorded them in his diary: the promotion of several of the churchmen whom he most admired and of some of his closest friends was no doubt welcome; but what he felt about the ejection of Sancroft and others is less clear-cut. He was relieved that a schism had been avoided, and ruefully observed that the clergy's own doctrine of passive obedience had now worked against them, but there is an undertone of frustration at the high-minded detachment of Sancroft and others.[79] Like so many of the English, Evelyn was a reluctant revolutionary, desperate to avoid popery, but equally reluctant to overturn the rightful succession.

In the years left to him, Evelyn's interest in spiritual and moral reform continued, as did his habit of setting clergymen to work, this time under the more formal auspices of the Boyle lectures. His service as a trustee of these lectures was just one of the ways in which he kept abreast of contemporary intellectual life: he helped Bentley, Wotton, and Woodward; he admired the exchanges of those two 'great men', Edward Stillingfleet and John Locke, but was shrewd enough to recognise that Locke was getting the better of the argument.[80] Meanwhile he was working on *Numismata*, transcribing his sermon notes, revising his diary, and preparing devotional works and advice for his beloved grandson. When John Evelyn died the Church of England was a very different institution from the church of the 1630s or even the 1660s, but Evelyn was no less at home in it.

Although he was 'no man of the church', Evelyn was 'a son of the church and greatly concerned for her'.[81] Not that his filial service was ever slavish or unquestioning. The Church of England suited his outlook: its structure, doctrines, worship, and sacraments spoke to both his head and his heart. The church let him be the sort of Christian that he wanted to be. It had the cachet of a minority church: in the Interregnum and under James II it was a church under siege, and indeed for much of the seventeenth century devout Anglicans, rightly or wrongly, perceived themselves as under assault on all sides, from Catholics, Dissenters, atheists, the apathetic, and the immoral. Evelyn's formative religious experience in the 1650s had perhaps fostered a taste for that mixture of self-congratulation and self-pity so often found in minority groups. He had no difficulty in imagining a church devoid of its temples, priests, and altars; he could and did at times practice that interior devotion, that private individual service of God, suitable to those living under persecution or in the midst of the ungodly.

Evelyn was his own man. Whether we judge by those divines whose friendship he cultivated as each generation gave way to the next, or by those whose writings he recommended and read, Evelyn was never in the pocket of a clerical clique, but enjoyed a wide and generous appreciation of the heritage of the English church. What else are we to make of this intimate of Archbishop Tenison who also welcomed the publication of a life of Archbishop Laud?[82] Evelyn's genuine admiration for the clerical state, his use of divines as spiritual counsellors, and his deference to ecclesiastical dignitaries have to be measured against his criticism of poor clerical performance, clerical wrangling, and weak leadership. We might be forgiven for suspecting that his stern judgments, moralizing, sermon notes, devotional compositions, spiritual counselling of others, and even his frequent allusions to his own lay status, reveal more than a hint of the cleric *manqué* about Evelyn. Whatever the merit of such speculation, he indisputably believed that every Christian was responsible for his or her own religion. As he told his grandson, the Christian had a duty to reflect and read, 'confirming you in the Christian faith, and inabling you to defend its doctrine, against the prophaneness & Errours of this Atheisticall & proflygat Age'.[83] An understanding of doctrine was significant, but as we have seen it was simply part of that full service which required holy living and the sublime moments offered by prayer and the sacrament. Although we have not yet sounded the depths of John Evelyn's piety, we have begun to discern some of the tensions that gave it its shape. The more we explore his religious life, the more we will see how one individual's remarkable archival legacy can illuminate the many small changes of emphasis and concern that make up the shifting sands of English religion in the seventeenth century.

NOTES

1 BL Add. MS 78298: to Thomas Keightley, 25 March 1651. I am grateful to the British Academy and the University of Wales Swansea for grants towards the cost of working on the Evelyn Papers.

2 BL Add. MS 78298: to John Cosin, 1 Jan. 1652; BL Add. MS 78515: 'Memoires for my Grand-son', fol. 19; also see Add. MS 78442: Evelyn to his son, 16 March 1673.

3 *Diary*, IV, 479.

4 BL Add. MS 78298: to Hamilton, 27 April 1671.

5 Ibid.

6 *A Devotionarie Booke of John Evelyn of Wotton, 1620-1706*, ed. by W. Frere (London: John Murray, 1936), p. 8. For the transcendent in groves see Evelyn, *Sylva*, 2nd edn (London, 1670), pp. 225-47, esp. p. 229. Evelyn's religious life has been described in F. Higham, *John Evelyn Esquire: An Anglican Layman of*

the Seventeenth Century (London: S.C.M. Press, 1968).

7   BL Add. MS 78442: Evelyn to his son, 16 March 1673. Evelyn's use of spiritual preparation before and meditation at the eucharist served as a spur to his religious zeal, see *Diary*, IV, 224.

8   John Bowle, *John Evelyn and his World* (London: Routledge, 1981), p. 3.

9   *Diary*, IV, 43.

10 Ibid., III. 82, 150, 147.

11 Ibid., III, 148-9; IV, 6.

12 Ibid., IV, 505; III, 378.

13 Ibid, IV, 630.

14 Ibid, IV, 56, 291, 560.

15 Ibid., IV, 505.

16 The volume is BL Add. MS 78364. I am preparing an analysis of these notes for publication elsewhere.

17 *Diary*, III, 552; BL Add. MS 78364, fol. 149. An earlier attempt to exploit Evelyn's diary as a source for the tenor of preaching is John Spurr, *The Restoration Church of England, 1646-1689* (New Haven & London: Yale University Press, 1991), ch. 6.

18 *Diary*, III, 629; BL Add. MS 78364, fol. [150].

19 BL Add. MS 78515, fol. 33ᵛ.

20 See 'Mary Evelyn and Devotional Practice', by Gillian Wright below; I am indebted to Dr Wright for sending me a copy of her illuminating chapter in advance of publication. See also Frances Harris, *Transformations of Love: the Friendship of John Evelyn and Margaret Godolphin* (Oxford University Press, 2003).

21 BL Add. MS 78385.

22 BL Add. MS 78440: Evelyn, 'Directions for the Employment of your time'.

23 BL Add. MS 78442: Evelyn to his son, 13 March 1673.

24 BL Add. MS 78385 H, fol. 5ᵛ; Add. MS 78385 A, fol. 6.

25 BL Add. MS 78440: Evelyn, 'Directions for the Employment of your time'.

26 BL Add. MS 78299: to Lady Berkeley, 12 Aug. 1682.

27 BL Add. MS 78442: Evelyn to his son, 13 March 1673.

28 BL Add. MS 78385 C, fol. 9ᵛ.

29 Graham Parry, 'John Evelyn as Hortulan Saint', in *Culture and Cultivation in Early Modern England*, ed. by Michael Leslie & Timothy Raylor (Leicester: Leicester University Press, 1992), p. 146.

30 BL Add. MS 78298, to William Pretyman, 2 Dec. 1651.

31 BL Add. MS 78316: James Stephens to Evelyn, 28 Feb. 1651.

32 *Diary*, III, 58-9.

33 I describe this process in *Restoration Church*, (see n. 17 above), pp. 115-20, 137-44; and 'Schism and the Restoration Church', *Journal of Ecclesiastical History*, 41 (1990), 408-24.

34 *Diary*, III, 37-9, 20; BL Add. MS 78364, fols 1-49.

35 BL Harleian MS 3783, fol. 150.

36 BL Add. MS 78298: to John Cosin, 25 April 1652; the reference is to I Kings 19. 18 and Romans 11. 4.

37 *Diary*, III, 214, 231.

38 BL Add. MS 78316; the 'Dr H' addressed can only plausibly be identified as Hammond.

39 BL Add. MS 78298: to Jeremy Taylor, 9 Feb. 1654.

40 *Diary and Correspondence of John Evelyn*, ed. by William Bray (London: Bohn, 1859), III, 105: Taylor to Evelyn, 12 May 1658. The original is now in the Houghton Library, Harvard University (MS Eng. 991).

41 *Diary*, III, 75, 76, 90. Richard Owen was not inflexible when it came to conforming to the Interregnum regime, being admitted to a living in Kent by the Triers in 1657, see A. G. Matthews, *Walker Revised* (Oxford: Clarendon Press, 1948), pp. 54-5.

42 BL Add. MS 78364, fol. [59].

43 BL Add. MS 78298, to Jeremy Taylor, 18 March 1655.

44 Ibid.: to Cosin, 1 Jan. 1652; for John Cosin the younger, see *Diary*, III, 26 n. 6, 632-6.

45 BL Add. MS 78298, to Keightley, 25 March 1651.

46 BL Add. MS 78364, fol. 67; *Diary*, III, 160.

47 BL Add. MS 78364, fol. 104: notes on sermons of 1658; *Diary*, III, 80-1.

48 BL Add. MS 78364, fol. 49; *Diary*, III, 60. Evelyn's presentation of the Interregnum must always be treated warily because from the 1680s onwards Evelyn weeded, revised, re-wrote, and perhaps reevaluated so much of the material for his own life, including his diary, sermon notes, and letterbook. My own portrait of the religious context of the 1650s can be found in my *Restoration Church*, pp. 14-20.

49 *Diary*, III, 67.

50 Ibid., 94-5.

51 BL Add. MS 78298, to Gaspar Needham, 16 June 1653.

52 Rand, quoted in J. M. Levine, *Between the Ancients and the Moderns: Baroque Culture in Restoration England* (New Haven & London: Yale University Press, 1999), p. 29; Michael Hunter, 'John Evelyn in the 1650s: a Virtuoso in Quest of a Role', in his *Science and the Shape of Orthodoxy: Intellectual Change in Late-Seventeenth-Century Britain* (Woodbridge: Boydell, 1995), pp. 67-97.

53 BL Add. MS 78298: to Hartlib, 4 Feb. 1660.

54 BL Add. MS 78298, to Taylor, 9 July 1661; Add. MS 78299: to Lady Sunderland, 7 Dec. 1688.

55 BL Add. MS 78298: to Cornbury, 9 Feb. 1665.

56 Hints of their relationship appear at BL Add. MS 78298: to Pierce, 20 Aug. 1663, to Obadiah Walker, 21 Aug. 1669, and *Diary*, IV, 73; Evelyn may have had a closer relationship with Sancroft, but clearly had a much warmer relationship with Tillotson and Tenison, both of whom he admired as preachers and pastors.

57 BL Add. MS 78442: Evelyn to his son, 16 March 1673; *Diary*, IV, 6.

58 BL Add. MS 78299, to Lady Sunderland, April 1679. For instances of Evelyn's own providentialism see *Diary*, III, 246, 311-12, 417, 464; IV, 512; and on the wider Anglican picture see my '"Virtue, Religion and Government": the Anglican Uses of Providence', in *The Politics of Religion in Restoration England*, ed. by Tim Harris, Paul Seaward, & Mark Goldie (Oxford: Blackwell, 1990), pp. 29-47.

59 BL Add. MS 78298, to Taylor, 9 Oct. 1656: to Bishop of Rochester, 12 Feb. 1672.

60 *Diary*, III. 608-9.

61 BL Add. MS 78299: to Lord –, Nov. 1688.

62 BL Add. MS 78299: to Bishop of Oxford, 19 March 1682.

63 BL Add. MS 78298: to his cousin George, 13 Jan. 1659.

64 BL Add. MS 78299: to Lady Clarendon, 27 Dec. 1686.

65 BL Add. MS 78366.

66 *Particular Friends: the Correspondence of Samuel Pepys and John Evelyn*, ed. by Guy de la Bédoyère (Woodbridge: Boydell, 1997), pp. 159, 162; *Diary*, IV, 475-9.

67 BL Add. MS 78298: to Davenport, 12 Jan. 1674.

68 *Diary and Correspondence*, ed. Bray, III, 143: Barlow to Evelyn, 21 June 1664; for Clarendon's part see BL Add. MS 78298: to Cornbury, 9 Feb. 1665; to the Dean of Ripon, 12 March 1666.

69 BL Add. MS 78298: to the Dean of Ripon, 12 March 1666.

70 For Davenport or Sancta Clara see, BL Add. MS 78298: to Davenport, 12 Jan. 1674, to Stillingfleet, 4 Aug. 1668; for Patrick McGinn see Evelyn's draft letter, 1671, BL Add. MS 78317, and Add. MS 78298: to Hamilton, 27 April 1671; for Clifford, see ibid., 14 Nov. 1671, and *Diary*, III, 577.

71 BL Add. MS 78298: to Thomas Barlow, 12 Dec. 1669.

72 Ibid.: to Durel, 2 Aug. 1672.

73 BL Add. MS 78299: to Godolphin, 23 May 1686; also see *Diary*, IV, 498, 504, 509-10, 512, 519, 540.

74 *Diary*, IV, 540-3.

75 Ibid., 478-9; also see 529-30, 531, 546-7, 576-7.

76 BL Add. MS 78299: to Sancroft, 10 Oct. 1688.

77 Ibid.: to Lord –, Nov. 1688.

78 BL Add. MS 78442: Evelyn to his son, 18 Dec. 1688, is the original letter, slightly amended in the letterbook copy in Add. MS 78299.

79 See *Diary*, IV, 648; V, 59.

80 BL Add. MS 78299: to the Archbishop of Canterbury, 10 April 1697; *Particular Friends*, p. 260.

81 BL Add. MS 78299: to Bishop of Oxford, 19 March 1682.

82 *Diary and Correspondence*, ed. Bray, III, 340-1: Evelyn to Tenison, 29 May 1694.

83 BL Add. MS 78515, fols 6-7. This begs the bigger question about the acquisition of the education and leisure needed to defend the church's doctrine. Evelyn did not have such high expectations of all women (see Gillian Wright's essay below) and he doubtless shared the pessimism of most clergy about the lower orders (see, for example, Patrick's sermon reported in *Diary*, IV, 229).

'ACTION TO THE PURPOSE'

Evelyn, Greenwich, and the Sick and Wounded Seamen

GILLIAN DARLEY

JOHN EVELYN'S APPOINTMENT as one of the four Commissioners for the Sick and Wounded and Prisoners of War in October 1664 brought together a number of strands in his life and satisfactorily confirmed him in royal favour. No other episode in Evelyn's life would so well combine his ambivalent personal ambitions, his humanity and his religious morality, his cultured and well-travelled eye, or his interest in administrative and built solutions to social and institutional problems. Organizing complex and highly urgent provision and keeping accurate records concentrated the often prolix Evelyn's mind as never before. The weight of huge responsibilities – immediate and all too visible – drew out an efficient, even exemplary, civil servant.[1] A new aspect of Evelyn's personality, deeply compassionate and impressively efficient, comes into sharp relief, but to date has been given comparatively little attention.

A stimulus to his work as a Commissioner from the earliest moment was his growing realization that a built solution existed to many of the problems with which he and his colleagues were dealing; a large naval hospital would provide long-term care and support for chronic invalids, the elderly, and even their dependents. A convinced if often disillusioned supporter of the monarchy, he had the breadth of experience and the architectural knowledge to conjure into being this statement of royal magnanimity. The conjunction of his experience as a Commissioner with his admiration for Paris, a fine and monumental city, suggested possibilities. Already in his anonymous tract, *A Character of England* of 1659 Evelyn had reflected unfavourably on London, which had 'nothing … of ornament, nothing of magnificence, no publique and honourable works, such as render our Paris and other Cities of France, renowned, and visited by all the World'.[2]

Evelyn, who turned forty in the year of the Restoration, was alternately restive and resigned to a bookish existence at the outer reaches of the court, as the months passed and he remained unrewarded for his tactful political behaviour and his loyalty to Charles II. Meanwhile Mary Evelyn's hopes (or perhaps, his) for a position at court, as Lady of the Jewels, were raised but then dashed. During the Interregnum her father Sir Richard Browne had been Evelyn's host in Paris and latterly his eyes and ears in France, looking out for books and in 1659 measuring out the Tuileries, the Palais Royal, and the Arsenal for him. Browne had returned after nineteen years overseas with empty pockets, but bearing the high regard of the exiled court, notably that of his 'true best friend', the Lord Chancellor Clarendon, and was quickly appointed Clerk of the Council, a position at the very heart of events.

John Evelyn's first official appointment was as a Commissioner of Sewers, a situation which he had already been offered in October 1658, and turned it down 'because there was an Oath to be taken of fidelity to the Government as now constituted without a King: I got to be excused'.[3] In October 1660 he could happily accept. But Browne's reassuring report of Clarendon's 'good satisfactions, as well to your concerns as to my owne', and of 'what esteem he professes to have for you',[4] was not to bear fruit for some time. Evelyn's next post, in May 1662, was rather more prestigious and interesting; he was invited to join the Commission for, as he put it, 'reforming the buildings, wayes, streetes, & incumbrances, & regulating the Hackny-Coaches in the City of London'.[5] His fellow Commissioners included John Denham, Surveyor of the Works, Hugh May, Paymaster of the Works, and Stephen Fox, Clerk of the Green Cloth and Paymaster of the Forces, as well as 'divers Gent: of Quality'. The committee, which met regularly until 1664, placed Evelyn in a forum which agreed on the urgency of major improvements to the fabric of London, in particular paving and cleaning major thoroughfares. Membership of the Commission gave him the status and the expertise to be nominated as a surveyor for the repairs to St Paul's and, all too soon afterwards, to draw up his own confident plan for the rebuilding of London, following the Fire.

The appointment to the second Commission for Sick, Wounded, and Prisoners in October 1664 was of an entirely different order of importance in Evelyn's life. His fellow Commissioners were Sir Thomas Clifford, given responsibility for Devon and Cornwall, Colonel Bullen Reymes, who was to look after Hampshire and Dorset, and Sir William Doyley, responsible for the eastern counties. These, together with Evelyn's own area of Kent and Sussex, were in the eye of the storm for any engagement with the Dutch. Each Commissioner received a salary of £300 per annum [Fig. 1].

The Commissioners with their Treasurer, Captain George Cocke, could learn from the experience gained by the first Commission for the Sick and Wounded, set up by Parliament in 1653 to deal with the aftermath of eleven years of war. Then the overriding problem had been obtaining supply. Naval debt had been mounting inexorably. Yet by December 1660 Samuel Pepys, Clerk of the Acts at the Admiralty, was able to report near solvency. This satisfactory position was short-lived. A second Dutch War was already indicated by the autumn of 1664, following sporadic engagements around

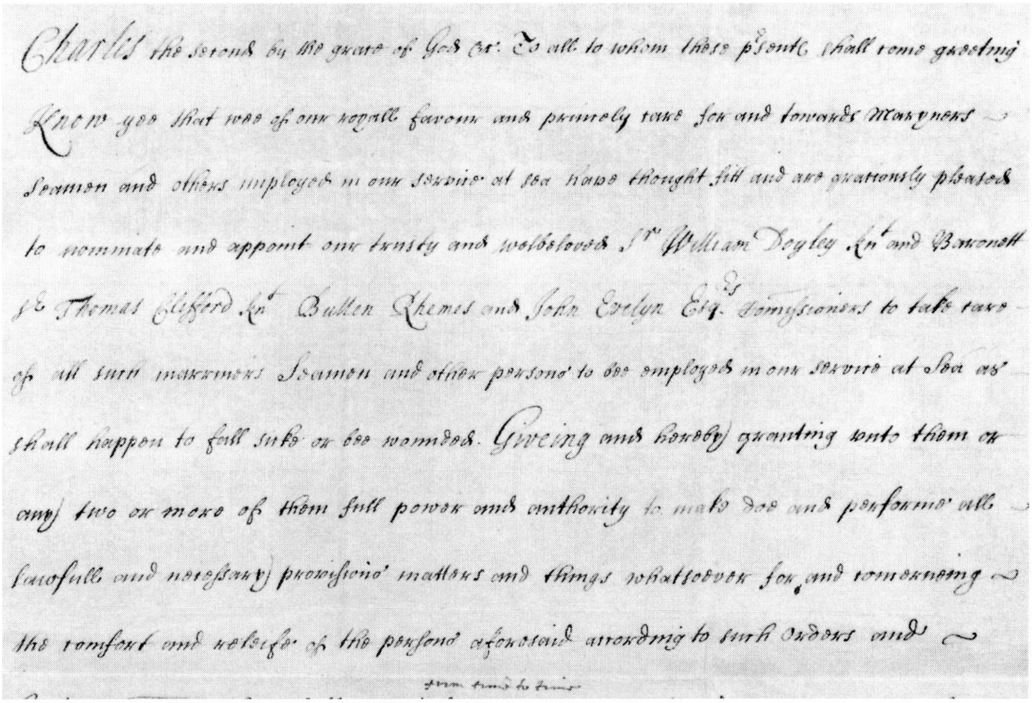
Charles the second by the grace of God &c: To all to whom these p'sents shall come greeting
Know yee that wee of our royall favour and princely care for and towards Maryners
Seamen and others imployed in our service at sea have thought fitt and are graciously pleased
to nominate and appoint our trusty and welbeloved Sr William Doyley Knt and Baronett
Sr Thomas Clifford Knt Bullen Rhemes and John Evelyn Esqs Commissioners to take care
of all such maryners Seamen and other persons to bee employed in our service at Sea as
shall happen to fall sick or bee wounded. Giveing and hereby granting unto them or
any two or more of them full power and authority to make doe and performe all
lawfull and necessary provisions matters and things whatsoever for and concerning
the comfort and releife of the persons aforesaid according to such Orders and
from time to time

Fig. 1: Commission for Sick and Wounded Seamen, 1664
(British Library, Add. MS 78320).

distant trading posts, and war was declared by the Dutch in the following January, by the English a month later. What seemed certain was that the fleets would meet in coastal waters and that every port had to prepare for an enormous influx of both wounded men and prisoners of war.

There was a flurry of meetings of the Commission in the early winter, to prepare accommodation, appoint officers and staff in the various towns, and to design administrative systems to handle large numbers, whether of the sick, wounded, prisoners, or dependents – the need for medical assistance or essential humanitarian relief being equally pressing. Half of all civil hospital beds were requisitioned, and in London the Savoy Hospital and Ely House were soon brought back into use. Hospital ships were a promising solution, but although several were requested, only the *Loyal Katherine* was at their disposal by the outbreak of hostilities. Typically, Evelyn found time to design a seal for the Commission depicting the Good Samaritan.

In January 1665, as the Dutch declared war, reality took hold; Evelyn went off to survey his district, of all the regions the most likely to be under sustained pressure. In March he received a harsh intimation of the horrors ahead when he went to meet the desperately burned survivors of the *London* which had blown up in an accident, killing many hundreds. In the coming months the man to whom he would turn with increasing regularity, and with growing pleasure in his company, was Samuel Pepys.

As a Commissioner Evelyn had to be hydra-headed; chasing for supply, billeting, and treating the sick, wounded, and prisoners of war. He was the single point of reference for all: encouraging, instructing, occasionally reprimanding a team of officers, surgeons, and physicians and their helpers in each of the many ports. Mayors and town officials had to be placated and reassured. The task required superhuman qualities to set against a continual and desperate shortage of funds for surgeons, nurses, landladies, and other contractors, and for payments to the men, let alone desperate widows and orphans. Added to this was the complex organization required for efficiently discharging the healthy, burying the dead, and identifying malingerers and false claimants. The onset of the plague – which had until then been held at bay by quarantine and water – ensured that 1665 would be Evelyn's *annus horribilis*. Circumstances and his own abilities and commitment soon ensured that he became the lead commissioner, to whom the others deferred and on whom they usually depended to represent their desperate case to the Treasury and at court. When he wrote to Robert Boyle at the time of his appointment, 'Farewell sweete repose, books, gardens and the blessed conversation you are pleased to allow',[6] he could not have envisaged what lay ahead.

The letters in the Sick and Wounded papers in Evelyn's archive vividly illustrate his central position in what became a prolonged crisis. In June 1665 Col. Reymes had called on the Commission's Treasurer Captain Cocke at Whitehall and reported back to Evelyn that 'he shrinks up his shoulder & says tis true, there is a Prive Seale signed for 20000; but it is a greate ways of and what to do in the interim is the question. Well I am resolved to try presently whether my rethorick will infuse pateince, and being but as yet a stranger amongst them tis possible for once, it may serve.'[7] Reymes, an entertaining and verbose correspondent, had many fewer prisoners and sick in his district (centred on Portsmouth) than either Doyley or Evelyn, yet his debt was already £1000. For his part, Doyley wrote to Evelyn that he was 'sorry to find you allso so full of troubles, my mysery continues and if an Engagement happen I am like to fill the country with sick men and Prisoners and all this I must abid without any great store of money sent me'.[8]

Their difficulties were both trivial and overwhelming. Bullen Reymes reported in a typical letter that he had no brandy for the sick (the only available anaesthetic) and that the nurses had barricaded the stairs against him, believing that he had received, and misappropriated, money from the King. The anecdotal evidence of major and minor incidents alike which sprang from his colleagues' correspondence merely corroborated Evelyn's own experiences. The Commissioners were snowed under by paperwork and the need to account for every penny while being themselves frequently in danger and increasingly in personal debt. The following year Reymes described, in a letter to Evelyn which also pointed out the need for another commissioner for Ireland, the special qualities he considered to be necessary for the job: 'Not every man, that can write well & ... accompt, is fitt for it. Hee must have judgement & discression how to behave him selfe in exegence, not possible to be foreseene & therfore no orders can be given before hand ... he must be of some resonable estate, that so his Poverty & want put him not upon indirect courses which we must answer for.' In Reymes' experience it had turned out 'a sad imployment'.[9]

By the autumn of 1665 Evelyn's own responsibilities included 2500 prisoners at Chatham, many of whom were sick, and over 600 sick and wounded men at Gravesend; while Dover Castle was full and those who could not be accommodated there were lying in the streets. He did not know what to do with captured Dutch officers, while the onset of the plague meant that private landlords were turning men out for fear of contagion. There was a desperate shortage of surgeons, both as a result of the poor and uncertain pay and as they themselves succumbed to illness. Petty disorder, with escaped prisoners and cheating landladies, was the norm. Evelyn's deputies and marshalls in the various towns around the Kent and Sussex coast were struggling with mayors and enraged citizens; letters of desperation poured down on Evelyn daily. There was no way of meeting even such basic needs as clothes for those washed ashore naked.

In a letter Evelyn wrote in early September to Clarendon's son, Henry Hyde, Viscount Cornbury, the Queen's Lord Chamberlain, he dealt in an eloquent first paragraph with niceties of the heart and the garden, and then adeptly changed tune. He begged leave 'to entertaine you a little with mine owne particular condition; since as contraries illustrate one another, it cannot but improve your happiness'. Then followed a terrible litany beginning with the estimated 7000 '(and possibly half as many more conceil'd)' who were victims of the plague that week in London and the incidences at Deptford (almost thirty households, including that of his nearest neighbour, which had finally persuaded his 'Couragious Wife', who was in the advanced weeks of pregnancy, to depart for Surrey). But

my Conscience, or something ... which I would have taken for my duty, obliges me to this sad station, 'till his Majestie take pitty on me, and send me a considerable refreshment for the Comfort of these poore Creatures, the Sick and Wounded Sea-men under mine Inspection through all the Ports of my district: For my owne particular, I am resolv'd to do my duty ... but the second causes should cooperate; for in summ, my Lord all will, and must fall into obloquy and desolation, unless our supplys be speedily settled on some more solid fonds to carry this important service on: My Brother Commissioner Sir William Doily after an accoumpt of £17000 is indebted above £6000, and my reckoning comes after it a pace: The Prisoners of Warr, our Infirmitories, and the Languishing in 12 other places: the charge of Sallaries to Physitions, Chyrurgeons, Officers, Medicaments, and Quarters, require speedy, and considerable supplies; lesse then £2000 a Weeke will hardly support us.

He begs Hyde to read his letter to his father, 'who I know has bowels, and may seriously represent it to his Majestie and my Lord high Treasurer'.[10]

In carefully measured language, using nothing but the baldest facts, Evelyn forcibly conveyed the burden borne by the commissioners over the past six months. The letter is testament to his literary, and diplomatic skills. Nevertheless he quickly wrote to Hyde again, three days later, to apologize 'for the Style, the Mistakes, and the length of mine of the ninth Instant', explaining that he had been unduly apprehensive; his servant was sick merely of 'a very ougly Surfeit' and he had been able to visit his wife who was 'within a fortnight of bringing me the seaventh sonne; and it is time my Lord he were borne; for they keepe us so short of moneys at Court, that his Majesties Commissioners had neede of one to do Wonders, and heale the sick and wounded by Miracle, 'till we can maintaine our Chyrurgeons'.[11] On reflection, Evelyn had decided that a little levity might better achieve his purpose.

Three weeks later, all levity again forgotten, he wrote to Sir Philip Warwick, secretary to the Lord Treasurer.[12] 'One fortnight has made me feele the uttmost of miseries that can befall a Person in my station, and with my affections: to have 2500 Prisoners, and 1500 sick and wounded men to take care of, without one peny of mony, and above £2000 indebted; It is true, I am but newly acquainted with buisinesses, and I now find the happy difference betweixt Speculation, and Action to the purpose; learning that at once, which others get by degrees'. Only the decision of the Duke of Albemarle and Lord Sandwich '(in pure Commiseration of me) ... to straine their Authority, and to sell (though not a full quorum) some of the Prizes, and breake bulke in an Indian-ship' had temporarily relieved the situation. Evelyn was becoming increasingly critical of the conduct of affairs ('is his Majestie resolv'd to maintaine the Armies of his Enemyes in his owne boosome?'), and by implication of the profligacy at court.

By October Evelyn had thrown all expedience and caution to the winds. He followed a letter to Sir William Coventry with one to the Lord Chancellor, assuring him that he had told Warwick and Coventry 'nothing which dos halfe reach the literall height of our deplorable Condition'; now it was 'nothing lesse than an indispensable necessity' that had caused him to approach Clarendon himself and ensure he was fully aware of the desperate situation.[13] Yet even in extremis Evelyn had hopes for the future – this time for himself; 'I am in hope that having pass'd through the most restlesse, perilous and intollerable condition which can happen to mortal-man, I may one day (through your Lordships favour) be thought on for some Employment which may not be the most servile under heaven.'

By the end of the month he had thrown all restraint to the winds, writing to Lord Ashley, Chancellor of the Exchequer, by now careless of his own reputation at court and future preferment, that the King was exposed to 'a greate deale of Dishonour, not to say Contempt, among those whose lives depend upon what they expect from us, and has beene indede very long due them'.[14] His Majesty was risking many lives (for, as Evelyn put it, the needs of the sick and wounded were 'altogether incompatible with delays'), as well as the 'Affections of a greate many men this winter'. He himself was at the end of his tether, prepared to risk all, 'I have no interest to serve … but my duty and common charity & therefore use no artifice in my expressions: I am frequently upon the place, converse with them and know their condition'. He begged Ashley to reserve a proportion of the prizes for the Commissioners' purposes, until 'some certaine Assignation be made us on the Royal-Ayde'.

The court was now at Oxford and his father-in-law kept him fully informed of the progress of his claims as they were passed along the chain of authority. Almost every key figure around the King and with any access to, or influence upon, supply had now received graphic and desperate letters from Evelyn. In early November he went in person to Oxford. The Duke of Albemarle, who had been in continual contact with Evelyn in these months, largely in connection with the accommodation of prisoners of war,[15] forcibly pressed the commissioners' case in a letter to Lord Arlington, while pointing out that responsibility for prisoners should be placed elsewhere.[16] Clarendon had discussed the problems of the Dutch prisoners with the King and was trying to get the Duke of York to intervene. The auguries seemed promising. Late that month, Browne reported encouragingly from the Council meeting of that afternoon, in which 'your good friend the Duke of Albemarle had soo fully prepared his Majesty and his RH that there was little difficulty upon the reading of your paper'.[17] But a month later Browne reported that all remained at a standstill.

In the long term, nothing was more essential (or economic) than purpose-built accommodation for the suffering men. Doyley had improvised hospitals in existing buildings at Ipswich and Harwich, as had Reymes at Porchester Castle. A barn at Gravesend had provided thirty extra beds in Evelyn's area, along with Chelsea Hospital and Leeds Castle near Maidstone, adapted to provide essential shelter for the prisoners. Even with provision in civil hospitals, the accommodation was woefully inadequate.

Throughout the period Evelyn still kept himself abreast of intellectual developments abroad. Samuel Tuke, Mary Evelyn's Catholic cousin and tutor to the children of Henry Howard, the future 6th Duke of Norfolk, was a warm supporter of his work, even while the two men carried on a permanent and often heated religious debate. From the moment of his arrival in Paris in 1664, Tuke sent Evelyn welcome and regular news. He kept him informed on matters of Royal Society interest (meetings of the French academies were, he had heard, tiresome, since they all talked at once, but he would endeavour to attend one) and on architectural topics such as Louis XIV's summons to Bernini. In return Evelyn sent him Robert Hooke's *Micrographia* and Thomas Sprat's history of their Society.[18]

In August Evelyn sent the newly arrived Wren to visit Tuke bearing a letter of introduction. Tuke wrote, 'I have & shall endeavour to serve him to the best of my capacity which God knows is very little, for I can neither furnish nor recommend.'[19] In October 1665 Tuke reported that Bernini had left Paris, leaving behind his designs for the finishing of the Louvre (and a marble head of the king), and in later letters that Dr.Wren and his companions would be returning with evidence of the 'wunders from here';[20] and again, 'he will be furnished with many of the *choisest plums* ... & I will so [order?] it that you shall have your share'.[21]

Evelyn was in little doubt that Chatham was the best location for a major naval hospital, and he began to seek a site. The diaries, substantially written up in the 1660s and therefore reflecting his current concerns, reveal him continually searching back in his memory for suitable models. The Abbot's Hospital in Guildford, a collegiate-style almshouse for twelve 'brothers' and eight 'sisters', all to be aged over sixty, was an example he knew well, since it was just a few miles from Wotton and built around the time of his birth. Another set of almshouses well known to him were those of the Trinity Company in Church Street, Deptford, originally built in 1613 as a single-storeyed foundation flanking the churchyard of St Nicholas and extended in 1664 on land given by Evelyn's father-in-law Sir Richard Browne (who later became Master of the company). Later Evelyn, who like his son John was to become a brother of Trinity House, commented 'it was a good & charitable work & gift but much better bestowed on the poor of that Parish than on the seamens widows, the Trinity Co being very rich & the rest of the poor of the parish exceedingly indigent'.[22]

Among other more appropriately scaled models available to Evelyn in 1665 were Christ's Hospital, Newgate, which had been built in the 1550s and would be burned in 1666, and the Charterhouse in Clerkenwell, to which he recorded a visit in 1657. On his travels earlier he had been impressed by the Charité in Lyons, and in Paris the Hôtel Dieu, the Charité, and the Hôpital S. Louis, the latter built between 1607 and 1612 for plague victims. He reserved his greatest admiration for the Gasthuis in Amsterdam, which was reputedly built by Queen Elizabeth I for English soldiers injured in the Netherlands. It was 'for state, order & accommodations one of the worthiest things that I thinke the world can show of that nature'.[23] Evelyn was very familiar with monastic and collegiate buildings in Oxford and elsewhere, and with palaces on their model such as Nonsuch (to which the Exchequer moved during the Plague) and Hampton Court.

During a coach-ride with Pepys in late January 1666, he revealed the extent of his plans. As Pepys noted, he 'intertained me with discourse of an Infirmery which he hath projected for the sick and wounded seamen against the next year, which I mightily approve of – and will endeavour to promote, it being a worthy thing – and of use and will save money'. Pepys was not, however, the first to hear of it.

A letter from Richard Evelyn suggests that the design for the Chatham infirmary had been drawn up early in the New Year. He thanked his brother for his letter,

by which I perceive […] proiect of the Infermary design'd at Woodcott hath so […] pleased his Matie that he hath ordered the finishing […] with speede, Mr Packer indeede wrote me word of meeting you at Chatham, & I now understand the occasion, I [doubt?] not, but his Invention, ioyned with your Direction will advance the Designe to be no lesse Profitable to the abatement of […] than Charitable for the Relief of the Distressed.[24]

Philip Packer, Paymaster of the Works, was also a friend from Oxford and the Royal Society and he had invited Evelyn to Nonsuch, where together they admired the extravagant and splendid Italianate ornament of the former palace, after which the brothers, their wives and children and friends spent several days together with 'extraordinary mirth & cheere ... after much sorrow & trouble during this Contagion, which separated our families'.[25] Out of that happy interlude came Evelyn's Chatham hospital scheme.

Browne had stressed how expedient it would be if Evelyn came back to Oxford to present 'your infirmary' to the King, backed up by the Duke of York's recommendation, but he also sounded a cautionary note: 'The King borrows money of all his servants. Ld. Arlington hath brought in 2000, Mr. Williamson 500, Mr Chiffing 500.'[26] Meanwhile Evelyn's deputy from Gravesend wrote to find out if he had yet been to Hampton Court (where the court had moved from Oxford), to present 'the proposals we discussed'[27] to the King. Four days later, in fact, Evelyn was there and was invited to return, which he did. Presumably he presented his scheme in greater detail on the second visit.

To date the only institution which Evelyn had designed was his Baconian college of like-minded men, 'who desire nothing more than to give a good example, preserve science & cultivate themselves, join in society together & resolve upon some orders and Oeconomie, to be mutualy observed', as he had written to Robert Boyle in September 1659.[28] His prototype Institute for Advanced Study was based on the Carthusian model (except that Mary

Evelyn was to be accommodated), with six cells, a chapel, and a central building serving for the library and dining room. Evelyn drew up a lengthy timetable for orders, prayers, recreation, gardening, and music, as well as sessions in which each would report back on their studies. Architecturally, the elevations of the scheme suggest his familiarity with the work of Roger Pratt and his contemporaries[29] [Fig. 2].

By 1665 Evelyn had become friendly with Hugh May and John Denham (to whom he dedicated the first edition of his translation of Fréart's *Parallel between Ancient and Modern Architecture* in 1664) from the meetings of the paving Commission. Wren and Hooke were already well known to him and he was often in their company at the Royal Society. But Evelyn's hospital was, thus far, little more than a rudimentary ground-plan for a vast quadrangle which he quickly sent to Pepys, with an apology for its hasty and rough nature[30] [Fig. 3]. The proposed scheme was to house five hundred and Evelyn estimated that the king's outlay of £1400 would be reimbursed within fifteen weeks by the savings made over the former arrangements. The practical and moral advantages included the treatment of sick men under a single roof, supervision leading to temperance, ease of administration and, eventually, the usefulness of the building as a workhouse or similar institution in peacetime. Meanwhile 'the clamours of landladys etc. to the reproch of the service will be taken away' and seamen would be entered and discharged and (if recovered) secured for further service. The building would be an engine of efficiency and economy.

The Duke of York had promised to pass the detailed scheme on to the King and, in addition, suggested a second hospital at Harwich. On 17 February Browne reported that 'Lord Arlington much desires to be fully informed of all the whole concerning the Hospital which he says shall be speedily put in hand; whatever shift is made for money', and three days later Evelyn presented the plan to the Commissioners of the Navy. Here for the first time he met a check to his ideas. The Commissioners, though encouraging, were also realists, telling him that they 'saw no money'. Evelyn and Pepys dined together after the meeting, Pepys no doubt reinforcing the message of caution.

Meanwhile Browne continued to send encouraging reports from White-hall, to which the court had now returned, in particular on the sustained interest of both the King and the Duke of York. Evelyn was encouraged to hurry down to Chatham 'to set out the ground & to proceed with all diligence'. His search for a suitable site was difficult because of ownership, ground levels, and other considerations, but he succeeded and sent a letter with detailed, and much refined, estimates to Pepys on 26 March.[31] Scaled down slightly, it still enabled him to point to enormous savings. Somebody must have advised him on the detailed costs and quantities, perhaps one of

Fig. 2: Evelyn's plan for a college, 1659
(British Library, Add. MS 78344).

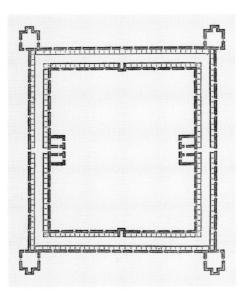

Fig. 3: Evelyn's plan for a
hospital at Chatham, 1666
(from *Diary and Correspondence
of John Evelyn*, ed. by William
Bray (1859), III, 176).

his fellow paving Commissioners or either of the two mathematicians and architect Fellows of the Royal Society, Christopher Wren or Robert Hooke.

Until then all the signs had been highly promising, but spring was the season of new naval engagements, the country remained at war, and supply was scarcely more forthcoming. From that moment onwards, nothing more was to be heard of the Chatham project – buried beneath an avalanche of weightier and intensely urgent problems. As far as Evelyn was concerned, it had been a highly worthwhile preparatory exercise towards an object of which he would never lose sight. The most tangible short-term result was the appointment in May 1666 of an extra Commissioner, Sir George Downing, with responsibility for the inspection of hospitals and arrangements for the prisoners. Evelyn did not welcome the appointment, noting that Downing had insinuated himself into favour, having once been a 'fanatic preacher' and 'not worth a groate, becoming excessive rich'.[32]

In spring 1666 the financial crisis facing the Commissioners was exacerbated with the prospect of unquantifiable numbers of new prisoners and sick and wounded. Men were now deserting after their recovery, so that the Commission had to perform a policing role in addition to everything else. By the autumn it was responsible for a vast number of permanent invalids, the exchange and repatriation of prisoners, and the pressing need to settle accounts. Finally it emerged that their Treasurer Cocke was a fraudster; he was eventually tried at the Guildhall in 1670.[33]

The end of the war in the summer of 1667 was far from marking the end of Evelyn's cares and responsibilities. From May all accounts had had to be authorized by the Treasury, making settlement slower still. As late as July 1669 he was called upon to explain his own Commission accounts, despite Pepys' admiration for his skills as a book-keeper, and they were not finally closed until 1675. When Evelyn published his retort to George MacKenzie's 1665 essay on the advantages of a solitary life over public service, *Publick Employment and an Active Life Prefer'd to Solitutde, and all its Appanages, Such as Fame, Command, Riches, Conversation &c. In Reply to a late Ingenious Essay of a contrary Title* (1667), he allowed his side of the debate to verge on ambiguity – conceding that when princes put private pleasure above duty the argument was severely compromised. It was in the dedication to Sir Richard Browne, and that exemplary man's long service to court and country, that the 'chief *design* of this little *Piece'* lay.[34]

In the meantime the country embarked on another ill-conceived war against the Dutch. In March 1672, just after the Stop at the Exchequer, Doyley, Reymes, and Evelyn were again appointed as Commissioners for Sick and Wounded Seamen and Prisoners of War. Inevitably they were better prepared for the task, systems of control were far more rigorous, and the new Commission document outlined their responsibilities with great care. Becoming less formal in its terms towards the end, it urged the Commissioners and their staff to hurry to the reception points and deal with everything 'in as husbandly and thrifty manner as you can', and be wary of deception.

A year later, despite all such precautions, Evelyn's district – which now included Margate and a number of towns which had not received the sick or prisoners before – was already £9000 in arrears. There was comfort to be gained from the fact that Lord Clifford, the new Lord High Treasurer, had formerly been one of the Commissioners. Nevertheless, Evelyn was still not immunized against the daily horror as his diary account of an operation on a seaman for a gangrenous limb showed; and in spite of his bravery and endurance the wretched man died.[35]

Another peace brought no change; many people were still owed money long after the sick had left. On the least suspicion of any mishandling of funds, all supply dried up. In the summer of 1674 even Evelyn found himself personally impugned, and the accusations were still rumbling on in 1681. The Navy Office wrote to say that the Deptford accounts were imperfect and in the draft of an unsent letter, probably to Danby, he tried to justify himself; 'never having been … deceived in the former war', he wrote, he was 'too confident of success in this'. The obvious moral rectitude of Evelyn, who as he protested had never accepted a bribe, colluded, or connived, was persuasive; he had been made desperately anxious by the responsibilities of his post, in which he had sustained the considerable personal financial loss of some £500.[36]

The single certainty to which Evelyn held throughout these tests of his honour and competence was the importance of an institution which could house the human casualties of war. He continued to search out exemplars: Hooke's new Bedlam, which he visited in April 1678, he considered 'magnificently built'. His thirst for information continually pursued his son, the younger John Evelyn, on his travels. While in Paris two years earlier he was sent to meetings of virtuosi, but found the conversation about 'philosophical things' beyond him. However, he reported, 'every week produces some new cut of the buildings and gardens hereabouts', and he listed the Carnavalet, Colbert, and Mazarin's mansions and the Invalides.[37] Louis XIV's great establishment was close to completion and Evelyn must have been unusually well informed on its appearance and plan.

Finally, over dinner on 14 September 1681, Evelyn heard the welcome news that Charles II planned to emulate the French king. Sir Stephen Fox, still a close friend, passed on the King's proposal that Chelsea College be bought for the nation and asked if he could mediate with the Royal Society in the sale of the building. Fox was acting on the King's obligation to his army of twenty years' standing, some of whom had enlisted in the 1650s, with a plan to provide both a barracks for a royal force and a home for deserving elderly soldiers – even though (or perhaps because) there had been fierce opposition in Parliament to a Standing Army.

Evelyn's ideas for the new establishment were fully formed: its personnel, accommodation (the library no doubt a personal touch), and rules (although much of the regulation followed military lines). Four hundred men would live under 'laws & orders as strict as in any religious convent', as he put it. Piety was enforced. The arcaded courtyards provided an architectural motif which served to emphasize the monastic model as well as being practical. Another model had now joined the Invalides, that of Kilmainham, founded in Dublin in 1680 by the Duke of Ormonde. By January 1682 the scheme for Chelsea had been refined on paper – thirty-two dormitories, each with a chimney, were proposed. In May, Evelyn accompanied Fox and Wren to see Archbishop Sancroft and present him with the 'plot & design'. Fox was the major funder and contributed over £13,000. At his funeral his generosity was ascribed to purely humanitarian motives: he had hated to see honourable men who had given their strength for the nation begging and 'did what he could to remove such a scandal to the Kingdom'. Wren, as Surveyor-General, was the architect, and Evelyn, we can assume, the man responsible for framing the brief, drawing on his extensive experiences as a Commissioner for the Sick and Wounded, his plan for the Chatham hospital, and his own wide and always current architectural knowledge. In August 1682 he went to examine the foundations at Chelsea having, as usual, prepared himself by an architectural visit to see a modest set of almshouses, Boone's in Lee, consisting of a school, chapel, and almshouse.[38] Wren's 'palatial' scheme was three-sided with a fine setting of canals and regal gardens, a Tuileries for old soldiers, but there were still no plans for the men of the King's Navy.

Yet Evelyn's perpetual pleas for a naval hospital had lodged somewhere in national and institutional consciousness, prompted by the example of the Invalides. James II signalled the availability of Webb's abandoned Greenwich Palace in 1687, and in late 1690 attention returned to the site when Dr Richard Lower's report on the feasibility of various sites and buildings for use as naval hospitals was refined to consider just two: Greenwich and Carisbrooke Castle, the latter quickly judged to be impractical. Meanwhile yet another Commission for Sick and Wounded Seamen (the fourth) struggled with many of the same problems of accommodation, organization, and supply. Evelyn, by now on the sidelines, had written to Lord Godolphin at the Treasury, pleading poverty: 'after so many yeares that their late Majesties so promiscuously scatter'd their Favours, I once little thought I should still be planting cole-worts. It was not so much a marke of my Ambition, as of my Desire to do my duty in something which might have been more usefull.'[39]

The palace was surveyed on June 1 1691 and the Commission asked to estimate the costs of conversion. Six weeks later the Queen gave consent. The Corporation of Trinity House (whose Master was now Samuel Pepys) were appointed Trustees, a caretaker was appointed, and work on the King Charles Building was planned to begin the following winter. The terrible aftermath of the Battle of La Hogue prompted Queen Mary to offer more buildings and land.[40]

The Queen's death on 28 December 1694 gave the project its necessary urgency. The involvement of the Surveyor-General, Sir Christopher Wren, along with Evelyn, Fox, and Pepys, meant that in many respects the model for Greenwich was bound to be Chelsea. The four men had been over this ground many times in the last thirty years, and despite their years all were to be involved in some major capacity in the planning and execution of the Royal Naval Hospital at Greenwich. Pepys wrote to Evelyn in November 1694 that he was 'recollecting his old thoughts on the matter', so that he could comment on the plans (as had Stephen Fox). He was confused by their variety, which ranged from a fairly basic conversion of the 'new' building there into an infirmary to a grandiose scheme with wings, 'an Invalides for the sea', with a complex range of accommodation for widows and orphans as well as the aged and incapacitated. There were many variants on the wards, dormitories, and cells, as well as the common areas. Commenting on that was, he considered, beyond his competence. Nevertheless 'the work is too near akin to me, and to the Commands I have heretofore had concerning it, to let it want any degree of furtherance I can give it'. He was adamant that the money must be voted from a Parliament 'as little disposed to deny as any I sat in'.[41]

In Evelyn's case the areas of expertise and experience that he had brought to Chelsea (via Chatham) were extended to Greenwich. In recognition of this, and of his huge burden so honourably discharged at the two Commissions, Godolphin was ready to offer him the appointment of Treasurer in February 1695.[42] Evelyn, despite his advanced age, accepted and went to look for examples, visiting Morden College in Blackheath, then under construction and perhaps designed by Wren. He was soon concerning himself, as a member of the committee, with the constitution of the Royal Foundation. He wrote to Samuel Travers, the Surveyor at Greenwich, that they need look no further than France; for 'if those of the *Invalides* ... were consulted; and especialy by what Orders and Establishment the *French* Kings late Colledge at *Brest* (erected about 10 Yeares since, upon a Designe in part like what is intended at Greenewich) is Govern'd; 'tis possible something might be found applicable to it'.[43] Alternatively the great London hospitals might provide suitable examples ('by long experience found sufficient') or the exemplary constitution of the little College at Dulwich.

Chelsea would provide a model for the establishment, 'according to which, the Edifice it Selfe ought at first to be proportion'd and contriv'd'; especially if his Majesty intended, as Evelyn felt he should, to set up a seminary for a thousand boys on the lines of the mathematical school at Christ's Hospital, with which Pepys was much concerned. Warming to the theme, he outlined a religious and educational programme for the boys, ending with a brief aside on the wider objective, an 'August and Princely Designe, for the comfortable Subsistance of Emerited and disabl'd Sea-men and Mariners, their Widdows, Children and Indigent Relations', and commenting that the support of such a project should be 'by an universal and permanent Contribution; which for being such, and of so universal Benefit, cannot but be very Easy and agreable to all the Nation in its great, and highest Concerne'.

In the New Year he wrote to William Vanbrugh, Secretary to the Commissioners of the Hospital, informing him that he would remain at Wotton (which was now his home) until such time as the building works had 'absolute neede of present Mony', having sent Travers his ideas on the Constitution. He had spent the last three months in London 'to no purpose'. In the meantime he deputed his son-in-law William Draper to appear on his behalf. Approaching his seventy-fifth birthday he recognized the danger signs; the loss of enthusiasm as a project matured and the difficulties in extracting the King's promised contribution, an annual £2000, from the Treasury. On 21 April 1696 the Grand Committee (including Draper, Evelyn's nephew William Glanville, and Pepys) had met to settle the plans for the hospital for seamen, and on 30 June at precisely five o'clock ('Mr Flamsted the Kings Astronomical Professor observing the punctual time by Instruments') Wren and Evelyn laid the foundation stone in front of the Commissioners. Godolphin was the first subscriber to pay his share: £200. But few followed his example, meetings were inquorate, and during the summer Evelyn told him that he was obliged to press the 'Greate persons' for money in person; 'accordingly I have ben with the *Duke of Shrewsbery*, Earles of Dorset, Pembroc, Lord Keeper, Lord Montague, and sevrall other noble men, knights and Gentlemen of the first Rank etc. My Lord, The[y] seeme to looke on and avoyd me, as one Carying the Pest about me.'[44]

Soon money worries became acute. With costs standing at £5000, by November the Treasurer had received just £800. Evelyn himself was out of pocket. After another six month stay in London on largely fruitless Greenwich business, he went back to Wotton. Draper, standing in for him, turned to Sir Stephen Fox. But Fox, who had dug so deep into his own pocket for Chelsea, could not do so again for Greenwich. The retirement of Godolphin from the Treasury at this moment was a blow. As subscriptions could not be relied upon, various duties had to be levied, from merchant seamen's wages, from the Navy, and from a number of other quarters. By November 1699 the finances were in credit, a major achievement on the part of Evelyn and Draper. Subscribers were rewarded with an (inaccurate) print of the Royal Naval Hospital. As the building progressed (with the King Charles building extended by the Base block behind) Evelyn was often on site. In June 1698 he went to see the foundations of the hall and chapel laid and in April 1700 he and Wren presented William III with the model and engraved plans of the hospital.

In August 1703 John Evelyn, approaching eighty-three years of age, finally resigned. The expenditure stood at £88,305 and receipts had been £89,879. The entire undertaking was in the black. The irony, as Christine Stevenson points out, was that the pensioners, here as at Chelsea, had paid for much of their 'charitable' accommodation themselves through deductions from their pay.[45] Yet the balance sheet was a triumph of careful accounting, and Evelyn's best answer to the small-minded officials who had hounded him for shillings as he had finalised his accounts as a Commissioner. On his retirement he joined the standing committee of governors (called directors), as did Fox, and handed the Treasurership formally over to his able and, by then, experienced son-in-law.

In early April 1705 the Evelyns mounted a family party to Greenwich, the hospital now being in operation and the building 'going on very magnificent'; eighty-one rooms were occupied and there were two hundred inmates. By the time of Evelyn's death the next year, there were three hundred pensioners in residence. William Draper's financial troubles as

Treasurer lay ahead.[46] But as John Bold points out, by the end of the first phase in 1710 '15 years of building work had produced half a Hospital – Les Invalides had been substantially completed in four'.[47]

After his active role in the initial planning of Chelsea, Evelyn's role at Greenwich was that of the experienced elder statesman and consolidator. He had no direct hand in the design or even the eventual constitution of the Royal Naval Hospital, but his leading role was a commemoration of, and a recompense for, the lost project for Chatham. Greenwich Hospital, in the capable hands of his protégé and friend Wren, would epitomize his ideals; it was Wren to whom he had dedicated his 1707 edition of Fréart's *Parallel,* with his own expanded *Account of Architects and Architecture*, and whom he praised there for his role in building, improving, and beautifying the 'Greatest Citty of the Universe'.[48] Evelyn's efforts, given form by Wren, to create a benevolent institution on a suitably generous scale and to provide England with an emblematic architectural set piece, reflected the long-held notions of responsibility, civic dignity, and order which he had outlined in *Fumifugium* many years earlier. He implicitly agreed with Wren's statement that architecture had its 'political use' and that 'publick Buildings [could become] the Ornament of a Country'.[49]

No single building better symbolized national pride and stability at the end of England's stormiest century than Greenwich Hospital, so easily mistaken (as Edward Hatton put it) for 'the Palace of a Prince [rather] than a Harbour for the Indigent'.[50] It is no exaggeration to give a great deal of the credit for that achievement to John Evelyn.

NOTES

1 J. J. Keevil, *Medicine and the Navy 1200-1900*, 4 vols (Edinburgh & London: Livingstone, 1957-63), II, 80-113.
2 In *The Writings of John Evelyn*, ed. by Guy de la Bédoyère (Woodbridge: Boydell, 1995), p. 79 (in which Evelyn disguises himself as a French visitor to London).
3 Evelyn, *Diary*, III, 223.
4 BL Add. MS 78306: Browne to Evelyn, 16 April 1661.
5 Evelyn, *Diary*, III, 318-19.
6 BL Add. MS 78298: to Boyle, 23 Nov. 1664.
7 BL Add. MS 78320: Reymes to Evelyn, 13 June 1665, from 'Paynters hall'.
8 Ibid.: Doyley to Evelyn, 10 July 1665, from Colchester.
9 BL Add. MS 78321: Reymes to Evelyn, 11 Feb. 1666.
10 BL Add. MS 78298: to Cornbury, 9 Sept. 1665. I have followed Douglas Chambers's transcription of this and the following letter, which he has generously allowed me to consult, ahead of publication.
11 Ibid.: to Cornbury, 12 Sept. 1665. The 'son' was to be a daughter, Mary.
12 Ibid.: to Warwick, 30 Sept. 1665.
13 Ibid.: to Clarendon, 2 Oct. 1665.

14 Ibid.: to Ashley, 26 Oct. 1665.

15 BL Add. MS 78320; including suggestions (17 Sept.) that Dutch prisoners be kept on board captured ships off Gravesend, and (27 Sept.) 'I understand Leeds Castle is a very fitt place for … Dutch prisoners', but insisting (4 Oct.) that none be quartered at Woolwich, Greenwich, or yards where 'the Kings servants are building of shipps'.

16 Ibid.: Albemarle to Arlington 4 Nov. 1665.

17 BL Add. 78306: Browne to Evelyn, 29 Nov. 1665.

18 Ibid.: Tuke to Evelyn, 11 July 1665.

19 Ibid.: 12 Aug. 1665.

20 On the basis of these links between Evelyn, Tuke, and Wren, Lisa Jardine has confirmed that Wren's Letter 'to a Particular Friend' was addressed to Evelyn; see Lisa Jardine, *On a Grander Scale: the Outstanding Career of Sir Christopher Wren* (London: HarperCollins, 2002), pp. 234-47. For the 'Letter', see Christopher Wren jr, *Parentalia: or Memoirs of the Family of Wrens* (London: T. Osborn & R. Dodsley, 1750), p. 351, and Lydia M. Soo, *Wren's 'Tracts' on Architecture and Other Writings* (Cambridge: Cambridge University Press, 1998), pp. 103-6.

21 BL Add. MS 78306: Tuke to Evelyn, 13 Jan. 1666.

22 Evelyn, *Diary*, III, 577.

23 Evelyn, *Diary*, II, 45-6.

24 BL Add. MS 78302: Richard to John Evelyn, n.d. [early 1666]. The original has suffered damage and some loss of text.

25 Evelyn, *Diary*, III, 426-8.

26 BL Add. MS 78306: Browne to Evelyn, [illeg.] Jan. 1666.

27 BL Add. MS 78321: Griffiths to Evelyn, 25 Jan. 1666.

28 BL Add. MS 78298: to Boyle, 3 Sept. 1659.

29 Michael Hunter, *Establishing the New Science* (Woodbridge: Boydell, 1989), pp. 181-4.

30 *Particular Friends: the Correspondence of Samuel Pepys and John Evelyn*, ed. by Guy de la Bédoyère (Woodbridge: Boydell, 1997), pp. 52 and 336: Evelyn to Pepys, 31 Jan. 1666 and fig. 3.

31 Ibid, pp. 60-5: 26 March 1666.

32 Keevil, *Medicine and the Navy*, II, 106; Evelyn, *Diary*, III, 444-5.

33 Keevil, *Medicine and the Navy*, II, 109.

34 *Public and Private Life in the Seventeenth Century; the Mackenzie-Evelyn Debate*, ed. by Brian Vickers (Delmar, N.Y.,: Scholar's Facsimiles and Reprints, 1986).

35 *Diary*, III, 610. One of Evelyn's deputies in the field was Samuel Pepys's perpetually needy brother-in-law, Balty, Balthasar de St Michel, based at Deal. He deluged Evelyn with hysterical letters: by May 1673 he was at his wits end, had 'pawned my credit' and owed £1250; by the following year his life was at risk (BL Add. MSS 78321-2: 9, 17, 27 May 1673, 1 March 1674). But a colleague suggested that he was being less than honest and had failed to share out earlier payments: 'it is no wonder that Mr Michel should write soe, who cares not what he doth, or says. And I cannot expect better fare from him then other people' (BL Add. MS 78322: Elnath: Hannam to Evelyn, 24 March 1674).

36 BL Add. MS 78322: Evelyn to –?, n.d.

37 BL Add. MS 78301: John Evelyn jr to his father, 15 Feb. 1676.

38 Evelyn, *Diary*, IV, 269-70, 288-9.

39 BL Add. MS 78299: to Godolphin, 31 July 1691.

40 John Bold, *Greenwich: an Architectural History of the Royal Hospital for Seamen and the Queen's House* (New Haven & London: Yale University Press, 2000).

41 *Particular Friends*, pp. 253-4: Pepys to Evelyn, 7 Nov. 1694.

42 BL Add. MS 78305: William Glanville jr to Evelyn, 12 Feb. 1695: 'to acquaint you that some ... since I put your Papers into my Ld G[odolphin's] hands desiring him to lay them before the King when his Lopp went next to Kensington his Lopp receiv'd them very kindly & order'd me to put them into the King's ... tho they have not yet been read I hope you will find a better effect of his ... yesterday he came to me & told me he had spoke to his Majesty in your behalf ... be Treasurer of Greenwich Hospitall which by reason of your vicinity to that town ... would be very fit for you especially since it would be a place of no manner ... I desird his Lp to tell me what your salary would be he said he thought it would not exceed 300L but would not deserve to another above 200L but in regard to you he thought the king would allow 300 he desird your answer speedily for he had not yet mentioned it to the rest of the Lds of the T[reasury] till he heard your resolution. ... Now I think I need say nothing to invite you to accept my Lds kindness with all cheerfullness it being an honorable Post & so ... your Charitable disposicion without mentioning many other real advantages ... I will therefore expect to hear from you tomorrow.'

43 BL Add. MS 78299: to Travers, 29 Dec. 1695.

44 Ibid.: to Godolphin, 3 Aug. 1696.

45 Christine Stevenson, *Medicine and Magnificence: British Hospital and Asylum Architecture* (New Haven & London: Yale University Press, 2000), p. 67.

46 For Draper and Greenwich, see also Carol-Gibson-Wood, 'Susanna and her Elders: John Evelyn's Artistic Daughter', below.

47 Bold, *Greenwich*, p. 136.

48 BL Add. MS 78299: to Wren, 20 Feb. 1697; Roland Fréart, *A Parallel of the Antient Architecture with the Modern*, trans. by John Evelyn, 2nd edn (London, 1707), dedication.

49 Wren jr, *Parentalia*, p. 351.

50 *New View of London*, 2 vols (London, 1708), II, 746.

JOHN EVELYN: REVOLUTIONARY[1]

STEVEN PINCUS

JOHN EVELYN'S EPITAPH records that he lived 'in an age of extraordinary events and revolutions'.[2] Of this Evelyn himself was well aware. When, in the 1680s, he came to rework his journal, Evelyn pointed to 'the effects of that comet 1618' which initiated an era of 'prodigious revolutions' in Europe, an era that had not yet come to an end.[3] While he was an enthusiastic supporter of the Restoration of 1660, he also looked forward with a caution tempered by long experience in politics to the events of 1688-9. Less than a month after the landing of William of Orange, he proclaimed that 'it looks like a revolution'.[4] In a letter to his son John jr who had taken up arms in support of the Prince of Orange, the elder Evelyn referred to 1688 as *Anno Mirabili*, noting emphatically that 'every moment is pregnant of wonders'.[5] Evelyn hoped fervently that 'a Parliament of brave and worthy patriots, not influenced by faction, nor terrified with power, may produce a kind of new creation amongst us'.[6] To promote just such a revolutionary regime, just such 'a new creation', Evelyn had himself penned an agenda for action. Writing in November 1688, he called not for the deposition of James II but for a revolutionary transformation of English society. He sketched out a plan to 'render this nation as happy as humane endeavour were with the blessing of God, capable to make it'.[7] Many, not all, of Evelyn's aspirations were achieved by the revolutionary regime. In the following decade he referred fondly to the events of 1688-9 as 'the wonderful Revolution'.[8]

Evelyn's call to transform English society in 1688, not just to transform or limit England's king, sits uneasily with the consensus of scholarly assessments. Virginia Woolf describes Evelyn as a conventional 'country gentleman of strong Royalist sympathies'.[9] Christopher Hill insists that Evelyn's 'loyalty was to church, order and property rather than to the person of the king'. It was thus possible for Evelyn to 'gloomily accept 1688 as the lesser evil'.[10] In this assessment of Hill's, if in no other, Jonathan Clark is able to agree. Evelyn's reaction to the events of 1688-9, Clark assures us, was that of a 'royalist'.[11] From the 1640s onward, Michael Hunter argues, John Evelyn showed 'an unwavering loyalty to the monarchy as the embodiment

185

of political stability'.[12] Evelyn, we can be sure, notes Richard Greaves, 'was in no sense a radical'.[13] W. G. Hiscock, in his critical biography of Evelyn, concludes that Evelyn was a Tory both because he supported the interests of 'small landowners' and because he adopted the political opinions of his patron Sidney Godolphin.[14] Craig Rose has recently claimed that John Evelyn's political views 'had something in common with those of unambiguous Jacobites'.[15] Given the steadiness and fundamental conservatism of John Evelyn's politics, then, it is hardly surprising that Joseph Levine has found that Evelyn 'played no role in the great events of 1688-9'.[16]

This image of John Evelyn as committed unwaveringly to the monarchy and Church of England, as standing against rather than for any profound alteration in English society, coincides perfectly with the vast majority of assessments of the events of 1688-9. The lively British and continental debate about the meaning and significance of the Glorious Revolution took a decisive turn with the publication of Edmund Burke's *Reflections on the Revolution in France* (1790). Far from transforming English politics and society, the events of 1688-9 restored normality in church and state after the unfortunate disruption of the reign of James II. 'The Revolution was made to preserve our ancient indisputable laws and liberties, and that ancient constitution of government which is our only security for law and liberty', Burke informs his readers. 'The very idea of the fabrication of a new government is enough to fill us with disgust and horror. We wished at the period of the Revolution, and do now wish, to derive all we possess as an inheritance from our forefathers. Upon that body and stock of inheritance we have taken care not to innoculate any cyon alien to the nature of the original plant.'[17] It was Burke's views, not those of his radical Whig antagonist Richard Price, which Thomas Babington Macaulay confirmed in his monumental *History of England*. Unlike continental revolutions, Macaulay assured his readers, 'our Revolution' was 'strictly defensive'. There was no hope for reform or transformation in 1688-9. 'As our revolution was a vindication of ancient rights, so it was conducted with strict attention to ancient formalities,' Macaulay explains, 'in almost every word and act may be discerned a profound reverence for the past.' In short, 'to us who have lived in the year 1848, it may seem almost an abuse of terms to call a proceeding conducted with so much deliberation, with so much sobriety, and with such minute attention to prescriptive etiquette, by the terrible name of revolution'.[18]

While twentieth-century historians have deployed less evocative language in their accounts of 1688-9, they have largely confirmed the assessments of their Whig forbears. There were 'no new ideas' in the Revolution of 1688-9, G. M. Trevelyan assures us. As a result 'the spirit of this strange Revolution was the opposite of revolutionary'.[19] 'Whatever modifications we may make to the classical Whig interpretation,' concedes Lord Dacre, 'in the end it is difficult to contest Macaulay's thesis that the English Revolution of 1688 saved England from a different kind of revolution a century later.'[20] For Jonathan Scott the significance of 1688-9 was that 'at last it restored, and secured, what remained salvageable of the Elizabethan church and state'.[21]

The range of Evelyn manuscripts now housed and catalogued in the British Library makes it possible to re-evaluate John Evelyn's politics, and in so doing to raise questions about the standard interpretation of the events of 1688-9. Against the view of the unwavering loyalist John Evelyn and a profoundly traditionalist England facing the uncomfortable reality of an aggressive and innovative Catholic monarch in 1688, I will suggest that Evelyn, and perhaps most Englishmen and women as well, were deeply disappointed with the Restored monarchy. That disappointment led Evelyn to call for a complete reorientation of English foreign policy, English political economy, and English religious life. Evelyn's revolutionary memorandum of November 1688 focussed less on constitutional arrangements or justifications for political resistance – a topic of so much recent scholarly debate – than it did on reorienting English society and culture. In fact he hoped that the events of 1688-9 would transform English politics and English society. I am suggesting that we look beyond his own guarded pessimism about post-revolutionary society – a pessimism no doubt borne out of his dashed utopian hopes of 1660 – to his aspirations for social transformation. I am suggesting, along with Joseph Levine, that we realize that John Evelyn as well as a great number of Englishmen and women 'did not like to be thought of as rebels … even as [he and] they adopted the possibilities of modernity'.[22] Evelyn's new idea in 1688 was that England could no longer be saved by narrowly conceived political or theological solutions. Perhaps we could better understand what was revolutionary in the Glorious Revolution if we similarly widened our interpretative focus.

John Evelyn was a young man at the outbreak of the Civil War. While he never took up arms for the King, his royalist sympathies were clear by the end of the 1640s. He looked back on the 1630s as a golden age. 'Never was there either heard or read of a more equal and excellent form of government than that under which we ourselves have lived during the reign of our most gracious sovereign's Halcyon days,' Evelyn proclaimed in his first publication.[23] His return to England in the 1650s did not signal approval of the new regime. He condemned the Protectorate of 'that archrebel Cromwell',[24] calling it one 'of the bloodiest tyrannies and most prodigious oppressors that ever any age of the world produced'.[25] Throughout the 1650s Evelyn worked tirelessly to promote the return of Charles II. He sent intelligence to the exiled King and his ministers,[26] wrote political pamphlets condemning the commonwealth regime, and attempted to persuade his school friend Colonel Herbert Morley to betray the Tower of London to the royalists.[27]

Unsurprisingly Evelyn looked to the possibility of the Restoration with unbridled enthusiasm. Charles II, because he had been 'mortified by so many afflictions, disciplined by so much experience, and instructed by the mis-carriages of others', was clearly the person 'most excellently qualified to govern' England.[28] Evelyn twice reassured Englishmen and women that the 'virtues and morality' of Charles II and his two younger brothers surpassed those of 'the most refined family in this nation'.[29] As a result, he was con-fident that under the restored monarchy 'the humble man will have repose, the aspiring and ambitious, honours. The merchant will be secure; trades immediately recover; alliances will be confirmed; the laws reflourish; tender consciences considered; present purchases satisfied; the soldier paid, main-tained, and provided for; and, what's above all this, Christianity and charity will revive again amongst us'.[30]

Evelyn's youthful optimism and unqualified support for Charles II did not, however, survive the 1660s. Observing Charles II and his government at close hand, occasionally serving his king in minor capacities, Evelyn became well aware that his aspirations would be dashed. Far from ushering in an era of political and cultural revival that he had hoped for, the restored monarchy, he came to believe, brought with it political and moral decay. Riding in a coach in January 1666 with his friend Samuel Pepys, he talked of 'the vanity and vices of the Court, which makes it a most contemptible thing'.[31] After the Fire of London and the disastrous Dutch raid on the Medway in June 1667 he was convinced that 'our ruin [is] approaching and all by the folly of the King'.[32] His near millenarian optimism dashed, he never recovered his respect for Charles II and his regime. Charles II's court 'was corrupted with the basest of men, pimps and knaves, who in time perverted his debonair temper with dissolute principles and there was no virtue at the bottom', he lamented on the eve of the Revolution of 1688. 'It all resolved into ease and luxury and with no regard to present or future farther than to put off impendent evil during his days, though at the certain ruin of all that should come after.'[33] Significantly his cultural analysis, his insistence on the moral malaise brought in with the restored monarchy, was, as Abigail Williams has recently shown, the hallmark of Whig rather than Tory cultural analysis in the late seventeenth and eighteenth centuries.[34]

John Evelyn did not respond to his disappointment with philosophical retreat. He did not act the part of a conventional Anglican royalist either by uncritical support for the regime or by adopting a lifestyle of contemplative withdrawal. Instead, after a brief political flirtation with the Catholic Lord Treasurer Thomas Clifford, he began to make new friends. While the attitudes recorded in his diary prior to his copying them over in the 1680s are of uncertain value, the notes of his acquaintances do provide a good guide to his activities in the 1670s. These reveal some surprising alliances. His most frequent dining companion, and one of his closest friends in the 1670s, was the Whig politician and eventual Lord Mayor Sir Robert Clayton.[35] Not only did Evelyn invariably dine with Clayton when the two were in London, but he also spent several days at Clayton's newly purchased country house at Morden.[36] The diary makes little mention of the topics he and Sir Robert discussed. However, Evelyn defended his Whig friend – a friend who described himself as an opponent of tyranny, a proponent of religious liberty, and a 'brave defender of the liberty and religion of his country'[37] – as a 'discrete magistrate and though envied, I think without much cause'.[38]

During the Exclusion Crisis Evelyn developed an intimate friendship with the prominent Whig politician the Earl of Essex. It was at the earl's 'earnest invitation' that he spent several days at Cassiobury in the spring of 1680.[39] Evelyn several times visited Essex in his London home where they conversed 'alone in his study'.[40] While Essex no doubt admired Evelyn for his gardening expertise, he also saw fit to discuss 'particulars of state relating to the present times'. He had a sympathetic listener. When Essex was dismissed from the Privy Council, 'being no great friend to the D[uke of York]', Evelyn commented that his 'integrity and abilities [were] not so suitable in this conjuncture'. Far from disparaging this Whig magnate, as did many an Anglican royalist during the Exclusion Crisis, Evelyn heaped praises upon him as 'a sober, wise, judicious and pondering person', who was 'very well versed in our English histories and affairs, industrious, frugal, methodical and every way accomplished'.[41]

Evelyn's friendships even extended to the ideological heart and soul of the Whigs. Even though he came to criticize the Earl of Shaftesbury as 'crafty and ambitious', it is clear that prior to the Tory reaction of the 1680s they had developed something of a friendship. They visited each other socially several times.[42] In the mid-1670s Evelyn had his son collect gardening advice for Shaftesbury while he was in Paris.[43] He developed a deeper and more long-lasting friendship in this period with Shaftesbury's secretary, John Locke. The two first came into contact when Locke replaced the deceased Benjamin Worsley on the Council of Trade, of which Evelyn was an active member.[44] His first impression was that Locke was 'an excellent learned gentleman'.[45] Greater intimacy bred greater appreciation. In the 1690s, Evelyn gushed to Samuel Pepys about Locke's *Essay Concerning Human Understanding*, claiming that 'so rare and excellent a piece' ought to be required reading for all intelligent readers.[46] He came to refer to Locke as 'our friend',[47] and urged that a medal be created to honour him since 'none will envy [his] being named among the most learned and deserving'.[48]

Unsurprisingly he placed John Locke among his short list of recipients of presentation copies of his *Numismata*.[49]

Given these associations, and the fact that Evelyn's brother George served as a Whig M.P. for Surrey in all three Exclusion Parliaments, it is perhaps to be expected that his own political views were not those of an Anglican royalist. While his criticisms of Charles II and his policies were always more temperate than those of the extreme Whigs, criticisms they were nonetheless. Evelyn, like the opposition leaders in the 1670s, worried that Charles II's army would not be used against foreign enemies but for 'another design'.[50] Similarly he expressed concern that the Cavalier Parliament was 'growing now corrupt and interested with long sitting and court practices'.[51] While he believed the authors of the 'papers, speeches, libels, publicly cried in the streets' took 'too shameful a liberty' in their denunciations of the Duke of York, he confessed that 'the people and Parliament had gotten head by reason of the vices of the great ones'.[52] Evelyn thought the spectacular revelations of the Popish Plot by Titus Oates, 'a vain and insolent man', were certainly exaggerated but contained 'something really true'.[53] Evelyn's political conclusions in 1679 bordered on the revolutionary. 'Unless we alter the entire scheme of our late politics, and go upon another hypothesis,' he wrote to his friend Sidney Godolphin, 'we shall run into a sudden and inevitable conclusion.'[54]

The First Whigs notoriously failed to achieve their ends. John Locke went into exile. Essex ostensibly committed suicide. Charles II and the Tories gained the ideological upper hand. Yet Evelyn did not become an advocate of the Tory reaction. Instead, he continued to enunciate his criticisms, always in a tone of moderation; doubting for example the legality of the surrender of London's charter in 1683, and noting that 'divers of the old and most learned judges were of opinion that they could not forfeit their charter'.[55] After the charter was surrendered, Evelyn remarked that he was 'not so well satisfied with these violent transactions and not a little sorry his Majesty was so often put upon things of this nature against so great a city, the consequences whereof might be so much to his prejudice'.[56] He similarly lamented the replacement of Lord Chief Justice Pemberton, 'the very learnedest of the judges and an honest man', with George Jeffreys, the staunchest of Tories, 'the most ignorant, though the most daring' man on the bench.[57] He had no stomach for the Rye House Plot to assassinate the King and Duke of York, but much sympathy with the alleged plotters and their grievances. Essex and Lord William Russell, Evelyn thought, were merely 'endeavouring to rescue the King from his present councilors and secure religion from Popery, and the nation from arbitrary government, now so much apprehended'; they were men who disapproved of 'some late councils and management of affairs in relation to France, to Popery, to the persecution of Dissenters'.[58] He even thought the republican Algernon Sidney, despite his being 'obstinately averse to government by a monarch', had 'very hard measure', praising him for his 'great courage, great sense, great parts, which he showed both at his trial and his death'.[59] Indeed his actions in the immediate aftermath of Lord Russell's execution were hardly those of an Anglican royalist, a Tory, or a future Jacobite. He invited to his house Russell's brother, Colonel John Russell, his aunt the Countess of Bristol, and his cousin the Countess of Sunderland.[60] With Lady Sunderland, whose opinions and commitments were invariably Whiggish despite her husband's notorious political vacillations, Evelyn maintained a 'long and worthy friendship'.[61]

Despite his profound disappointment with Charles II, Evelyn greeted his brother's accession with optimism and tempered enthusiasm. Like most Englishmen and women he was willing to look past James II's Roman Catholicism and focus upon his political qualities.[62] As soon as the old king had died, Evelyn wrote to his wife that 'certainly the prophane buffoons will be all discarded; the state and oeconomy of the court brought into a better form'. He hoped, perhaps a bit naively, 'that the King will not be so easy to the French as men thought'.[63] John jr quickly dashed off a poem celebrating the recent accession.[64] To his diary Evelyn, who was to become one of the new king's commissioners of the Privy Seal, confided that he 'begins his reign with great expectation and hopes of much reformation as to the former vices and prophaneness both of court and country'.[65] Like most in England, he revelled in James's promise not to alter the constitution in church or state, and thought his first six months as king were an unqualified success. 'I find that infinite industry, sedulity, gravity, and great understanding and experience of affairs in his Majesty,' he wrote in September 1685, 'that I cannot but predict much happiness to the nation as to its political government, and if he so persist (as I am confident he will) there could nothing be more desired to accomplish our prosperity, but that he were of the national religion: for certainly such a Prince never had this nation since it was one.'[66]

But James II did not so persist. After the defeat of the Duke of Monmouth's religiously-inspired rebellion in July 1685, Evelyn found very little to celebrate and much to castigate in James II's regime. When he met Judge Jeffreys upon his return from the trials of the rebels, Evelyn commented that the newly appointed Lord Chancellor was 'of nature cruel and a slave of this court'.[67] He praised the House of Commons for querying whether James could dispense with the oaths statutorily required of army officers.[68] James continued to use his dispensing power, the legality of which Evelyn very much doubted, and thus compelled the commissioners of the Privy Seal to ratify his actions. But Evelyn chose to absent himself, explaining to his friend Sidney Godolphin that 'I never have, so never will I (by the grace of God) do anything unbecoming an honest man'.[69] Inevitably the King was forced to sack his increasingly intransigent commissioners in favour of the 'zealous Roman Catholic' Lord Arundel of Wardour.[70] Evelyn objected vigorously to the creation of the new Ecclesiastical Commission, which he noted was given the 'full power of all ecclesiastical affairs in as unlimited a manner, or rather greater, than the late High Commission Court, abrogated by Parliament'.[71] When the Ecclesiastical Commission suspended Evelyn's friend Henry Compton from his duties as Bishop of London, the diarist noted the action was 'universally resented'.[72] Evelyn was no more enthralled with the Ecclesiastical Commission's forced eviction of the Magdalene College fellows, an eviction that only demonstrated that 'princes have long hands'.[73] Evelyn was disgusted by the King's creation of 'a mighty land army' that 'was doubtlessly kept and increased in order to bring in and countenance Popery'.[74]

Evelyn did not believe that James II was pursuing a few bad policies. He was, in fact, convinced that the King had broken the promise he made at his accession and was pursuing 'violent courses' toward the 'destruction of an excellent government both in church and state'.[75] While he was pleased with the acquittal of the seven bishops in June 1688, he did not rest content that an Anglican Revolution had taken place. In August, he counted himself among 'the whole nation' who were 'disaffected and in apprehensions'.[76] When James II appeared to reverse course in the autumn, abrogating the hated Ecclesiastical Commission, restoring the Magdalene College charter, and rescinding the writs to elect a packed Parliament, he still did not regain confidence in his prince. He noted with alarm that James II had 'called over 5000 Irish, 4000 Scots' to bolster his army and 'retains the Jesuits about him'. All of this, he recorded, 'gave no satisfaction to the nation, but increasing the universal discontent, brought people to so desperate a pass as with utmost expressions even passionately seem to long for and desire the landing of that Prince [of Orange], whom they looked on as their deliverer from popish tyranny'.[77]

Evelyn, like a large proportion of the English nation, had ceased to trust the king or his government. New policies could not satisfy them. Only a radical reorientation of English politics and English society could yield improvement. Evelyn, who had been informed about the Prince of Orange's plans by his friend Thomas Tenison in early August,[78] prayed on 31 October for 'his Majesty to hearken to sober and healing counsels'.[79] After William landed, Evelyn feared the 'beginnings of our sorrows, unless God in his mercy prevent it'. He hinted that it was no longer possible for James to correct the problem. 'Nothing in likelihood', Evelyn noted, could promote 'some happy reconciliation of all dissensions amongst us' except 'a free Parliament'.[80] Within a month, the former royalist conspirator had decided to throw in his lot with William. After spending the month of November at his son's London residence, Evelyn dispatched John jr to Oxford and the Prince of Orange.[81] John jr spent five days in Lord Lovelace's regiment 'in defence of our English Athens', which he described significantly as 'my five days' rebellion'. Evelyn, hardly acting like an Anglican royalist or a Tory passive obedience man, had sent his own son to take up arms against the King of England 'for the Nassovian hero, the primitive religion and the liberty of my country'.[82] Having lived through the political anarchy of the late 1650s, he did not greet the prospect of civil war without trepidation; he greeted it with desperation. In the autumn of 1688 Evelyn and the nation thought that William of Orange represented the last best hope.

This was the context in which Evelyn drew up his hitherto unnoticed agenda for revolutionary change, having been twice bitterly disappointed by Stuart monarchs; having suffered through political and religious persecution under the commonwealth; having served in government in various capacities; and knowing that there were limits to the politically possible. He drew up his agenda, convinced that radical change was necessary but unsure as to whether the political will or skill existed with which to carry it out. In short, he drew it up as an old man sceptical that change was possible, but absolutely convinced that it was necessary.

His agenda was not a republican one. He was anxious to retain the monarchy – he explicitly argued for a 'regency' – and even was willing to retain the current King if only in name. But a narrow focus on constitutional arrangements should not obscure the profundity of change he desired. In fact he had little to say about constitutional issues. Like the Bill, but not the Declaration of Rights, he insisted that 'no prince within the prospect of the crown of England should hereafter marry with a Papist'.[83] Like both the Bill and Declaration of Rights, he warned against 'armies and despotic designs'. He also made it clear that no royal dispensing power could justify placing Catholics in military or civilian offices. Like the Declaration and Bill of Rights, he desired that parliamentary elections should be free. But he went beyond those documents, calling for 'a reform made in the representatives sent to Parliaments, by fewer burgesses and more knights'.[84] Presumably he was reacting to the reforming of the corporation charters under Charles II and James II. However, it is possible that he already envisioned a broader programme of electoral reform that he outlined in the 1690s.[85] He also hoped to increase Parliament's authority by insisting 'that the militia and navy be put into the hands of such as the king shall recommend *if approved by the Parliament and that it be strictly exercised by experienced officers*'.[86]

However, the bulk of Evelyn's agenda was not narrowly constitutional. Instead he hoped for a wide-ranging series of reforms in English state and society. He called for a reorientation of English foreign policy; a rethinking of political economy; and a comprehensive reformation of manners. He also called for a reversal of later Stuart Francophilic policies. Whereas so much recent scholarship has emphasized England's relations with the Scotland and Ireland, Evelyn was far more concerned with his nation's place in Europe. He did not hope for an Anglo-Scottish union, but instead hoped 'that, if it were possible, Holland and England were made one people inseparably to be united'. 'What even were more desirable,' he added in a clear reference to the struggle against Louis XIV that had already begun on the continent, 'the supreme magistrate of this nation should declare himself the head and defender of all protestants in Europe and insert it in his title.'[87] He hoped that the post-revolutionary English regime would be fully and permanently committed to the continental struggle against France, an aspiration that distanced him from the blue-water policies of the Tories in the 1690s and beyond.

Evelyn also demanded that attention be paid to a bundle of issues that can best be grouped as political economy. He called for 'a public register of estates and a new census or domesday survey [to be] made for the more equal raising of public taxes'.[88] Such a register was clearly preparatory to a land tax, hardly a form of taxation favoured by Tories. He also wanted 'the revenue allotted for the royal state and pompous part of government' to be 'only so great as to maintain its magnificence without endangering enslaving of the subject'. He wanted to limit the power of the executive, but not the size of government, for he hoped 'the rest' would be 'religiously applied to the public, especially the navy'. The administrators of this expanded state apparatus 'of what condition whatsoever' were to be paid 'ample salaries' and not take 'any fees, for themselves, clerks, and under officers whatsoever'. The suggestion that 'no more criminals be transported but [be] condemned to public works at home' was as much evidence of Evelyn's conviction of labour's centrality to producing prosperity as it was of his distaste for Judge Jeffreys's West Country assizes in the wake of Monmouth's rebellion. Finally he insisted that the state make a significant effort to promote economic innovation. He advocated the creation of 'a standing committee ... of fit persons to receive and make report of all projects convertible to the public benefit without ridiculing or discouraging the proposers'.[89]

That Evelyn's post-revolutionary agenda included a vast array of proposals regarding religious life will come as no surprise. However, the range and content of his suggestions were not those to be expected from a staunch defender of church, order, and property. 'Let our episcopal church remain as it ought with all its ancient rites, as the stable and national profession,' he suggested, but 'with indulgence to all sober dissenters'. To be sure he excluded Socinians and Quakers from the benefit of his toleration, but this proposal already went much further than anything imagined by the high churchmen. He did not propose to ban Roman Catholic practice but only to limit the number of priests to a 'competent number'. Not only did he call for an expansion of religious liberty, but he also wanted an enrichment of religious and moral life. He wanted the parochial clergy to be 'better provided for where the livings are not sufficient for a decent maintenance', implying his discomfort with pluralism. 'That a public library be erected and furnished with such books as the Convocation or Bishop of the Province shall think fit at the public charge, one in every county,' reflected his deep concern for lay learning. He was not concerned only for wealthy parishioners. He demanded that 'some better expedient be found out for the charging of parishes to maintain their poor'. Concern for the nation's manners ranked high among his priorities. He wanted to prevent under-age marriages, hoped that 'the stage and filthy interludes be reformed', and wanted the London and Southwark fairs which were 'occasions of much dissolution and villainy' abolished.[90] Evelyn, in short, called for a complete overhaul of English social, religious, and moral behaviour.

The agenda he set out in November 1688 was not a conservative one. His vision was broader than merely reversing the pernicious innovations of James II. He did not hope merely to restore the ancient constitution in church and state. If William III could bring about these reforms, Evelyn was certain, he would not simply be remembered as a good king. His achievements 'would outdo the splendour of all the heroes of antiquity, and reign in the hearts and minds of posterity as long as 'tis Christian, that is, till time shall be no more'.[91] What were the origins of these calls for revolutionary transformation? Why did he call for reforms in foreign policy, political economy, and religious life? What do they tell us about Evelyn's political commitments on the eve of the Revolution?

Evelyn was not an insular man. Not only did he travel widely on the continent in the 1640s, but he maintained a lifelong fascination with European cultural and political affairs. He took every opportunity to meet and discuss politics with European diplomats when they came to England. His diary is filled with conversation and dinners with residents, envoys, and ambassadors from the United Provinces, Poland, Denmark, Sweden, Venice, and France.[92] Throughout his life he reflected deeply on England's proper role in Europe.

He might have devoted a great deal of energy to 'transposing French cultural ideas to England', as Michael Hunter has noted, but he never embraced French culture.[93] Indeed, from the 1650s he came to fear and loathe French power. In his 1652 pamphlet exploring the state of France, he maintained that 'the crown and King of France are at this present day more opulent and mighty than ever they were'.[94] In fact, he claimed, all the nations of Europe 'seem at this instant epoch of time, to conspire as it were, and defer to the present *grandezza* of the French empire'.[95] The power and potential of France was already so great that he thought 'it were high time she were now a little observed, and a *Non Ultra* fixed unto her proceedings and future aspirings'.[96] While he was impressed with the rapid growth of French political power, he did not admire French politics. He lamented that 'as for the Parliaments of France (besides the name and formality) there is in truth no such thing in nature'.[97] He pitied the French 'plebeians' for 'their incomparable poverty and excessive oppression'.[98] He criticized the growing power of the French monarch, commenting that the French government only retained 'a shadow of the ancient form'.[99]

These criticisms were not restricted to the political realm. Cultural imperialism, Evelyn was sure, was merely the stalking horse for political dominion. ''Tis not a trivial remark,' he warned, 'that when a nation is able to impose and give laws to the habit of another (as the late Tartars in China) it has (like that of language) proved a forerunner of the spreading of their conquests there.'[100] England, Evelyn feared, had succumbed to '*la mode de France*'. London, he mourned, was overwhelmed by 'armies and swarms' of French accoutrements that 'hang in the ears, embrace the necks and elegant waists of our fair ladies, in the likeness of pendants, collars, fans, and petticoats, and the rest of those pretty impediments, without which heaven and earth could not subsist'.[101] When, in October 1666, Charles II briefly began wearing a new 'Persian'-style vested suit, Evelyn hoped his invective against French culture was beginning to take effect. However, he soon lamented that it was 'impossible for us to leave the Monsieur's vanities in good earnest'.[102] 'We have submitted to, and still continue under the empire of the French', he and his daughter Mary jointly concluded in the 1670s or early 1680s.[103]

This antipathy for France dramatically accelerated in the 1680s. At the same time that he was distancing himself ideologically from the Tory reaction, he was reacting with horror at French expansionism and English inaction. He was certain that Louis XIV was in a position to make a 'fair game for an universal monarchy'.[104] 'The French (who 'tis believed brought in the Infidel) disturbing their Spanish and Dutch neighbours and almost swallowed all Flanders' were, Evelyn was convinced, 'pursuing [Louis XIV's] ambition of a fifth and universal monarchy'.[105] All of this was made possible by England's 'pseudopolitic adherence to the French interest'.[106] Unsurprisingly, Evelyn coupled his political denunciation with cultural criticism. He must have nodded approvingly when his friend John Tillotson preached against 'the vain and servile complements crept in in this late depraved age, in this nation, from the imitation of the French and other nations'.[107] France, he scribbled furiously in his diary, 'had now the ascendant and we [are] become quite another nation'.[108] His overall assessment was one of damning criticism of the restored monarchy. 'All this blood and disorder in Christendom had evidently its rise from our defect[s] at home,' he wrote dejectedly, 'in a wanton peace, minding nothing but luxury, ambition and to procure money for our vices.' 'We were wanton mad,' Evelyn concluded, to suffer 'the French to grow so great and the Hollanders so weak.'[109]

Evelyn briefly, very briefly, hoped that the death of Charles II and the accession of James II would lead to a complete reorientation of English foreign policy and English cultural tastes. The Revocation of the Edict of Nantes in France and James II's failure to support the persecuted Huguenots convinced him that little had changed. 'All the Reformed Churches in Christendome [are] now weakened and utterly ruined, through our remissness and suffering them to be supplanted, persecuted and destroyed; as in France, which we took no notice of,' he remarked caustically in October 1685, 'the consequence of this time will show.'[110] 'So mighty a power and ascendant here, had the French ambassador,' Evelyn thought, that it explained the long delay in publishing the brief for relief of French Protestants along with the crown's active suppression of works denouncing the French persecution.[111] Meanwhile he thought he could detect the same old French political tricks aimed at achieving universal dominion on the European scene. Just as England's 'terrible war' with the Dutch in the 1660s was 'begun doubtless at the secret instigation of the French &c to weaken the States and Protestant interest',[112] so now the Danish king's encroachment on Hamburg was a 'French contrivance to embroil the Protestant princes in a new war'.[113] Unsurprisingly, Evelyn thought his dinner companion Everard van de Weede, Sieur de Dijkveld, a 'prudent and worthy person', when he openly 'deplored the stupid folly of our politics, in suffering the French to take Luxembourg: it being a place of the most concern to have been defended for the interest of not only the Netherlands but of England also'.[114]

John Evelyn called for a revolution in English foreign policy in November 1688 because he had come to believe that the foreign policy of both Charles II and his brother James was disastrous for England and Europe. Convinced that 'Louis le Grand is to be the Universal Monarch', he demanded a radical shift in English political alignments.[115] Alliance, even amalgamation, with the Netherlands was the best hope of putting a halt to the hitherto inexorable advance of the French King. Evelyn was predictably a great supporter of the Nine Years War. While he did at times complain and complain bitterly about the war effort, his complaints were about shortcomings in the administration of the war effort, not about the justice or necessity of the war itself. He was convinced, as he informed his son, that William and Mary were engaged in a 'necessary and decisive war with France', that it was on 'the firm prosecution and fortunate event of [this war that] all our public and private happiness depends'.[116]

John Evelyn had an enduring and passionate interest in the emerging field of political economy. Although he had made himself into a virtuoso in the 1650s, he was well aware that he was descended from a family of manufacturers. Near his brother George's house in Surrey 'stood formerly many [gun]powder mills, erected by my ancestors', he proudly informed John Aubrey, 'who were the very first that brought that invention into England; before which we had all our powder out of Flanders'.[117] It was perhaps pride in this family connection that propelled his fascination in all things commercial. Throughout his life he sought out and conversed with experts on trades, shipping, and manufacturing.[118] In the late 1650s he dined with the Dutch ambassador Willem Nieupoort, who 'laughed at our Committee of Trade, as composed of men wholly ignorant of it, and how they were the ruin of commerce by gratifying some for private ends'.[119] Sir Thomas Modyford, the former governor of Jamaica, told him how easy it could be to conquer the Spanish possessions in the West Indies.[120] Evelyn maintained a long-standing friendship with Sir William Petty, of whom he thought 'there were not in the whole world his equal for a superintendant of manufactures and improvement of trade; or, for to govern a plantation'; 'If I were a Prince, I should make him my second counselor at least'.[121] During James II's reign he developed a close friendship with the great traveller and East India merchant Sir John Chardin, so close that he stood godfather to Chardin's son.[122]

Evelyn not only talked about commerce, he read about it avidly. 'As to trade', he advised his friend Samuel Pepys, 'it were a noble collection, could we procure all that has been printed (which would make a very useful and considerable volume, because for most part published by wise and knowing men) since Henry the 8th's time to this. They are commonly in the bulk of pamphlets, but in my opinion of much esteem.'[123] In fact his library catalogue for 1687 reveals that he assembled just such a collection: works on commerce by Roger Coke, John Houghton, Slingsby Bethel, Henry Robinson, and Gilbert Burnet, among many others.[124]

He was also active in making economic policy. In the late 1650s he made a significant investment in East India Company stock, and was at least initially active in its general court.[125] After the Restoration, he predictably served on the Royal Society's Georgic Committee devoted to the improvement of English husbandry.[126] In 1670 he was appointed to the Council for Foreign Plantations,[127] participated in a variety of discussions, ranging from the government of troublesome New England to the diversification of West Indian production, and came to know two other radical economic thinkers,

Silias Titus and Benjamin Worsley.[128] The Earl of Shaftesbury later invited Evelyn to participate in the newly amalgamated Council of Plantations and Foreign Trade, where he came into contact with John Locke. Here again he was drawn into discussions of colonial matters, serving on the committee 'to examine the laws of his Majesty's several plantations and colonies in the West Indies'.[129] Charles II turned to him for advice for improvements in naval engineering,[130] and he was able to put his King in touch with the most innovative shipwrights, in part, because he was a younger brother of Trinity House, London's early modern shipping fraternity.[131] The range and depth of his interest in commercial matters suggests that Michael Hunter was overly pessimistic when he claimed that Evelyn's 'commitment to useful knowledge ... waned' after the 1650s.[132]

By the 1680s interest in political economy had ceased to be ideologically neutral. In fact, though little noticed by early modern historians, debates over England's proper attitude to trade generated profound divisions within the political nation in the years leading up to the Glorious Revolution, and these divisions would have enduring consequences. Two competing visions of political economy came to be clearly enunciated in the 1680s. The first, most closely associated with Josiah Child, the East India Company, and eventually the regime of James II, was that property was based on land, and was thus necessarily finite. 'The principal advantage and foundation of trade in England is raised from the wealth which is gained out of the produce of the earth,' Child contended;[133] the world therefore had a necessarily finite economy totally 'derived out of this principal stock of good husbandry'.[134] Agriculture and the fisheries, a kind of farming of the sea, were the fundamentals of trade, which in turn consisted merely of merchants buying 'commodities purely to sell again, or exchange the commodities of one nation, for those of another, for no other end but that of their own private benefit or profit'.[135] Since no wealth was created by human labour, international trade was necessarily a zero-sum game: 'whatever weakens' Italy, France, or Holland 'enriches and strengthens England'.[136]

Against the view of Child and the East India Company, a second interpretation of political economy emerged. This argued that property was created by human labour, and was hence potentially infinite. John Locke was sure that 'if we rightly estimate things as they come to our use, and cast up the several expenses about them, what in them is purely owing to nature, and what to labour, we shall find that in most of them **99/100** are wholly to be put on the account of labour'. No wonder he was convinced that for states 'the honest industry of mankind' and 'numbers of men are to be preferred to largeness of dominions'.[137] 'What we call the wealth, stock, or provision of the nation,' insisted Sir William Petty, whom Evelyn so much admired, was 'the effect of the former or past labour' of that nation's people.[138]

The conflict between these opposing views of political economy came to a dramatic head in the 1680s. Sir Josiah Child successfully took control of the East India Company and purged it of his ideological enemies. In early 1685 his political economic ideas achieved legal sanction in the landmark case of East India Company *v.* Thomas Sandys. In this case, pitting the East India Company against an interloper into the area of trade in which it claimed a monopoly, the court was able to enunciate the crown's economic vision. 'As to manufactures,' the creation of goods by human labour, argued Evelyn's *bête noir* Chief Justice Jeffreys for the majority, 'the public weal is little concerned therein.'[139] Land, not manufactures or exchange, was what mattered; 'the King is the only person truly concerned in this question, for this island supported its inhabitants in many ages without any foreign trade at all, having in it all things necessary for the life of man'.[140] Property and livelihood depended on land. Trade was a luxury, not necessary for England's welfare, and therefore it was well within the King's prerogative to regulate all foreign trade as he saw fit.

John Evelyn was not an idle observer of these developments. He could not have made his own views more clear. Just when Child was establishing his hegemony over the East India Company, he chose to sell off the stock he had held in the company since the 1650s.[141] Earlier that year he informed Pepys that 'all wise men know' that Child's company was 'neither so rich, wise or powerful as they would be thought intrinsically, and that it is the credit and estimation the vulgar has of them, which renders them considerable'.[142] When he chose to visit Child's new lavish seat at Wanstead in 1683, he commented that the East India Company governor was 'most sordidly avaricious'.[143] By contrast he dined on the same day with James Houblon, a Whig merchant recently purged from the company by Child, whom he termed a 'rich and gentile French merchant'.[144]

Evelyn's own discussions of political economy presaged his sympathy for those who thought that property was created by labour. In his treatise on *Navigation and Commerce*, he argued that humans could not live alone on the basis of natural endowments, but were required to engage in 'labour and industry';[145] 'it is not the vastness of territory, but the convenience of situation; nor the multitude of men, but their addresses and industry which improve a nation'.[146] Where Child feared that excessive wealth would produce luxury, Evelyn thought that only prosperity could generate power: 'Riches and plenty, with the love and prosperity of a people, be the glory of a Prince, and the nerves of a state.'[147] Where Child saw the Dutch as a people to be feared and loathed, Evelyn praised their industry and virtue. Dutch 'extraordinary industry' prepared their towns for trade, and made them 'ravishing' to the eye.[148] Indeed the Netherlands provided proof that wealth was based on labour and good economic policy rather than natural resources.

Holland 'affords neither grain, wine, oil, timber, metal, stone, wool, hemp, pitch, nor almost any other commodity of use', he noted, 'and yet we find, there is hardly a nation in the world which enjoys all these things in greater affluence'; it was all the 'affects of industry'; 'indeed it is that alone, which has built and peopled goodly cities, where nothing but rushes grew; cultivated an heavy genius with all the politer arts; enlarged and secured their boundaries, and made them a name in the world, who, within less than an age were hardly considered in it'.[149] Dutch 'grandeur' was based on 'their admission of foreigners, increase of hands, encouraging manufactures, free and open ports, low customs, toleration of religions, natural frugality, and indefatigable industry';[150] by contrast, those countries that pursued dominion rather than exchange, that followed the policies advocated by Child and the East India Company, were doomed to failure. Venice, for example, was 'a glorious city' when its governors devoted their energies to commerce alone, but slid quickly into decline when they changed 'their industry into ambition', seeking to expand their territorial control.[151] Similarly, despite the King of Spain's massive dominions in the West Indies, Evelyn was sure 'he could neither be rich nor safe' because of his failure to generate wealth through industry.[152] He criticized France as well for discouraging gentlemen to pursue 'any trade or mechanic calling'.[153]

It was this preference for a political economy based on industry rather than land, on domestic manufactures rather than imperial possessions, which provides the background for his thinking in November 1688. Trade properly understood, he explained to Pepys during the Tory reaction of the 1680s, lacked 'any public encouragement' and languished 'under insupportable difficulties'.[154] He hoped that the post-Revolutionary regime would change the direction of English economic policy, that a new Council of Trade would promote economic innovations, that all available labour would be deployed at home rather than in the plantations, and that revenue would be generated by taxing the land, for which he demanded a complete and accurate land register. He called for government frugality and increased expenditure on the navy so that it could protect foreign trade. In short his political economic agenda, a Revolutionary agenda, was very similar to that of John Locke and the Whig critics of Child's Tory East India Company.[155]

Despite, or perhaps because of, the economic difficulties of the 1690s, Evelyn continued to think of England not as an agrarian but as a 'mercantile nation',[156] and reaffirmed his commitment to the principles of 'the incomparably judicious and learned Mr. Locke'.[157] He continued to call for a powerful Council of Trade, 'composed of a wise, public spirited, active and noble president, a select number of assessors, sober, industrious and dexterous men of consummate experience'. This Council would not only aim to protect trade during the naval war with France, but would promote 'the manufactures of the kingdom'.[158] In the 1690s struggle between the Tory East India Company and the Whig proponents of the Bank, he made it clear where his sympathies lay. He eagerly noted the creation of the Bank, supported by his friends Locke, James Houblon, and Sidney Godolphin, and proudly remarked on how quickly the subscription 'was filled and completed', and how it was 'put under the government of the most able and wealthy citizens of London'.[159] He was disappointed when Parliament 'let fall' their plans to remodel the East India Company so as to reverse Child's 1682 reforms.[160] Later he noted with disgust 'what prodigious bribes have been given by some of the East India Company out of the stock'.[161] Throughout the revolutionary decade Evelyn, though no longer active in making economic policy, remained deeply interested in issues of political economy and his ideological commitments were closer to those of John Locke than Josiah Child, to the Junto Whigs than those of the Jacobites.

Evelyn's deep commitment to the Church of England is well known. His diary is filled with sermon notes and discussions with eminent churchmen.[162] Yet the nature of his lay Anglicanism has never been subjected to much scrutiny. What was the nature of his religious thinking in the years immediately preceding and following the Revolution of 1688-9? What explains the precise nature of the demands he set out in his Revolutionary agenda of November 1688?

The young John Evelyn, whose image so dominates the historiography, was a conventional lay Anglican. It was in the 1630s, the high water mark of Laudianism, that the Church of England was 'in her greatest splendor, all things decent, and becoming the peace, and the persons that governed'.[163] When the Lord Protector Oliver Cromwell proscribed any public activities of Church of England clergymen in 1655, he thought it 'the mournfullest day that in my life I had seen, or the Church of England herself, since the Reformation'.[164] 'Never was religion so perverted', was his lament.[165] During this period of iniquity he increasingly entrusted his spiritual welfare to 'Laud's protégé', Jeremy Taylor – a divine who insisted on the absolute unlawfulness of Presbyterian ordination – whom he called his 'ghostly Father'.[166]

While Evelyn's religious practices and tastes in the 1640s and 1650s were perhaps typical of a wide range of lay Anglicans, deeply disappointed with political defeat and religious proscription, his views and connections evolved significantly in the years after the Restoration. The key to that transformation was his intimacy with John Wilkins of Wadham College and future Bishop of Chester. Already in the mid-1650s he referred to the warden of Wadham as 'my excellent and dear friend',[167] and his admiration and sympathy with Wilkins's views on a variety of matters only grew with time. In the 1660s he ranked Wilkins among the greatest men in Europe 'for parts and ingenuity'.[168] When it came time to appoint a tutor for his son John jr he turned to Wilkins for advice.[169] Their increasingly intimate friendship was remarkable because the Bishop of Chester's views were so different from those of Evelyn's earlier religious confidant, Jeremy Taylor. Wilkins, though 'exactly conformable himself' to the Church of England, was notorious for being 'very tender to those that differed from him'.[170]

Throughout the 1670s, 1680s, and 1690s Evelyn developed a new set of clerical friendships with those who might be described as John Wilkins's disciples and fellow travellers. Almost all of these men would become bishops after the Revolution of 1688-9. William Lloyd, who preached Wilkins's funeral sermon, became an intimate and favourite of Evelyn's when preacher at St Martin's in London.[171] He thought Lloyd 'one of the most deep learned divines of the nation, in all sorts of literature', high praise indeed from a virtuoso.[172] Lloyd, who had done so much to stoke the flames of the Popish Plot, who had openly sided with William III in the decisive days of December 1688 and January 1689, remained Evelyn's friend throughout. He consulted with Lloyd about 'affairs' in December 1688 and dined with him after he had become almoner to Queen Mary.[173] They shared a great admiration for John Tillotson. Evelyn listened to the Whig sympathizer Tillotson often from the late 1670s, commenting that he preached 'excellently' and 'incomparably'.[174] During the Exclusion Crisis he turned to Tillotson for advice on matters of clerical patronage.[175] When Tillotson was preferred to the see of Canterbury after the Revolution, he clearly approved. In a comment replete with meaning, he noted that Tillotson was 'far politer than the old man', Sancroft.[176] Tillotson in turn sent Evelyn, with whom he exchanged medicinal recipes, his 'most hearty respects'.[177] A third cleric whom Evelyn admired, this time with less personal intimacy, was Edward Stillingfleet. Frequently he commented that Stillingfleet had preached 'excellently', 'incomparably', 'learnedly', or 'admirably'.[178] Tillotson, Stillingfleet, and Lloyd were all close associates of John Wilkins, members of his 'club for a comprehension and limited indulgence for dissenters in religion'.[179]

Evelyn also greatly admired two other men who were preferred to episcopal sees after the Revolution, men renowned for their low churchmanship. He made a point of hearing Simon Patrick preach, either at Whitehall or in Covent Garden. He returned from both places convinced that Patrick had treated his subject 'most profitably', or with 'an incomparable discourse'.[180] It was in the mid-1670s that he 'first heard that famous and excellent preacher', Gilbert Burnet, and he was duly impressed; Burnet spoke 'with such a flood of eloquence and fullness of matter as showed him to be a person of extraordinary parts'.[181] Later he developed a real friendship with the controversial Burnet, offering to lend him 'an heap of old letters and dispatches' in the hopes that 'some passage or other might occur to give light to that desiderate and excellent work you are now finishing'.[182] The finished product, Burnet's *History of the Reformation*, he thought 'excellent',[183] and the two visited or dined together several times in 1670s and 1680s.[184] Soon after Burnet's triumphant return from political exile with William's revolutionary army in 1688, Evelyn was writing to him in friendly terms, recommending an engraver.[185] The friendship clearly continued, for Ralph Bohun assured Evelyn in 1701 that he was 'well thought of' by Burnet.[186]

Evelyn's greatest clerical friend was the London preacher and future Archbishop of Canterbury, Thomas Tenison. From the 1670s onwards he attended as many of Tenison's sermons as he possibly could. His notes on them far and away outnumber those of any other preacher in his book of sermon notes.[187] 'I esteem this doctor to be absolutely one of the most profitable preachers in the Church of England,' Evelyn wrote of him in 1683.[188] From the mid-1680s the two frequently exchanged visits and views about politics and religion.[189] Tenison christened Evelyn's granddaughter Jane and officiated at the wedding of his daughter Susanna.[190] It was with Pepys and Tenison that Evelyn dined and presumably discussed recent developments a week prior to the eagerly anticipated arrival of William III.[191] He later extolled his friend's 'exemplary holy life, great pains in constant preaching' and his constant promotion of 'the service of God both in public and private: so as a man of more universal and generous spirit, with so much modesty, prudence and piety I never met with'.[192] So when Tenison was translated from the see of Lincoln to that of Canterbury in late 1694, Evelyn could not but 'thank God and rejoice, he being most worthy of it both for his learning, piety and prudence'.[193]

Was Evelyn expressing a religious preference by praising these preachers and maintaining these friendships? It is, of course, true that he did praise some high churchmen and future non-jurors. He very much appreciated Thomas Ken's passionate preaching, Thomas Sprat's elegant style, and Henry Compton's churchmanship.[194] However, he was never as enthusiastic about these men as he was about the low churchmen. Other high churchman and non-jurors he despised. Samuel Parker, the high church Bishop of Oxford and political ally of James II, he castigated as a 'violent, passionate, haughty man', whose only redeeming quality was that he failed to convert to Rome.[195] The Oxford preacher Robert South, who would become one of the leading critics of the Williamite episcopate after the Revolution, Evelyn dismissed as 'an ill natured man'.[196] More positively, it was the low church-men whom he recommended to his nearest and dearest. The best guide to understanding communion, 'this great and dreadful mystery', he told his son, were the two treatises on the subject by Simon Patrick.[197] He advised his wife that 'you should constantly (as you do) use the directions and monthly devotions only prescribed in Dr. Patrick's *Christian Sacrifice* with what your own pious heart will suggest', and thought that she could also profit from reading Tillotson's sermons and Patrick's *Devout Christian*.[198] When the Countess of Sunderland wrote Evelyn requesting a list of books 'fit to entertain your more devout and serious hours', Evelyn included in his list works by Burnet, Stillingfleet, Tenison, Patrick, and another future Williamite bishop Edward Fowler.[199] Almost two decades later he recommended Tillotson's sermons, Stillingfleet's works, and the devotional writings of Patrick to his beloved grandson.[200]

Whether or not it makes sense to speak of latitudinarians in the 1660s and 1670s, it was clear to Evelyn and many others that there was a real and profound division within the Church of England by the 1680s and 1690s. Late in his life Burnet tried several times to capture the differences between high and low churchmen. The attitudes of the low churchmen – and among these Burnet counted himself, Lloyd, Tenison, and Tillotson – were, above all, 'very moderate'.[201] This moderation consisted of three things. First, they were committed to a programme of comprehension and toleration, to a broader Church of England, and large scope for legal religious worship outside the national church. Second, they came to defend political resistance, convinced that 'there is a full power in the legislature to settle the Crown, and to secure the nations'. Unlike their high church opponents, these clergymen knew 'of no unalterable or indefeasible right, but what is founded on the law'.[202] Third, they were deeply devoted to pastoral reform, to a reformation of English manners from the ground up. They thought that high churchmen had spent too much energy magnifying 'the authority of the clergy' and asserting 'the rights of the church' in their bitter struggle with Dissent, to the neglect of the moral lives of their parishioners.[203]

Evelyn clearly perceived this division, and just as clearly indicated where his religious preferences lay. The immediate post-revolutionary period was, he noted, a 'time of very great division and dissension in the nation', with 'the moderate and sober part' of the church 'for a speedy reformation of diverse things, which were thought might be made in our liturgy, for the inviting in of Dissenters', and their opponents, 'the more stiff and rigid', 'for no condescension at all'.[204] To the Countess of Sunderland he expressed his preference for the 'moderate (and I think) wiser Church of England men', as against 'those of the higher strain'.[205] Evelyn's low church friendships in the 1680s and his commitment to the ideological programme of these friends go far to explain the religious content of his November 1688 Revolutionary agenda. His call for toleration and for the reformation of English manners were also the desiderata of his clerical friends.

While he had looked upon the proliferation of Protestant sects in the turbulent 1640s and 1650s with utter contempt, by the 1680s he had come to rather more charitable conclusions. In the late 1670s he criticized a sermon delivered at Whitehall 'against our late schismatics' for being 'a little over sharp'.[206] He praised Simon Patrick for 'setting forth the love we ought to have to our fellow Christian and to all mankind', a topic which at the height of the Exclusion Crisis must have sounded very much like a call for toleration.[207] Tenison, who clearly deeply influenced his moral compass over the last two and a half decades of his life, lectured his auditors 'against peevishness and want of sweetness and easiness of temper'.[208] Some time in the 1680s – for we cannot date the entry in Evelyn's diary precisely – he became committed to these views, declaring that there might be 'some relaxations' in the enforcement of religious uniformity 'without the least prejudice to the present establishment, discreetly limited'.[209]

Evelyn's commitment to the reformation of English manners was of much longer duration. Like his low church friends, he believed that since good works and moral behaviour could and would promote salvation, it was the responsibility of the church and state to do everything possible to improve the manners of Englishmen and women. They drew from an anti-Calvinist theology puritan conclusions about the moral life. The low churchmen were relentless in their preaching 'against the sin of drunkenness and all in-temperance, either of the palate or any other excess', including excesses of 'apparel' or 'words'.[210] Just after the Revolution Tillotson proposed, just as Evelyn himself had done in November 1688, that 'a new body of ecclesiastical canons' should be created, which gave a 'more effectual provision for the reformation of manners both in ministers and people'.[211] 'It is not imaginable', Evelyn himself complained to the Countess of Sunderland, how prevalent were 'prophane and filthy communications, atheistical, negligent and extravagant talk, which passes now amongst our most generous youth fit neither for Christians nor heathens to speak or hear'.[212] His interest in the construction of public libraries throughout the nation can be directly traced to Tenison. It was he who in 1684 had expressed to Evelyn 'his intention of erecting a public library in St Martin's parish, for the public use'. Evelyn enthusiastically joined him and Christopher Wren in the project, which he deemed 'a worthy and laudable design'.[213]

Evelyn's interest, like those of the low churchmen in general, was never merely in reproving the lower orders. He wanted to improve the manners and quality of life of the entire nation, believing that a happier nation was a more productive nation, as well as a more blessed nation. Thus he praised Tenison for his catechizing,[214] Lady Mordaunt for her charity to the poor,[215] and all his favourite preachers for their plain, easily accessible style. Charac-teristically he took his model for public welfare from the United Provinces. While high churchmen forever castigated the Dutch for their religious pluralism, Evelyn argued for Anglo-Dutch union and English imitation of

Dutch welfare practices. 'It is most remarkable,' he gushed about Amsterdam, 'what provisions are here made and maintained for public and charitable purposes, and to protect the poor from misery, and the country from beggars.'[216] Over the course of the 1670s and 1680s Evelyn had found new religious advisers and friends. He became committed to their agenda of religious liberty and moral reform.[217] Like them he rejected puritan theology in favour of Nonconformist morality. Far from being unwavering in his religious sentiments, he became a convert to limited religious toleration and an enthusiast for a religion devoted more to moral improvement rather than strict and unchanging uniformity.

By November 1688 John Evelyn had become convinced that England needed a revolutionary change. Whether or not he ever wanted to dethrone James II, he had clearly decided that England's state, society, and religious culture needed to be radically transformed. He thought that it needed not just to preserve all that was valuable in its traditions, but also to modernize, to embrace a modern foreign policy, political economy, and religious culture.

Two aspects of Evelyn's career might lead one to doubt his revolutionary credentials. First, one might point to his passionate anti-Catholicism. Perhaps his turning against James and his willingness to support William was no more than a visceral reaction to a Catholic monarch. He was then no modern, no revolutionary, but a reactionary defender of England's protestantism. Second, he was far less enthusiastic about the events of 1688-9 than he was about the Restoration of 1660. He never voiced the near millenarian enthusiasm that pervaded his writings of the late 1650s and 1660s, and was at best a reluctant revolutionary. Both of these claims do have some merit, but neither makes sense of the full range of Evelyn's interests and activities.

One need not look far for evidence of Evelyn's distaste for Roman Catholicism. When it became clear to him and to the nation as a whole that the Duke of York was a Catholic convert, he worried 'what the consequence of this will be'.[218] He lamented that Titus Oates's exaggerations and lies had discredited the Popish Plot, while the Rye House plotters had brought Protestantism into disrepute.[219] After James II's accession he bemoaned the elaborate new Catholic chapel at court and deplored that 'the Romanists [are] swarming at court with greater confidence than had ever been seen in England since the Reformation'.[220] He never had anything good to say about Catholic theology, terming one popular piece of Catholic apologetic published during James II's reign 'a most undecent blasphemous piece',[221] and was particularly enthusiastic in praising his clerical friends for preaching anti-Catholic sermons.[222]

However, Evelyn's anti-Catholicism never amounted to blind prejudice, and never determined either his politics or his social relations. His revolutionary agenda did demand that no future monarchs marry Catholics, but he did not want to bar Catholics from the throne or court, nor did he place them beyond the pale of religious toleration. In fact he was initially an enthusiastic supporter of James II, hoping that he would reform the nation's manners and reverse Charles II's Francophilic foreign policy. Evelyn turned against him, not for his religion, but for his policies. James was undone, he later commented, 'after a short and unprosperous reign by his own indiscreet attempting to bring in Popery' – to make the country Roman Catholic, not to have Catholicism tolerated – 'and make himself absolute in imitation of the French'. James, he thought, had succumbed to the 'impatience of the Jesuits and [the] zeal of the Queen to subdue the kingdom and religion to the Roman'.[223] Evelyn was not a bigoted anti-Catholic; he chiefly detested the aggressive French and Jesuit political style. It was the Jesuits, not all Roman Catholics, whom he blamed for 'fomenting our disorders in church and state from 37 to 60', for their 'destructive, immoral, and pernicious' principles, for aiming to trick James II and later the Anglican episcopate.[224]

Many of Evelyn's closest friends were in fact Catholics. The Catholic Lord Treasurer Thomas Clifford favoured him 'even to intimacy and friendship'; he was 'my great friend, and loved me', Evelyn wrote afterwards.[225] He was friendly throughout his life with various members of the Catholic Howard family. His son was 'much brought up amongst Mr Howard's children at Arundel House', and in return Henry Howard had two of his sons spend time with the Evelyn family.[226] Evelyn and the Catholic Earl of Bristol also appear to have had a close friendship.[227] He even hosted the Catholic nuptials of his wife's Catholic kinsman, Sir Samuel Tuke.[228]

Evelyn did not imagine or desire that a post-Revolutionary England would pursue aggressive anti-Catholic policies. In a note written in September or October 1688, he made clear that while he anxiously desired that England would at last declare war on France, he hoped that war would be conducted in the context of a multi-confessional alliance.[229] In fact he praised William and Mary for pursuing his recommended policy of tolerance for Catholics in fact if not in law. 'The Roman Catholics,' he wrote to Lady Tuke with some satisfaction, have 'never been more at ease and less disturbed in all my observations than here at present'.[230]

Just as he was happy with the toleration allowed for Catholics and others after the revolution, so he was happy with the Revolution itself. Having been bitterly disappointed in the aftermath of 1660, he viewed the new regime with scepticism. Before William defeated the Jacobites in Ireland, he complained bitterly of 'the indiscreet government of affairs amongst us'.[231] After the battle of the Boyne, he and Pepys agreed the management of the navy to be lacking; hampered, presumably unlike that administered by Pepys, 'by negligence and unskillful men'.[232] But these complaints reveal not the bitter criticism of a Jacobite, but the anxious concern of a supporter of the Revolution. While his high hopes for both sons of Charles I were never met, the scepticism with which he greeted the post-Revolutionary monarchs was soon overcome. He was indeed saddened that Mary never 'showed some (seeming) reluctancy at least, of assuming her Father's crown and made some apology, testifying her regret that he should by his misgovernment necessitate the nation to so extraordinary a proceeding'.[233] But in his eyes this was her only fault. To William Lloyd he extolled the 'truly Christian and royal virtues and endowments of that incomparable princess'.[234] To Tenison he remarked that she was 'universally beloved',[235] 'such an admirable creature', he added in his diary, 'as does if possible outdo the renowned Queen Elizabeth herself'.[236] Like the rest of the nation, he was slower to warm to William; but warm he did. When his army defeated the Jacobites in Ireland, he wrote that 'one may say of him as of Caesar, *Veni, vidi, vici*, for never was such a kingdom won in so short an expedition'.[237] The foiled 1696 assassination plot gave him a chance to reflect on the stark choice that confronted the nation; it would 'have been very fatal to the ... whole nation, had it taken effect; so as I look on it as a very great deliverance and prevention by the Providence of God'.[238] While he had noted the deaths of both James II and Charles II with the bitterness of disappointment, William's death provoked his fears for the future, seeming to threaten 'the interests of the whole nation in this dangerous conjuncture'.[239] The revolutionary monarchs had succeeded – unlike Charles II and James II – in promoting the national interest.

He found more to praise in post-Revolutionary England than the new monarchs. He no doubt celebrated the new regime's Declaration of War against the aspiring universal monarch Louis XIV. He was also pleased that the new regime was committed to the promotion of his political economic programme.[240] He was naturally overjoyed that his clerical friends now had control of the Church. He also developed some new, decidedly Whiggish, friendships. He dedicated his *Acetaria* to the Junto Whig Lord Chancellor Somers, 'a most excellent lawyer, a very learned man in all the polite literature and an excellent pen and was master of an handsome style of easy conversation'.[241] He doted on the young and talented William Wotton, who became a national celebrity for his defence of the moderns against the ancients and notorious for his commitment to Whig principles.[242] Richard Bentley also benefited from Evelyn's patronage and friendship in the 1690s. He was instrumental in having Bentley appointed the first Boyle lecturer in 1692.[243] Bentley's 'excellent' discourse against Epicureanism solidified his admiration,[244] and he later turned to Bentley for help in assembling his *Numismata*. Bentley's Whig sociability made him the bane of Tory

Oxford.[245] Yet Evelyn was thrilled to be invited to join weekly evening meetings involving Christopher Wren, John Locke, and the no less Whiggish Isaac Newton.[246] These post-revolutionary friendships, with John Locke, with two successive Whig Archbishops, as well as with the Whig Lord Chancellor and two young Whig intellectuals, were not those of a closet Jacobite, or a reluctant revolutionary.

Evelyn's agenda of November 1688 was written by a man who demanded profound changes in England, but was sceptical that those changes were possible. He thought that the only hope for English and European political survival lay in war with France, and perhaps union with the United Provinces. He feared that only significant reorganization of England's economy would make such a war possible. While he did not specifically advocate the creation of the Bank of England, he did outline a series of proposals that made clear his preference for a commercial rather than an agrarian political economy. England's future, he knew, lay in manufacturing not imperial expansion. Labour, not conquest, was the key to realizing its potential as a commercial nation. He also came to sympathize with the religious program of the low churchmen. The reformation he called for had much more in common with the Whigs Burnet, Tillotson, and Tenison than with the more exclusive reformation desired by the high churchmen. He wanted to improve the lot of all Englishmen and women, rich and poor, Anglican and Noncomformist.

John Evelyn, it turns out, was not a conventional royalist. While in the 1650s he deeply believed that the nation's woes could be ameliorated by the restoration of the hereditary monarch, he had lost faith in that monarch by the 1670s. His disappointment first in Charles II and then in James II forced him to subtly readjust his political thinking. He had once believed that the rightful monarch would inevitably promote England's national interest. In the face of disappointment he turned to legislative solutions. In November 1688 he insisted that Parliament should have the right to approve military appointments. He also wanted to limit the king's discretionary funds, making it clear that he expected Parliament to be less an event and more of an institution. He implied that the only way to guarantee that future monarchs would protect the national interest abroad was to create a new kingdom, not British but Anglo-Dutch. He also came to believe that the moral life of Englishmen and women, about which he cared so deeply, could not be improved from the top down. The morals of monarchs could not be counted on. 'Powerful preaching', he told Lady Sunderland, had failed to improve the nation.[247] Only by passing legislation and turning to the nation's representatives could the country's moral future be protected.

Evelyn's revolutionary commitments, like the nature of the events of 1688-9 themselves, have been obscured by the preoccupations of early modern historiography. By focussing narrowly on theories of resistance and anti-Catholicism, historians have missed the profound changes that took place in the English political nation in the later seventeenth century. They have sought too hard to find the concerns of the Elizabethans and the early Stuarts in the minds of their descendants. These concerns, to be sure, were there. But so were new concerns. Fears of French imperialism, concerns about the proper organization of the English economy, and divisions within the Church of England dominated political debate in the 1670s, 1680s, and 1690s. Constitutional arrangements and anti-Catholicism were only part of the discussion in the revolutionary years. The Revolutionary agenda set by John Evelyn and a range of other men and women in the years preceding and following 1688 was one which called for a radical reorientation of English foreign policy, the creation of a new set of modern financial institutions based on a commercial rather than an agrarian economy, and the reformation of the Church of England along low church principles.

NOTES

1 I am grateful for the comments and criticism of Susan Stokes, Abby Swingen, Blair Worden, Adam Fox, and Mark Knights. I have also benefited from discussions of Evelyn with Frances Harris and John Spurr.
2 John Aubrey, *The Natural History and Antiquities of the County of Surrey Begun in the Year 1673*, 5 vols (London: E. Curll, 1719), IV, 131. Since Aubrey predeceased Evelyn, the notation of the epitaph must be the work of the editor.
3 Evelyn, *Diary*, II, 7.
4 Ibid., IV, 609.
5 BL Add. MS 78442: Evelyn to John Evelyn jr, 18 Dec. 1688. In his diary he calls 1688 'annus mirabilis tertius', after 1588 and 1660: Evelyn, *Diary*, IV, p. 566.
6 BL Add. MS 78442: Evelyn to John Evelyn jr, 18 Dec. 1688.
7 BL Add. MS 78299: Evelyn to Lord ?, Nov. 1688. In November 1688 very few people were calling for the deposition of James II. William III's *Declaration* did not. Mark Goldie has argued that calling for a regency, as Evelyn did, prior to mid-December 1688 was no sign of Tory or proto-Jacobite sentiment. Indeed Evelyn's proposal called for far more innovation than did the 'Instructions' written by the Whig Thomas Erle; see Mark Goldie, 'Thomas Erle's Instructions for the Revolution Parliament, December 1688', *Parliamentary History*, 14 (1995), 337-47 (p. 341).
8 John Evelyn, *Memoires for my Grand-Son*, ed. by Geoffrey Keynes (Oxford: Nonesuch Press, 1926), pp. 72-3.
9 Virginia Woolf, 'Rambling Round Evelyn', in *The Common Reader* (New York: Harcourt, Brace, 1925), p. 118.
10 Christopher Hill, 'John Evelyn', in *Collected Essays* (Amherst: University of Massachussetts Press, 1985), I, 251.
11 J. C. D. Clark, *English Society 1660-1832*, 2nd edn (Cambridge: Cambridge University Press, 2000), p. 83.
12 Michael Hunter, 'John Evelyn in the 1650s: a Virtuoso in Quest of a Role', in

Science and the Shape of Orthodoxy: Intellectual Change in Late Seventeenth-Century Britain (Woodbridge: Boydell, 1995), p. 70. Mark Jenner has similarly highlighted Evelyn's commitment to church and king in his elegant reading of *Fumifugium*: 'The Politics of London Air: John Evelyn's *Fumifugium* and the Restoration', *Historical Journal*, 38 (1995), 535-51.

13 Richard Greaves, *Secrets of the Kingdom* (Stanford: Stanford University Press, 1992), p. 220.

14 W. G. Hiscock, *John Evelyn and his Family Circle* (London: Routledge & Kegan Paul, 1955), p. 129.

15 Craig Rose, *England in the 1690s* (Oxford: Blackwell, 1999), p. 197. To be fair, elsewhere Rose claims that Evelyn was 'a life-long constitutional royalist' (p. 71) My only quibble with that assessment is that it does not allow for the ways in which Evelyn's views developed over the course of the second half of the seventeenth century.

16 Joseph Levine, *Between the Ancients and the Moderns* (New Haven & London: Yale University Press, 1999), p. 9.

17 Edmund Burke, *Reflections on the Revolution in France* (Harmondsworth: Penguin Books, 1968), p. 117.

18 Thomas Babington Macaulay, *The History of England from the Accession of James II* (New York: Harper & Brothers, 1849), II, 611-14.

19 G. M. Trevelyan, *The English Revolution 1688-89* (Oxford: Oxford University Press, 1938), pp. 3, 5.

20 Hugh Trevor-Roper, *From Counter-Reformation to Glorious Revolution* (Chicago: University of Chicago Press, 1992), p. 247.

21 Jonathan Scott, *Algernon Sidney and the Restoration Crisis, 1677-83* (Cambridge: Cambridge University Press, 1991), p. 27.

22 Levine, *Between the Ancients and the Moderns*, pp. 28-9. John Dixon Hunt has also called Evelyn's *Elysium Britannicum* an 'essentially modern' undertaking; see his 'Evelyn's Idea of the Garden', in *John Evelyn's 'Elysium Britannicum' and European Gardening*, ed. by Therese O'Malley & Joachim Wolschke-Bulmahn (Washington, D.C.: Dumbarton Oaks, 1998), p. 274.

23 *Of Liberty and Servitude*, trans. by John Evelyn (London: M. Meighen & G. Bedell, 1649), sigs. [B1ᵛ-B2ʳ].

24 Evelyn, *Diary*, III, 220.

25 John Evelyn, *An Apologie for the Royal Party* (1659), in *The Writings of John Evelyn*, ed. by Guy de la Bédoyère (Woodbridge: Boydell, 1995), p. 95. See more detailed criticisms in John Evelyn, *A Panegyricke to Charles II* (London: John Crooke, 1661), p. 4; and *Diary*, III, 244.

26 Evelyn, *Diary*, III, 59, 200.

27 Ibid., III, 237-8.

28 Evelyn, *An Apologie* (1659), in *Writings*, p. 105.

29 Ibid., pp. 105-6; the second time was in response to Marchamont Needham's 'wicked forged paper': Evelyn, *Diary*, III, 243.

30 Evelyn, *An Apologie* (1659), in *Writings*, p. 106.

31 *The Diary of Samuel Pepys*, ed. by Robert Latham & William Matthews (London: Bell, 1972), VII, 29.

32 Ibid., IX, 484 (16 March 1669). In his darkest moments in 1667 Evelyn even feared that 'we should soon see ourselves fall into a Commonwealth again'; ibid., VIII, 556.

33 BL Add. MS 78299: Evelyn to Lord ?, Nov. 1688.
34 Abigail Williams, 'Whig Literary Culture: Poetry, Politics and Patronage, 1678-1714' (University of Oxford D.Phil, 2000), pp. 160-6.
35 Among other mentions: Evelyn, *Diary*, IV, 81, 125, 147, 170, 173, 180, 182, 183, 187, 190, 198, 219, 248, 292.
36 Ibid., IV, 121.
37 Aubrey, *Natural History and Antiquities of the County of Surrey*, III, 75-7; V, 293.
38 Evelyn, *Diary*, IV, 186.
39 Ibid., 199.
40 Ibid., IV, 238, 260.
41 Ibid., IV, 200-2.
42 Ibid., III, 519; IV, 18, 82, 88. For the criticisms of Shaftesbury, see IV, 328 (13 July 1683). It should be noted that these were ones of political style rather than of political diagnosis. In this he probably shared the views of his friend Essex. For the differences between Shaftesbury and Essex, see Mark Knights, *Politics and Opinion in Crisis, 1678-8* (Cambridge: Cambridge University Press, 1994), pp. 48-64.
43 BL Add. MS 78301: John Evelyn jr to Evelyn, 15 Feb. 1676.
44 Evelyn, *Diary*, III, 628, IV, 25.
45 Ibid., III, 628.
46 *Particular Friends: the Correspondence of Samuel Pepys and John Evelyn*, ed. by Guy de la Bédoyère (Woodbridge: Boydell, 1997), pp. 213-15: Evelyn to Pepys, 26 Feb. 1690. He even sided with Locke when he was criticized by Stillingfleet: BL Add. MS 78299: Evelyn to Tenison, 10 Sept. 1697.
47 *Particular Friends*, p. 246: Evelyn to Pepys, 7 July 1694.
48 *Numismata: a Discourse of Medals, Antient and Modern* (London: Benjamin Tooke, 1697), p. 260.
49 BL Add. MS 78314: Benjamin Tooke to Evelyn, 11 Jan. 1698.
50 Evelyn, *Diary*, IV, 13, 136.
51 Ibid., IV, 154.
52 Ibid., IV, 172.
53 Ibid., IV, 174.
54 BL Add. MS 78298: Evelyn to Godolphin, 6 March 1679. I have relied on the transcriptions provided me by John Spurr and Mark Knights. To both of them I am exceedingly grateful.
55 Evelyn, *Diary*, IV, 319-20.
56 Ibid., 341-2.
57 Ibid., 342.
58 Ibid., 329, 323, 332.
59 Ibid., 352-3.
60 Ibid., 333-4.
61 Ibid., 594. See also ibid., 185, 246.
62 This point I establish at some length in my forthcoming monograph, *The First Modern Revolution*.
63 BL Add. MS 78431: Evelyn to Mary Evelyn, 8 Feb. 1685.
64 John Evelyn jr, *To the King: a Congratulatory Poem* (London: R. Bentley, 1685).
65 Evelyn, *Diary*, IV, 437.

66 Ibid., IV, 474-5, 479.
67 Ibid., 484.
68 Ibid., 489.
69 BL Add. MS 78299: Evelyn to Godolphin, 23 May 1686. For specific instances of his refusal to act see Evelyn, *Diary*, IV, 509-10, 512.
70 Ibid., IV, 540.
71 Ibid., 519.
72 Ibid., 524.
73 BL Add. MS 78539: Evelyn to Ralph Bohun, 27 Oct. 1687.
74 Evelyn, *Diary*, IV, 582.
75 Ibid., IV, 536.
76 Ibid., 597.
77 Ibid., 599-600.
78 Ibid., IV, 592.
79 Ibid., 603.
80 Ibid., 606.
81 Ibid., 606, 609.; Hiscock, *John Evelyn and his Family Circle* (see n. 14 above), p. 149.
82 BL Add. MS 78301: John Evelyn jr to Evelyn, 15 Dec. 1688. John jr, it should be noted, heaped scorn on 'the passive obedience men, who trembled for their plate and their libraries'.
83 BL Add. MS 78299: Evelyn to Lord ?, Nov. 1688. For the Bill of Rights, see Lois Schwoerer, *The Declaration of Rights, 1689* (Baltimore: Johns Hopkins University Press, 1981), pp. 28, 270-1. Interestingly Evelyn did not specifically bar a Catholic from inheriting the throne.
84 BL Add. MS 78299: Evelyn to Lord ?, Nov. 1688. See also Schwoerer, *Declaration*, pp. 296-7.
85 For Evelyn's later hopes for Parliamentary reform, see BL Add. MS 78299: to Godolphin, 16 June 1696; Add. MS 78431: to Mary Evelyn, 11 Nov. 1695.
86 BL Add. MS 78299: Evelyn to Lord ?, Nov. 1688.
87 Ibid.
88 Ibid.
89 Ibid.
90 Ibid.
91 Ibid.
92 Evelyn, *Diary*, III, 229, 236, 254-5, 377, 497, 502, 504-5, 515. These are but a few examples taken from one volume of the diary. They could be multiplied.
93 Hunter, 'Evelyn in the 1650s' (see n. 12 above), p. 68.
94 *The State of France* (London: M.M., G. Bedell & T. Collins, 1652), pp. 1-2.
95 Ibid., sig. [B11ᵛ].
96 Ibid., pp. 94-5.
97 Ibid., p. 15.
98 Ibid., pp. 72-3. France, for Evelyn, became the benchmark of rural poverty. So, for example, he noted that the people in Rutland lived 'as wretchedly as in the most impoverished parts of France, which they much resemble being idle and sluttish'; Evelyn, *Diary*, III, 122.
99 *State of France*, p. 14.
100 Evelyn, *Tyrannus* (1661), in *The Writings of John Evelyn* (see n. 25 above), p. 163. In *Mundus Muliebris: or, the Ladies Dressing-Room Unlock'd, and her*

Toilette Spread (London: R. Bentley, 1690) Evelyn attributed the fall of the Roman Empire to the spread of 'Asiatick' manners: sig. [A4ʳ].

101 *Tyrannus*, in *Writings*, p. 164.

102 Evelyn, *Diary*, III, 465, 467. He had indeed called upon the King to take the lead in rejecting French fashion: *Tyrannus*, in *Writings*, p. 167.

103 John and Mary Evelyn, *Mundus Muliebris*, 1690, p. 22. For Mary's role, see Evelyn, *Diary*, IV, 423-4.

104 Evelyn, *Diary*, IV, 380.

105 Ibid., 331.

106 Ibid., 369.

107 Ibid., 308.

108 Ibid., 339. Three years later he expressed these cultural sentiments with respect to gardens: BL Add. MS 78299: to Robert Berkeley, 16 July 1686.

109 Evelyn, *Diary*, IV, 331.

110 Ibid., 478. For further extensive discussions of the persecutions in France, see ibid., 447-8, 484-7, 493, 498, 575, 581.

111 Ibid., 508, 510.

112 Ibid., III, 404-5. De Beer notes that this entry for 1665 was a 1683 addition.

113 Ibid., IV, 524-5.

114 Ibid., 548-9.

115 *Particular Friends*, p. 175: Evelyn to Pepys, 15 March 1687.

116 BL Add. MS 78432: John jr to Mary Evelyn, 16 Dec. 1692, reporting on a letter sent him by his father.

117 Aubrey, *Natural History and Antiquities of the County of Surrey* (see n. 2 above), I, sig. A5: Evelyn to Aubrey, 8 Feb. 1676. The best discussion of the Evelyn family gunpowder mills is in *Gunpowder Mills: Documents of the Seventeenth and Eighteenth Centuries*, ed. by A. G. Crocker and others, Surrey Record Society, 36 (2000), pp. 1, 75.

118 Notes from his 1650s conversations with tradesmen are preserved in his abortive History of Trades: BL Add. MS 78341.

119 Evelyn, *Diary*, III, 187.

120 Ibid., IV, 46.

121 Ibid., 58, 531.

122 Ibid., 520-1, 561.

123 *Particular Friends* (see n. 46 above), p. 114. Evelyn to Pepys, 8 July 1680.

124 BL Add. MS 78632: library catalogue, *c.*1687. Political economy should thus be added to Hunter's description of the 'serious arsenal of book learning' acquired by Evelyn: Hunter, 'Evelyn in the 1650s' (see n. 12 above), p. 72.

125 Evelyn, *Diary*, III, 201-2.

126 Ibid., III, 374.

127 BL Add. MS 78393: Commission for Foreign Plantations, 30 July 1670; Evelyn, *Diary*, III, 570-1.

128 Evelyn, *Diary*, III, 580-1, 602-3.

129 Ibid., III, 624, 629.

130 Ibid., IV, 12.

131 Ibid., 6.

132 Hunter, 'Evelyn in the 1650s', p. 79.

133 Josiah Child, *A Discourse of the Nature, Use and Advantages of Trade* (London: Randal Taylor, 1694), p. 7. I have quoted from this 1694 pamphlet because it

is the clearest and most concise statement of Child's views. He was, however, well known to enunciate these positions throughout the 1680s in printed works, declarations at Court and in the committee of the East India Company, and in his letters of instruction to factors in the East. These general propositions are elaborated at greater length in the chapter on political economy in my forthcoming book on the Revolution of 1688-89. In the meantime see Steven Pincus, 'The Making of a Great Power? Universal Monarchy, Political Economy, and the Transformation of English Political Culture', *The European Legacy*, 5 (2000), esp. 536-8.

134 Child, *A Discourse Concerning Trade and that in Particular of the East Indies* (London: Andrew Sowle, 1689), p. 8.

135 Ibid., pp. 10-11.

136 Child, *Discourse*, p. 3.

137 'Second Treatise of Government', in *Political Writings of John Locke*, ed. by David Wootton (New York: Mentor, 1993), pp. 281-2.

138 Sir William Petty, *The Political Anatomy of Ireland ... to Which is Added Verbum Sapienti* (London: D. Brown & W. Rogers, 1691), p. 9. I am grateful to Ryan Frace for this reference.

139 EIC *v.* Sandys, in *A Complete Collection of State Trials*, ed. by T. B. Howell (London: T. C. Hansard, 1811), X, 523.

140 Ibid., p. 534.

141 Evelyn, *Diary*, IV, 297.

142 *Particular Friends*, pp. 129-30: to Pepys, 28 April 1682.

143 Evelyn, *Diary*, IV, 305-6.

144 Ibid. Houblon later was a great supporter of the Bank of England, and in 1689 was an early and avid supporter of crowning William III: Roger Morrice, Entering Book, 2 Feb. 1689, Dr. Williams Library, MSS 31Q, p. 454.

145 Evelyn, *Navigation and Commerce* (London: Benjamin Tooke, 1674), p. 5.

146 Ibid., pp. 15-16.

147 *Tyrannus*, in *Writings* (see n. 25 above), p. 169. See also *State of France*, p. 32. Evelyn did frequently decry luxury. However luxury he thought was the result not of wealth, but of bad moral leadership.

148 Evelyn, *Diary*, II, 46.

149 *Navigation and Commerce*, pp. 6-7.

150 Ibid., p. 64.

151 Ibid., pp. 7-8.

152 Ibid., p. 15.

153 *State of France* (see n. 94 above), p. 77.

154 BL Add. MS 78299: to Pepys, 19 Sept. 1682.

155 It is true that James II was occasionally rumoured to be advocating a land register at the high point of his flirtation with Dissent, but nothing ever came of it; see Yale University Library, Osborn MSS 1, Box 2, Folder 28: Owen Wynne to Edmund Poley, 14 Oct. 1687.

156 BL Add. MS 78299: to Godolphin, 16 June 1696.

157 *Numismata*, p. 230.

158 BL Add. MS 78299: to Godolphin, 16 June 1696.

159 Evelyn, *Diary*, IV, 177, 185-6. For the support of Locke, Godolphin, and Houblon, see Bank of England Archives, G7/1, p. 1; M1/3.

160 Evelyn, *Diary*, V, 90.

161 Ibid., 209.
162 We now know these were supplemented by book of longhand sermon notes, BL Add. MS 78364.
163 Evelyn, *Diary*, II, 19-20. The entry was obviously written much later.
164 Ibid., III, 164.
165 Ibid., 197.
166 Ibid., 149. For Jeremy Taylor, see Anthony Milton, *Catholic and Reformed: the Roman and Protestant Churches in English Protestant Thought, 1600-1640* (Cambridge: Cambridge University Press, 1995), pp. 491-3.
167 Evelyn, *Diary*, III, 105-6. Three days later he referred to Wilkins as 'obliging and universally curious'; ibid., III, 110.
168 Ibid., 416.
169 Ibid.
170 William Lloyd, *A Sermon Preached at the Funeral of the Right Reverend Father in God John Late Lord Bishop of Chester* (London: A. C. for Henry Brome, 1672), p. 34.
171 Evelyn, *Diary*, IV, 169.
172 Ibid., IV, 172.
173 Ibid., IV, 240-1, 454, 612; V, 8, 12.
174 Ibid., IV, 107, 131, 244, 373.
175 BL Add. MS 78299: Evelyn to William Sancroft, 18 April 1680.
176 Evelyn, *Diary*, V, 80.
177 BL Add. MS 78318: H. Pawnan(?) to Evelyn, 14 Feb. 1692.
178 Evelyn, *Diary*, IV, 9, 34, 53, 134, 238, 277, 368.
179 Anthony Wood, *Athenae Oxonienses*, ed. by Philip Bliss, 4 vols (London: Lackington et al, 1820), IV, 512-13. The entry for Tillotson is not in the original edition, but added by Wood in manuscript to his own copy.
180 Evelyn, *Diary*, IV, 160, 297, 520.
181 Evelyn, *Diary*, IV, 47-8. Evelyn was clearly impressed by later sermons as well, see for example: ibid., IV, 309.
182 BL Add. MS 78299: to Burnet, 30 Aug. 1680.
183 *Particular Friends*, p. 119: Evelyn to Pepys, 6 Sept. 1680. See also Evelyn, *Diary*, IV, 241.
184 Evelyn, *Diary*, IV, 124, 205, 300-1.
185 BL Add. MS 78299: to Burnet, 23 Jan. 1689.
186 BL Add. MS 78314: Ralph Bohun to Evelyn, 19 March 1701.
187 In his sermon notes, BL Add. MS 78364, Evelyn recorded eleven of Tenison's sermons; Tillotson was next with five (excluding the vicar of Deptford, Evelyn's home parish). See also Evelyn, *Diary*, IV, 106, 279, 351, 530, 537, 573.
188 Ibid., IV, 307-8.
189 Ibid., 366, 372, 388; V, 105; BL Add. MS 78299: Evelyn to Jael Boscawen, 17 Sept. 1686.
190 Evelyn, *Diary*, V, 84, 138.
191 Ibid., IV, 603.
192 Ibid., V, 65-6.
193 Ibid., 198.
194 On Ken: see ibid., IV, 543, 577; on Sprat, IV, 131, 167, 188; on Compton, whose talent, Evelyn thought 'is not in preaching', see IV, 9, 97, 379.
195 Ibid., IV, 574.

196 Ibid., III, 532.

197 BL Add. MS 78442: Evelyn to John Evelyn jr, 16 March 1673.

198 BL Add. MS 78431: Evelyn to Mary Evelyn, 30 July 1685.

199 BL Add. MS 78299: to Lady Sunderland, 12 Sept. 1686.

200 Evelyn, *Memoires for my Grand-son*, pp. 49-50.

201 *A Supplement to Burnet's History of My Own Time*, ed. by H. C. Foxcroft (Oxford: Clarendon Press, 1902), p. 463.

202 Gilbert Burnet, *The New Preface and Additional Chapter* (London: D. Midwinter & B. Cowse, 1713), pp. 12-13.

203 *Supplement to Burnet's History of My Own Time*, p. 506.

204 Evelyn, *Diary*, V, 6.

205 BL Add. MS 78299: to Lady Sunderland, 12 Jan. 1690.

206 Evelyn, *Diary*, IV, 131.

207 Ibid., 224.

208 Ibid., 296. I will show elsewhere that Evelyn's friends Burnet, Tillotson, Tenison, Stillingfleet, Patrick, Moore, and Cumberland agitated for comprehension and toleration in the wake of the Revolution. These quotations highlight what we know Evelyn heard.

209 Evelyn, *Diary*, III, 607-8. De Beer dates the passage from 1680-85. Mark Knights has suggested that Evelyn's letter to Godolphin in March 1679 reveals similar sentiments: *Politics and Opinion in Crisis*, p. 200.

210 Evelyn, *Diary*, V, 15. This example is taken from a sermon by Tenison.

211 BL Add. MS 4236, fol. 19ᵛ: John Tillotson, 'Concessions which will probably be made by the Church of England for the Union of Protestants', 13 Sept. 1689.

212 BL Add. MS 78299: to Lady Sunderland, 15 April 1679.

213 Evelyn, *Diary*, IV, 367-9, 455.

214 Ibid., 259-60.

215 Ibid., 140.

216 Ibid., II, 45-6.

217 I have found no clear evidence about Evelyn's views on political resistance during the period in which so many of the low churchmen developed elegant justifications for their rejection of passive obedience. The fact that his son had belittled the Oxford 'passive obedience men' is perhaps telling. While it is true that Evelyn had specifically rejected resistance on religious grounds in his manuscript history of religion, that was an early statement of his views. Late in life he commented that the manuscript was 'hastily put into chapters many years since' and was 'full of errors'; Evelyn, *Memoires for my Grand-son* (see n. 8 above), p. 64.

218 Evelyn, *Diary*, IV, 7, 87, 154.

219 Ibid., 320, 331.

220 Ibid., 419, 535; BL Add. MS 78431: Evelyn to Mary Evelyn, 5 March 1685.

221 Evelyn, *Diary*, IV, 243. The tract was *Contemplations on the Life and Glory of Holy Mary the Mother of Jesus*. Evelyn's annotations in his copy of *Present State of the Controversie* (1687) in the British Library (unpress-marked as yet).

222 Evelyn, *Diary*, IV, 188, 198, 529, 532-3.

223 Evelyn, *Diary*, V, 475.

224 Evelyn (trans.), *The Pernicious Consequences of the New Heresie of the Jesuites* (London: J. Flesher for Richard Royston, 1666), sigs. [A4-A5]; BL Add. MS

78299: Evelyn to Lady Berkeley, 26 Nov. 1683; Evelyn, *Diary*, III, 393, 397; BL Add. MS 78299: Evelyn to Sancroft, 10 Oct. 1688.

225 Evelyn, *Diary*, III, 571; IV, 9.

226 Ibid., III, 326, 329; IV, 142.

227 Ibid., III, 295.

228 Ibid., 373. Evelyn also wrote in praise of Tuke's play *Adventures of Five Hours* (1663): see Geoffrey Keynes, *John Evelyn: a Study in Bibliophily*, 2nd edn (Oxford: Clarendon Press, 1968), p. 259.

229 BL Add. MS 78307: note, Sept./Oct. 1688.

230 BL Add. MS 78299: to Lady Tuke, 14 June 1693.

231 Evelyn, *Diary*, V, 22.

232 Ibid., 70; see also 24, 27, 29, 30.

233 Ibid., IV, 623-4. It is significant that Evelyn here claims that the nation deposed James II for his misgovernment.

234 BL Add. MS 78299: to Lloyd, 5 Feb. 1695.

235 Ibid.: to Tenison, 7 Jan. 1695.

236 Evelyn, *Diary*, V, 205.

237 Ibid., 28-29.

238 Ibid., 233.

239 Ibid., 491.

240 It should be noted that Evelyn's friendship with the moderate Tory Sidney Godolphin was not inconsistent with his own commitment to Whig political economy. Godolphin himself worked closely with Whigs on economic matters: PRO, SP 105/82, f. 21: Charles Montagu to George Stepney, 6/16 Oct. 1690.

241 Evelyn, *Diary*, V, 135, 361, 408.

242 Ibid., 184; BL Add. MS 78299: Evelyn to Pepys, 7 July 1694. The clearest statement of Wotton's Whig principles can be found in William Wotton, *The Case of the Present Convocation Consider'd* (London, 1711), pp. 22-4.

243 Evelyn, *Diary*, V, 88-9.

244 Evelyn, *Diary*, V, 94; this was his Boyle Lectures.

245 See Joseph Levine, *The Battle of the Books* (Ithaca: Cornell University Press, 1991), pp. 53-4.

246 *The Correspondence of Richard Bentley*, ed. by Christopher Wordsworth, 2 vols (London: John Murray, 1842), I, 152: Bentley to Evelyn, 21 Oct. 1697.

247 BL Add. MS 78299: to Lady Sunderland, 15 April 1679.

MARY EVELYN AND
DEVOTIONAL PRACTICE[1]

GILLIAN WRIGHT

MARY EVELYN, eldest daughter of John and Mary Evelyn, died of smallpox in March 1685, aged nineteen. In his diary, John describes the news of her illness as 'a wonderfull affliction to me, not onely for her beauty, which was very lovely, but for the danger of loosing one of extraordinary parts & virtue'. In his reflections on Mary's abilities and accomplishments after her death, John enlarges on the subject of his daughter's diligent piety:

> How unexpressable losse I and my Wife sustain'd, the Virtues & perfections she was endow'd with best would shew; of which the justnesse of her stature, person, comelinesse of her Countenance and gracefullnesse of motion, naturall, & unaffected (though more than ordinaryly beautifull), was one of the least, compar'd with the Ornaments of her mind, which was truely extraordinary, especialy the better part: Of early piety, & singularly Religious, so as spending a considerable part of every day in private devotion, Reading and other vertuous exercises, she had collected, & written out aboundance of the most usefull and judicious periods of the Books she read, in a kind of Common place; as out of Dr. Hammonds *N.Test*: and most of the best practical Treatises extant in our tonge.[2]

A paper headed 'A Note of what Bookes and papers were found written by my late Daughter Mary E. after her decease: 1685', includes references to seven manuscripts on religious subjects, several of which, such as 'A parchment book with some loose papers in it, containing Collections out of History, divinity &c by way of Commonplace' and 'A Paper book stich'd with some in loose papers being prayers translated by her out of French &c', testify clearly to the habits of spiritual reading and transcription ascribed to Mary in John Evelyn's diary.[3] Unfortunately, however, only a few of the manuscript items described in the list are still extant in the Evelyn archives. It is possible, as Frances Harris has suggested, that other papers may have been passed on to later generations of Evelyn women, and thus lost to the family collections.[4] Whatever the reason, some of the most intriguing items in the list of Mary Evelyn's papers, including both the parchment book of commonplaces and the translations of French prayers, are now missing.

Of the documents which remain, the most substantial witnesses to Mary

Evelyn's devotional practice are two small notebooks and two loose papers, all probably written between 1679 and 1683. Three of these documents are now included in a composite volume, BL Add. MS 78440; the other is catalogued separately as Add. MS 78441. The latter is a small notebook, compiled by Mary Evelyn, with a title-leaf dated Friday 31 August 1683; though in a prefatory note she explains that the ensuing text is based on notes made on loose pages in London the previous winter, now transferred to a single notebook for fear lest they be lost. This notebook is entitled 'Miscelania', with the explanatory subtitle, 'Book of several designes and thoughts of mine for the regulating my Life upon many occasions'. Its contents include meditations and resolutions on subjects such as her daily timetable, prayer, preparation for communion, and the moral dilemmas posed by worldly activities such as theatre-going, playing cards, and dancing. Of the three documents in Add. MS 78440 cited in this article, the most substantial is Mary Evelyn's book of sermon notes, which covers a period from May 1679 to November 1683, and refers, in varying levels of detail, to thirty-six sermons, heard mostly at Deptford Church. The other two documents, both undated, are a paper by John Evelyn, headed 'Directions for the Employment of Your Time', and Mary's own 'Necessary Additions to those Directions of my Father when I was at Sayes Court'. John's 'Directions' are not explicitly addressed to Mary, but they are clearly intended for one of his daughters, and Mary's known piety, as well as the existence of the 'Necessary Additions' document in her hand, makes her the most likely candidate. She also refers in her 'Miscelania' to 'my Fathers Directions in the paper he gave me'.[5] The 'Necessary Additions' appear from their content to have been produced while Mary was staying with friends in London, and needed to adapt and re-apply her father's instructions to take account of the different social and spiritual conditions which obtained in these different circumstances.

This discussion of Mary Evelyn's devotional practice relies heavily also on the chapters on Anglican lay piety in John Spurr's book, *The Restoration Church of England*.[6] The kind of devotional practice to which Mary Evelyn's papers testify is closely consistent with the emphasis on holy living promoted within Restoration Anglicanism, promulgated in sermons and in treatises such as, perhaps most famously, *The Whole Duty of Man* and Jeremy Taylor's *Holy Living*. Put simply, this is a theology which stresses that true faith must issue in good works and a good life, and consequently takes a great interest in how good Christian living can be understood, organized, and practised. Another essential aspect of this theological emphasis is its insistence on the integration of private devotional practice into the institutional and ceremonial life of the church. Hence the importance ascribed in the devotional treatises to subjects such as preparation for communion or attendance at prayers.

Three aspects of Mary Evelyn's writings clearly illustrate her affinity with the holy living movement in the Church of England: her reading, her use of the vocabulary of holy living, and, more broadly, her attitude to the Church itself, as indicated by her comments on church structures and ceremonies and her awareness of how the Church of England was defining its own teaching and institutions in careful distinction both from Roman Catholicism and from the various strands of Protestant nonconformity. This article examines each of these aspects of Mary Evelyn's writing, and also considers the question of Mary Evelyn's engagement with the theological material she had encountered through books and sermons. Was this a critical engagement, and if so, to what extent? How did she respond to the spiritual instruction she had read and heard?

One of the main concerns of John Evelyn's 'Directions for the Employment of your Time' is to make recommendations about his daughter's reading, both sacred and secular. Sacred reading receives considerably more attention than secular, and John's most specific prescriptions concern his daughter's reading of the Bible.[7] Mary is to read 'One Chapter & Psal: Morning & Evening, getting some practical *Texts* by *heart*; which will both furnish you for *prayer*, and *Life*'. In no case other than the Bible does John specifically prescribe frequency of reading, or memorizing texts. However his suggestion that knowing the Bible will furnish Mary for prayer and life is in line with his habitual assumption – consistent, evidently, with traditional humanist principles – that reading is no mere passive exercise but a practical activity which should result in perceptible benefits for the reader. Hence he recommends that Mary should copy out devotional passages, and that she should use books such as Simon Patrick's *The Devout Christian* and 'Bish: Andrews' to supplement her own private prayers.[8] The other spiritual books specified in John's 'Directions' are, with one exception, all by contemporary or near-contemporary Church of England writers.[9] These 'Devout & usefull *Bookes*' are *The Whole Duty of Man*, *The Ladies Calling*, John Wilkins' *Of Natural Religion*, William Cave's *Primitive Christianity* and *The Lives of the Primitive Fathers*, Simon Patrick's *Parable of the Pilgrim* and *Mensa Mystica*, John Pearson's *Exposition on the Creed*, and Henry Hammond's *Paraphrase on the New Testament*.[10] In the case of both Pearson and Hammond, however, John advises Mary to read only part of the text. Of Pearson's *Exposition* he recommends that she should read only the summary paragraphs on each article of the creed; 'the rest' he writes, 'you neede not reade, it being *critical*'. Similarly, he says that she should read the New Testament alongside Hammond's paraphrase 'without the *Notes*, which are Likewise *Critical*', adding, however, 'unless where you are in any doubt, &c: beseeching *God* to direct you in the right, & ever remembering that all our *Reading*, & *Praying* signifies nothing without the improvement of our *Lives*'. Again, this is reading *for use*, and the use which John envisages is expected to find expression in practical, holy living.[11]

Two points of interest are apparent from John Evelyn's choice of books on his daughter's behalf. One is that he was keen for her to be well-informed about the historical basis for her religion. Thus, for example, he recommends Cave's *Lives of the Primitive Fathers*, 'because you will see, how the *Church of God*, has ben govern'd in all ages'. The second is that many of these books are key texts in the holy living movement: principally, perhaps, *The Whole Duty of Man* and the works by Simon Patrick. Similarly, in Mary Evelyn's own papers, her references to books she has read already or resolves to read in the future are consistently to 'holy living' books: again, principally, *The Whole Duty of Man*, and the works of Simon Patrick.[12] In the 'Necessary Additions' she resolves to read in *The Whole Duty of Man* every evening, while in the 'Miscelania' she plans to read chapter three of *The Whole Duty of Man* – the chapter on the Lord's Supper – as part of her self-preparation every time she receives communion, as well as using some of the prayers from Simon Patrick's *The Devout Christian*.[13] Moreover, many passages in the 'Miscelania' which do not explicitly cite a source can nonetheless be shown to correspond closely to the instructions of these and similar devotional treatises. For example, Mary's meditation on prayer, and her insistence that she should not neglect her own private prayers just because she is also attending public prayers, closely follow *The Whole Duty*'s teaching that 'this of private prayer is a duty which will not be excused by the performance of the other of publick. They are both required, and one must not be taken in exchange for the other.'[14] Similarly, when she argues that special Sunday prayers should be in addition to, not instead of, her usual morning and evening prayers, justifying her argument by analogy with the burnt offerings required by God of the Israelites in Numbers 28, there is an exact precedent for this biblical comparison in Simon Patrick's *Mensa Mystica*.[15]

Her soul-searching as to whether it is acceptable for her to go to the theatre, given that she is staying in a household where theatre-going is considered harmless, is resolved in a compromise: she will do so when socially necessary, in order to avoid offending her companions, but she will not go on Saturday evenings, for otherwise experience shows that inappropriate thoughts linger in her mind and disrupt her preparation for Sunday. This compromise has possible precedents in the *Mensa Mystica*, which enjoins 'That we are to lay aside (some time before we come to the Lords Table) all our worldly employments though never so innocent', and in François de Sales's advice on how to negotiate pastimes which are lawful but dangerous. De Sales writes, 'dance & play according to the rules I have prescribed thee, when to comply with civil company thou shalt find it fit in wisdom and discretion. For compliance, as a branch of charity, maketh indifferent things good, and dangerous tolerable, and even taketh away the mischief from those things that are in some sort evil.'[16] Although what Mary says on this issue is so similar to Patrick and de Sales, and although she cites both these writers elsewhere in the 'Miscelania', she does not name them, or anyone else, as authorities for the compromise she has reached about theatre-going. The impression conveyed by Mary's spiritual writing is that the teaching in the books she has read has been so completely assimilated that it can be articulated and presented, in effect, as her own thought. This non-acknowledgement of sources is one example of a narrative practice which pervades the 'Miscelania' and the sermon notes: Mary's tendency to suppress distinctions between quotation, allusion, paraphrase, and analysis, such that the one runs seamlessly (or nearly so) into the other. Thus in the sermon notes it is often difficult to tell whether Mary is actually quoting the words of the preacher, or summarizing what he has said in her own words. The teachings of the treatises become her own convictions; the preacher's words, once heard by Mary, seem to become her own words.

The vocabulary used in both the sermon notes and the 'Miscelania' provides further evidence for the influence of 'holy living' teaching on Mary Evelyn. In the 'Miscelania', indeed, she prays: 'deny me not the meanes to grow better, by enabling me dayly to performe a Methodical course of Holy Living'.[17] The sermon notes consistently indicate that this devotional approach was strongly favoured by the preachers she heard, including the vicar of Deptford, Richard Holden, the preacher she cites most frequently.[18] For example, Mary concludes her notes on a Christmas Day sermon by Holden with the precept: 'Every article of our Faith hath a direct Tendency to Piety & a Godly Life'.[19] On 27 February 1681, Holden is said to have preached that 'Knowledge is a good Foundation but 'tis Practise & Obedience Crowns the Work'.[20] Another sermon, not by Holden this time, on the text 'My yoke is easy and my burden is light' (Matthew 11.30), concludes: 'So God is not onely Glorified by Faith & Praise & thanksgiving, but by Justice & Charity & al the Actions of a Holy life. For though St Paul did say that Faith was Imputed to Abraham for righteousness yet St James says he was Justified by Works for again faith without Works is Dead.'[21] Her notes on another sermon, heard in April 1683, include a reference to 'our tyme which God gave us here to work out our salvation'.[22] Working out one's salvation, a phrase from Philippians 2.12, was a favourite concept among holy living writers, and Mary Evelyn seems to have taken it to heart: in a prayer in her 'Miscelania' she confesses that she has 'mis-spent a great part of that pretious tyme allowed for the working out my salvation, In vain, unnessecary, sinfull Actions, nay Sometymes in Absolute Laziness & sloth'.[23] In fact, the entire 'Miscelania' manuscript, which has the heading 'Rules for spending my precious tyme well', is testimony to Mary Evelyn's commitment to working out her salvation through the practice of careful self-examination and self-regulation advocated in books such as *The Whole Duty of Man*. The references to 'precious time' also recall John Evelyn, for whom this was a favourite phrase: he uses it, for example, in his 'Directions' to Mary when enjoining her to 'be not *long* in *dressing* or *Un-dressing*, which trifles away much *precious* time'.[24]

In both the 'Miscelania' and the sermon notes, the importance of the institutions and ceremonies of the Church of England to Mary Evelyn's devotional practice is apparent. Again, in accordance with the teachings of writers such as Patrick, her own private devotions are conceived as being complementary to her participation in public church events.[25] Hence her careful deliberations as to how to spend her Saturdays, especially the Saturday before the communion service; hence too, the very existence of the sermon notes, which, according to the 'Miscelania', she subsequently used alongside the Bible as aids to meditation.[26] It is also evident from the sermon notes that she was aware of at least some of the points of devotional practice on which the Church of England differed from other denominations. Her first sermon note, for instance, is on Richard Holden's sermon at Deptford on Romans 16.17: 'Now I beseech you brethren, mark them which cause divisions and offences, contrary to the doctrine which ye have learned, and avoid them'.[27] In Mary's account, Holden's sermon begins with a closely-argued justification of the use of set forms of prayer, and concludes with a defence of the Church of England's communion service:

There are many among you that contemn several holy rights and devote ceremonies of the Church because they have beene abused in former ages and by other nations, as the Sosinions who would (at the Benediction) sit because they believed Jesus to be no more than wholy man and as papists who kneele (as much at t'other side) because they imagine Bread to be the very body of Christ; now, Because these with Superstition have brought that holy institution to foolishness, ought we that know the right Contemn or Not follow it because it was or is corrupted by others.[28]

She was also in church to hear the reading of Charles II's declaration to all his loving subjects on the occasion of the Rye House plot, described by Mary as 'being founded upon Schismatical & wicked dissenting Principles'.[29] The preacher that morning, a Mr Jackson, 'Exorted us to be Lovers of one another & to Joyne unanimously in the Love of Christ & the Church that so by our well compacted strength we might be able to breake the Chaine of our Sinns & those especialy which disturbe the Discipline & harmony of the Church Millitant'. Here Mary risks one of the very few value-judgements in her sermon notes, referring to 'the Excellent reasons he pressd upon us to live together in unity & Brotherly accord'.[30]

That same sermon, indeed, occasions the only other example in the sermon notes of Mary stating an opinion about what she has heard at church.

Here she writes, 'truly 'twas a very good Sermon suitable to the Concerns of this Day' – suitable, apparently, not only to the denunciation of the Rye House Plot, but also because this was a communion Sunday, and because it was the anniversary of the Great Fire of London.[31] There is no equivalent in Mary's writing to her father's occasionally rather caustic comments on the quality of the preaching he heard – for example, his comment that Mr Smith, the curate at Deptford, was 'a good man, but had not the talent of Preaching'.[32] However, there are two references to Mr Smith – presumably the same man – in Mary's sermon notes: and on each occasion she transcribes only the biblical text, without reporting on the sermon itself.[33] Arguably this omission is in itself a value judgement. Moreover, John Evelyn's comments on the style and quality of sermons tend to occur in his diary, rather than in his own manuscript volume of sermon notes, which, like Mary's, concentrate on summarizing content.[34] Indeed, such value judgements as occur in his sermon notes are commonly of the same sort as Mary's, explaining why the message of this particular sermon was appropriate to the time. But the structure and conventions of Mary's sermon notes are much more flexible than John's, and are much less obviously governed by a sense of propriety; and so it is at least worth remarking that she makes no overt attempt to criticise or qualify what the preachers have said. Similarly, on no occasion in the 'Miscelania' does she attempt to criticize or qualify the teaching of the devotional handbooks. In this respect, her writing is conformist. It is also conformist in the respect already described: her habit of blurring the distinctions between her own voice, and the voices of the preachers she had heard and the books she had read, such that the tendency of her texts is towards producing one consistent ideology, one single voice. Her own analysis is continuous with, and often indistinguishable from, received wisdom.

While conformist, her writing is also both thoughtful and innovative. The very existence of the 'Miscelania' and the 'Necessary Additions' document is evidence of her determination to think through the teaching she has received, and to extend or modify it in new situations. In the 'Necessary Additions' she resolves to avoid ten o'clock prayers 'because of Crowding through Westminster Hall among the Lawyers & other Inconveniencies', deciding to rise at six a.m. to attend the earlier morning prayers instead. She is also prepared, occasionally, to differ from her father, at least on matters of timing. In the 'Miscelania' she writes: 'above all I wish that He would direct me to some *Confessor that would be a very great Comfort to my weake & unsteady Disposition*'.[35] John records in his diary that after Mary's death he found amongst her papers 'one letter to some divine (who is not named) to whom she writes that he would be her Ghostly Father & guide ... well I remember, that she often desired me to recomend her to such a person, but (though I intended it) I did not think fit to do it as yet'.[36] It is likely that in this wish Mary was influenced by *The Whole Duty of Man*, which advises anyone who has doubts about his spiritual worthiness 'not to trust to his own judgment, but to make known his case to some discreet and Godly Minister, and rather be guided by his'.[37] So on this occasion, when there is a difference – admittedly a very small one – between her father's wishes and the advice of the books he's recommended to her, Mary does not shrink from articulating her own opinion.

It is also probably fair to say that Mary's approach to the teaching she has received has a rather more writerly emphasis than her sources would necessarily have warranted. The only writing John mentions in his 'Directions' is copying – 'transcribing *Devotions*, and sometimes things into your *Receit-book*' – and his only other comments on this activity concern her deportment as she writes; there is nothing about writing as an intellectual or spiritual activity.[38] For Mary, however, writing is evidently an important devotional exercise. When in the 'Miscelania' she vows to read *The Whole Duty of Man* as part of her self-preparation for communion, she says that she will conduct the self-examination which is an essential part of this preparation by 'carefully writing downe in a Separate Paper, what sins committed & mercies received since last Communicating'.[39] *The Whole Duty* itself does not recommend that the intending communicant should use writing as a tool of self-examination; it appears rather to assume a process of silent introspection, or else confession to a 'discreet and Godly Minister'. Mary not only makes the point about writing down her sins, but says she will read the document over every day, presumably until her next communion.

Elsewhere in the 'Miscelania' she opens a six-page section with the declaration 'Here begins Meditations after Reading the Holy Scriptures, & some short Comments upon several Chapters & verses: either of my own or out of Books & what I have remembered of Sermons'.[40] Here again she does not seem to draw clear distinctions between her own comments, extracts from books, or recollections of sermons; all appear to be equally valid and useful to her as spiritual aids. This impression is confirmed over the ensuing six pages, where, while biblical passages are carefully identified in the margin, there is only one citation of a contemporary theological book, Simon Patrick's *Aqua Genitalis*.[41] With that one exception, Mary's densely-packed meditations on Christ's sacrifice, the punishment of sins, the glorification of God, etc., are laid out with no indication of what comes from where. For her, it is all useful spiritual material, and by the act of writing it down she both confirms and extends its usefulness. Finally, her use of writing as a spiritual activity can also be seen in the sermon notes: not just in the mere existence of the notes, but in various local details. Thus, having summarized a sermon on the parable of the fig tree, she applies it to herself, praying that she may by God's grace lead a good life, and not be cut down like the unprofitable fig tree.[42] On fol. 4 of the sermon notes manuscript she experiments with writing summary headings – 'inconstantia' and 'spiritus' – in the outer margin beside the notes to which they apply. Presumably this was intended to facilitate future use of the notes for meditation.[43] Another strategy which she uses several times is to transform her report on a sermon at the last into a prayer, with the simple addition of the words 'amen, amen' – or, on one occasion, 'which I beg for Christ his sake amen, amen'.[44]

In his obituary on Mary in his diary, John Evelyn is careful to memorialize his daughter's habitual piety, her dedication to prayer, fasting, and spiritual reading, and her typically meticulous preparation for monthly communion. He emphasizes, however, that the extent of her literary activities had been largely unknown to her family until after her death:

Having some days after opened her Trunks, & looked into her Closset, amazed & even astonished we were to find that incredible number of papers and Collections she had made of severall material Authors, both Historians, Poets, Travells &c: but above all the Devotions, Contemplations, & resolutions upon those Contemplations, which we found under her hand in a booke most methodicaly disposed.[45]

Amazed he may have been, but Mary Evelyn's writings nonetheless represent an application of the devotional practice prescribed for her by John himself in the 'Directions for the Employment of your Time'.[46] The devotional practice to which they testify was consistent with his precepts, even as it exceeded his expectations.

NOTES

1 I should like to acknowledge the invaluable assistance of Victoria Burke of the University of Ottawa, in the research for this essay.
2 Evelyn, *Diary*, IV, 421.
3 BL Add. MS 78440.
4 Unpublished conference paper, University of Reading, 19 November 2001.
5 BL Add. MS 78441, fol. 7.
6 John Spurr, *The Restoration Church of England, 1646-1689* (New Haven & London: Yale University Press, 1991), especially chs 6 and 7. For an outline of 'holy living' principles and practices, see esp. pp. 284-5.
7 Recommended secular reading includes Plutarch, Seneca, Epictetus, the English histories, the herbals, and the natural histories. Presumably the classical works were to be read in translation. In his diary, John Evelyn mentions his daughter's reading of classical poets, both Greek and Latin, but the only foreign languages which he explicitly attributes to her are French and Italian (Evelyn, *Diary*, IV, 423, 421). She appears to have read François de Sales in the original French; see n. 13, below.
8 'Bish: Andrews' is Lancelot Andrewes, *Directions to Pray*, first published 1630, as *Institutiones piae, or, Directions to Pray, also a Short Exposition of the Lords Prayer, the Creed, the 10 Commandments &c*; later published as *Holy Devotions, with Directions to Pray* (1655 and three subsequent editions).

9 The exception is the Presbyterian William Bates, whose tract *The Harmony of the Divine Attributes* is on John's list. He also appears to identify Bates as the author of a tract called 'The reasonableness of Christian Religion' (likewise recommended to Mary). John Spurr suggests this probably denotes Bates's *The Divinity of the Christian Religion, Proved by the Evidence of Reason and Divine Revelation* (1677).

10 Apart from *Directions to Pray* and *On the Reasonableness of the Christian Religion*, all of the books recommended by John Evelyn to his daughter also appear in the much longer catalogue of spiritual literature which he compiled for Anne Spencer, Countess of Sunderland, in a letter of 12 Sept. 1686 and entitled 'The Protestant Ladys Library'. I owe this reference (from his letterbook, BL Add. MS 78299) to Douglas Chambers. *The Whole Duty of Man* and *The Ladies Calling* were both published anonymously, but have traditionally been attributed to Richard Allestree. Apart from *The Whole Duty of Man*, all the spiritual treatises mentioned in the 'Directions' are listed in the Evelyn library catalogue of *c*. 1687 (BL Add. MS 78632). My quotations from the treatises in this article follow the editions cited in the catalogue.

11 This emphasis on reading for practical benefit is also heightened by the method of selective reading which John advocates in the case of Pearson and Hammond. Both the *Exposition* and the *Paraphrase* are works of dense and extensive scholarship. The *Exposition*, for instance, in the 1669 copy owned by John Evelyn (now BL Eve. B. 23), extends to 398 folio pages. Pearson divides the Apostles' Creed into twelve sections, and then considers each section point by point. His erudite text is crammed with references to the Bible, the classical writers, the Church fathers, medieval exegetes, and Roman Catholic writers (the latter typically so that they can be refuted). Each sub-section concludes with a 'recollection of all', designed 'to deliver the summ of every particular truth, so that every one when he pronounceth the Creed may know what he ought to intend, and what he is understood to profess, when he so pronounceth it' (sig. A3^r). It is these summary paragraphs, with their emphasis on practical application, which Mary is instructed to read. Selective reading of Pearson's *Exposition*, unsurprisingly, seems to have been common practice, and was indeed provided for in the structure of the book: see *Exposition*, sig. A3^{r-v}, and Ian Green, *Print and Protestantism in Early Modern England* (Oxford: Oxford University Press, 2000), p. 11. Hammond, comparably, anticipates that the 'less curious *Reader*' of his *Paraphrase* will confine his attention to the main text, ignoring the learned annotations 'which of necessity contain many things above the understandings of the more ignorant' (1671 edn, sig. A4^{r-v}). If John's concern to guide Mary away from 'critical' texts seems somewhat patronizing, it is worth noting that she was probably only thirteen years old at the time the 'Directions' were drafted; see n. 13 below.

12 In the 'Miscelania' (BL Add. MS 78441, fol. 13^v) she also cites François de Sales's *La Vie Dévote*, which, although Roman Catholic, has a lot in common with these Anglican treatises. See Spurr, *Restoration Church* (see n. 6 above), pp. 372-3, and Louis Martz, *The Poetry of Meditation* (New Haven & London: Yale University Press, 1962), p. 6, and passim. Elizabeth Clarke's recent study of George Herbert provides an excellent example of how the spirituality of de Sales could be accommodated within the seventeenth-century Church of England; see Clarke, *Theory and Theology in the Poetry of George Herbert* (Oxford: Oxford

University Press, 1998), pp. 71-126.

13 BL Add. MS 78441, fol. 7ᵛ. John's 'Directions' paper, which seems to have been prepared before Mary became a communicant, recommends that, once started, she should take communion once a month – this on the authority of Simon Patrick. Since his diary records his daughter Mary's confirmation on 16 April 1679 (*Diary*, IV, 167), the 'Directions' can probably be dated to late 1678 or early 1679, when Mary (born 1665) would have been thirteen.

14 BL Add. MS 78441, fol. 7; *The Whole Duty of Man* (1682), pp. 109-10.

15 Ibid., fol. 7; *Mensa Mystica* (1667), pp. 184-5.

16 *Mensa Mystica*, p. 195. I quote the 1675 English translation of de Sales, *An Introduction to a Devout Life*, p. 291. However, Mary's one direct reference to de Sales, elsewhere in the 'Miscelania', cites the French title, *La Vie Dévote*, and provides a page reference which corresponds to the 1644 Paris edition (see BL Add. MS 78441, fol. 13ᵛ). A principle similar to de Sales's is to be found in *The Ladies Calling*, which teaches: 'As for the entertainments which they find abroad, they may be innocent, or otherwise according as they are managed. The common entercourse of Civility is a debt to Humanity, and therefore mutual visits may often be necessary, and so (in some degree) may be several harmless and healthful recreations which may call them abroad' (1673 edn, 12°, pt 2, p. 152).

17 BL Add. MS 78441, fol. 5.

18 For Holden, whom Mary consistently refers to as 'Mr Holding', see de Beer's note, Evelyn, *Diary*, IV, 4.

19 In BL Add. MS 78440: sermon notes.

20 Ibid.

21 Ibid. The name of the preacher in this note is unclear, but it is not Holden.

22 BL Add. MS 78441. fol. 7ᵛ.

23 Ibid., fol. 5. See Spurr, *Restoration Church*, pp. 294 and 296.

24 See also Theodore Hofmann and others, *John Evelyn in the British Library* (London: British Library, 1995), p. 13.

25 When Mary is at home in Deptford, there are three distinct but compatible levels of devotion: her own private prayers and readings, family prayers, and church services. When she is in London, in a household where there are no family prayers, she arranges to say prayers with a friend.

26 BL Add. MS 78441, fol. 14.

27 The text is cited in full from the Authorized or King James Version of the Bible. Mary provides an abbreviated version of the verse, and no reference.

28 BL Add. MS 78440: sermon notes.

29 Ibid.

30 Ibid.

31 Ibid.

32 Evelyn, *Diary*, IV, 243.

33 BL Add. MS 78440: sermon notes.

34 John Evelyn's folio volume of sermon notes is now BL Add. MS 78364.

35 BL Add. MS 78441, fol. 13.

36 Evelyn, *Diary*, IV, 431; my elision.

37 p. 79.

38 As described below, John Evelyn's account of his daughter's death stresses that the discovery of her 'Devotions, Contemplations, & resolutions upon those Contemplations' among her effects was a surprise to her family. In an earlier

part of his obituary, he praises her writing for its 'maturitie of judgement, and exactnesse of the periods, choice expressions, & familiarity of style', but seems here to be referring specifically to her letter-writing skills.

39 BL Add. MS 78441, fol. 7ᵛ.
40 Ibid., fol. 14.
41 Ibid., fol. 16ᵛ.
42 BL Add. MS 78440: sermon notes.
43 This provision of headings is, evidently, a very typical commonplace-book strategy, but I suspect she may also have been influenced here by *The Whole Duty of Man*, which has a similar layout.
44 BL Add. MS 78440: sermon notes.
45 Evelyn, *Diary*, IV, 431.
46 She also writes in the 'Miscelania': '*And I intend to beg all my Fathers Prayers & Devotions till I have got all into my hands* and when my wishes are Accomplished I shall prize them more then the finest things this World can afford' (BL Add. MS 78441, fol. 13).

SUSANNA AND HER ELDERS

John Evelyn's Artistic Daughter

CAROL GIBSON-WOOD

IN 1701, following his recent election to the Royal Society, the Yorkshire antiquary Ralph Thoresby was in London visiting other virtuosi and their collections. Thoresby noted that these included 'the famous Mr. Evelyn, who has published a great number of very rare books'. It was not his books that the elderly Evelyn showed Thoresby, however, but drawings, paintings, and etchings; and these were not examples he owned by Carlo Maratti or Wenceslaus Hollar, but works done by members of his own family. Thoresby writes that, in addition to showing him prospects he had drawn in Italy and miniatures executed by his wife, Evelyn 'afterwards carried me in his coach to his son Draper's at the Temple, and showed me many curious pieces of his ingenious daughter's performance, both very small in miniature and as large as the life in oil colours, equal it is thought, to the greatest masters of the age'.[1] This 'ingenious' daughter was Susanna, and in this paper I want to consider both her activities as a painter, and the aesthetic values held by virtuosi like John Evelyn and Ralph Thoresby which allowed her paintings to be compared to those of 'the greatest masters of the age'. Since virtually nothing has been written on Susanna Evelyn, I will also provide biographical material that has been extracted from the Evelyn Papers at the British Library.

Susanna, the youngest child of John and Mary Evelyn, was born in 1669, when her mother was about thirty-four years old and her father nearly fifty.[2] Only three of her siblings were still alive when Susanna arrived: brother John was fourteen, and sisters Mary and Elizabeth were just three-and-a-half, and eighteen months old. The younger John Evelyn was admitted to the Middle Temple in 1672, then travelled abroad and married in 1679; consequently, the household at Sayes Court during Susanna's childhood consisted of three little girls and their parents. How the girls were educated remains unclear. Their accomplished mother must have taken charge of much of their education, but more formal tutoring may also have played a role, and professional masters were certainly employed to teach the eldest daughter Mary singing and dancing.[3]

Although Ralph Bohun, who remained a family friend after serving as tutor to John junior, was not directly involved in the girls' education, he sometimes wrote to them and also maintained a regular correspondence with their mother in which he expressed an interest in their progress. From this correspondence, we can gain some insight into Susanna's early character in relationship to that of her sisters, to whom she was regularly compared. Her mother described her as a 'sincere rough girle', who was 'more backward in accomplishments' than her sisters, of whom she considered Mary to be superior in manner and abilities.[4] In 1682 she told Bohun, with apparent exasperation, that the thirteen-year-old 'Sue shufles about at the old rate[,] do what we can[,] and how to change her method growes to[o] hard for me'.[5] A year later, Bohun referred to the two older girls as exhibiting their mother's talents between them, Mary being very learned, musical, and an outstanding writer, and Elizabeth having social and organizational skills that would make her an admirable household manager and mother. As for Susanna, he noted simply that 'there are some accomplishments that may fall to Mrs. Susan's share, but I have no room to be particular'.[6] The picture of Susanna which emerges is one of a rather aimless and undistinguished girl, of whom her parents seem to have had no great expectations. Because her sisters were precocious, Susanna was allowed to be ordinary.

This situation changed dramatically in 1685, however, when Susanna was fifteen. In March Mary caught smallpox and died. This was a severe blow for both parents, who had regarded Mary as a perfect daughter and exceptional person – witty and learned, skilled at languages and music, and a model of piety and virtue. John Evelyn lamented her death in unusually strong terms in both his Diary and letters, while Mary senior's correspondence with Bohun reveals that she was nearly overcome by this loss, and continued to compare her surviving daughters unfavourably to the superior merits of their deceased sister.[7]

Bohun spent time with the family after Mary's death, and evidently had a serious talk with Susanna before leaving. In a messily written letter [Fig. 1], whose numerous blots and crossings-out contrast sharply with the fine hand of her late sister, Susanna wrote to Bohun:

The great trust you put in me at parting and youre good councill upon all occasions oblige me to give you thanks and tho I have not been cerious [sic] and descerning enough hitherto yet I hope my endeavours to please my father and mother and to performe my duty in all kinds will gain me your good opinion in time [.] you were very wise to my deare sister whose memorie is very frech [sic] amongst us and whose virtues I must never hope to reach yet I will doe my best to imitate her in all I can.[8]

It was in this period immediately following Mary's death that Susanna first took up drawing, perhaps as part of her new programme of personal improvement. Her mother wrote to Bohun that 'Sue ... is very good and

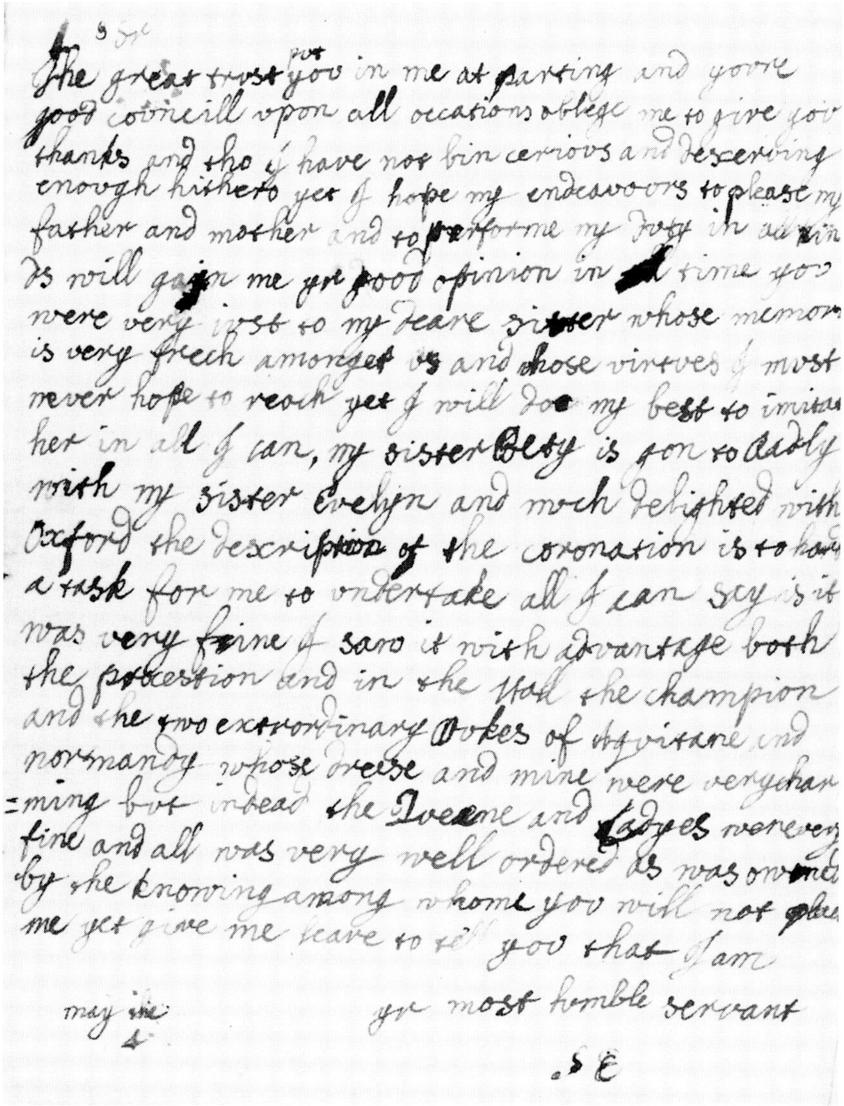

Fig. 1: Letter from Susanna Evelyn to Ralph Bohun, 4 May [1685]
(British Library, Add. MS 78539).

employs her time well to a minute[.] she now drawes and will I believe succeed well enough being much pleased with the entertainment.'[9]

But family afflictions were not over that year. In July, Elizabeth eloped with the nephew of a neighbour, an event which shocked and offended her parents. Evelyn promptly removed Elizabeth from his will. This proved to be an unnecessary punishment, however, for less than a month later she was dangerously ill with smallpox and, after begging her parents' forgiveness for her undutiful behaviour, died.[10]

Elizabeth's death actually seems to have shaken her mother out of her severe depression over Mary's demise, for both parents regarded the double loss as a certain sign of divine judgement. Mary senior's letters from this period suggest that she may have felt that Elizabeth's death signalled God's displeasure that she did not accept more readily His will in taking young Mary from her, while John, who seemed more inclined to regard Elizabeth's death as a just reward for her disobedience, wrote that: 'I hope God will be more gracious to my onely remaining Child [Susanna], whom I take to be of a more discrete, sober and religious temper: that we may have that comfort from her, which is deny'd us in the other'.[11] In any case, Susanna inevitably became more precious to them, as their only surviving daughter. But with the contrasting examples of both sisters now immortalized, one the model of perfection and the other of folly, the pressure on Susanna not to disappoint her parents must have been enormous.

Unlike Mary, Susanna was neither intellectual nor musical; but she did prove to have a set of skills which her gifted sister had apparently lacked – drawing, painting, needlework, and related arts. These were skills which her virtuoso father in particular valued highly. As a young man, he had himself drawn and etched prospects, and had taken pride in his wife's occasional artistic productions, such as a miniature copy of Raphael's *Entombment of Christ* that she presented to Charles II.[12] In association with the early Royal Society's 'history of trades' project in 1662, Evelyn had published *Sculptura*, an account of the history and techniques of engraving, and translations of Fréart de Chambray's treatises on architecture and painting in 1664 and 1668, and had an interest in writing on other artistic techniques.[13] Although he did not amass a major collection, he also purchased numerous prints and paintings both abroad and in England, and Samuel Pepys, soon after meeting Evelyn in 1655, identified him as being someone who was particularly knowledgeable about painting.[14] An inventory taken at Wotton in 1702 gives some idea of the types of pictures Evelyn owned: they included religious and allegorical paintings by Italian masters such as Paolo Veronese, Carlo Maratti, Guido Reni, and Rosso Fiorentino; several 'low life' subjects by the Anglo-Dutch painter Egbert van Heemskerck; and numerous still-lifes, perspective pieces, landscapes, and seascapes. These shared wall space with portraits of family members by contemporary English painters including John Riley and John Closterman, and works executed by himself, his wife, Susanna, and Princess Louise Hollandine of Bohemia.[15]

The eclecticism of John Evelyn's picture collection registers his diverse attitudes to painting. An appreciation of history paintings by Italian masters had developed during his continental sojourn as a young man, where he had visited all the major collections in Rome, for example, and commissioned works (including copies of earlier paintings) from Carlo Maratti.[16] Pictures of Dutch genre and landscape subjects were readily available on the open market in London in the late seventeenth century, and appealed to a wide range of buyers, while patrons of Evelyn's social rank would typically commission portraits of family members. The mechanics of painting, and its usefulness in recording natural appearances and phenomena, were of interest to members of the early Royal Society, and related to an appreciation of verisimilitude and high finishing in general, as manifested in *trompe l'oeil* still life and perspective pieces.[17] I will return to the relevance of Evelyn's attitudes to painting at the conclusion of this paper, when considering the wider significance of Susanna's artistic activities.

Susanna's early progress in drawing was reported to Ralph Bohun in a series of letters from Susanna and her mother. In early November of 1685, Mary affirmed that 'Sue … draws very well for the time she has given to it', and told Bohun that they planned to spend part of the coming winter in London primarily for the benefit of Susanna's improvement;[18] this 'improvement' may have included her receiving instruction from a drawing master. Several of Susanna's letters to Bohun seem never to have reached their destination, a circumstance which her parents attributed to her poor handwriting; 'wee tell her she writes so ill a hand the post cannot convey her letters by the superscription[,] at which she is not very well pleased', her mother noted.[19] In a letter which Bohun did receive, however, Susanna says, 'I have no newes to tell you but what you know allready only that I have undertayken to draw and am com[e] but a little way in it yet[,] but my father gives me great incorigement to go on and says I doe very well for the time I have learnte.'[20] In the following months, her mother reports successively that 'she draws visibly better every day', then 'she really draws very well', 'she improves mightily in drawing', and (in 1689) 'Sue advances in her drawing and begins to paint in Oyle[.] she is very industrious in all her works[,] never Idle[,] her father is much satisfied with her ingenuity.'[21]

Susanna must have had a professional drawing master during at least part of this time, at Sayes Court, in London, or both. I have found no documentation recording her masters, but she might have learned drawing and miniature painting from someone like Alexander Browne, who gave lessons to Samuel Pepys's wife and other genteel ladies.[22] Oil painting was a less common accomplishment for young women; she may have been taught by John Riley or John Closterman, who executed portraits of several Evelyn family members, including Susanna.[23] Although Evelyn's household accounts do not record payments made to drawing or painting masters, they do include expenditures on 'things for Mrs. Susan', which included brushes, oil, and pigments, for her painting.[24]

In the summer of 1689, when she was twenty years old, Susanna accompanied her brother and sister-in-law to Tunbridge Wells, an outing which gave rise to her father's fullest recorded comments on the importance he attached to her artistic skills. Susanna and her mother corresponded while she was away and, although only Susanna's letters survive, they indicate that John Evelyn was sending comments to his daughter via his wife, to which Susanna responded. He was clearly very concerned about Susanna ignoring her art while she was at the Wells, and seems to have asked how much drawing she had done there. On 5 August, Susanna wrote:

pray let my father know I have not to[o] much time on my hands, and that it would have bin impossible for me to compasse any drawing for you know the morning is spent on the walks & by the time one has dressed din'd & bin at the greene there is not much time to spaire[.] the little worke I carried I shall bring back undone & therefore I hope he will excuse me.[25]

In another letter from Tunbridge Wells written a few days later, Susanna refers to this issue again by asking her mother to assure her father that she is impatient to return to her usual work, and quite bored with 'doeing nothing but dres[s] and santour frome morning til night'. She also says 'pray let my father know I should take it for a high favour if he would write t[w]o or three lines to me and I am very glad any thing I doe pleases him'.[26] In response, John Evelyn wrote his longest recorded letter to his daughter. It begins, 'Child, I was (you may imagine) in no small fret, when I heard you were persuaded to abandon your selfe so to the Waters, as to putt off all thoughts of your pencil, 'til your coming home again'; it goes on to both entreat her to spend a little time drawing each day and inform her of a picture auction advertised in Tunbridge Wells that she might attend, and, before giving her his affectionate blessing, ends with an amusing poem written on her behalf:

> shall Walk, & Talke, & fatal Raffle
> Thyne Ingenuity all baffle?
> Drink, Dresse, & Dice, damned Daunce
> Now we have Warrs with pagan France,
> From Morn to Night take up thy Tim
> So as thou hast none to Designe?
> O Wicked Wells, Good Child, come home,
> And fall againe to point & Loome

> If thou forget Cromatick pencil
> And then to worke againe do wincell
> Fear – better thou hads't learn'd to Spin,
> Than ever Tunbridge to have seene.[27]

In a subsequent letter to her mother, Susanna asks her to thank her father for his advice; although she again protests that she cannot possibly find time for drawing at the Wells, she describes how she has enjoyed attending the picture auctions there.[28] She did not purchase any prints, as her father had suggested, but rather found the sales entertaining events, because of the amusing comments about the pictures supplied by the auctioneer, Edward Millington[29] [Fig. 2]. Two years later, Susanna was in Bath with her mother for the sake of their health. On this occasion, it was Susanna herself who lamented, in a letter to her father, the resulting sacrifice of time from her painting and drawing.[30] By this date, both John and Susanna Evelyn clearly regarded her artistic pursuits as more than an improving diversion.

Evelyn's fullest tributes to his children in his Diary occur at some rite of passage – sadly, this was usually their death. But in Susanna's case, he provided his most extended character sketch on the occasion of her marriage in 1693. It reads:

She is a good Child, religious, discrete, Ingenious, & qualified with all the ornaments of her sex: especially has a peculiar talent in Designe & Painting both in oyle & Miniature, & a genious extraordinary, for whatever hands can pretend to do with the Needle: Has the French Toung, has read most of the Greek & Roman Authors, Poets, using her talents with great Modesty, Exquisitely shap'd, & of an agreable Countenance: This Character is due to her, though coming from her Father.[31]

Although she was clearly a very different type of person from her deceased sister Mary, Susanna had not disappointed her parents in her character or accomplishments, and her marriage to William Draper in 1693 was also an honourable one. Not only was Draper respectable, wealthy, and of upstanding character, but the new household in which the married Susanna found herself was also one in which drawing and painting were encouraged. Draper's mother, also called Susanna, with whom the couple lived for several years, was herself an amateur artist. Soon after her marriage, while staying at the house of in-laws in Buckinghamshire, Susanna wrote to her mother that 'We at this place are all workers for we see nobody to disturb us. ... My mother [in-law] paints all day as long as she can see which way of spending the day I believe wo'd please my Father.'[32] John Evelyn admiringly described the elder Mrs Draper as a 'pictrisse', and Mary Evelyn characterized her as 'a vertuosa and a good natured woman without affectation'.[33] But although Susanna was twenty-four when she married, and her mother-in-law was reportedly both kind to her and supportive of her habitual pursuits, Susanna's frequent letters to her mother in the years immediately following her

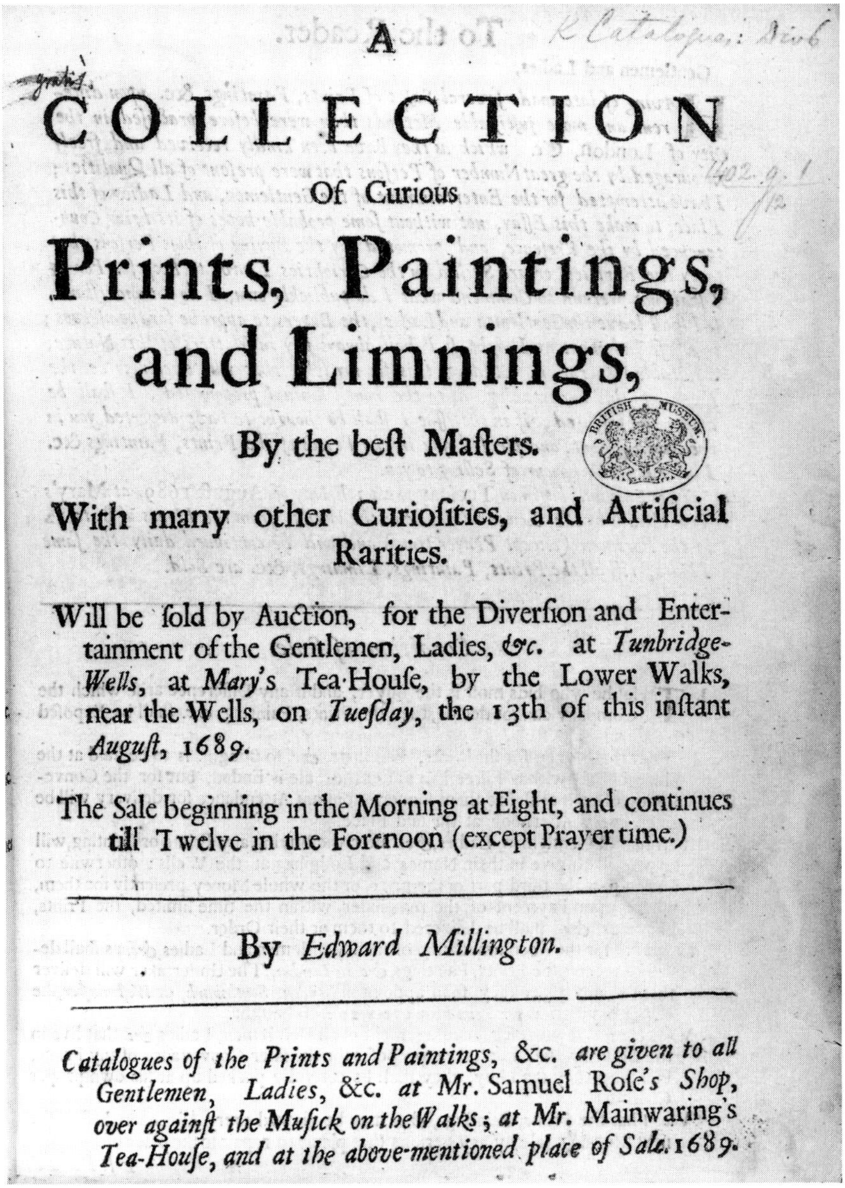

A

COLLECTION

Of Curious

Prints, Paintings,

and Limnings,

By the best Masters.

With many other Curiosities, and Artificial Rarities.

Will be sold by Auction, for the Diversion and Entertainment of the Gentlemen, Ladies, *&c.* at *Tunbridge-Wells*, at *Mary's* Tea-House, by the Lower Walks, near the Wells, on *Tuesday*, the 13th of this instant *August*, 1689.

The Sale beginning in the Morning at Eight, and continues till Twelve in the Forenoon (except Prayer time.)

By *Edward Millington.*

Catalogues of the Prints and Paintings, &c. *are given to all Gentlemen, Ladies,* &c. *at* Mr. Samuel Rose's *Shop, over against the Musick on the Walks; at* Mr. Mainwaring's *Tea-House, and at the above-mentioned place of Sale.* 1689.

Fig. 2: Auction catalogue of Edward Millington, Tunbridge Wells, 13 August 1689 (British Library, 1402.g.1(12)).

marriage often include indications that she was nonetheless extremely homesick. That she was similarly missed by her parents is expressed in a letter from her father, who says: 'I give you many thanks for your kind, & constant Correspondence with your Mother, who continually languishes after you, as I my selfe do also not a little.'[34]

John Evelyn's messages to his absent daughter are seldom so tender, however, and it was not he but Mary Evelyn who wrote regularly to Susanna during the 1690s, although Mary's side of the correspondence has not survived. Susanna's letters to her mother are full of news and gossip – about friends and relatives, Susanna's successive pregnancies and babies, the state of everyone's health, and details of women's fashions as Susanna shopped for items requested by her mother – all communicated in a direct, unstudied, and run-on prose.[35] Ralph Bohun had characterized Susanna's earlier epistolary style as conveying 'much news in a little compass',[36] and this did not change in her adult life. She had little interest in writing or reading, and seems to have led an active much more than a contemplative life. In her only extant reference to literature, for example (in a letter of 26 April 1695, referring to books by Mary Astell which she had perused after her mother seemingly requested that she purchase them for her in London), she remarks that, in *A Serious Proposal to the Ladies*, she thinks Mary Astell 'uses to[o] many hard words considering she writtes to women who are not as Learned as her selfe', and 'as for the other Booke the little I have read of it showes me that unless I were well read in philosophie I shall not much edifie by it'.[37]

On the infrequent occasions when she wrote directly to her father, Susanna was extremely self-conscious about her shortcomings as a writer, but eager to please him in what he consistently encouraged – her drawing and painting. For example, as a new bride touring parts of southern England with her husband, she included in a letter to her mother an uncharacteristically fulsome description of the pleasant situation and grounds of a relative's house in which they were staying near Henley-on-Thames. Equally uncharacteristically, John as well as Mary Evelyn wrote back, the former responding that 'I am exceedingly pleas'd with your description of the place you are in: Could you not, exercise your Tallent, by takeing a Landskip of it before you come away?'[38] It was clearly with some trepidation that Susanna returned his letter, telling him :

With some difficulty deare Father I obtain of my self to trouble you with a letter & have hardly couradge to undertake it but my hopes are that you will looke on it as an intention to pay my dutty & let that excuse the defects both of stile & hand[.] you will easily believe my Aprehensions are great to writ to my Father who is so good a Judge of both & I must confess had I bin capable of following yours & my Mothers Examples I shd have bin perfect in all things but I am sensible how far I fall short of my parents but shall never impute the faults I am guilty off to any want of instruction.

... I will Endeavour to obey your commands in the Landskip[.] I feare I shant come off very well my sckill in that being but little & the want of your invention to contracht the object into a compass of the eye will make it dificult to keep a proportion the extent of it being large but I will doe my best to compass it.[39]

The invention of her father's which Susanna did not have with her must have been some sort of *camera obscura*, and the development of such optical devices at the Royal Society was an activity in which Evelyn took a particular interest. Both Prince Rupert and Christopher Wren had invented instruments for casting planes and objects into perspective which they brought to the Royal Society in the 1660s, and Robert Hooke had worked on 'improving' these so that they could be used for drawing and painting.[40] Hooke demonstrated the use of a 'dark box for painting', that is, a *camera obscura*, at the Royal Society in 1670, and a few years later produced a small, portable version which he recommended for the use of travellers.[41] It was perhaps this sort of device which Evelyn owned.

Recording landscapes and prospects was frequently practised by male virtuosi, including John Evelyn; Susanna excelled in portraits, but also painted flowers, biblical subjects, and 'Indian pictures'. Some are listed in Evelyn's inventory of Wotton from 1702,[42] and others are mentioned in Susanna's letters; unfortunately none of them can be identified with certainty today. Like other genteel women painters of the period, Susanna primarily copied works which had been painted by other artists; these were displayed at home, or given to family members and friends. Her father played an active role in both asking her to execute specific works, and borrowing originals for her to copy. Susanna's letters to her mother include numerous comments, some of which are directed to her father, on current artistic projects, the most significant of which I will summarize below.

Susanna and her husband spent the summer of 1694, and subsequent summers with increasing numbers of children, at Sayes Court, which John and Mary Evelyn had recently vacated. One of Susanna's first undertakings there was to produce a copy of the portrait of Margaret Godolphin, commissioned from Matthew Dixon in 1673, presented by her to Evelyn, and hung in the parlour at Sayes Court [Fig. 3]. At the request of her father, who wanted a copy of the portrait to retain when he presented the original to Lord Godolphin, Susanna began the picture in June of 1694, but was not very confident of her ability to carry it out successfully because of its large size.[43] Perhaps she wished to abandon it, for in August her father wrote 'I still recomend to you the copying of Mrs Godolphins Picture, 'tis all I need to impose upon you for this sumer of that kind; my intention being to present it to my Lord, being unwilling to part with the Originall, unless it be for another of your hand, because I know you will equal, if not exceed it'.[44] Susanna did not complete the painting before she had her first child in

Fig. 3: Margaret Godolphin. Engraving by W. Humphreys after the portrait by Matthew Dixon for the frontispiece of Evelyn's *Life of Mrs Godolphin* (1847) (British Library).

September and spent the winter in London, where she worked instead on a 'little pickture' (that is, a miniature) for Lord Godolphin, and also promised to undertake something for her brother.[45] The picture of Margaret Godolphin is not mentioned again until the following June, when the Drapers were again at Sayes Court, and Susanna was expecting another child. She seems to have asked a painter named Mrs Berinclaw to put the finishing touches on the picture, so that she would be freed from this obligation to pursue other projects. In particular, she hoped to borrow, through her father's agency, a painting of Robert Boyle from which to execute copies, but her father refused to do this until the picture of Mrs Godolphin was completed. Her remarks to her mother portray Evelyn as unsympathetic to her situation:

Mrs Berinclaw is to come this weeke to finish Mrs Godolphins pickture which I shall be glad of for I cant get my Father to borrow the Boyel till that is done so that I loose a great deale of time & fine weather for he does not consider that within three months I shall be so neare my time that I shall be thinking of Leaving this place in order to fitt my affairs for my Lying In. … I hope when the other is done I shall prevail with him to get it for me but my deare mother knowes his old way of fancying things can be done in a moment. I intend to keep my promiss with my Brother & had begun

243

one all this time had I mett with any thing fitt to Copie. I was in hopes Mrs Berinclaw co'd have furnisht me but hers are all put up her house being a sad little hole not fitt to hang them in. I have tried other friends but cant get one so that I think to copie the Boyel in a Less Volum for him.[46]

Her father arrived in Deptford for a visit the next week, and seems to have been sufficiently satisfied with the picture of Margaret Godolphin to obtain the loan of the other picture.[47] This may have been the portrait of Robert Boyle by Johann Kerseboom which had been presented to the Royal Society in 1692.[48] By the end of August Susanna had finished a small copy of the painting for her brother, despite another personal setback – her infant son Thomas, whom Evelyn described as 'a very hopefull, strong and lovely Child',[49] had died in July. She gave birth to a daughter, Mary, in early September.

Evelyn seems to have asked her to execute a copy of the Boyle portrait for Lord Godolphin, for at the beginning of December she reported that she was 'very bussy beginning my Lord's picture of the Boyel',[50] and her father, visiting her in London later that month, took a particular interest in its progress. Susanna again described to her mother his anxieties over its completion, and sought her collusion in alleviating them:

I am very bussy every Morning at my pickture. my Father stands by according to custome [and] is full of feares that I will not finish so soone as he woo'd have me ... wee are going Satterday next to Adscomb to my great grief being very much sett upon finishing my pickture. I hope to stay but a weeke or ten day at most [.] it co'd not be avoided. ... I desire my Father may not know I goe for he will be very uneasy about the pickture & indeed I am much vext that it happen. I have kept my going from his knowledg & mean to make great hast back again.[51]

By February, Susanna had begun another copy of the Boyle portrait, to be retained for hanging in the Drapers' newly acquired London house.[52] A year later she tells her father that she is hard at work on another unidentified picture, and apologizes about yet another which was seemingly not carried out as he wished.[53] All of these references suggest that it was John Evelyn who most consistently both encouraged and vexed her about her painting.

In addition to pursuing her own work in the 1690s, Susanna had various contacts with professional painters, notably when an artist was engaged to carry out a family commission. Being based in London, she was conveniently located to oversee such business for her father as well as herself, and had probably become acquainted with London painters, studios, and picture shops through him, for John Evelyn had dealt with numerous London artists over the years. For example, already in 1648 he had commissioned a portrait of himself from Robert Walker (*fl.* 1641-58), now in the National Portrait Gallery, to be given to his young bride (originally painted with an image of Mary in place of the skull). And his activities at the early Royal Society had included membership on a subcommittee which was to confer with three of the most eminent London painters of the 1660s – Peter Lely (1618-80), Samuel Cooper (*c.*1608-72), and Robert Streeter (1621-79) – with the aim of writing a comprehensive history of painting and its techniques.[54] Evelyn had also played an important role in advancing the career of the young and previously little-known sculptor Grinling Gibbons (1648-1721), and had patronized the painters John Riley (1646-91) and John Closterman (1660-1711) for portraits of several Evelyn family members.[55] He seems to have been on good enough terms with both Riley and Kneller to serve as their mentor in other portrait commissions, for in January of 1689 he recommended both artists to Gilbert Burnet.[56] In June and July of 1689, at the request of Samuel Pepys, Evelyn had his portrait painted by Sir Godfrey Kneller, at the artist's London studio. Perhaps at her father's suggestion, Susanna went to look at the portrait, which was either still in Kneller's studio or already hanging in Pepys's library, on her way to Tunbridge Wells later that summer. 'Pray tell my father I saw his pickture,' she wrote to her mother, '& think it very like & finely painted'[57] [Fig. 4].

Susanna's letters from 1694 and 1695 indicate that she was in touch with the painter John Closterman on behalf of her father, and also overseeing the progress of a portrait being painted of her nephew Jack, who spent some of his holidays from Eton with the Drapers.[58] One of her very rare art-critical comments concerns a portrait of her husband executed in 1695/6 by an unspecified painter, of whose mannered style she did not approve. She wrote that: 'my spouses pickture is finisht but so little like him that wee have no encouragement to have any more done. I must owne the woork is soft & fine but I have no esteeme for a friends pickture if it be not very like.'[59] These comments register Susanna's clear position in the contemporary debate about the role of face painting – should the artist record the sitter's physical appearance 'warts and all' (as did John Riley), or adapt it to an idealized, fashionable template of appearance (as was the practice of many other painters)?

Susanna seems to have been acquainted with the miniaturist Susannah Penelope Rosse, whose father Richard Gibson had been drawing master to Princesses Mary and Anne, and whose numerous remaining miniature paintings, some of them only about an inch in height, demonstrate that she was a highly accomplished artist. In July of 1694, when she was seven months pregnant with her first child, Susanna reported that:

wee have had Mrs. Rose & her Daughter most part of last week with us. She has began to draw my cosen Tukes & Mrs Goldings & my pickture at her owne desire so that we are like to be set in her gallery of Beauties especially mine being taken at a good time my cheeks being very shallow but what I loose in one part is made up in another being very much improved in bigness.[60]

245

Fig. 4: John Evelyn, by Sir Godfrey Kneller
(V & A Picture Library; private collection).

This 'gallery of Beauties', unlike those of Lely and Kneller to which Susanna implicitly and facetiously compares it, was clearly not a professional commission, and the circumstances of its proposal suggest a certain degree of friendship between the two painters.

After 1696 Susanna wrote to her mother less frequently, and only once mentions her painting, asking her in the summer of 1697 to 'let him [her father] know I paint every day'. This summer schedule is confirmed in a letter from William Draper to John Evelyn, in which he reports that Susanna 'spends about the first four hours of every working day' on her arts, and has 'dead colour'd two Coppyes of your Picture'; but which picture this was is unclear.[61] She probably had less time to write letters or paint pictures in this period with her increasing domestic responsibilities; she gave birth to seven more children over the next ten years.

In 1700, following the death of his uncle and aunt, Sir Purbeck and Lady Temple, William Draper inherited the estate of Addiscombe, near Croydon. The Drapers took up residence there, but decided to pull down the ancient mansion and have a new one built, for they had inherited not just the estate, but also a considerable fortune.[62] While the building was proceeding, they spent the summer of 1702 at Wotton where, John Evelyn noted, 'my family was above thirty'.[63] The new house was nearing completion a year later when Evelyn, now eighty-two years old, went to see and approve it.[64] It no longer stands, but a nineteenth-century photograph reveals that it was a substantial pile, presenting a façade defined by a disturbingly monumental Ionic order. Nicholas Hawksmoor was involved in assessing the value of the work done in December of 1703, and the younger Edward Strong has been suggested as possibly responsible for the design of Addiscombe House.[65] William Draper would have known both architects through their contemporary work at Greenwich Hospital; John Evelyn held the position of Treasurer to the Commissioners at Greenwich Hospital from 1696, and Draper took over this office from his father-in-law in 1703.[66]

To decorate the grand staircase and saloon of their new house, the Drapers chose the young James Thornhill, who would later gain fame for his work at Greenwich Hospital and St Paul's Cathedral, as well as at other residences, both private and royal. The paintings at Addiscombe were destroyed before they could be recorded in photographs, but descriptions of them identify the subject matter as including a *Feast of Bacchus, Bacchus and Ariadne, The Judgement of Paris*, and other mythological subjects and landscapes on the walls.[67] This would have been one of Thornhill's very first independent jobs and may have led, I would suggest, to Draper recommending him for the important Greenwich commission in 1707, for he was relatively unknown at that date.[68] Thornhill's sketchbook (preserved in the British Museum) includes both the sketch of a ceiling plan inscribed 'Draper', and several drawings of Bacchus and Ariadne that Edward Croft-Murray has associated with the Addiscombe project.[69] Susanna, with her interest in painting, probably played a significant role in selecting these subjects. A few years earlier, when she and her husband were decorating the rooms of their London house, she had described to her mother the much more modest paintings they had commissioned from a Dutch painter as overdoors and chimney pieces,[70] but no letters written by her between 1700 and 1707 survive; Thornhill's work at Addiscombe is therefore not mentioned in her extant correspondence.

Susanna's own activities as a painter are also undocumented after 1700, and I have been able to retrieve only a few facts about the rest of her life, which I will summarize here; these derive mainly from her letters to her sister-in-law Martha, and nephew Jack (Sir John Evelyn after 1713)[71] who, following the deaths of her brother in 1699, her father in 1706, and her mother in 1709, became Susanna's main correspondents. In 1707, Susanna's eldest daughter Mary, twelve years old, died suddenly of what was then diagnosed as a stroke, at Addiscombe.[72] Other afflictions followed, for her husband William Draper died in 1718, leaving a major financial problem behind him, in the form of a large debt owing to Greenwich Hospital, of which his eldest son and heir William unsuccessfully tried legally to clear himself. The next year, Susanna and her five remaining children (William, John, Susanna, Evelyn, and Sara) left for France, where they spent about three years. The youngest daughter Sara died in France, and Susanna suffered additional worries over the conduct of her son John, who developed a reckless and extravagant lifestyle. The Drapers did not move back to Addiscombe, presumably for financial reasons, and the house was let for much of the eighteenth century.[73] With her nephew's assistance, Susanna managed to secure a naval position for the problematic son John, but he died in 1732 leaving more debts. Her daughter Evelyn married someone named Clarke in about 1722, and it was this daughter's family which eventually inherited Addiscombe House, for Susanna's son William seems to have remained single. William was a traveller and antiquarian, whose letters to his cousin Sir John Evelyn often include detailed accounts of his activities on the Continent.[74] He mentions his mother only once, in a letter sent from his sister's house at Ockley in 1755, where he tells Sir John that his mother sends her regards to the family at Wotton. Susanna would have reached her eighty-seventh year by this date.[75]

Susanna Draper's correspondence is clearly of interest for the insight it provides into the dynamics of the Evelyn family, but it is also significant, I would suggest, for its contribution to our understanding of the status of 'amateur' painting in England at the end of the seventeenth century. In considering this issue, I would like to build upon parts of Kim Sloan's discussion in her excellent book *A Noble Art*, the publication of which coincided with an exhibition, held at the British Museum, devoted to amateur artists and drawing masters *c*.1600-1800. First of all, Sloan points out that although numerous ladies and gentlemen painted in the seventeenth century, 'there are few contemporary written references to indicate how they learned or what their families thought of their work', and cites Samuel Pepys's remarks on his wife's progress in limning as a unique documentation.[76] To this evidence, we may now add John and Mary Evelyn's comments on the artistic activities of both Susanna and her mother-in-law, to build up a slightly fuller picture of the genteel practice of painting in this period. Although frustratingly brief, these references nonetheless tally with Pepys's, in testifying to the high value placed upon women's artistic skill by well-educated family members. Furthermore, they provide some information about the range of subjects undertaken and media employed, and how both the elder and younger Susanna Draper found time to paint while attending to their domestic and social responsibilities.

Sloan also rightly notes that modern art historians have traditionally given priority to professional painters in constructing progressive histories of 'great' art, and have given a pejorative sense to the term 'amateur' that is very different from the meaning assigned in the seventeenth and early eighteenth centuries.[77] These points too can be given additional force with reference to the significance of assessments of Susanna's painting by her contemporaries. The terms 'amateur painter' and 'professional painter' were not actually used in that period at all, and the earliest history of British art, Bainbrigg Buckeridge's *An Essay Towards an English School of Painters* of 1706, unlike its modern counterparts, includes accounts of genteel painters such as Anne Carlisle and Thomas Flatman, alongside those who practised painting as a trade. Painting for financial reimbursement marked a difference in social class, but not a difference in the aims and nature of painting, or the criteria for its assessment. Producing copies of paintings was a widespread practice among all types of painters, for example, and not necessarily regarded as an activity inferior to painting from the life or producing an original composition.

For virtuosi like Evelyn, Pepys, and Thoresby, good painting demonstrated sound technique, and accuracy of representation; hence, when Samuel Pepys says that a painting by his wife Elizabeth was 'mighty finely done', we should not assume that the qualifier 'for a woman' or 'for an amateur' was implicit for him. Similarly, John Evelyn's belief that Susanna could excel, in her copy, Matthew Dixon's portrait of Margaret Godolphin was not simply a naive expression of parental pride. I would also maintain that Ralph Thoresby's remark that Susanna's paintings equalled those of the greatest masters of the age was not just a trope. These statements by well-educated English viewers should not be discounted simply because their aesthetic values do not accord with current ones; rather, it is surely our duty as historians to take into account their views, and the activities of *vertuose* like Susanna Evelyn, in constructing accounts of the visual culture of early modern England.

NOTES

1 *The Diary of Ralph Thoresby, F.R.S.*, ed. by Joseph Hunter, 2 vols (London, 1830), I, 340.

2 Evelyn records her birth on 20 May 1669, and her baptism on 25 May 1669; Evelyn, *Diary*, III, 528.

3 Evelyn, *Diary*, IV, 272.

4 BL Add. MS 78539: Mary Evelyn to Ralph Bohun, 11 Feb. 1684: 'they [Sue and Betty] yet give way to Moll who to be just to, has the start of both, in good Meene and taking wayes. she sings very well and pleases universally. God keepe her from the small pox.'

5 BL Add. MS 78539: Mary Evelyn to Bohun, 22 Aug. 1682.

6 BL Add. MS 78435: Bohun to Mary Evelyn, 29 Oct. 1683.

7 BL Add. MS 78539: Mary Evelyn to Bohun, 21 July 1685: 'Sue and she [Betty] both spend their time very well. I hope much good of them, you are sensible I loved them all yet some distinction might reasonably be allowed the Eldest, as first and for many reasons something to be preferred well God be praised for those which remaine and I pray heartily he will spare them yet awhile', Mary Evelyn to Bohun, 3 June 1685; 'she [Betty] and Sue endeavour by keeping close to me to suply for her [Mary] but tho I must acknowledge them good Children and deserving nothing yet reaches what I never must see againe.'

8 BL Add. MS 78539: Susanna Evelyn to Bohun, 4 May 1685.

9 Ibid.: Mary Evelyn to Bohun, 20 May 1685.

10 Evelyn, *Diary*, IV, 460-4.

11 Ibid., IV, 462.

12 Ibid., III, 287.

13 Michael Hunter, 'John Evelyn in the 1650s: a Virtuoso in Quest of a Role', in *Science and the Shape of Orthodoxy: Intellectual Change in Late Seventeenth-Century Britain* (Woodbridge: Boydell, 1995), pp. 67-98.

14 *The Diary of Samuel Pepys*, ed. by Robert Latham & William Matthews, 11 vols (London: Bell, 1972), VI, 243.

15 BL Add. MS 78403. In this inventory of 1702, Evelyn lists the portrait of the Viscountess Mordaunt as being by Princess Sophia, but in his *Diary* for 1641 (I, 26) he recorded that this portrait was by Sophia's sister Louise Hollandine, who was renowned for her abilities as a painter.

16 The 1702 inventory (BL Add. MS 78403) includes, for example: 'A Madonna, the Babe, St. Catherine, St. Sebastian. By Carolo Maratti, the Popes chiefe painter copyed for me by him at Rome, from the Original of Correggio, which I borrow'd of Cardinal Fr. Barberini:1646', and 'A large Emblem Original, of Maratti, representing the Church, & Reason submitting to Faith, with severall Figures, rarely painted, which with the former I brought from Rome.'

17 A distinctive sensibility to painting among English virtuosi was first identified and analysed by Walter E. Houghton, jr, 'The English Virtuoso in the Seventeenth Century', *Journal of the History of Ideas*, 3 (1942), 51-73 and 190-219 (205-11).

18 BL Add. MS 78539: Mary Evelyn to Bohun, 7 Nov. 1685.

19 Ibid.: Mary Evelyn to Bohun, 9 Nov. 1685.

20 Ibid.: Susanna Evelyn to Bohun, 27 Nov. 1685.

21 Ibid.: Mary Evelyn to Bohun, 8 Oct. 1686, 21 Oct. 1686, 10 March 1689, 14 July 1689.

22 On Browne, see Antony Griffiths, 'Early Mezzotint Publishing in England II: Peter Lely, Tompson and Browne', *Print Quarterly*, 7, no. 2 (June 1990), 131-45 (134-6).

23 In his *Diary*, John Evelyn recorded, 20 Sept. 1685, that 'My Wifes & Daughter Susans pictures were drawn this Weeke' (IV, 475); the finished paintings were probably those by Riley and Closterman that hung, along with other family portraits by the same artists, in the Great Parlour at Wotton in 1702 (BL Add. MS 78403).

24 The account drawn up by John Strickland for 1 April – 30 June 1689, for example, includes 'For Picturs pinccaills oyle and Coolers and Severall other things for Mrs. Susan: 00-16-09'; see BL Add. MS 78408.

25 BL Add. MS 78433: Susanna Evelyn to her mother, 5 Aug. 1689.

26 Ibid.: 16 Aug. 1689.

27 BL Add. MS 78299: Evelyn to his daughter Susanna, 14 Aug. 1689.

28 BL Add. MS 78433: Susanna Evelyn to her mother, 26 Aug. 1689.

29 A copy of the catalogue for the auction on 13 Aug. 1689 by Edward Millington that Susanna attended is at BL press-mark 1402.g.1 (12).

30 'If I dide not hope my mother would receive good by the Bath should very unwillingly consent to spend so much money & time mearely on my account espescialy when I consider I shall not be able to say much for my self bathing & drinking watters not allowinge me any time to paint or draw but I hope if it please God to give me health I shall at my returne make up all my Idle houres': Susanna Evelyn to her father, 25 July 1691, BL Add. MS 15949, fol. 128.

31 Evelyn, *Diary*, v, 138.

32 BL Add. MS 78433: Susanna Draper to Mary Evelyn, 21 Aug. 1693.

33 BL Add. MS 78539: Mary Evelyn to Bohun, 7 April 1695.

34 BL Add. MS 78299: John Evelyn to his daughter Susanna, n.d. [betw. 24 Oct. and 28 Nov. 1693].

35 67 letters from Susanna to her mother, dating from 1689 to 1707, are in the Evelyn Papers, BL Add. MS 78433.

36 BL Add. MS 78435: Bohun to Mary Evelyn, 13 Dec. 1687.

37 BL Add. MS 78433: Susanna Draper to Mary Evelyn, 26 April 1695. Susanna's full comments about Mary Astell in this letter read as follows: 'that of the proposalls to the Ladyes I have read and thinke it a very pretty Fancy but wholly impracticable. her notions are very holly and good but such as I feare few will imittate. if I might venture to find faults I think she uses to many hard words considering she writtes to women who are not as Learned as her selfe and as for the other Booke the little I have read of it showes me that unless I were well read in philosophie I shall not much edifie by it. when Mr. Draper went to bye the bookes she was in the Shope. he sayes she is an agreable sort of a wooman and lookes younge. she was talking to a young Gentleman but upon his coming in went away.' Mary Astell's *A Serious Proposal to the Ladies for the Advancement of their True and Greatest Interest* was first published in 1694, with a second edition in 1695. The 'other book' referred to by Susanna would have been her *Letters Concerning the Love of God* (1695).

38 BL Add. MS 78299: Evelyn to his daughter Susanna, n.d. (betw. 24 Oct. and 28 Nov. 1693).

39 BL Add. MS 78300: Susanna Draper to Evelyn, 12 Oct. 1693.

40 In November 1663 Prince Rupert (Honorary F.R.S.) presented to the Society

'an Instrument of his Highnesses Invention, for casting any Platform into Perspective'. In discussing it, reference is also made to 'an instrument of Dr. Wrens Invention for casting any naturall Object into Perspective', and Hooke suggests that, with some additions, the Prince's model could be used for both types of perspective drawing. In the following meetings, Hooke reported on the progress being made in constructing this 'improved' version of 'Prince Rupert's Perspective Engine', and he presented the completed version to the Society on 23 Dec.: Royal Society, 'Journal Book', vol. 1 (1660-64), fols. 225-6, 233, 239, 251, 252; reproduced in Thomas Birch, *History of the Royal Society*, 4 vols (London: A. Millar, 1756), I, 329, 333, 334, 348.

41 Hooke demonstrated the use of the 'dark box' several times in May, June and July of 1670; Royal Society, 'Journal Book', vol. 3 (1667-71), fols 272-3, 275, 276-7, 279. On 19 Dec. 1694 he presented a paper on 'An Instrument of Use to take the Draught, or Picture of any Thing'; William Derham, *Philosophical Experiments and Observations of the late eminent Dr. Robert Hooke* (London, 1726), pp. 292-6.

42 These include: 'Flowers of my Daughter Drapers painting', and 'The V. Mary w St. Joseph, carrying into Egypt: painted from an original by my Daughter Draper'; the inventory also lists a number of drawings by Susanna, including two in crayons 'comparable to the originals', a drawing of 'a Duke of Venice', and '2 drawings of my daughter one a Madonna & Child the other a fig: after a drawing of Parmegian. very rarly done': BL Add. MS 78403.

43 'My Duty to My Father who I desire may know I have begun Mrs. Godolfins pickture. how well I shall end I know not but am full of feares haveing never undertaken any so large. I will doe my best'; 'My Mother paints Indian picktures & I a mornings Mrs Godolfins which I feare I shall not performe so well as I wo'd it being so much beyond the bigness I am used to'; BL Add. MS 78433: Susanna Draper to Mary Evelyn, 14, 19 June 1694.

44 BL Add. MS 78299: Evelyn to Susanna Draper, Aug. 1694.

45 'My Dutty to my Father & tell him I am finishing my Lrds little pickture'; 12 March 1694/5: 'I will paint a pickture for my Brother as soon as I possibly can but at present am very bussy finishing my Lrds which I hope will be done in a few days more'; 'I stay till my Father comes to towne to Borrow me the pickture of my Lord Boyel which I intend to copie in less for my Brother': BL Add. MS 78433: Susanna Draper to Mary Evelyn, 31 Jan., 26 April 1695. Although Robert Boyle was not a lord, it seems most likely that he was the sitter referred to; it is also possible that the picture of Boyle was owned by Godolphin and that Susanna means 'my Lord's Boyle' in this letter; see also the wording of n. 52 below.

46 BL Add. MS 78433: Susanna Draper to Mary Evelyn, 4 June 1695.

47 Evelyn presented the Dixon portrait to Godolphin later in 1695. A draft letter, written in September to accompany the picture, includes the following remarks by Evelyn: 'Tho your Lordship be furnish'd with a Collection of Choice and excellent Pictures ... yet I am perswaded you will not lesse Esteeme the piece I make bold to send you. For tho it is not the hand of a greate Master, it is yet not onely an Original, but of such an Original as no Copy has yet at all approach'd, Except what my owne daughter but now finish'd for me': BL Add. MS 78307.

48 But see n. 45 above. On portraits of Boyle, see R. E. W. Maddison, 'The Portraiture of the Honourable Robert Boyle, F.R.S.', *Annals of Science*, 15

(1959), 141-214. None of the portraits listed by Maddison include a Godolphin provenence.

49 Evelyn, *Diary*, v, 215: 'Dyed my Grandson and Godson Tho: Draper of a Convulsion fit at Nurse, just as they were about to have weaned it ... to the very greate Griefe & affliction to us all, & especially to my poore daughter, now big with another.'

50 Susanna Draper to Mary Evelyn, 6 Dec. 1695, BL Add. MS 78433.

51 BL Add. MS 78433: Susanna Draper to Mary Evelyn, 23 Dec. 1695.

52 'I have bin & still am very bussie a painting my Lrd Godolfins picture of Boyel & have done one & half the other which will help to fill our empty house which we are by degrees furnishing', BL Add. MS 78442: Susanna Draper to John Evelyn jr, 25 Feb. 1696; 'I am hard at worke at my second pickture in hopes before Easter to compass it', BL Add. MS 78433: Susanna Draper to Mary Evelyn, 28 Feb. 1696.

53 Susanna says that she has nothing to say for herself 'about the other [picture] onely hope you will pardon me & I promiss to make up all in this I have now in hand', BL Add. MS 78300: Susanna Draper to Evelyn, 25 Feb. 1697.

54 The formation of this subcommittee was first proposed by Thomas Povey (F.R.S.) on 22 Aug. 1666; on 19 Dec. 1667 Povey read a paper to the Royal Society which described a technical process he had observed Streeter using, outlined the larger writing project he envisioned, and again urged collaboration between practising painters and Royal Society Fellows. The subcommittee, consisting of Povey, Sir Philip Carteret, Sir Theodore de Vaux, John Evelyn, Thomas Henshaw, William Croone, Edmund Wylde and Robert Hooke, was appointed on that occasion, and met on 2 Jan. 1668; Royal Society, 'Journal Books' and 'Classified Papers'. Povey's paper and the appointment of the subcommittee are also included in Birch, *History of the Royal Society* (see n. 40 above), II, 227-30.

55 The 1702 inventory of Wotton, written by John Evelyn, includes portraits by Riley of John Evelyn jr and his wife, and by Riley and Closterman of Susanna and of John jr's sister-in-law; BL Add. MS 78403.

56 In a letter to Burnet dated 23 Jan. 1689, Evelyn wrote: 'This is Mr. Rylie our Apelles, and first of English Painters, who desires the honour of making your Picture ... Let our Lysippus then obtaine this favor: he comes not now to Importune you, for I have told him, and Mr. Kneller, another greate Artiste (who has ben with me to bespeake the same favour) how precious your Moments are at present; but to give you your owne time and leasure, when he may waite on you whith his Crayons'; BL Add. MS 78299. I am grateful to Douglas Chambers for pointing out this reference.

57 BL Add. MS 78433: Susanna Evelyn to Mary Evelyn, 29 July 1689.

58 Ibid.: 14 June 1694: 'when I was last in towne I was with Mr. Closterman about his pickture. he said it should be done a forenight. he had not done with the papers my father left with him but said all sho'd be returned together. I will shortly send to him againe'; and 12 March 1695: 'the childs picture is done so I believe 'tis Mr. Stricklands fault tis not sent'. The portrait may be that listed in the 1702 inventory of Wotton as hanging in the 'Great Parlour' there: 'My Grandson Jo. Evelyn at length, by Houseman. Closterman'.

59 BL Add. MS 78433: Susanna Draper to Mary Evelyn, 5 March 1696.

60 Ibid.: 2 July 1694.

61 BL Add. MS 15949, fol. 28: William Draper to Evelyn, 4 Aug. 1697.

62 In his *Diary* for 13 March 1700 (V, 385-6), Evelyn recorded that Lady Temple 'left my son-in-law Draper (her nephew) the mansion house of Addiscombe, very nobly and completely furnished, with the estate about it, with plate and jewels, to the value in all of about £20,000'. In a letter to Bohun, 8 Jan. 1702, Mary Evelyn wrote that: 'my sonne and Daughter Draper are at Adscomb preparing to pull downe the house being resolved to build notwithstanding the prospect of great taxes': BL Add. MS 78539.

63 Evelyn, *Diary*, V, 508-9.

64 Ibid., 541.

65 Hawksmoor is recorded as having measured joinery work done at Addiscombe in December 1703: BL Add. MS 38480, fol. 406. The manuscript is a volume of the Liverpool Papers, and includes various documents of the Draper family; the Earl of Liverpool made Addiscombe House his residence for many years. However, Kerry Downes, in *English Baroque Architecture* (London: Zwemmer, 1966), p. 52, says that Strong was the mason, and probably also the designer, of Addiscombe House.

66 On the progress of Greenwich Hospital during these years, and the roles of Evelyn and Draper, see John Bold, *Greenwich: an Architectural History of the Royal Hospital for Seamen and the Queen's House* (New Haven & London: Yale University Press, 2000), pp. 108-29, and Gillian Darley's essay above.

67 Edward Walford, *Greater London: a Narrative of its History, its People, and its Places*, 2 vols (London: Cassell, 1882-4), II, 136-7.

68 Thornhill's only other known early commissions were the sets for Thomas Clayton's opera *Arsinoë* in late 1704, and decorative works for Stoke Edith, Herefordshire, in 1705; it has been suggested that he may have assisted the aged Antonio Verrio in painting the Queen's Drawing Room at Hampton Court between 1702-4, however; Edward Croft-Murray, *Decorative Painting in England*, 2 vols (London: Country Life, 1962), I, 69-70.

69 Croft-Murray, *Decorative Painting*, I, 266.

70 BL Add. MS 78433: Susanna Draper to Mary Evelyn, 22 April 1696.

71 BL Add. MSS 78442 and 78463.

72 Her death is described by William Draper in a letter to Mary Evelyn, 6 Sept. 1707, BL Add. MS 78433.

73 It was the residence of Lord Chancellor Talbot until his death in 1737, then Lord Grantham (d.1786) and Charles Jenkinson, 1st Earl of Liverpool (d.1808). Ownership of the property descended through members of the Clarke family, until it was sold in 1809 to the East India Company; H. M. Vibart, *Addiscombe: Its Heroes and Men of Note* (London: Constable, 1894), pp. 9-13.

74 These letters are in BL Add. MS 78463. A number of letters sent to the younger William Draper (including one from George Vertue) are located in Add. MS 38480.

75 In Evelyn, *Diary*, I, 36, de Beer states (without citing a source) that Susanna Draper died in 1754, but this is not consistent with her son's letter of 1755.

76 Kim Sloan, *'A Noble Art': Amateur Artists and Drawing Masters c.1600-1800* (London: British Museum, 2000), p. 42.

77 Ibid., p. 7.

ADVICE TO LETTER-WRITERS

Evidence from Four Generations of Evelyns

SUSAN WHYMAN

LET US OBSERVE the ten-year-old son of John Evelyn as he writes a letter in 1665. There is no letter-writing manual at hand, just a pen made from the third left feather of a goose and a pot filled with ink made from oak-tree galls. John jr writes in Latin and carefully forms each letter using a large italic script. He struggles to keep his lines straight and his sentences centred. He opens with greetings to his 'Dearest Father', and leaves deferential space before closing with 'Ever your most obedient son'. The body of the letter contains many compliments. John jr may be young, but he clearly under-stands epistolary conventions.[1]

Historians have no difficulty in finding the output of letter writers like John's son, John jr. A mammoth cornucopia of family letters tumbles from the shelves of the British Library – for example, the Wentworth, Blenheim, Portland, Coke, and Trumbull Papers. Smaller gems are found in local record offices. Correspondence is most prolific for elite families and often extends throughout the lives of individuals and over many generations. Each family archive is marked by epistolary patterns relating to forms of address, handwriting, format, and dating practices. One of the most common features in collection after collection is the survival of children's first letters sending compliments to family members. These stilted formulaic epistles are then corrected, dissected, discussed, circulated, and finally saved by proud or unhappy kin.[2]

At first glance, these children's letters seem conventional and uninterest-ing. Why were they fussed over and even saved at all? In fact, their regular appearance tells us that we are witnessing something central to a culture based on sociability and conversation. I will argue that these first epistolary efforts were a rite of passage that provided entry into polite society. These letters-in-training may seem artificial to us, but they taught self-discipline and served as models for courtesy letters in a society based on patronage networks. They also shed light on the process by which an increasing number of men and women learned how to use the English language in an elegant manner.

Today I will use the diamond in the crown of the British Library's letter collections – the Evelyn archive – to show how the writing and preservation of family letters was encouraged over four generations. Basic literacy was taught by tutors, schoolteachers, or writing-masters, some time between the ages of four and eight.[3] But letter-writing as an indispensable lifelong skill was nurtured, monitored, and enshrined by family mentors. Since letters were so important, each generation was taught that they should be carefully preserved. I believe that the massing of these archives was not just random, but was part of a concerted family policy. Letters were collected no less purposefully than portraits or parcels of land.[4]

In family after family, we find an organized programme of copying outgoing letters, assembling letterbooks, keeping drafts, and endorsing standardized data about each letter. When self-set targets went unmet, writers expressed guilt. Thus Evelyn complained about letters 'which I intended to transcribe, but they grew to[o] fast upon me'.[5] A delight in filing, ordering, and transcribing engaged each proud generation.[6] Usually, one family member assumed the role of guardian of the letters and left marks of editing the collection. In the case of the Evelyns, the diarist taught his family how to assemble their papers. But it was his grandson Sir John Evelyn who assumed the role of editor, adding notes, and listing his favourite letters in the flyleaf of his grandfather's letterbooks.[7] It is common to find letters bearing double and even triple endorsements. They form an intricate conversation between loved ones over several generations.[8]

John's son, John jr, lived at a time when a convergence of historical factors was producing a diverse letter-writing public. The Evelyn archive contains several thousand letters to and from a broad range of people from the sixeenth to the eighteenth centuries.[9] No longer reserved for diplomacy and business use, more people were just 'scribbling' letters for many different reasons. After the Restoration in 1660, the post office was reorganized, and it now carried private letters throughout England, Wales, Scotland, Ireland, and abroad. A provincial post was also developing along with mail boats to and from the continent.[10] By the 1680s, the London penny post had hundreds of collection places, and deliveries were made up to eight times a day.[11]

By the 1720s, literacy rates had risen to about forty-five per cent for men and twenty-five per cent for women. For London women, it was nearer forty-eight per cent.[12] Rising geographic, social, and economic mobility led to separation of families, who needed to stay in touch.[13] At the same time, there was an outburst of printed matter, the development of new literary forms, and an increased respect for an improved, stable English language. The rise of a polite culture that stressed self-expression and manners was of critical importance.[14] Letter-writing played a crucial role in its development, as elite families like the Evelyns trained children to use letters in new polished ways.

Our first sets of letters between father and son are from the 1630. In

1634, Evelyn's brother George at Oxford sends a letter to his father Richard signed 'yo'r obedient sone'. Richard drafts his own answer on the back of the original and saves them both. Richard also writes to his 'loving sonne John', begging him to attend to learning. In 1635, John admits 'my father being ... extreamely displeased at my Writing so ill a Character, I put my selfe to the Writing Schoole for a Moneth or two, till I had redressed that in some measure'.[15]

We have even more evidence for the diarist's intense concern about the letter-writing skills of his own son John jr (1655-99),[16] and his grandson John (1682-1763).[17] Evelyn's small cramped hand covers every inch of space of scores of letters to children and grandchildren. Our first reply from his son John jr, at the age of ten, is in Latin. Its large boyish print is accompanied by a note from his tutor: 'Mr John presents you with his duty & a distick of verses ... they are according to your desire, wholy his own & your letter must divide your prayse between him & his phrase book.'[18] A triumvirate of father, tutor, and son cooperated in a process in which the child mastered epistolary conventions in Latin, French, and English, first at home, and later at Oxford. On the back of another letter dated 30 Jan 1666[/7] a proud father writes a note for later readers: 'Jack was but 12 years old when he writ this'. This is a precocious letter, studded with showy verses, describing John jr's travels to Oxford. It is labelled 'The Oxford Gazette', like a newspaper, and reveals heady but arrogant exuberance.[19] As he matures, John jr simplifies his forms of address. He closes simply with 'your dutifull son' and drops the adjectives 'most humble' and 'obedient'.[20] He obviously knows his epistolary etiquette. When he asks for money, he hopes, 'Sr, you will pardon me if I beg not in latine. I reserve that for a letter of thanks.'[21]

At the age of eighteen, John jr's sister Susan, with less education, cannot control her ink and covers her page with blots. When asked to describe her travels to the coronation, she admits in phonetic spelling: It is 'to[o] hard a task for me to undertake all I can say is it was very feine'.[22] Here we see early signs of gender difference in epistolary ability. We should note, however, that both sexes are assigned the task of describing travels and experiences through letters.[23] Though the gap may widen according to education, daughters' skills are equally encouraged.

Susan's sister Mary (1665-85) is a more gifted correspondent. At the age of eleven, she confesses, 'I wish I could writt better',[24] but by the age of seventeen, she pens an elegant epistle to her brother. She offers him a thousand thanks, though his generosity is 'so much beyond what I ever could have expected'. Her closing words and signature are framed by respectful one-inch spaces, so as to present her letter prettily.[25] These letters which seem so formal are the necessary accoutrements of any polite person who must give and receive favours.

As we read them, we see John's sons and daughters trying to understand how the genre of letter-writing works. At first, they comprehend only formal features like overall design and appropriate length. At this stage, the texts strongly resemble spoken language. As youngsters mature, they observe situations that give rise to expected types of letters. They replace stilted compliments with personal sentiments and are learning to become authors.[26] Both sexes are expected to participate in this process, yet once boys receive a classical education, they have an increasing advantage over their sisters. In many collections we find mandatory Latin letters penned at school from sons to fathers. I have examined seven from Evelyn's son and thirteen from his grandson. The latter agrees to write to his grandfather at least one Latin letter per month, 'follow[ing] strictly the method of composition prescribed by you'. This is done by the diarist's 'command' not 'request', notes Evelyn, as he crosses out the word 'petitionem' and replaces it with 'mandatum'.[27]

As boys learn to express themselves in Latin, boring as it may be, their command of English also expands.[28] The constant translating and polishing of words results in a deep intimacy with language at the most formative stage of development. Most important, the first formal exercise in composition at school is the imitation of Cicero's letters. The significance of this overlooked pedagogical technique cannot be ove-remphasized. It shows that letter-writing was used as a foundational skill for all later learning. Furthermore, schoolboys experienced this basic method for over three hundred years.[29] As Evelyn put it, the goal of John jr's education was 'an intire conquest of the two learned Languages:[and] an Easy & Natural style of writing'.[30] Elegant epistles that seemed artless, penned at home and then in school, were crucial to achieving this end.

This becomes clear when we observe Evelyn monitoring his grandson John's letters from Oxford. 'Pray forget not to write Latine letters,' Evelyn warns, ''til you have gotten a style: Cicero & the 2d Pliny ... are excellent,'[31] as are 'admirable examples in Erasmus'.[32] Following Cicero's rule that subject and purpose determine each letter's character, we find set types such as thank you notes to patrons, and letters of praise that use classical rhetoric and tropes.[33] For example, shortly after John arrives in Oxford, Evelyn gives a sentence-by-sentence description of a letter that he expects John to send to his friend Francis Godolphin. Godolphin is to be married and John must present his congratulations handsomely. Evelyn carefully writes the proper form of address and title. He thinks that cupids and doves will make suitable themes for felicitations to the fair lady. This letter, he warns, is important to the Evelyn family, for it will 'conciliate and cement that family's further kindness'. Evelyn knows 'of no more acceptable & proper method of your expressing your gratitude, than by Epistles, or Verses, or both'.[34]

Emotional ties bind the diarist to the Godolphins. Francis's mother

Margaret was Evelyn's most intimate soulmate and she died after giving birth to Francis.[35] Under the late Stuarts the Godolphins will grow even more powerful, becoming the Evelyns' most influential kin and patrons. Some time after the diarist's demand for a letter to Francis, young Godolphin is made a Teller of the Exchequer. He will 'certainly rise every day higher', notes Evelyn, '& may be able & disposed to do you seasonable kindness'. At this point, Evelyn orders John to write Francis another 'Latine Epistle (becoming your breding)'. John must send the original or a copy left open, so that his grandfather may read it first. Though clearly helpful, this must have put pressure on our fledgling letter-writer.[36]

In another action that becomes habitual, Evelyn shows John's epistles to Godolphin to friends outside the family. 'That it was all your owne', he writes, 'some that I have shew'd it to (and are great judges) would hardly believe. … They could not mend it; style & matter & contexture so highly pleasing them.'[37] This procedure in which Evelyn literally put words into his grandson's mouth is repeated with the Bishop of Norwich. The Bishop is so impressed with John's letter that he sends the boy a book. John then writes an elegant letter of thanks which the diarist copies and saves, noting it 'is shew'd & spoken of to severall for your style & handsome Addresse to your extraordinary commendation'.[38] Further epistles are ordered and sent to John's uncle, to Oxford officials, and to Samuel Pepys.[39] Each of the elders' proffered scripts is accompanied by a request to show no one his instructions.[40] Thus Latin letters are not just academic exercises, they are used for practical purposes in polite society. Indeed, grandfather is giving grandson a passport into a world of patronage and power.

This circulation of manuscript letters creates webs of intimate social networks among family and friends, as well as a community of writers and readers.[41] In 1701, Evelyn encloses a sealed letter to John's Vice Chancellor with the order: 'Deliver it to him with your owne Acknowledgements, as well as mine.' A copy of the enclosure is written on the bottom of the letter, so that the boy will know its contents. This simple act produces a complex chain of interactive letter-writers who circulate, then read, then respond to texts in overlapping acts of reading and writing.[42] Interestingly, John's grandmother Mary, a brilliant letter-writer, does not comment on her grandson's epistles. That is her husband's job, not hers.[43]

Evelyn criticizes as well as praises the boy's Latin, inserting more exact and concise wording.[44] John's style may be 'excellent', but Evelyn wishes he 'tooke a little more time & care in writing your epistles'.[45] 'Either your ill penn, or paper, or both render'd your lett'r in some places hardly legible.'[46] John's attempt to please is displayed in a draft of a Latin letter with corrections in every line and doodling on the bottom.[47] But by 1705 his flourishes, spacing, and flowing hand are becoming more representative of an elegant eighteenth-century epistle. The whole presentation is that of a well-polished gentleman with regard for the outer appearance of letter and person.[48]

The final letters under scrutiny are written in the eighteenth century by Sir John Evelyn's children – the great-grandchildren of John Evelyn. Their more regular patterns of spelling, punctuation, and handwriting show a shift in epistolary format as well as constant mentoring by kin. The eldest, John (1706-67), at the age of eleven writes his 'leater' from 'Eaton' in a modern flowing hand with carefully drawn initials.[49] By now the Godolphins have become so intimate that John's brother Charles (1709-49) is sent to live with the Countess of Godolphin at the age of ten. Thus Charles has two sets of taskmasters who monitor his letters. In 1725, Lord Godolphin is glad to receive Charles's letter from abroad written in French, though he doubts it is 'of your own composing'.[50] At the age of fifteen, Charles's large script is made up of carefully rounded letters. A mentor underlines and corrects mistakes in spelling and grammar.[51] This shows the trends toward standardization that have been evolving in contrast to the varied forms of earlier generations.[52] The free-flowing, ornamental round hands of Sir John's sons are worlds apart from the tight scrawl of the diarist.

At the age of fourteen, however, their sister Mary resists epistolary conventions. Her over-sized letters laced with blots and crossed-out lines show her difficulty in stifling her independence. Someone has underlined her many misspelled words and inserted those that she left out. Thirteen years later, however, we see her writing a typical polite letter that varies little from those of her siblings. Her letters give visual proof of her acculturation to social conventions.[53]

The Evelyn case study demonstrates the almost obsessive importance that literate families placed on teaching epistolary skills. In every generation, letter-writing was fostered at an early age. Children learned to write fluently, master conventions, organize content, and present themselves as polite persons. Elders set high standards, which they passed on to their children, and constantly reinforced them through mentoring and praise. They did this because they saw letter-writing as more than just a useful skill. Unlike music, art, and drawing, which were also taught, letter-writing was the first visual proof that a child was assenting to, or resisting, social conventions and norms. In a culture that prized language, conversation, and manners, letter-writing was a measurable prerequisite for entry into the adult world.

Thus, at the age of thirteen in 1695, the diarist's grandson John wrote to his father in flourished cursive letters: 'My love to my sister, and tell her that I shall be very glad when she can write that I may hold correspondence with her.'[54] This sentence shows that at the first possible time of written self-expression, entering epistolary networks was a natural and expected birthight for literate children. As John Locke advised, all types of learning might become delightful activities if taught at home at an early age when the mind was uncluttered.[55]

Scores of children's letters in other archives confirm their claim to being rites of passage. Likewise, most literate children had epistolary mentors, including parents, siblings, and godparents. They were specifically appointed to read, correct, and monitor first epistles and their corrections still exist. Since elite boys left home for public school at an early age, letter-writing may have been more intense for this group. But both sexes were expected to write letters at regular intervals. Lapses were considered a breach of duty.

Not surprisingly, children's letters in different collections have a tendency to look alike. They are filled with large unjoined letters that reveal slow, painful copying, and paper is often ruled. Blots and crossed-out words flourish, while margins are violated by unexpected length of words. Spelling is phonetic, but forms of address are scrupulously correct. These letters illuminate the process by which politeness was learned. In fact, the entire life cycle was filled with epistolary rituals. As children became parents they offered their own advice and the pattern reoccurred. Clearly, literate families felt that letter-writing helped their children to function in a society that depended upon social relationships.

It was purposeful family training, not modern letter-writing manuals, which produced early epistolary skills. Clearly, the primary models in the minds of young Evelyns were the family letters that they had a duty to write and receive. They also found ideal examples in letters of their Evelyn ancestors, which young ladies were asked to copy. Hence, Mary Evelyn's letters of the 1660s were transcribed into books by her great-granddaughter Mary in 1730.[56] In other family archives, we see similar young women copying letters and absorbing their contents and style.[57]

Letter-writing manuals may have been helpful to non-elites. Or they may have may have been read for impractical reasons: to enter a restricted social world, for romantic entertainment, or for literary interest.[58] The Evelyns, however, had little need for French models or business formularies. Better examples were found in classical antecedents, as Douglas Chambers shows in his essay. They were also located in contemporary literature, as well as popular and elite culture, in both printed and manuscript form.[59]

In fact, the boundaries between storytelling and real letters were constantly transgressed. Thus when Evelyn's grandson John wrote a letter describing his travels, he noted: 'I have run through each of the things I saw in some order, and have offered to your eyes events of daily life in a rude and incomplete account, as if putting together a story.' He hastened to add that he hoped he had not strayed 'too far beyond the proper bounds of a letter'. As Evelyn youngsters wrote letters, they learned to use narrative by telling stories about their daily lives. In this sense, their letter-writing was a pre-condition, along with other factors, for the eighteenth century world of letters. Just as children's epistles taught manners, so letter-writing, generally, provided a training ground for a free and easy command of the English language. Since the Evelyns wrote family letters outside of institutions, it might empower them as individuals, but it also indoctrinated them in the values of polite society.

In practice, letter-writing was always a two-edged sword. As Evelyn children matured, the epistolary format provided opportunities for free self-expression. It also gave them practice in the art of manipulating language to attain personal goals. This was particularly important for some women[60] and middling-sort letter-writers[61] who had educational disadvantages and less opportunity to write. Yet if schooling inequities led to difficulties with spelling, grammar, and presentation, this did not stem the flow of polite letters to and from women and middling-sort writers.

Within elites, public school and university widened the gap between brothers and sisters, but the earlier equality in nurturing letter-writing gave women an epistolary foundation for life. In the late seventeenth century, it spawned a generation of female letter-writers. By the eighteenth century, women's letters would even be published.[62] It is not surprising that John Evelyn's wife Mary, her daughter Mary, and her great-granddaughter Elizabeth wrote as easily as their brothers, and they may have been less constrained by classical formulas. In contrast, John jr's wife, Martha, the daughter of a wealthy Levant merchant, still spelled phonetically and crossed out mistakes as an adult. Her different early background was revealed in her letters. They indicate that rank could override gender when it came to letter-writing.[63]

The Evelyns and other elite families used letters to meet a broad range of personal, social, and dynastic needs. I have focused on the ritual role of conventional children's letters because they illuminate the larger social framework in which they were written. They help us to look at personal letters as material artefacts that evolved over time into showcases for polite breeding. In this role, they introduced young people to society, connected them to patronage networks, and gave them a new respect for the English language. They were saved because their owners read them, treasured them, and saw them as valuable possessions. We are the latest generation in a chain of privileged readers who may use them to understand the past.

NOTES

1 BL Add. MS 78301: John Evelyn jr to his father, 13 Dec. 1665.

2 It is rare to find a family archive without children's letters. Good examples may be found in the correspondence of the Cottrell-Dormer, Hatton, and Trumbull families.

3 David Cressy, *Literacy and the Social Order: Reading and Writing in Tudor and Stuart England* (Cambridge: Cambridge University Press, 1980); R. S. Schofield, 'The Measurement of Literacy in Pre-Industrial England', in *Literacy in Traditional Societies*, ed. by Jack Goody (Cambridge: Cambridge University Press, 1968), pp. 311-25; Margaret Spufford, 'First Steps in Literacy: the Reading and Writing Experiences of the Humblest Seventeenth-Century Spiritual Autobiographers', *Social History*, 43 (1979), 407-34; Keith Thomas, 'The Meaning of Literacy in Early Modern England', in *The Written Word: Literacy in Transition*, ed. by Gerard Baumann (Oxford: Clarendon Press, 1986), pp. 97-133. For the educational process see Edmund Coote, *The English School-Master* (London: R. Roberts, 1687); Richard Mulcaster, *The First Part of the Elementarie which Entreateth Chefelie of the Right Writing of our English Tung* (London: T. Vautroullier, 1582); William Kempe, *The Education of Children in Learning* (London: T. Orwin, 1588); J. Brinsley, *Ludus Literarius: or, the Grammar Schoole* (London: T. Man, 1612), and later editions of these works.

4 For a case study, see S. Whyman, '"Paper Visits": the Post-Restoration Letter as Seen through the Verney Family Archive', in *Epistolary Selves*, ed. by R. Earle (Aldershot: Ashgate, 1999), pp. 15-36.

5 John Evelyn, *Memoires for my Grand-son*, ed. by Geoffrey Keynes (Oxford: Nonesuch Press, 1926), pp. 64-5; cf. BL Add. MS 78515, the original manuscript.

6 Harold Love, *Scribal Publication in Seventeenth-Century England* (Oxford: Clarendon Press, 1993), pp. 198-200.

7 BL Add. MSS 78298-9, in which Sir John Evelyn lists some 'remarquable' letters in each volume.

8 For example, in BL Add. MS 78301, the letter of 18 Sept. 1671 bears the annotations of three generations.

9 Theodore Hofmann and others, *John Evelyn in the British Library* (London: British Library, 1995), p. 17. The correspondence includes hundreds of drafts, copies, and letters over eight generations. Evelyn's two folio letterbooks contain autograph copies of over eight hundred of his selected letters.

10 Post Office Archive, Acts file; M. M. Raguin, *British Post Office Notices 1666-1899* (Medford, Mass.: Raguin, 1991); J. W. M. Stone, *The Inland Posts, 1392-1672: A Calendar of Historical Documents* (London: Christie's – Robson Lowe, 1987); Post Office, *The Post Office: an Historical Summary* (London: HMSO, 1911); Howard Robinson, *The British Post Office: a History* (Princeton: Princeton University Press, 1948).

11 William Dockwra, *The Practical Method of the Penny Post* (London: George Larkin, 1681); BL Harl. MS 5954, fol. 20; T. Todd, *William Dockwra and the Rest of the Undertakers: the Story of the London Penny Post 1680-2* (Edinburgh: C. J. Coudland & Sons, 1952).

12 Cressy, *Literacy and the Social Order*, pp. 129, 176; Kathryn Shevelow, *Women and Print Culture* (London: Routledge, 1989), p. 30; *Kissing the Rod: an*

Anthology of Seventeenth-Century Women's Verse, ed. by Germaine Greer and others (London: Virago Press, 1988), pp. 1-31.

13 E. Wrigley, 'A Simple Model of London's Importance 1650-1750', *Past and Present*, 37 (1967), 44-70; S. Whyman, *Sociability and Power* (Oxford: Oxford University Press, 1999).

14 Paul Langford, *A Polite and Commercial People* (Oxford: Oxford University Press, 1989); Lawrence Klein, *Shaftesbury and the Culture of Politeness* (Cambridge: Cambridge University Press, 1994).

15 BL Add MS 15948, fol. 2: Richard to George Evelyn, 30 June 1634, and draft of answer 10 July 1634; BL Add. MS 78302: Richard to John Evelyn, 15 Dec. 1635; Evelyn, *Diary*, II, p. 13. There are letters of Evelyn's grandfather George and father Richard in BL Add. MSS: 78272 and 78274.

16 BL Add. MS 78442: Evelyn to John Evelyn jr, 1673-93.

17 BL Add. MS 78462: Evelyn to (Sir) John Evelyn, 1698-1701.

18 BL Add. MS 78301: John Evelyn jr to his father, 13 Dec. 1665.

19 Ibid.: 30 Jan. [1667] and [1667].

20 Ibid.: 4 Jan. 1676.

21 Ibid.: 24 Sept. 1672.

22 BL Add. MS 78359: Susanna Evelyn to Ralph Bohun, 4 May n.y.

23 BL Add. MS 78307: Francis Godolphin to John Evelyn, 5 July 1690; Add. MS 78299: Evelyn's reply, 9 Aug. 1690. I thank Douglas Chambers for this reference.

24 BL Add. MS 78442: Mary jr to John Evelyn jr, 1 March 1676.

25 Ibid.: 24 Nov. 1682.

26 Bodleian Library, Oxford, North MS d. 4, fols 4-14; Martin Nystrand, *The Structure of Written Communication: Studies in Reciprocity between Writers and Readers* (Orlando, Florida: Academic Press, 1986), pp. 155, 158.

27 I am indebted to Allan Ronald for his research and translations of Latin letters. BL Add. MS 78301: John Evelyn jr to his father, 22 Aug. 1672; Add. MSS 78442, 78462: (Sir) John Evelyn to his grandfather, 23 May, 2 Oct. 1699.

28 Harris F. Fletcher, *The Intellectual Development of John Milton* (Urbana, Illinois: University of Illinois Press, 1956), I, 182.

29 T. W. Baldwin, *William Shakspere's Small Latine & Lesse Greeke* (Urbana, Illinois: University of Illinois Press, 1944), II, 239-87; J. Brinsley, *Ludus Literarius* (London: T. Man, 1612), pp. 166-71; Fletcher, *Milton*, I, 206; [William Kempe], *The Education of Children in Learning* (London: T. Orwin, 1588), sig. G1; Giles Constable, *Letters and Letter-Collections* (Turnhout: Editions Brepols, 1976).

30 BL Add. MS 78462: John Evelyn to (Sir) John Evelyn, 12 June 1699.

31 Ibid.: 8 Apr. 1699. On this, see also Edward Greg's essay above.

32 Ibid.: 26 Oct. 1700.

33 For example, BL Add. MS 78302: Sir John Evelyn to his grandfather, 17 June 1700.

34 BL Add. MS 78462: John Evelyn to (Sir) John Evelyn, 26 March 1698; 18 April 1698; 26 Oct. 1700.

35 John Evelyn, *The Life of Mrs Godolphin*, ed. by Harriet Sampson (Oxford: Oxford University Press, 1939).

36 BL Add. MS 78462: John Evelyn to (Sir) John Evelyn, 26 May 1699, 26 Oct. 1700.

37 Ibid.: 12 June 1699.

38 Ibid.: 6 June 1701; BL Add. MS 78301: (Sir) John Evelyn to his grandfather, 17 June 1700.

39 BL Add. MS 78462: Evelyn to (Sir) John Evelyn, 5 Aug. 1699, 19 Apr. 1701; 6 June 1701; 19 Dec. 1701; 2 Dec. 1701.

40 For example, ibid.: Evelyn to (Sir) John Evelyn, 26 March 1698.

41 Margaret Ezell, *Social Authorship and the Advent of Print* (Baltimore: Johns Hopkins University Press, 1999); Peter Beal, *In Praise of Scribes: Manuscripts and their Makers in Seventeenth-Century England* (Oxford: Clarendon Press, 1998).

42 For reading see *A History of Reading in the West*, ed. by G. Cavallo, R. Chartier, & L. Cochrane (Oxford: Polity Press, 1999); Alberto Manguel, *A History of Reading* (London: Flamingo, 1997); Michel de Certeau, *The Practice of Everyday Life* (Berkeley: University of California Press, 1984); J. Raven, H. Small, & N. Tadmor, *The Practice and Representation of Reading in England* (Cambridge: Cambridge University Press, 1996); BL Add. MS 78462: Evelyn to (Sir) John Evelyn, 19 Dec. 1701.

43 BL Add. MS 78462: Mary Evelyn to (Sir) John Evelyn, 1706-8.

44 Ibid.: Evelyn to (Sir) John Evelyn, 7 Oct. 1699; Add. MS 78301: 2 Oct. 1699.

45 BL Add. MS 78462: Evelyn to (Sir) John Evelyn, 19 April, 13 May 1701.

46 Ibid.: 4 April 1701.

47 Ibid.: (Sir) John Evelyn to his grandfather, 1 April 1700 (draft); fair copy in Add. MS 78301.

48 BL Add. MS 78301: (Sir) John Evelyn to his grandfather, 9 Aug. 1705.

49 BL Add. MS 78471: John Evelyn to his father, 22 Sept. [1717].

50 BL Add. MS 78469: Francis, 2nd Earl Godolphin, to Charles Evelyn, 25 April 1726.

51 BL Add. MS 78472: Charles Evelyn to Sir John Evelyn, 14 Oct. 1726, 6 Nov. 1731.

52 Cary McIntosh, *The Evolution of English Prose: Style, Politeness, and Print Culture* (Cambridge: Cambridge University Press, 1998); *Sociolinguistics and Language History: Studies based on the Corpus of Early English Correspondence*, ed. by Terttu Nevalainen & Helena Raumolin-Brunberg (Amsterdam: Rodopi, 1996); David Graddol, Dick Leith, & Joan Swann, *English: History, Diversity and Change* (London: Routledge 1996).

53 BL Add. MS 78477: Mary to Anne Evelyn, 30 May 1724; Mary Evelyn to Sir John and Lady Evelyn, 16 June 1737.

54 BL Add. MS 78442: (Sir) John Evelyn to his father, 18 Aug. 1695.

55 John Locke, *Some Thoughts Concerning Education* (London: A. & J. Churchill, 1693).

56 BL Add. MS 78439: Mary Evelyn's letters 1657-1670s, in the hand of Mary Evelyn, daughter of Sir John Evelyn.

57 For example, Bodl MS Facs.54: letters from relations and friends of Esther Masham, 1722.

58 Roger Chartier, 'Introduction: an Ordinary Kind of Writing' and 'Secretaires for the People?', in R. Chartier, A. Boureau, & C. Dauphin, *Correspondence: Models of Letter-Writing from the Middle Ages to the Nineteenth Century* (Princeton: Princeton University Press, 1997), pp. 1-23, 59-111. For manuals generally see K. Hornbeak, 'The Complete Letter Writer in England 1586-1800', *Smith College Studies in Modern Languages*, 15 (1934), 1-150, and Jean Robertson, *The Art of Letter-writing* (London: University Press of Liverpool, 1942).

59 It is not surprising that the printer Richardson started with real letters and framed them into a letter-writing manual on the suggestion of two booksellers. The manual, in turn, led to the development of the novel, *Pamela*.

60 *Writing the Female Voice: Essays on Epistolary Literature*, ed. by E. Goldsmith (London: Pinter, 1989), p. xii; Ruth Perry, *Women, Letters, and the Novel* (New York: AMS Press, 1980), 68-70; Patricia M. Spacks, *Boredom: the Literary History of a State of Mind* (Chicago: University of Chicago Press, 1995), pp. 83-109; Mary Favret, *Romantic Correspondence: Women, Politics, and the Fiction of Letters* (Cambridge: Cambridge University Press, 1993).

61 Middling-sort letter-writing lies outside the limits of this paper but is covered in forthcoming publications.

62 For example, Lady Mary Wortley Montagu, *Letters of the Right Honourable Lady M—y W—y M—e:. Written during her Travels in Europe, Asia, and Africa* (London: T. Brecket & P. A. De Hondt, 1763); R. Brimley Johnson, *Bluestocking Letters* (London: John Lane, 1926).

63 BL Add. MS 78432: Elizabeth to Mary Evelyn, 12 July [1695], 20 Aug. [1697]; Martha to Mary Evelyn, 13 Aug. 1692, 6 Nov. 1695. Martha (d.1726) was a younger daughter of Richard Spencer, Turkey merchant (d.1667). Her mother remarried Sir John Stonehouse a year after Spencer's death; *The Historical Register ... XI, For the Year 1726 ... with a Chronological Diary* (London: R. Nutt [1726]), p. 36; Evelyn, *Diary*, IV, 189-96.

SIR JOHN EVELYN

His Grandfather's Heir

EDWARD GREGG

THE DIARIST John Evelyn left his grandson and namesake not only his Wotton and Deptford estates, but much more. In many ways his grandson was his intellectual as well as his legal heir: he was to follow a career and pursue interests surprisingly similar to those of his grandfather. The journals which 'young Jack Evelyn' kept sporadically are neither as extensive nor as personally revealing as his grandfather's *Diary*, but they help to establish that the younger Evelyn became very much the man the elder set out to shape.

The diarist took a great interest in the education of his grandson and ultimately exercised an unusual degree of control over it. In part his interest sprang from his continuing sense of disappointment in his only surviving son, young John's father, compounded by the loss of his four other sons, one of them a boy of exceptional promise, in infancy or childhood. Young John himself was the second son of the marriage of John Evelyn jr and Martha Spencer, an elder son Richard having been born in December 1680 and dying in September 1681. The younger John was born on 1 March 1682, followed by two sisters, Martha Maria, who was born on 28 June 1683 and lived only two months, and Elizabeth, born 26 November 1684. After their marriage John Evelyn jr and Martha Evelyn lived with his parents and young John was accordingly born at Sayes Court in Deptford. It was only in April 1684 that the young parents set up housekeeping in London, 'wholy without my approbation', complained the diarist, 'upon pretence of his applying himselfe more seriously to his studying the Law'.[1] The first major decision taken in young John's education was to send him to school, unlike his father, who had studied only with tutors until he entered university. In 1689, therefore, young John was 'putt to a French School in Greenwich', next door to Deptford, and he apparently lived with his grandparents until 1691, when, through the influence of Dr Thomas Tenison (later archbishop of Canterbury) 'he was removed to a School in King's Street near Golden Square'.[2] At that time his father was chief clerk of the Treasury, a position from which he was dismissed in June 1691.The loss plunged him into despondency and led in the next year to prolonged ill-health.[3] In December 1691 the grandfather attended 'a very pretty Act or exercise of the Schoole boys where was my Grandson: Speeches & Orations, verses in Gr: Lat: French: ending with a consort of voices of the boys, & then exercises in Mathematics'.[4]

In the spring of 1692, however, through the patronage of his father's close friend, Sidney, Lord Godolphin, John Evelyn jr was appointed one of the chief commissioners of the revenue for Ireland,[5] a renumerative position but one which meant taking up residence in Dublin. The younger Evelyns decided to take their daughter, who was only eight, with them, but to leave 'Jack' in England under the supervision of his grandparents. At the age of ten Jack was ideally suited to enter Eton, which was undoubtedly selected because Dr Henry Godolphin, younger brother of Lord Godolphin, had been a fellow there since 1677 (and in 1695 would be appointed provost). In June 1692 Evelyn took his grandson to Eton for the first time and in July both the parents and grandparents visited him there.[6] From Chester on the day before his family's embarkation for Ireland, John jr wrote that 'Eaton has by this time I suppose dryed up Jack's Tears'.[7]

At Eton young Jack was certainly not among strangers. Apart from Dr Godolphin and his wife Mary, there was also the family of Jael Boscawen, sister of Sidney and Henry Godolphin, who resided frequently in Lord Godolphin's homes in St James's and Windsor, and who had been largely responsible for rearing his only son, Francis (four years older than young Jack), whose mother had tragically died in childbirth. There are indications that young Jack frequently visited Mrs Boscawen and her children, Hugh, Dorothy, and his future wife Anne; in 1693, John Evelyn jr asked his father to convey his greetings to 'Mrs Boscawen, whose care of, and kindnesse to my young hopes at Eton lays constant and unanswerable obligations on me and my wife'.[8]

Letters from the diarist and his wife Mary, as well as from young Jack himself, kept his family in Ireland apprised of the boy's success at Eton: 'I am transported at the account my Mother gives of Jack's progresse in his book', John Evelyn jr wrote his father in January 1693.[9] In December that year, the diarist noted that Jack had come home for Christmas and '12 [*sic*] years old, gotten into the 3d forme & a very pregnant hopefull fine Child, whom I pray God to blesse'.[10] Certainly the grandfather worked assiduously to encourage his grandson: in January 1694 young Jack informed his father that 'my Grandpapa is making me a little Library at Deptford in my Aunt [Susanna] Draper's closet, which much pleases me'.[11] Others commented on the young boy's intellectual interests, not always favourably; 'the Eton Schollers will have another week of liberty', Mrs Boscawen notified the diarist in June 1694, 'neither will he that is such a lover of his book be thankfull for it, as others was'.[12] It was during this school holiday that, accompanied by the steward of the Deptford estate, Jack Evelyn paid a courtesy call on one of his

grandfather's oldest friends, Samuel Pepys: 'I had a very kinde visit yesterday from our pretty Ætonian, conducted by Mr [John] Strickland,' Pepys
notified the senior Evelyn, 'but could not get the Little Knave to dine with
mee, as being elsewhere bound. But I hope he will make me amends another
day.'[13]

By 1695, young Jack was deeply immersed in the studies of both Latin
and Greek and was acquiring the knowledge of ancient authors, history, and
mythology which was such a great part of his grandfather's life, and mastery
of which was considered the hallmark of the educated Englishman. He was
sending his father Latin odes of his own composition, although he reassured
him that 'I have not quite forgott my French, for sometimes I read a chapter
in the Testament, sometimes some other Book.'[14] Certainly his grandfather
basked in the reflected light of young Jack's success. In April 1696 he noted
in his diary that 'I went to Eaton, din'd with Dr Godolphin the Provost.
The Scholemaster assured me that there had not ben in 20 yeares a more
pregnant youth in that place than my Grandson.'[15]

In May 1696 Jack Evelyn's family returned from Ireland, his father
'Indispos'd', in the diarist's words.[16] Although he retained his positions
as commissioner of the Irish excise and one of the chief commissioners of
the Irish revenue, he did not feel well enough to see 'my Patron', Lord
Godolphin.[17] The nature of his illness remains unclear; in October 1697,
the diarist referred to 'my distressed miserable son, & sicke daughter', the
context making it clear that while Martha Evelyn was physically ill, the same
may not have been true of her husband.[18] In May 1698 Sir Hans Sloane, one
of the most eminent physicians of the day, examined the younger Evelyn and
reported to his father that 'He is in a very deep melancholy & does believe
his distempers to be much worse than really they are. ... In short 'tis as
plain as anything can be, that he being young may receive advantage from
medicines could he be prevailed with to take them.'[19] Politicians in England
and Ireland began to discuss the disposal of his offices in case of his death.[20]
Although young Jack spent Easter 1697 with his parents in Berkeley Street
rather than join his grandfather at Wotton ('He improves so fast', John jr
notified his father, 'that he is not far from being at the head of the School'),[21]
he continued to live primarily with his grandparents; when, in November
1697, he wanted permission to leave Eton to witness William III's triumphant progress through the City in celebration of the treaty of Ryswick, it
was his grandfather, not his father, to whom he appealed.[22] When John
Evelyn jr finally died in March 1699, his burial at Wotton was attended
neither by his father, nor by his son, who had entered Oxford in the previous
month.[23]

Having completed his studies at Eton in September 1698, young Jack had
subsequently studied 'Arithmetick and Algebra' under Dr John Arbuthnot,

later the author of *John Bull*, until February 1699,[24] when he went to Oxford to take up residence in his grandfather's old college, Balliol (his father had been a fellow-commoner of Trinity). Balliol was a relatively small and poor college at the end of the seventeenth century, and the diarist was easily the brightest star in Balliol's crown, to the extent that the master, Dr Roger Mander, personally accompanied young Jack from London, which they left on 17 February, arriving in Oxford the next day. Jack's first report to his grandfather, written three days later, was in English; all his subsequent letters from Oxford were in Latin (a practice which he had begun with his father, John Evelyn jr, in 1696).[25] The grandfather was thrilled: 'Pray forget not to write Latine Letters 'til you have gotten a style', he enjoined his grandson. 'The Translating Latine into Greek, & Gr: into Latine is of infinite advantage for the obtaining perfection in those so necessary Tongues.'[26] He proudly forwarded young Jack's letters to Pepys and 'The Club in York Buildings', and reported that 'Everybody is pleased with your Epistles & the style, easy & natural, & still recommend the Imitation of Cicero and Pliney.'[27]

On his arrival at Oxford, Jack Evelyn was apparently discontented to find himself placed in the lodgings of his tutor, Edward Strong, rather than in his own rooms, but was sternly reprimanded by his grandfather: 'one whose businesse is to improve himself in Learning may beare with some In-conveniences, without showing great discontents'.[28] Further letters, long, laborious, and written in his cramped hand, exhorted young Jack to call upon those at Oxford whose acquaintance might prove valuable and whose company educational. At the end of March 1699, he urged Jack to call on Thomas Hoy, M.D., who in September of the previous year he had successfully recommended to Robert Spencer, 2nd Earl of Sunderland, and to Archbishop Tenison for appointment as Regius professor of physic at Oxford, '& make some civil excuse that you did it not sooner'.[29] While Jack was in Oxford, his grandfather was working hard in London to establish his reputation with men whose acquaintance and support might be useful in the future. A prime example was John Moore, then bishop of Norwich and from 1707 bishop of Ely, to whom Evelyn showed his grandson's letters. In April 1701, he reported to Jack that Moore spoke 'so extraordinarily kindly of you', and in July that 'he lets you know, that his whole Library is at your Service, who may challenge free access when ever you please'.[30] The younger Evelyn remained close to Bishop Moore until the latter's death in 1714.[31]

While at Oxford, the younger Evelyn's principal study was mathematics and his 'master' was a Scotsman, John Keill, who had been incorporated from Edinburgh at Balliol in 1695 and was later Savilian professor of astronomy from 1711 to his death in 1721.[32] Keill reported directly to Evelyn's grandfather, who in turn assured Jack that 'I am exceedingly pleased with … the progresse Mr Keil has assured me you have maintained in your

Mathematicks.'[33] This progress was achieved against a background of frequent absences from Oxford. In August 1699 Jack was invited to join a family party composed of his mother and sister and his aunt and uncle, Elizabeth and Simon Harcourt, on a journey to Bath, apparently his first prolonged trip. His grandfather was less than enthusiastic: 'I heare you are designed to waite on your Mother to the Bath nor am I averse to it provided you stay not too long in that unpleasant & unwholesome ayre & place, where there is so little vertuous & profitable Conversation'; he suggested his grandson should also visit Bristol (which he did) '& above all the Duke of Beaufort's delicious & princely Seate'.[34] In his 'Short Account' which he wrote in 1759, four years before his death, Sir John Evelyn was to recall that he 'stayed above a month' in Bath, 'during which time he dined at Badminton with the old Duke of Beaufort, father of the great grandfather of the present Duke, and at Longleat with Lord Weymouth'. In September 1699 Jack Evelyn visited Worcester and at Christmas he spent several weeks with his family in London and Wotton. In the autumn of 1700 he spent two months at Wotton and Addiscombe, the home of his aunt and her husband, Susanna and William Draper. In addition, his maternal grandmother, the wife of Sir John Stonehouse, lived at Radley and he 'was often at this place but 3 miles from Oxford near Abingdon'.[35]

In late October 1700, while he was at Balliol, Jack Evelyn fell victim to smallpox. The news had a devastating impact on his grandfather, 'having lost two beautifull daughters about your yeares'. However, the master of Balliol, Dr Mander (who had also become vice-chancellor of the university) and Jack's tutor, Edward Strong, wrote daily reports of his condition to Simon Harcourt, who kept the Evelyns informed.[36] The attack was relatively mild and the eighteen-year-old quickly recovered, to the relief of his mother and grandparents, especially when Jack spent 'part of this winter' with his family in Dover Street.[37] When he left Oxford at the end of the following year, his grandfather sent a special letter of thanks to Mander and instructed Jack: 'I would also have you present your Tutor (Mr Strong) with a Ginny Extraordinary from me, not as a recompence, but as a small token of my thanks for his prayers & care of you.'[38]

The decision to leave Oxford was taken by the younger man, without the approbation of his grandfather. In reply to Jack's letter of 19 November, Evelyn wrote on 2 December: 'I question not at all your Seduity and dilligence since that time of you being returned, but the many large interruptions caused through your many absences, & by your Sicknesse, leaving you so short a continuance at the University (hardly in all amounting to two years compleate) does seem to those who conjecture of the progress which most others make in so narrow a Compasse, to expect greater things from you, or wonder at your quitting Oxford so soon.'[39] Jack's mother (who continued to make her home with her father and mother-in-law), however, reassured her son that even if he ignored his grandfather's arguments, he would be no less welcome to the old man should he decide to return home.[40] On 27 December, the diarist noted 'My Gr. Son came from Oxford for alltogether', without further comment.[41] To Pepys he wrote, 'he is now neere 20 yeares old, as I am of 80. And there are some polishings which I should rather he had learne here (and whilst I am here) than when in the country.'[42]

Normally a young man of Jack Evelyn's rank and education would complete his 'polishings' abroad on the Grand Tour. By the end of 1701, however, such a trip might prove exceedingly hazardous because of the impending War of the Spanish Succession. Fighting between Franco-Spanish and Imperial armies had already broken out in Italy, and it was only a matter of time before the Maritime Powers declared war on Louis XIV and Philip V. All five of John Evelyn's sons were dead and so were those of his brothers; Jack was the sole remaining male heir and too important to the future of the Wotton estate to risk. Both Evelyn's and his wife's 'tendernesses have determin'd against venturing him further from home'. Pepys, when consulted by his old friend, lauded the grandson ('hee being indeed a jewel'), but advised risking the hazard of a voyage, reminding Evelyn of how foreign travel as young men had benefited both of them and suggesting that such a trip would be much more suitable for Jack as a bachelor than later, when he might be married with a family.[43] In the event the younger Evelyn never left Great Britain, nor did *his* eldest son ever venture abroad.

Instead, Jack Evelyn embarked on a series of domestic tours which were to continue throughout his life and are one of the principal themes of his journals. The first took place in August and September 1702 when his uncle, William Draper, and he toured the West Country, going as far as Cornwall, where a special visit was paid to Godolphin, 'the ancient seat of the family from whence they take their name'.[44] In the summer of 1703 he visited Portsmouth and in May and June 1704 (again accompanied by his Uncle Draper) made a major expedition to the north as far as Durham, visiting a dozen great homes and other points of interest, including Nottingham, York, and Cambridge. All this was, in the words of his grandfather, 'to supply the present unfavourable period from travelling foraine Countrys'. In addition to practising his languages (Latin and Greek, French, Italian, and Spanish), he also continued his studies in 'History and Chronoloaelogy, Mathematikes, and the study of the Civill Law'. For relaxation he played the flute and attended fencing school. 'In summ,' his grandfather informed Pepys in January 1703, 'finding him so moderatly and discreetly dispos'd, (studious, and mindfull of his owne Improvement), I give him free Liberty.'[45]

It was probably about the time that Jack Evelyn left Oxford that his grandfather began to compose a series of papers which were ultimately published under the title *Memoires for my Grand-son*, 'one in whom I at present find all those good & Laudable qualitys & Inclynations which nourish & support my Hopes that you will so Improve those Vertuous dispositions & Talents to the Glory of Almighty God & the Benefit of your Country & Relations as becomes an honest, Religious and worthy man'.[46] The *Memoires* demonstrate how transcendently important the future of the Wotton estate was to the old man, and contain detailed practical advice on how his grandson should manage his future family, his stewards and other servants, and his income. He strongly urged Jack to follow his policy at Wotton of planting 'Timber Trees, Oaks, Ash and Elms, frequent Copses … the planting of Timber-trees being in truth the onely best and proper Husbandry the Estate is capable of'.[47] Evelyn had already noted his grandson's interest in gardening and it was to be expressed not only at Wotton, where he continued and expanded his grandfather's planting in consultation with the most eminent gardeners of the day,[48] but also in his detailed journal descriptions of the various gardens and parks he visited during his travels.

The *Memoires* and the 'Promiscuous Advices' which accompanied them urged Jack to maintain his intellectual interests, pointing out that his education had been 'something above that of most ordinary Country Gents'.[49] This he was to do, being elected to the Royal Society in 1722 and the Society of Antiquaries in the next year. He also honoured his grandfather's great interest in building the Royal Hospital at Greenwich by contributing funds to support Sir James Thornhill's painting of the Banqueting Hall there, where, his Uncle Draper told him, 'You will see your Name & Summe in gold Letters.'[50] In parallel with his grandfather's involvement with Greenwich, when Jack Evelyn was seventy-one in 1753 he became one of the first Trustees of the newly established British Museum, and he was instrumental in the decision to house the Museum in Montagu House rather than build a new building.[51] One of the most detailed sections of the *Memoires* dealt with the care and maintenance of a gentleman's library, including purchasing, binding, and book-presses; the grandson had already shown himself a bibliophile and the grandfather uncharacteristically had complained of the number and cost of the books Jack had ordered sent to Balliol when he went to Oxford.[52] In 1716 he was to build a magnificent new library at Wotton to house both his own collections and those of his grandfather.[53]

The greatest contrast between the adult Sir John Evelyn and his grandfather was the degree to which religion was central to their lives. For the elder Evelyn, religion was of paramount importance, a fact reflected throughout his writings; while the grandson duly obeyed his grandfather's injunctions in the *Memoires* to maintain a strict regime of religious devotion, both for himself, his wife and children, and his household, the lack of religious commentary in his journals suggests that he was an observant, albeit hardly enthusiastic, Anglican.[54]

The most important and lasting way in which John Evelyn shaped his grandson's future was the exceptional care which he took to ally his dynasty to the house of Godolphin. In his *Memoires,* Evelyn told his grandson: 'If you conveniently may obtaine any creditable Office by Favour or purchase, there is nothing more desirable & profitable for young men to Advance themselves by.'[55] Evelyn's well-known attachment to Margaret Blagge, who married Sidney Godolphin in 1675 and died in childbirth in 1678,[56] led to his continuing interest in Margaret's only child, Francis, who because his father never remarried was largely brought up by Jael Boscawen. Sidney Godolphin continued his political career, being created a baron and first lord of the Treasury in 1684. Although he lost his Treasury position under James II, he regained it under William III and headed the Treasury for the better part of William's reign. He had served as 'patron' of Jack Evelyn's father, a role which the grandfather hoped he would continue playing. In 1698, Evelyn urged his grandson, still at Eton, to compose a congratulatory ode in Latin to present to Francis Godolphin in celebration of his marriage to Lady Henrietta Churchill, the eldest daughter of John Churchill, Earl of Marlborough: 'The reason why I injoyn you to compose a few lines in felicitating young Mr Godolphin's Nuptials is, the very great Obligation I have to that family, & the use I shall have of its continual favour & Friendship in your behalfe in due time.'[57] A year later Evelyn urged Jack to write again to Francis Godolphin, this time to congratulate him on his appointment as a Teller of the Exchequer (at £2000 per annum), pointing out that his friendship might be of use later.[58] There can be little doubt that by this time, Evelyn had in mind a marriage alliance for his grandson.

On 8 March 1702 William III died and was succeeded to the throne by his sister-in-law, Princess Anne of Denmark, an event which guaranteed that Marlborough and his close friend and political ally Sidney Godolphin, would be the dominant figures in the new government. On 7 May, the day before Godolphin was formally appointed Lord Treasurer, Evelyn wrote to him, asking him 'to take my Grandson into your Favour & patronage'.[59] The following month he wrote to Jael Boscawen, formally proposing the marriage of his grandson to her younger daughter, Anne.[60] Mrs Boscawen's reply four days later was highly encouraging: 'What I desire in the disposing of my child is a good famely, a sober vertuous yong man & a competent future, & these things I take to meet in your Grandson.'[61] She also agreed with Evelyn that the marriage should be delayed for some time, presumably while Jack completed his 'polishings', and there negotiations seem to have rested.

Godolphin for his part was undoubtedly in favour of the proposed marriage, but in acting as a political patron for Jack Evelyn, he refused to place family considerations before more pressing political necessities. Evelyn conducted a relentless campaign on his grandson's behalf; in June 1703, he wrote to Mrs Boscawen, discussing the financial incumbrances on his estate and, adding of his grandson: 'He is young, more than ordinarily knowing for his age of the most Usefull Learning: Sober, Industrious, & as yet Untainted; and has no reason to despair of Emerging (continuing Virtuous), especially should his Lordship receive him into his Patronage.'[62] It was not until January 1704 that Godolphin found a suitable position available and made Jack treasurer of the revenue of stamped paper, a minor office with an annual salary of only £300.[63] Rather than being discouraged, both Evelyns seem to have taken this minor appointment as a harbinger of better things to come. In September 1704 Mrs Boscawen assured the elder Evelyn that her brother 'said indeed … that he should be glad to do anything for your Grandson, that might make you more easy, & perticulerly in relation to this Marriage, which he seems to approuve of, & like as well as we doe, & when he did give him this little imployment, he told me himself, it was the rather done, with the prospect of it'.[64]

On 16 March 1705 the diarist noted, 'I waited on my L. Treasurer to whom was proposed my G—sons marriage with his Niece, which he much approved of.'[65] In late June he noted that 'My L. Treasurer made my Gr—son one of the Commissioners of the prizes the sallary 500 pounds per Annum', to be held in tandem with his other office.[66] On 8 July, Jack Evelyn, accompanied by his uncle Sir Simon Harcourt, who as solicitor-general had been part of Godolphin's administration since 1702, went to Windsor to wait on the Lord Treasurer. Undoubtedly one reason for their journey was to hammer out the details of the marriage contract (which Evelyn noted was 'now far advanced') with Godolphin.[67] At the end of the month, the diarist recorded: 'The Marriage Settlement of my Gr: son with a Daughter of Mrs Boscawen, sister to my L. Treasurer, now finished, stays onely for the comming back of Sir Sym: Harcourt to examine the deeds & seale: he being yet in the Circuit.'[68] Before the end of August, Harcourt had returned to London and the marriage settlement which John Evelyn had so carefully planned was completed, '& given to be Ingrossed, giving him my Intire Estate, reserving onely the possession of it during my life, and the absolute disposure of the personal Estate, to be disposed of by my Will: &c: The lease of the House, & intire furniture of my house at London I gave absolutely to my deare Wife.'[69] On 16 September Evelyn noted that his grandson and his fiancée received communion together in the Chapel Royal at St James's Palace, and two days later they were married in the chapel of Lambeth Palace; the ceremony was conducted by the Archbishop of Canterbury,

Thomas Tenison, who had placed young Jack Evelyn in his first London school in 1691. The jubilant grandfather recorded that they were, 'with aboundance of Relations on both sides, most magnificently Entertained with supper that night, by her Mother'. Evelyn spent the rest of the week 'receiving Visites of greate persons'. On 26 September he and his wife 'invited as many of the Relations of Mrs Boscawen, and of my L. Treasurer as were in Towne [&c], to the number of 18 to Dinner, which was as greate as the solemnity of Marriage of my Grandson &c required'.[70]

John Evelyn, now in his eighty-sixth year, realized that this was the last opportunity which he would have to direct his grandson's future: 'I have Maried you into a very honest & worthy Family and Relations', he conuded his *Memoires for my Grand-son*. 'And given you private Instruction how to Govern your selfe & Treat your Wife as becomes in a Christian and Gentleman'.[71] He died on 27 February 1706, only five months after his grandson's wedding, but knowing that he had allied him with the Boscawens, the Godolphins, and (through Francis Godolphin's marriage to Henrietta Churchill) the Churchills, three of the most influential families in Augustan England. In October 1708, thanks to his connection with the Lord Treasurer, Jack Evelyn was appointed joint postmaster-general (with Sir Thomas Frankland) at a salary of £1000 per annum. Godolphin and the Whigs fell from power in 1710, but Evelyn managed to retain his office, thanks to the influence of his uncle, Harcourt, who became a baron and lord keeper (and from 1713, lord chancellor) in the new, Tory administration. In August 1713 Evelyn was created a baronet at Lord Harcourt's behest.[72]

The death of Queen Anne in August 1714 and the accession of the first Hanoverian monarch, George I, entailed another political upheaval. The Tories, including Harcourt, were abruptly dismissed from office immediately upon the new king's arrival in England and were replaced by Whigs. Evelyn's brother-in-law, Hugh Boscawen, became comptroller of the household (replacing Evelyn's maternal uncle, Sir John Stonehouse) and his cousin-in-law, Francis, Earl of Godolphin (his father had died in 1712) became cofferer of the household. Their combined influence, however, was insufficient to prevent Sir John Evelyn's dismissal from the Post Office in February 1715. He was not to regain political office until September 1721 when he was appointed a commissioner of the Customs (at £1000 per annum), a position he held until his resignation a few months before his death in July 1763. Undoubtedly, the influence of Lord Godolphin and Viscount Falmouth (as Hugh Boscawen had by then become) was again deployed on his behalf, but in all probability Sir John's appointment was also largely influenced by the fact that Harcourt (who had been elevated to a viscountcy ten days earlier) had struck an alliance with Robert Walpole and the Whig administration. Sir John Evelyn's journals and surviving correspondence, however, demonstrate that his marriage, which proved exceptionally happy, and the connections which came with it, helped determine the future course of his life.

John Evelyn had largely succeeded in his goal: to mould his grandson and to make him a pillar of the community: 'we are Christians', he had written to young Jack in 1699, '& born for the good of our Country, Relations, & dependants'.[73] He would have rejoiced in the knowledge that his grandson so comported himself that a local historian of Surrey could write, nearly seventy years after his death, that Sir John Evelyn 'lived here universally beloved and respected'.[74]

NOTES

1 Evelyn, *Diary*, IV, 375.
2 BL Add. MS 78516: 'Short Account of Sir John Evelyn', aft. 1751; Add. MS 78531: Evelyn to Jael Boscawen, 29 June 1691: 'Dr Tenison has plac'd our little Jack in a Schoole of his not far from the new Church, & near my Son's, where the boy is much pleased.'
3 Evelyn, *Diary*, V, 93, 103.
4 Ibid., V, 79.
5 BL Add. MS 78301: Evelyn jr to his father, 19 Sept. 1692.
6 Evelyn, *Diary*, V, 103, 110.
7 BL Add. MS 78301: Evelyn jr to his father, 23 Aug. 1692.
8 Ibid., 25 Feb. 1693.
9 Ibid., 14 Jan. 1693.
10 Evelyn, *Diary*, V, 162.
11 BL Add. MS 78442: Jack Evelyn to his father, 3 June 1698.
12 BL Add. MS 78309: Jael Boscawen to Evelyn, 12 June 1694.
13 *Particular Friends: the Correspondence of Samuel Pepys and John Evelyn*, ed. by Guy de la Bédoyère (Woodbridge: Boydell, 1997), p. 242: Pepys to Evelyn, 22 May 1694.
14 BL Add. MS 78301: Jack Evelyn to his father, 18 Aug. 1695.
15 Evelyn, *Diary*, V, 236.
16 Ibid, V, 240 and n. 1.
17 BL Add. MS 78301: Evelyn jr to his father, 12 July 1696.
18 Evelyn, *Diary*, V, 269.
19 BL Add. MS 78685: Sloane to Evelyn, 17 May 1698.
20 E.g., BL Add. MS 28881, fols 282-3: Christopher Carleton to John Ellis, 29 May 1697: 'Poor Mr Evelin wee are told is again relapsed, if he should go off, I must pray your assistance to succeed him.'
21 BL Add. MS 78301: Evelyn jr to his father, 2 April 1697.
22 BL Add. MS 78462: Evelyn to his grandson, 1 Nov. 1697.
23 Evelyn, *Diary*, V, 318-19.
24 BL Add. MS 78516: 'A Short Account of Sir John Evelyn'.
25 BL Add. MS 78301: Jack Evelyn to his grandfather, 21 Feb. 1699; Add. MS 78442: Jack Evelyn to his father, 14 Jan. 1696. On this see further Susan Whyman's essay above.
26 BL Add. MS 78462: Evelyn to his grandson, 8 April 1699.
27 *Particular Friends* (see n. 13 above), pp. 263, 273: Evelyn to Pepys, 14 Jan.

1699, 22 July 1700; BL Add. MS 78462: Evelyn to his grandson, 26 May 1699.

28 BL Add. MS 78462: Evelyn to his grandson, 20 March 1699.

29 Ibid.: Evelyn to his grandson, 26 March 1699. See also Evelyn, *Diary*, V, 298 and n. 2.

30 Ibid.: Evelyn to his grandson, 4 April, 2 July 1701.

31 BL Add. MS 78514 A: Journal of Sir John Evelyn, 10 Feb. 1713, 15 July 1714. These journals are presently being edited for publication by Edward Gregg and Clyve Jones.

32 BL Add. MS 78516: Sir John Evelyn, 'Short Account'; cf. L. S. Sutherland, 'The Curriculum', in *The History of the University of Oxford*, V: *The Eighteenth Century*, ed. by L. S. Sutherland & L. G. Mitchell (Oxford: Clarendon Press, 1986), 473, n. 1; see also, *DNB*, X, 1198-9.

33 BL Add. MS 78462: Evelyn to his grandson, 14 June 1701.

34 Ibid.: Evelyn to his grandson, 5 Aug. 1699.

35 BL Add. MS 78516: Sir John Evelyn, 'Short Account'.

36 BL Add. MS 78462: Evelyn to his grandson, 26 Oct. 1700; cf. Evelyn, *Diary*, V, 431-2, 434.

37 BL Add. MS 78482: Mary Evelyn to her grandson, 10 [Nov. 1700]; Martha Evelyn to her son, 14 Nov. 1700; BL Add. MS 78516: Sir John Evelyn, 'Short Account'.

38 BL Add. MS 78462: Evelyn to his grandson, 19 Dec. 1701.

39 Ibid.: 2 Dec. 1701.

40 Ibid.: Martha Evelyn to her son, 8 Dec. 1701.

41 Evelyn, *Diary*, V, 484.

42 *Particular Friends*, pp. 287-8: Evelyn to Pepys, 10 Dec. 1701.

43 Ibid., pp. 289-90: Pepys to Evelyn, 24 Dec. 1701.

44 BL Add. MS 78516: Sir John Evelyn, 'Short Account'; his account of this journey, 'Iter Occidentale', 1702 (BL Add. MS 78512), is the first of his surviving journals.

45 *Particular Friends*, pp. 293-4: Evelyn to Pepys, 20 Jan. 1703.

46 *Memoires for my Grand-son*, ed. by Geoffrey Keynes (Oxford: Nonesuch Press, 1926), p. 4.

47 Ibid., p. 17.

48 BL Add. MS 78498: George London to John Evelyn, 5 April 1708; London and Henry Wise to Evelyn, 13 April 1708.

49 *Memoires for my Grand-son*, p. 39.

50 BL Add. MS 78463: Draper to Evelyn, 14 April 1707. The name of 'John Evelyn Esq.' and his £100 gift are still there, but as it was made six years before his baronetcy was conferred in 1713, visitors may assume it refers to his more famous grandfather.

51 BL Add. MS 78477: Anne Evelyn to Sir John Evelyn, 4 Feb., 5 April 1754.

52 BL Add. MS 78462: Evelyn to his grandson, 8 April 1699; *Memoires for my Grand-son*, pp. 50-4.

53 BL Add. MS 78462: Evelyn to his grandson, 8 April 1699; *Memoires for my Grand-son*, pp. 50-4.

54 BL Add. MS 78498: correspondence of Evelyn and James Moore, 1716.

55 *Memoires for my Grand-son*, pp. 9-11.

56 See W. G. Hiscock, *John Evelyn and Mrs Godolphin* (London: John Murray, 1951).

57 BL Add. MS 78462: Evelyn to his grandson, 26 March, 18 April 1698.

58 Ibid.: 22 May 1699.

59 BL Add. MS 78307: Evelyn to Godolphin, 7 May 1702 (copy).

60 BL Add. MS 78531: Evelyn to Jael Boscawen, 22 June 1702.

61 BL Add. MS 78309: Jael Boscawen to Evelyn, 26 June 1702.

62 BL Add. MS 78531: Evelyn to Jael Boscawen, 17 June 1703.

63 Evelyn, *Diary*, v, 556.

64 BL Add. MS 78309: Jael Boscawen to Evelyn, 21 Sept. 1704.

65 Evelyn, *Diary*, v, 587-8.

66 Ibid., 601-2.

67 Ibid., 602.

68 Ibid., 605.

69 Ibid., 606.

70 Ibid., 609-10.

71 *Memoires for my Grand-son*, p. 69.

72 Evelyn's connections with the leading figures of both parties were recognized by contemporaries. A week before Godolphin was dismissed, Dr William Stratford of Christ Church wrote to Edward Harley (son of Robert Harley, who was engineering 'the Great Changes'): 'Who is it that at this time dares open your father's letters? I thought [Sir Thomas] Frankland had been his servant, the other [John Evelyn] indeed is Lord Treasurer's nephew, but he too is now near allied to Sir Simon [Harcourt]. But methinks either of them might discern the weather well enough, not to offer at any such thing': HMC *Portland MSS*, vii, 9: Stratford to E. Harley, 1 Aug. 1710.

73 BL Add. MS 78462: Evelyn to his grandson, 9 May 1699.

74 Thomas Allen, *A New and Complete History of the Counties of Surrey and Sussex*, 2 vols (London, 1829), ii, 221.

THEIR 'OWN SWEET COUNTRY'

The Evelyns in Surrey

ISABEL SULLIVAN

'SURREY is the Country of my birth, and my delight': John Evelyn's letter to John Aubrey in the latter's posthumous *Natural History and Antiquities of the County of Surrey* states a recurrent sentiment in the diarist's writing, and is his own brief and personal contribution to the earliest published history of Surrey.[1] Evelyn was resident in Surrey for a small proportion of his life, in early childhood and old age, yet his affection for his 'own sweet country of Surrey', rural yet civilized, and conveniently close to London, is clear.[2] He was also conscious of the county's significance to his family's identity, and of their place in the county's history. They had lived and risen to landed power and eminence in Surrey over the previous two generations, and they have continued to be a presence in the county. Fittingly, the future survival of his own *oeuvre*, following on the success of the publication of his diary in 1818, owes much to the interest of a later county historian, William Bray, in the manuscripts preserved in Evelyn's Surrey home. This is an account of Evelyn's Surrey connections [Fig. 1].

The family had achieved some modest status in the county by the mid-sixteenth century. John Evelyn (d. 1568), a parishioner of Kingston upon Thames, one of the principal Surrey towns, appears to have held a respectable amount of land in the neighbouring parish of Long Ditton.[3] His son George Evelyn (1526-1603), grandfather of the diarist, would achieve a far more considerable fortune for his family in the gunpowder business. Although the diarist believed that his family 'were the very first' to bring the artificial manufacture of saltpetre to England from the continent, its introduction is more accurately attributed to a German, Gerrard Honrick, who sold his advice to the English government in 1560. The politically crucial English gunpowder industry was established by a tender issued in 1562.[4] Gunpowder was principally used for military and naval purposes before the late seventeenth century,[5] and it was Surrey businessmen who took advantage of proximity to London and plentiful woodland for the manufacture of charcoal to take up the new contracts. Surrey became the sole centre for its manufacture until the Civil War, and George Evelyn was awarded one of the first contracts

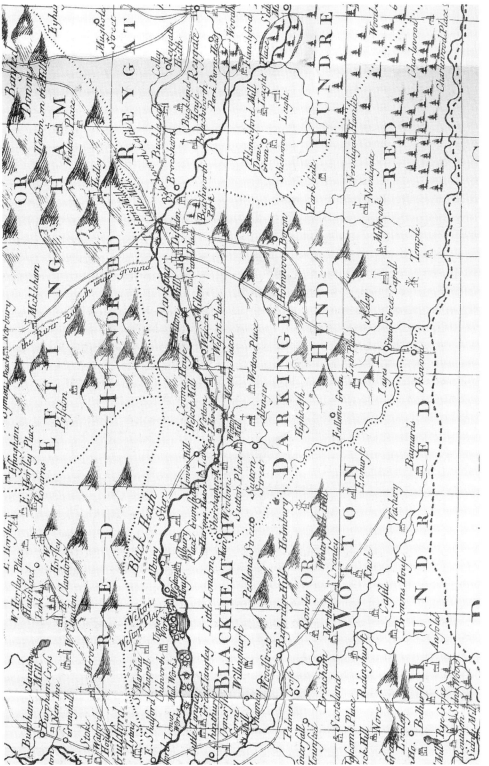

Fig. 1: Detail from the county map in Aubrey's *Natural History and Antiquities of the County of Surrey* (1819), I, showing Wotton (centre), Shere, Albury Park, the Chilworth gunpowder mills and Deepdene (Surrey History Centre).

in the early 1560s. His gunpowder works are believed to have been at Tolworth in the parish of Long Ditton, near Nonsuch Park.[6]

George Evelyn did not have a monopoly: in 1589 a patent for supply of gunpowder to the Tower of London was granted both to George Evelyn and his second son John, and to Richard Hill of Shere in Surrey. They did not work as partners, and indeed there appears to have been some rivalry between them which was brought before a commission in 1591.[7] Hill's mills are probably those formerly at Wotton mentioned by the diarist, as there is no evidence that the Evelyns worked mills at Wotton.[8]

By his death in 1603, business success had enabled George Evelyn to purchase several substantial Surrey estates, both further land in the Kingston and Long Ditton area (including Norbiton Hall, 1588), and new areas in the west of the county at Hill Place (Horsell, Bisley, and Chobham, 1567), in Wotton (1579-95) and in Godstone (1589). Two marriages, first to Rose Williams, then to Joan Rogers (*née* Stint), had given George Evelyn twenty-four children.[9] Three Surrey branches to the family as well as a branch established in Wiltshire, at West Dean, emerge through the inheritance of George Evelyn's surviving sons.

Thomas Evelyn (b. 1551), eldest son of George Evelyn (d. 1603) and Rose Williams, inherited the Long Ditton estate, and a share in gunpowder manufacture. The estate included the manor of Long Ditton and the patronage of Long Ditton church. Sir Thomas Evelyn (1587-1659), Thomas's son, is distinguished for his long-standing battle with the puritan minister of the parish, Richard Byfield; Byfield accused Evelyn of refusing to release money for the repair of the church, and for maintaining a 'prelatical' household chaplain who was luring away the congregation, while Evelyn claimed that Byfield slandered him and his wife in his sermons.[10]

Political rivalry of a fairly polite kind existed between Sir Edward Evelyn (1626-92), grandson of Thomas (b. 1551), and the diarist's brother George during the election of April 1685. Although George Evelyn was the favoured candidate of the county voters, the sheriff called the election during the absence of his party during an afternoon storm, enabling Edward Evelyn and the elderly and deaf Sir Adam Browne, the Duke of Norfolk's candidates, to win the day. Edward was described by the diarist as 'an honest gentleman', who was 'much in favour' with James II.[11] He died in 1692 without male heir. This branch of the family does not feature much in Evelyn's diary. Visits to Long Ditton by the diarist are to the Hatton cousins, children of Mary (1550-1612), the only surviving daughter of George Evelyn's first marriage, who married a local landowner Richard Hatton.

In 1589 George Evelyn had purchased the Godstone estate including the manor of Marden, the house Lee Place with its mills, and land in Bletchingley, in the south-east of Surrey. Godstone parish already supported an industry in fullers earth extraction, and there may also have been some quarrying of local firestone by this period.[12] The estate was left to George's younger sons by his first marriage, John (1554-1627) and Robert (b.1556), along with shares in the gunpowder business. The gunpowder was clearly lucrative, but subject to risk both physical and economic: every default on monthly supply to the Tower of London was subject to a penalty of £50.[13] Robert Evelyn, complaining of 'in-supportable losses … and dangers … almost to the whole overthrowe of his estate',[14] sold his share of both the business and the Godstone estate to John and left England for Virginia in 1609.

John's gunpowder works were established at Lee Place in Godstone by at least 1613.[15] His second son John (1591-1664) could afford to build a new home at Lee Place at the impressive cost of £9000, although the results of this expenditure were only faintly praised by his cousin the diarist.[16] John Evelyn continued to work gunpowder, with increasing difficulties in obtaining payment from the government, until he lost the monopoly in 1636.[17] He was the first Evelyn to take a Surrey seat in Parliament in 1628, for the borough of Bletchingley, and was knighted in 1641. Unlike his cousin and namesake Sir John Evelyn of Wiltshire, who was an outspoken radical, he was a moderate Parliamentarian in the Civil War. He was on good terms with his royalist Wotton cousins; the diarist notes of his attendance at a forty-first wedding day feast of Sir John Evelyn that 'there was much company of friends'.[18] The diarist admired the fine knightly monument to Sir John and his wife Thomasine at Godstone church [Fig. 2], and William John Evelyn, Sir John's descendant, commissioned a replica for the library at Wotton House.

John (1591-1664)'s second son John (1632-71), although he succeeded in retaining the eminence achieved by his father to become high sheriff of Surrey in 1666, was notoriously extravagant, and ultimately scandalous, in leaving part of his estate to his local mistress Mary Gittings. Lee Place is said by Aubrey to have been 'demolished' by his neglect, so it is now uncertain quite how grand the original Evelyn home had become. Marden Park and other Evelyn lands were sold by Mary Gittings to Sir Robert Clayton in 1672.[19] Clayton, who became Lord Mayor of London, would soon eclipse the Godstone Evelyns' importance in the area, with a grand new house at Marden and the development of stone quarries. The Evelyn family retained some estates in the parish until 1734, although they continued afterwards to live nearby at Nutfield and over the county border in Kent.

The third branch of the family was established at Wotton, a rural parish with a small scattered settlement in the south of Surrey, where Evelyn family members have held and managed the land ever since. George (1526-1603), grandfather of the diarist, had purchased part of the manor of Wotton in

Fig. 2: Monument of Sir John Evelyn and his wife Thomasine in the
chancel aisle of Godstone Church (from J. M. Hobson,
Photographic Survey of Surrey, 1903).

1579, and moved from Long Ditton to live at Wotton House, manor house
of Wotton, in the early 1590s, possibly on retirement from business. He is
buried in the Evelyn chapel at Wotton church, which stands alone in the
parish, below the ridge of the North Downs at White Down.

Perhaps at Wotton George saw himself reaping the benefits of his earlier
entrepeneurial success by enjoying the status of a more traditional landed
gentleman. He handed this on to Richard (*c.*1580-1640), only surviving son
of George's second wife Joan Stint, as he settled the Wotton estate on him
in 1595. Despite the diarist's pride in his innovative industrialist forebears,
the Wotton branch was founded on land and its associated conservative
sympathies.

Following his inheritance in 1603, Richard Evelyn expanded the estate
by purchases of further neighbouring manors. By 1622, he owned the seven
manors of Wotton, Abinger, Paddington Pembroke, Paddington Dean,
Milton, Westcott, and Westland, covering most of the parishes of Wotton
and Abinger and part of Dorking. Family estate deeds from the medieval
period show that the land here has always been highly valued for its timber.[20]
Richard could earn a substantial living from it, with an estimated value of
£4000 a year.[21] The estate comprised the Tillingbourne valley and the slopes

of the Greensand hills, including Leith Hill, the highest point of south-east England: 'the extent and circumference of vista I take to be much beyond ... any that I have observed either in England or elsewhere' wrote the diarist to Aubrey.[22]

Richard Evelyn was a justice of the peace for Surrey from 1621 and served as sheriff for Surrey and Sussex in 1634 in very grand style (with one hundred and sixteen liveried attendants instead of the more usual thirty or forty), although he is described by his son as little inclined to public office and its attendant expenses.[23] Richard married Eleanor Stansfield, heiress to a Sussex estate, the diarist being their second child. The diarist's brother George (1617-99) inherited the Wotton estate on Richard Evelyn's death in 1640.

George was educated locally at the Royal Grammar School in Guildford and remained a Surrey country gentleman for the rest of his life. The youngest brother Richard (1622-69) also remained in the county, first at a family house Baynards to the south-west of Wotton in Ewhurst, and then at Woodcote Park, Epsom, following his marriage to the heiress Elizabeth Mynne. George was a moderate royalist and remained in Parliament during the Civil War.[24] According to Aubrey, he lived 'very hospitably' at Wotton: and indeed, a surviving letter from George to his daughter Mary indicates as much, in enjoining her not to exceed '25 stone of beef per week' in the Wotton house-keeping.[25] The diarist would describe his brother's funeral as attended by 'above 2000 people ... all the Gentlemen of the County doing him the last honour'.[26]

George's long tenure of Wotton saw frequent visits from his far more cosmopolitan brother. John had been raised by his Stansfield grandparents in Sussex and educated at Lewes. A visitor to Wotton, he identified with his native place but imbued it with qualities of the pastoral which his brother is unlikely to have shared. His recollections of early childhood are of a rustic idyll; at the home of his brown-complexioned wet-nurse, 'a most sweet place towards the hills, flanked with wood, and refreshed with streams', he learnt a love of solitude 'sucked in with my very milk', and received his earliest education 'at the Church porch' in Wotton.[27] (The parish's less than sophisticated care of the Wotton church register was less appealing: he complained how it was 'miserably torn and abused (by those who ought to have preserved and continued it)', and undertook to bind the volume in his own monogrammed binding.)[28] Wotton equally served as the scholar's place of withdrawal from the *negotium* of London life. Three years after George Evelyn inherited the Wotton estate, in 1643, he permitted his brother to build what he describes as 'a study ... a fishpond, an island and some other solitudes and retirements', in the grounds of the house.[29]

George himself presumably had sufficient aspirations for his country home, then a moated Tudor construction,[30] to encourage the diarist and his

Fig. 3: Wotton House, south side, showing the mount, portico, fountain
and stream [mid-19th century] (Surrey History Centre).

cousin George (son of the Robert Evelyn who had emigrated to America in
c.1609) to landscape the grounds of the mansion on a much larger scale,
including an artificial terraced hill with portico, and probably make alterations to the interior in subsequent years.[31] The site at the junction of two
valleys fed by tributaries of the Arun and Wey rivers at different levels lent
itself to the creation of Italianate water features described by the diarist as
'all the Amoenities of a Villa, and Garden, after the Italian Manner'.[32] The
private gentleman's mansion thus became a model of the forefront of garden
design in England [Fig. 3].

Wotton was 'within little more than 20 miles from London and yet so
securely placed, as if it were an hundred', but the diarist also acknowledged
its 'good Neighbourho[o]d'.[33] Indeed, many Surrey houses with new
fashionable gardens were quite readily accessible from the 'solitudes' of
Wotton, and the diarist describes many local visits, including to his friend
Henry Howard's 'villa' at Albury Park to the west of Wotton, the garden of
which he also helped to design, and the much-praised 'amphitheatre' garden
and hermitage of Charles Howard at Deepdene in Dorking to the east.

The diarist came into his brother's Wotton estate in 1699, George having
settled the estate on him after the death of his surviving son in 1691. Sir John
Evelyn, 1st Baronet (1682-1763), grandson of the diarist, inherited Wotton
on the latter's death in 1706, and built a new library there: an oil painting by

George Lambert shows the house and terraced hill during the 1st Baronet's tenure.[34] Sir John Evelyn's son John, the 2nd Baronet (1706-67) inherited Wotton in 1763, and was succeeded by his son, Sir Frederick Evelyn, 3rd Baronet (1733-1812), in 1767. Frederick's death without heir in 1812 led to its inheritance by John Evelyn (1743-1827), of the former Godstone branch of the family, after the life term of Frederick's wife, Mary. Wotton, undergoing various 'modern' re-facings over the years, continued as the principal family home.

The continuous residence of the Evelyns at Wotton had secured the survival of a large quantity of family records there by the time of Sir Frederick and Mary Evelyn, and this is the core of the archives now held at the British Library (family and estate records, including the manuscripts of Evelyn the diarist) and at Surrey History Centre (principally deeds and manorial records). The first to take a serious interest in these records, as in an astonishing number of the other estate archives of Surrey, was William Bray, the family's solicitor and Surrey neighbour, and an indefatigable historian of his native county.[35]

The Evelyn and Bray families had lived within walking distance in neighbouring parishes for almost two hundred years when William Bray became the solicitor to the family at Wotton in about 1758. Sir Reginald Bray of Worcestershire, the most politically eminent family member, was Chancellor of the Duchy of Lancaster and Privy Councillor during Henry VII's reign, and was granted the manor of Shere Vachery and Cranleigh in Surrey in 1496. Further manors adjoining those of the Wotton estate were acquired, to include most of the parish of Shere, with a large area of heathland rich in ironstone and later exploited for forestry. Although the family flourished during the sixteenth century, it went into some decline during the seventeenth and early eighteenth centuries. 'What remained of a once very considerable estate' was inherited by William Bray's eldest brother George in 1740, now burdened by debts.[36] Only by tight financial management and assistance from his brother William was he eventually able to buy back some of the family's earlier possessions.

William Bray, a younger son born in 1736, would eventually inherit the Shere estate from his brother only in 1803. He was articled to John Martyr, an attorney in Guildford during the 1750s, and while at Guildford he began his habit of diary-keeping, which would continue until a few days before his death. Bray's early diaries provide us with a picture of Guildford in the mid-eighteenth century, where he enjoyed card-playing, syllabub parties, bowling, and dancing. He was sworn in as attorney at King's Bench in 1757, and began dividing his time between Surrey and London. By 1758 he is recording breakfasting at Sir John Evelyn's and taking tea there after a visit to Shere.[37] He was appointed as assistant to the Board of Green Cloth in 1761 through the patronage of Sir John Evelyn, 2nd Baronet, who had been appointed as a clerk the previous year. The Board was responsible for the provisioning of the Royal Household, a far from onerous duty before the introduction of reforms in 1782: Bray commented of the early years that 'nothing could be pleasanter than our situation at the Board of Green Cloth',[38] which occupied them between the hours of eleven in the morning and three in the afternoon. In his portrait by John Linnell Bray chose to be depicted proudly holding his appointment to the Board of Green Cloth, received some seventy years before. Bray supplemented his activities with a legal practice including stewardship of Surrey manors, administration of charities, and directorship of the Equitable Assurance Society (1774-1827).

He also seems to have found plenty of time for the pursuit of a wide range of interests, including antiquarian study and travels though England. His position well equipped him for his most lasting role, as the county's historian. As attorney to Lord Onslow and to Jane More Molyneux of Loseley, as well as the Evelyns, Bray was gaining access to rich accumulations of Surrey family archives from the 1760s onwards, which he would use in the completion of Owen Manning's <i>History and Antiquities of the County of Surrey</i> after Manning's death in 1801. Bray was the first to study and publicize the Loseley Manuscripts, probably the most significant family archive in the county, and his endorsements to be found on a large number are evidence of the thoroughness with which he examined them. He was evidently already privy to the Evelyn records while working on the second volume of the <i>History and Antiquities</i>, published in 1809, and his own bound collections of copy and original records may include some material he used at Wotton: the extent of migration of documents which passed through Bray's hands is still being discovered in collections held at Surrey History Centre.[39]

Friendship with the Evelyn family continued for the whole of Bray's life. He must have been the obvious candidate when Mary Evelyn, widow of Sir Frederick Evelyn, 3rd Baronet, sought advice on John Evelyn's diary and the possibility of its publication. In unpublished 'Recollections' of 1 March 1829 Bray gave his account of the beginning of the project: 'in the library was a very curious MSS ... it was well known to be in ... [Lady Evelyn's] possession, had been seen by many of the family and Lady Evelyn was desirous of publishing it if it should [be] likely to keep up the literary reputation which the writer had obtained and would be likely to please the public. By her desire I perused it, thought it well deserved publication, and by her ladyship's desire I undertook to select what was most likely to answer the proposed end.'[40]

The library was then in 'a confused state', the books having been removed when threatened by a fire in the stables adjoining the house, and replaced 'merely by the servants, in great confusion'; Lady Evelyn wanted 'a proper person' to arrange them and Bray found William Upcott, librarian at the London Institution, who performed the work and gave him 'considerable assistance'. Upcott's now better-known version of the 'discovery' of the Evelyn manuscripts is that he found that the ladies of the house had been regardlessly using the 'old letters' to make dress patterns and for kindling.[41] This was indignantly denied by Bray in 1822 in a letter to the *Morning Chronicle*, as a 'ridiculous story', insulting to the reputation of Lady Evelyn, who had died in 1817 before the diary was published.[42]

Bray worked, 'rising at 4 o'clock in the summer and so getting 3 hours or more every day, not interfering with my attendance at the Green Cloth, or in my practice in my profession', and completed the edition in 1818. He continued to work on the Evelyn archives afterwards, incorporating a selection of letters of John Evelyn and Richard Browne for a second edition of the diary, and composing a history of the various branches of the Evelyn family, on which he was still working shortly before his death at Shere in 1832.[43]

Bray's errors of transcription and over-zealous editing of passages in the diary which he must have considered detrimental to Evelyn's 'literary reputation' have earned criticism. He was still making excisions from the second edition in 1827, when he sent a note to John Bowyer Nichols, the publisher, of two paragraphs of doubtful taste he wanted omitted: one describing how one of Evelyn's companions killed a goat of an alpine peasant and refused to pay for it, and the other when Evelyn went to see torture inflicted on a criminal.[44] However, his achievement in gaining attention for the great resource of Evelyn's diary and ultimately the rest of the family archive is undeniable. In his own words: 'the success it met with was most flattering; perhaps there never was a book so universally well received. It was read by everyone and everyone was delighted'.

NOTES

1 John Aubrey, *Natural History and Antiquities of the County of Surrey Begun in the Year 1673*, 5 vols (London: E. Curll, 1719), I, sig. A3: Evelyn to Aubrey, 8 Feb. 1676.
2 Evelyn, *Sylva*, 4th edn, ed. by John Nisbet (London: Doubleday, [1908]), II, 166: 'my own sweet country of Surrey, inferior to none for pleasure and salubrity of air'.
3 Helen Evelyn, *History of the Evelyn Family* (London: Eveleigh Nash, 1915) is my principal source for background information on the family.
4 *Victoria History of the County: Surrey*, II, 306-29, describes the Surrey industry.
5 Gunpowder was not used for blasting until after 1665: see introduction to *Gunpowder Mills: Documents of the Seventeenth and Eighteenth Centuries*, ed. by A. G. Crocker and others, Surrey Record Society, 36 (2000), 2.

6 Probably at Myllclose, a plot bordering Nonsuch Park on the other side of the Hogsmill river, an area later used by the Earl of Worcester, Keeper of the Park, who had a licence for gunpowder in the seventeenth century; and in the eighteenth century by William Taylor: see C. F. Titford, 'The Great Park of Nonsuch', *Surrey Archaeological Collections*, 64 (1967), 74-5.

7 See S[urrey] H[history] C[entre] G52/8/9 for William Bray's notes on the relationship of George Evelyn and Richard Hill. The dispute between Evelyn and Hill was heard before Sir George More of Loseley in 1591 (for letter from Hill's employer Charles, Lord Howard, concerning the hearing in the Loseley MSS, see SHC 6729/3/35). PRO E 133/7/1048 (papers in Regina *v.* John Powell, 1592), has not been studied but also appears to relate to George Evelyn or his son George (d. 1637) and allegations concerning supply or offer of supply of gunpowder to the Spanish, which may be from Richard Hill.

8 Richard Hill owned moieties of the manor of Abinger and the manor of Paddington Dean, which were later Evelyn possessions; see SHC 6330.

9 George Evelyn's tomb in the Evelyn chapel, Wotton, depicts him kneeling with his two wives, with 'innumerable children' below (Ian Nairn, Nikolaus Pevsner, & Bridget Cherry, *The Buildings of England: Surrey*, 2nd edn (Harmondsworth: Penguin, 1971), p. 542. A full account of the descent of the Evelyn estates from George (1530-1603) is a complex one; in particular there are some inconsistencies in accounts of the descent of Godstone and West Dean (apparently due to the preponderance of the names George and John) between Owen Manning and William Bray, *History and Antiquities of the County of Surrey*, 3 vols (1804-14), II, 329, and Helen Evelyn, *Evelyn Family*, pp. 196-220. The fuller family tree, Godstone and Wotton branches, is provided in the former.

10 Helen Evelyn, *Evelyn Family*, pp. 519-23.

11 Evelyn, *Diary*, IV, 434.

12 J. Jacques, *Bygone Godstone* (Chichester: Phillimore, 1992), introduction, pp. [7-8].

13 By a patent of 7 Sept. 1599 for ten years for making of saltpetre and gunpowder, Richard Harding, Robert Evelyn, John Wrenham, and Symeon Turner were to deliver at the Tower yearly 100 lasts of good, perfect, serviceable corn gunpowder, by monthly portions, for which they were to receive 7d per pound, subject to penalty of £50 for every default; and they might sell to her subjects at 10d per pound (Manning and Bray, *History and Antiquities of ... Surrey*, II, 327).

14 Helen Evelyn, *Evelyn Family*, p. 197.

15 VCH, *Surrey*, II, 312, n. 4.

16 Evelyn, *Diary*, II, 219.

17 The Chilworth manufactury of the East India Company appears to have taken over: Aubrey, *Natural History and Antiquities of the County of Surrey*, IV, 56, says that there were eighteen powder mills at Chilworth in 1673; the monopoly was abolished altogether by the Long Parliament in 1641. See VCH, *Surrey*, II, 312-18, for an account of the controversies relating to the contracts during the Evelyns' time.

18 Evelyn, *Diary*, II, 237.

19 For records of the Godstone estates of the Evelyn family, see inter alia the Clayton archives, SHC K60 and K61.

20 SHC 6330.

21 Evelyn, *Diary*, II, 2.

22 Aubrey, *Natural History and Antiquities of the County of Surrey*, I, sig. A4ᵛ.

23 Evelyn, *Diary*, II, 2.

24 See A. R. Mitchell, 'Surrey in 1648', *Surrey Archaeological Collections*, 67 (1970), 67-83, for discussion of George's refusal to represent Parliament's case to the people of the county following violent suppression of a gathering of Surrey people to bring a petition asking for the restoration of the King 'to his due honour' in May 1648.

25 Cited in Bray's summaries of George Evelyn's letters to Mary, SHC G52/7/2/1.

26 Evelyn, *Diary*, V, 360.

27 Evelyn, *Diary*, II, 6.

28 SHC WOT/1/1; Evelyn's memorandum is dated 1697.

29 Evelyn, *Diary*, II, 81.

30 As illustrated by the diarist in 1640; see BL Add. MS 78610 A and B.

31 Nairn, Pevsner, & Cherry, *Buildings of England: Surrey*, p. 543, suggest that a Tuscan Doric doorcase in the entrance hall is of this period. References to the development of the Wotton garden, 1649-52, are in Evelyn, *Diary*, II, 551, III, 24, 60-1.

32 Aubrey, *Natural History and Antiquities of the County of Surrey*, I, sig. A3ᵛ.

33 Evelyn, *Diary*, II, 5.

34 Dated 1739; now belonging to Lord Camoys.

35 Details of Bray's career are taken from Julian Pooley's as yet unpublished article for the *New DNB*. Family details are taken from the introduction to the Bray archives, SHC G85. Further information has been kindly provided by Mr Pooley verbally.

36 SHC G85/26/1/43.

37 For Bray's diaries, see SHC G85/1/1-77. For diary extracts, 1756-1800, by F. E. Bray, see *Surrey Archaeological Collections*, 46 (1938), 30-58.

38 SHC G52/1/6/1.

39 Bray's collected volumes most obviously include Sir Frederick Evelyn's (printed) county treasurer's accounts (SHC G85/2/4/1). Conversely, he refers to the (permanent) removal to Wotton of Loseley MSS which related to a 1591 commission of Sir George More and others to enquire into George Evelyn's gunpowder business (SHC G52/8/9, p. 23).

40 SHC G52/1/6/2.

41 Upcott's account appears, inter alia, in Helen Evelyn, *Evelyn Family*, pp. 186-7.

42 SHC G52/12/9.

43 SHC G52/8/9 and G52/7/2/1 are draft versions of the history. A draft and a presentation copy are BL Add. MSS 78581 and 78582.

44 SHC Z/300/7: copy of an original at the Beinecke Rare Book and Manuscript Library, Yale University.

INDEX

Index